The Essential Paul Simon

The Essential
Paul Simon

Timeless Lessons for Today's Politics

Edited by John S. Jackson
With a Foreword by David Yepsen

Southern Illinois University Press
Carbondale and Edwardsville

15 14 13 12   4 3 2 1

Frontispiece: U.S. Senator Paul Simon stands on the dock at his home in Makanda,
Illinois, in May 1987. *Daily Herald* file photo; used with permission.

Library of Congress Cataloging-in-Publication Data
Simon, Paul, 1928–2003.
The essential Paul Simon : timeless lessons for today's politics / edited by John S.
Jackson ; with a foreword by David Yepsen.
    p. cm.
Includes bibliographical references and index.
    ISBN-13: 978-0-8093-3192-5 (cloth : alk. paper)
    ISBN-10: 0-8093-3192-6 (cloth : alk. paper)
    ISBN-13: 978-0-8093-3193-2 (ebook)
    ISBN-10: 0-8093-3193-4 (ebook)
1. United States—Politics and government—1945–1989. 2. United States—Politics
and government—1989– 3. United States—Politics and government—Philosophy.
4. United States—Foreign relations—1945–1989. 5. United States—Foreign
relations—1989– 6. United States—Foreign relations—Philosophy. I. Jackson, John S.,
1940– II. Title.
E83.5.S566 2012
320.973—dc23   2012007401

Printed on recycled paper. ♻

The paper used in this publication meets the minimum requirements of American
National Standard for Information Sciences—Permanence of Paper for Printed
Library Materials, ANSI z39.48-1992. ∞

Contents

Education and Literacy

Civil Rights

Immigration

Hunger

Gambling and Taxes

Taxes

Social Security and Public Pensions

Jobs and Economic Development

6. Culture, History, and Politics

Foreword

During his lifetime, Illinois senator Paul Simon wrote a trove of material: columns from his early newspaper and state legislative careers, newsletters to constituents written as a congressman and then as a senator, essays written as lieutenant governor of Illinois, and op-eds and radio commentaries from his time as director of the public policy institute he founded at Southern Illinois University. His presence in an office was often evidenced by the thwacking of an old Royal typewriter.

Many of those writings later grew into one of the twenty-two books he authored. This book is an attempt to unlock all that material for new generations of readers, as well as for Paul's old friends. It grew out of discussions in our office about how many who knew Paul are, as they say, "getting up there" in age. Current students and newcomers to Illinois weren't around when he was in his heyday.

At the same time, the troubles facing the world, the country, and Illinois are ones Paul frequently commented upon. His writing style was that of the classic newspaperman he was: outline the facts of a problem, discuss the different points of view, and then offer a series of bullet-point solutions for people and policy makers to adopt in order to fix things.

Read some of his pieces today, and he could just as well be writing for a blog or Facebook page, although his writing was a lot more civil than much of what you read on the Internet.

Corruption, deficits, financial mismanagement, hunger, the water crisis, the environment, and world peace were favorite topics of his, and those issues are alive and well and remain with us today. The only thing you'd have to do to freshen up many of Paul's columns is just add a few more zeroes to any numbers he used. Deficits and debts are higher, the money in politics is bigger, poverty is greater, and global temperatures are rising. Had people done some of the things he suggested years ago, we wouldn't be having a repeat of those discussions today.

At the same time we were talking about the problem of keeping Paul Simon's thoughts and legacy alive, archivist Walter Ray and other colleagues at Morris Library at Southern Illinois University Carbondale were busy filing, cataloging, and storing all those writings as part of the new Simon archive in the Special Collections section of the library. That archive made it possible for a researcher to methodically examine Simon's works to find the material that is still relevant today.

Dr. John Jackson, our colleague here at the institute, took on that task. Jackson is ideally suited for the work. He is a respected political scientist of long tenure here at the university. He knows Illinois, particularly southern Illinois. He knows politics and public policy, and he knew Simon well for many years. As a university official in the mid-1990s, Jackson helped Simon create the institute that today bears the senator's name.

Jackson has assembled an anthology of what he believes are the "essential" works of Simon's, the works that can still speak to us today.

David Yepsen
Director, Paul Simon Public Policy Institute

Introduction

Paul Simon started out as a journalist who then became a politician. But despite the extraordinary demands on his time and energy that came from being a public official for over forty years, Simon never gave up his writing. He wrote constantly and obsessively about public policy, politics, government, the major issues of the day, and the human condition. He wrote eloquently about the problems of common people and what government could and should do for the people it serves. He wrote cogently about the challenges of trying to apply religious principles and private morality in public life. He wrote candidly about how the state legislature, Congress, and the federal government worked and pointed out where they served the people well and where they failed miserably.

Simon won much of his early recognition and notoriety by penning a scathing indictment of the Illinois General Assembly and all its petty failings and blatant corruption. He was a crime fighter in Madison and St. Clair Counties before he became a corruption fighter in the Illinois legislature. He earned early on the reputation for a fearless truth-telling and unbending morality, which became his trademarks throughout his career. Like all reformers, he had his enemies and his detractors, but throughout four decades in politics, he had far more friends and admirers than enemies, and his supporters kept him in public office for most of his adult life.

Simon was first elected to the Illinois House in 1954, a position he held until 1962; he then moved up to the Illinois State Senate, where he served from 1963 to 1969. As lieutenant governor from 1969 through 1972, he faced a unique situation in which he served with Richard Ogilvie, a Republican, even though he was a Democrat elected separately, an anomaly that cannot happen under current law (Pensoneau). He ran for governor in 1972 and lost to Dan Walker in the Democratic primary. That loss was followed by two years out of government, during which time he taught at Sangamon State University (now the University of Illinois at Springfield) and was a guest lecturer at the John F. Kennedy School of Government at Harvard. Then Simon ran for the U.S. House and won election in 1974 from the 24th District in deep southern Illinois. In 1984, he challenged then-incumbent U.S. senator Charles Percy, a race many thought he could not win, but he did so by swimming strongly against a national Republican tide that was led by the Reagan landslide over Walter Mondale. He next ran for the Democratic nomination for president in 1988; however, he failed to generate enough interest and support, especially in the Iowa caucuses on which he had pinned most of his strategy. However, he was easily reelected to the Senate in 1990 with a record-setting victory margin over his Republican opponent, Lynn Martin. Simon served in the Senate for two terms and retired from office in 1997. Illinois was always his base, and it treated him well over his long and productive career. He still stands as one of the most successful and admired public officials in the history of the Prairie State.

Paul Simon always had a keen interest in history. From his earliest schoolboy days he read history, and as an adult he wrote informed treatises about lessons that could be drawn from history. Two of his best books were about Abraham Lincoln and Elijah Lovejoy the first, one of our greatest presidents; the other, a crusading newspaper publisher who was killed because of his abolitionist beliefs and writings. Paul explored their early lives and the forces that shaped them, and he extrapolated from that some of the enduring lessons of their lives. Simon's writings about pivotal and courageous leaders evidenced his deep admiration if not outright hero worship for those who shaped history. After his election to the U.S. House in 1974, Simon was constantly surrounded in Washington by the history and symbols, legends and heroes of America's past. He reveled in his life in Congress and in the access he had to the U.S. Capitol and its many resources, such as the Library of Congress. There the staff knew him well, and he was a frequent and welcome visitor.

In addition, he was in Washington when a lot of history was being made, and Simon had a place at the table in helping to shape some of that history. He spent twenty-two years in the U.S. Congress, ten in the House of Representatives and twelve in the Senate. From that insider's privileged perspective, he wrote about what Congress was doing at the time and what he thought it should be doing to tend to the common good and the public interest. Often there was a considerable gap between what those in Congress were doing and what Simon thought they should be doing. Usually this gap took the form of legislators settling for the short-term path of least resistance to get past the next election and Simon advocating more long-term and more difficult solutions to the nation's problems. Simon often called for courage in leaders and eschewed public opinion polls and what he termed the "finger to the wind" type of leadership. His critique of Congress was often trenchant, but he still loved the institution and its history and respected most of the people in it.

Paul Simon believed deeply in the value of public discussion, debate, and discourse. He was deeply committed to the Burkean, or "trustee," view of what representation is all about. Like the English philosopher Edmund Burke, Simon believed that leaders had to exercise their best judgment and do what they thought was right for the common good and for the best interests of the nation as a whole. He thought the representatives should follow the dictates of their conscience above all else and not exploit the lowest common denominator among their constituents. Simon felt that public officials too often pander to the prejudices, fears, and selfishness of the people they are elected to represent. He believed that leaders should lead—that is, they are elected to try to get things done, not just to hold the title and the position of power. Often this means making hard, sometimes unpopular choices. When leaders make these unpopular choices, they are then obligated to go home and explain their votes and decisions to the people and to try to convince at least a majority that they were right in their calculations. If they do not accomplish this public education function, they run the real risk of not being reelected in the next election. In fact, Paul Simon lost one election, for governor of Illinois in the Democratic primary of 1972, and he almost lost his seat in Congress in the general election of 1980, partially because those were bad years for well-known Democrats and also because he stuck his neck out on some controversial issues but failed to convince his public that he had taken the best position, a failure that his opponents exploited. However, he rebounded from both electoral setbacks, winning his first term in Congress in 1974 and a U.S. Senate seat in 1984, and his electoral success rate with the people of southern Illinois and all of Illinois was one of the best of any elected official in the state's history.

Paul Simon's abilities to explain himself and to keep a working majority of the people on his side depended heavily on his commitment to rational, honest, and nonpartisan discussion and discourse. Writing his columns and books was a fundamental part of that strategy, and the body of work they represent also reflects a succinct summary of a life lived and explained in the public domain. Writing is what Paul Simon did, week after week, year after year, obsessively. He did not have what one could call a hobby per se, but reading widely and writing steadily was what he did for fun. He could no more give up his writing than he could have given up his Pepsi-Cola. He simply had to try to educate the public, to speak out, to try to explain himself and his views. He wanted people to know what was going on in their government and how it related to their daily lives. He wanted to convince them that this far-off and esoteric stuff of government was indeed important to them, to their well-being, and to the future of the state, nation, and world. Simon believed that making his case was a part of the essence of leadership. He deeply believed in representative government and in the Founders' concept of the United States as a republic, and this public discourse function was an essential part of the bargain.

Not restricting himself to just the legislative branch, Paul Simon also wrote about the U.S. Supreme Court and the presidency. He had a particularly good platform from which to observe the Court since he was a member of the Senate Judiciary Committee and was deeply enmeshed in the early fights over presidential nominations to the Supreme Court. Both Ronald Reagan and George H. W. Bush sent up nominations that Simon considered to be too ideological and too partisan for his view of what the Court should be all about. He let the presidents know where he stood and explained his reasoning to the public. He served with Presidents Gerald Ford, Jimmy Carter, Ronald Reagan, George H. W. Bush, and Bill Clinton. He never hesitated to give them his advice, to compliment them where they did right, by his lights, and to tutor and correct them when they went astray, whether they wanted to hear from him or not. On very few matters was there much doubt about where Paul Simon stood and why.

One of Simon's enduring interests was American foreign and defense policy. Even as a member of the Illinois House, he started taking trips overseas and sending back home a written report to his people telling them what he was seeing and learning and why it should matter to them. Then as well as now, legislators were often criticized and condemned for their travel. Paul maintained that most legislators did not travel enough to be well informed about the issues they would have to vote on, particularly in the foreign and defense policy fields. He started this world travel tradition well before he was elected to Congress. Who has ever heard of an Illinois state legislator taking very public trips overseas and then carrying on a constant conversation with his audience back home telling them what he was seeing, who he was meeting, and why foreign and defense policy and trade policy was important to their daily lives? Paul Simon's slice of national history came during a volatile and violent era that saw the United States almost constantly engaged in war in some part of the world. He served in the U.S. Army in the Counter Intelligence Corps in Germany during the Korean War era, and that experience of serving in and traveling around Europe left an indelible mark on his thinking. He came back home and wrote about that during his time at the *Troy Tribune*, and he submitted articles to other Illinois newspapers as well, always telling them that foreign and defense policy were important to the folks back home, even in the smallest towns and most isolated places.

Paul Simon was in public office during the Vietnam War and its immediate aftermath. At first, like many other political leaders in Illinois and throughout the nation, he was a supporter of President Lyndon Johnson and his policies in Vietnam. Then slowly Simon changed and became more and more skeptical about the war and the practicality of realizing its stated objectives. By the time it ended under President Ford, Simon, like many Americans, was ready for American troops to come home. However, Simon was no isolationist. He constantly advocated a vigorous American foreign policy, one that was marked by energetic engagement with the world. He believed in and constantly supported a strong military; however, he was even more firmly committed to what we now call "soft power"—the use of diplomacy, cultural and educational exchanges, and mutual aid to build up the economies of other nations so they will not foster violence and foment hopelessness and resentment among their people and especially among the young (Nye). For Simon, hunger, ignorance, poverty, and deprivation were the biggest threats to world peace.

From that perspective, he also wrote about, and often criticized, American military involvement in subsequent conflicts in Grenada, Panama, Bosnia, Kosovo, Iraq, and Afghanistan. He was a longtime and consistent critic of our attempt to isolate and punish Cuba with a trade embargo. The idea of isolating an entire nation, particularly one only ninety miles off our coast, and trying to cut them off from the world made no sense to Simon, and he worked until his death on the prospect of changing our Cuban policy. Simon was a committed internationalist. He wrote multiple times about the hotspots around the globe, especially the Middle East and Africa. He wanted the people of his congressional district and state to know what was going on in some of the more obscure parts of the world, and he was deeply committed to the proposition that voters should care about a world that was much bigger than their neighborhood, town, or state.

Paul Simon also was interested in and wrote about all kinds of domestic issues and policies. Several of those he wrote about and worked on seemed to be particularly keen interests and personal burdens of his, including his hallmark issues of world hunger, literacy, water resources and policy, public education, language instruction, student loans, prison reform, access for those with disabilities, jobs, the deficit, the draft, and the need for a system of public service for all. There are multiple columns in his archive on each of these subjects. Some of them, like world hunger, water resources, public debt and the deficit, and foreign language instruction, subsequently became books after Simon had written columns on the same subjects. (See the appendix for an annotated bibliography of all of Paul Simon's books.)

Simon was a person who thought and wrote a lot about the political process and how to improve it. He wrote about his experiences running for office and the importance of campaigns in a modern democracy. Paul saw campaigns as the opportunity to do civic education on a mass basis, and thus the power and role of the media were extremely important parts of the equation. He also worried over the power and role of the many interest groups that are so active and so powerful in the American political system. He was especially concerned about the importance of money in American politics: how much it takes to run for office, how rapidly the amounts necessary to be competitive have grown, and how much time and energy candidates must devote to raising money and to begging their friends, supporters, and interest groups for campaign donations. Simon hated raising money and fretted over the pervasive and potentially corrupting influence of big money in campaigns. How to raise that money without compromising one's principles, the boundaries between asking for a campaign donation and selling out completely, and the promises one must make in order to raise money were all issues Simon was concerned about. The vast gap between those who were "politically articulate" because they had a lot of resources as compared to those who had few resources and thus little or no voice in Washington was a major problem for him. Paul Simon was a reformer in this field, and it was one of the subjects he devoted a great deal of effort to after he left public office. In the late 1990s, along with Mike Lawrence, Simon was able to use his platform at the Paul Simon Public Policy Institute at Southern Illinois University to develop a viable campaign finance and ethics package and get it adopted in the Illinois General Assembly, a body not usually noted for its interest in electoral reform.

Paul Simon was a social liberal, a true progressive in all of his values and basic instincts, who was also deeply committed to the proposition that deep budget deficits and massive amounts of borrowed money were irresponsible public policy. He was frugal personally, and that frugality carried over to how he wanted government to operate. He was not a small government conservative and definitely did not believe in starving the government until it could be "strangled in the bathtub," as archconservative Grover Norquist once famously advocated, but Simon did believe that government had limits and that there were some areas where the government could play only a very limited supporting role or no role at all. Simon clearly believed it when he claimed to be a "pay as you go Democrat," a label that he frequently used for himself. Under this mandate, he advocated a long list of Progressive programs, especially those that helped ordinary people and especially the more vulnerable in society.

Simon greatly admired Hubert Humphrey and quoted him often on the subject of the necessity of governmental help for the very old, the very young, the disabled, and the dispossessed elements of society. Simon thought such programs and policies were necessary in order to "establish justice, insure domestic tranquility, provide for the common defense, promote the general welfare, and secure the blessings of liberty to ourselves and our posterity," in the words of the preamble to the U.S. Constitution. But, Simon believed just as adamantly that we should pay for the public services we want and demand of our government. In Simon's worldview, it is not fair just to pass those costs along to our children and grandchildren. The budget deficit and accumulated mountains of public debt simply reflect that this generation of leaders and voters have been irresponsible and even dishonest about the real needs of the state or nation and who should pay the bills. According to Simon, we need to pay our own bills and support the taxes necessary to pay those bills as they come due. Simon was conscientious about his own personal finances, and he generalized that same ethic to the government. This line of reasoning led him to be a strong advocate for the Balanced Budget Amendment for the federal government, a position that was unusual for anyone on the liberal side of the continuum in his day. Equally defying the conservatives, he maintained that their penchant for cutting taxes and borrowing money was also irresponsible and dishonest.

Paul Simon the journalist often wrote "the first cut of history," as all jour-nalists do, but he also frequently wrote from a keen historical perspective. He typically thought about the long view and the big picture. He tried to connect the short term and small stuff to the long term and the big stuff. That is a tall order. Sometimes he failed. Some of his writing was time-bound, some parochial and prosaic, some apparently written hurriedly just to meet the need for filing another column that week. Every columnist will admit that the omnipresent discipline of the deadline will force the production of some less-than-memorable work. But many of Simon's writings are of lasting quality, cogently addressing the momentous issues of the day. Often those issues are ones we are still fighting about and struggling with. Many of his insights are timeless, worthy of preserving for the next generation and for future generations who did not know Paul Simon personally. He was truly the everyman sage, the Prairie Populist with the horn-rimmed glasses, bow tie, and jug ears, or an "Illinois Original," as biographer Robert E. Hartley called him. In appearance and demeanor, Simon appeared to be a caricature straight out of the 1950s and 1960s. He could have been a line drawing in a Herblock cartoon. However, much of what he wrote is about the enduring themes of history, politics, and the human condition.

Simon continued this tradition and commitment well after he left public office. After twelve years in the U.S. Senate and ten years in the House, he returned to southern Illinois and established the public policy institute that now bears his name at Southern Illinois University. There he continued to write, to lecture, to teach students, and to travel the world in his peripatetic attempt to discuss the issues in order to help both the public and political officials make more informed and more rational decisions. He wrote articles, letters to the editor, columns, and books virtually up until the day of his untimely death on December 9, 2003. After that, his voice was stilled, but this volume is an attempt to bring his thoughts and wisdom to a new and larger audience and to remind his old friends and supporters again of why they had so much appreciation and admiration for the essential Paul Simon. I was a friend and supporter of Paul Simon's for over thirty years. I first met him through our mutual friends Randall and Mae Nelson (the chair of the SIUC Department of Political Science and his wife) when Simon ran for governor in the Democratic primary in 1972. The Nelsons were his Jackson County coordinators in that campaign. I was already impressed with him because of his record as lieutenant governor and especially because of the courage he had shown in trying to negotiate the treacherous conflict in racially divided Cairo, Illinois. Townspeople there had frequent demon-strations and counter-demonstrations and occasionally traded gunshots; Simon had bravely tried to mediate in this deeply polarized situation. I also met Dick Durbin, who was at that time one of Simon's staffers, as he came to Carbondale and gave us a stack of computer printouts listing all the names of those in Jackson County who had voted in the last Democratic primary. We tried to call all of them and urged them to vote for Simon;

however, our efforts were too little to stop the Dan Walker tide, and Simon lost (Pensoneau and Ellis). I thought then and still think today that Simon was the best candidate in that race.

As a result of that early effort for Paul Simon, I was invited to be a part of his campaign advisers and supporters when he moved to Carbondale and started the quest for the congressional office late in the fall of 1973. Keith Sanders, who was then a professor in speech communication at SIUC and later became the executive director of the Illinois Board of Higher Education, Roy Miller, also a colleague in political science, and I did some of his earliest polling in that race. I also occasionally drove him to various political rallies, town meetings, and other events in the district during that campaign. Simon, of course, won that one, and from then on I became an occasional unofficial adviser to him, especially on polling and issues related to higher education, although many others filled that role as well. Sometimes he took my advice, and sometimes he did not. Paul had a strong sense of what he needed to do, and while he would listen to other points of view, he made his own choices. For example, Keith Sanders and I wrote a long memo advising him not to leave the House and run for the Senate in 1984. Fortunately, he thanked us and ran anyway.

Much later, I was dean of the College of Liberal Arts at SIUC when Simon decided to retire. My friend and colleague Joe Foote, then dean of the College of Mass Communications and Media Arts, and I urged him to come to Carbondale and set up a public policy institute. Joe and I also wrote all the internal documents that were required to get this institute set up and funded. This time he listened to or at least agreed with us, and we were delighted when he gave the go-ahead to our plan. Later I served in the provost's and chancellor's offices while Paul was trying to establish the public policy institute during its start-up phase, so I was able to facilitate some of that early effort. Then after I left the SIUC central administration, Paul called me in Little Rock, where I was teaching for a term at the University of Arkansas Little Rock, and offered me a staff position at the institute. I was glad to join him, Mike Lawrence, and all the other fine staff at the institute in January 2002, and I have been on the staff ever since. Mike Lawrence became director of the institute after Paul's death in December 2003, and I was pleased to continue to work with Mike during his almost five years in that role. I chaired the committee that brought David Yepsen to the director's job in April 2009, and I have enjoyed working with him and the staff since then. This book is an effort to repay some of my personal debt to Paul Simon and to mark my enormous respect for him as a person and as a public servant.

It is important to set out the limits of this study. Morris Library at Southern Illinois University Carbondale is the official repository for Paul Simon's congressional papers, which cover the entire twenty-two years he served in the U.S. House and Senate in Washington. This collection also includes many of Simon's personal papers, covering correspondence with constituents, family, and friends; scrapbooks kept by his mother, Ruth; and drafts of his many books and articles. I am indebted to Pamela Hackbart-Dean, the director of the Special Collections Research Center at Morris Library, and her staff for their crucial and cheerful support in assembling this book. Special thanks go to Walter Ray, who is the curator of the Simon papers. Nobody knows more about Paul Simon's work than Walter Ray, and he was unfailingly helpful in all facets of the development of this anthology. With Ray's help, I have reviewed all of the writings in the Paul Simon collection at Morris Library.

It is also important to note that there is another collection of Paul Simon's papers located at the Abraham Lincoln Presidential Library in Springfield, Illinois. This collection is focused on Simon's years in the Illinois House and Senate and as lieutenant governor of Illinois. The collection at the Lincoln Presidential Library was not reviewed in assembling this current work; however, there were many items from Simon's years of holding public office in Illinois also available in Morris Library, and as the reader will see, some items from Simon's early career were included in this book. Walter Ray believes that we have almost all of the *Troy Tribune* columns in Morris Library, and I have read all of those. We were also assisted by Jeanne Sagovac at the Tri-Township Public Library in Troy in reviewing some of the *Troy Tribune* articles. Some of those are included, although Simon's early years are not the focus of the book.

After Simon was elected to public office, he started writing a column that received wider circulation, and many of those early pieces are also in the Simon collection at Morris Library. Simon's biographer, Robert Hartley, summarized the wide array of columns he produced: "In January [1955], he began a commentary called 'Sidelights from Springfield,' which he wrote almost weekly during every session of the legislature until 1969 when he became lieutenant governor. . . . He wrote simply, in short sentences and with easily understood words and usage. He preferred to write about one subject at a time, rarely mixing topics in a way that might confuse a reader. . . . If he wrote on more than one subject in a column, he clearly separated them. He was not bashful about proclaiming his position on issues but did not use the column to mention every legislative initiative he sponsored. Simon spoke directly to readers of all education levels and stations in life" (51).

Simon used the title "From the Statehouse" for his columns written while he was lieutenant governor, and he produced a total of fifty-one of those during the four years in that office (Hartley 152). Simon continued his inveterate column-writing when he went to Washington, using the title "P.S./ Washington" for these columns. His reports from Washington as well as the wide assortment of other outlets he wrote for in the remainder of his life are all stored in the Special Collections section of Morris Library, and they make up the bulk of the selections included in this anthology.

I also want to thank Natalie Bohnhoff, Emily Burke, Matt Baughman, Pam Gwaltney, Barton Lorimor, Chris Rich, and David Yepsen of the Paul Simon Public Policy Institute for crucial assistance in the development of this work. Sincere appreciation is also extended to Paul Simon's children, Sheila Simon, the current lieutenant governor of Illinois, and Martin Simon, a respected photographer in Washington, D.C., the former and current chairs of the Paul Simon Public Policy Institute's Board of Counselors. In their official capacities as chair of the board, as well as unofficially as Paul's children, both Sheila and Martin encouraged the project at every stage. Thanks also are extended to Mike Lawrence and Robert Hartley, who read and corrected earlier drafts of this manuscript as external reviewers for SIU Press. Both reviewers offered very good and timely advice on the development of the book and topics to include. It is a better book because of the advice they offered. In addition, Dr. David Kenney, who knows a great deal about this era and Paul Simon's role in it, gave the manuscript a meticulous reading, and it benefited significantly from his suggestions. Finally, my appreciation is extended to the staff of SIU Press, especially Julie Bush, Karl Kageff, and Barbara Martin for their untiring devotion to this project. The advice of all of these people is much appreciated; however, whatever errors remain are solely my own.

Finally, thanks are extended for permission to reprint from the multiple sources where Paul Simon's columns were originally published. These include the *Chicago Tribune*, the *Chicago Sun-Times*, the *Daily Herald*, *Parade Magazine*, *Harper's Magazine*, the *Washington Post*, *Columbia Journalism Review*, *The Cresset*, *The Lutheran*, and *Illinois Heritage*, published by the Illinois State Historical Society. Reprints from those sources were all done with permission.

The Essential Paul Simon

1

The Early Days

Chapter 1 includes several selections from Paul Simon's early career. These selections start with columns from the *Troy Tribune*, which was the first newspaper Paul bought and edited at the tender age of nineteen. The newspaper was essentially defunct when Paul purchased it, and he had to start from scratch to rebuild the paper's physical facilities as well as its subscription and advertising base. The job required him to be owner, editor, publisher, reporter, and advertising salesman all at the same time. It was a difficult and trying time for the neophyte newspaperman, but it also offered an invaluable education in journalism and the newspaper business. Those were lessons that followed Paul Simon the rest of his life, and from the beginning he always identified himself as a journalist first and foremost, no matter how far his political career carried him. One of the reasons he consistently seemed to get good coverage from the media and to enjoy a good image with newspeople was that he was so clearly one of them with deeply engrained values honoring freedom of the press and the right of the public to know what was going on with their government.

Another insight we gain from these first columns is a palpable sense of life in the small town of Troy, Illinois, in the late 1940s and early 1950s. This is midwestern America in the Truman and Eisenhower eras, and Paul's columns reflect the pace and the atmosphere of that day. The motto below the masthead of the *Troy Tribune* boasted that it was "A Progressive

Newspaper in a Progressive Town." Troy was a place of small-town values and sensibilities where a local citizen was not too busy to jump into his car and show Paul to his destination. It was also a place where the people wanted more "personal items"—that is, small-town news and gossip—to appear in their newspaper. The second column in the series also shows that Paul was already taking an interest in local politics and the ways in which national politics had a direct impact on the life and interests of the local newspaper subscribers. He writes about Congressman Melvin Price, who became a powerhouse in Congress and was legendary for his long service to that congressional district and for his ability to bring home federal largesse to the local constituency. Simon in that era also commented in a neutral way about the Democratic and Republican candidates for president in 1948, and his studied bipartisanship became one of the hallmarks of his later political career.

The next two columns in this section show the early salvos in Simon's fights with organized crime in Madison County. When he arrived in Troy, he was surprised to observe that both illegal gambling and prostitution were openly available in the county, and he quickly decided to take them on and try to clean up the county. These articles show his methods of publicly declaring that the law was obviously being broken and challenging the state's attorney and the sheriff to do something about it. These articles and others like them led to the crusading newspaper editor image that Paul Simon acquired early in his first years in Troy, and that image stayed with him for the remainder of his career.

An article published in *Harper's Magazine* in 1964 shows the beginning of Paul's career as a crusading reformer. By then, he had been elected to the Illinois House and then the Illinois Senate, and he had not been favorably impressed with what he found there. It was a legislative process where all too many legislators seemed to have their hands out, and the pursuit of personal enrichment took precedence over any thought for the common good. The article, coauthored with Alfred Balik, was the first time Simon came to national attention, as the article garnered a lot of headlines. It was a journalistic bombshell that put the Illinois General Assembly in the spotlight in a very unflattering way. Some of Simon's colleagues were not amused, and they called him a traitor and worse in their response to his criticisms. From that day on, his relationships with some of his colleagues were strained or broken, and he was certainly never accepted into the tight-knit club of insiders who ran the legislature for their own benefit and for the enrichment of the narrow interests they represented. This did not deter

Paul Simon, who had come to the legislature as a reformer and corruption fighter, and he remained a reformer throughout his long career in both the state and national legislative bodies he served in for four decades.

INTRODUCTORY COLUMNS IN THE *TROY TRIBUNE*

"TROJAN THOUGHTS," JULY 1, 1948, VOLUME 1, NO. 2

One thing that is very apparent to a newcomer to Troy is the very friendly spirit which can be seen in almost everything done around Troy.

When I first came here for any period of time was during my Easter vacation. I worked around the shop here a little and looked the situation over somewhat. Although the Lions Club had given me a royal welcome the time I had been here for their meeting, the place was still a little strange. I felt a little uneasy. I was quite sure everything would turn out alright, but there were those thousand and one other possibilities that kept creeping into my mind. Would they resent having some young fellow take over the paper? Are the people here friendly? etc.

With these and many other questions on my mind, I walked out of the shop to the car and I thought I would drive out to Fred Wakeland's to ask him some questions about different things around Troy. I asked a fellow standing in front of the Post Office how one could get to Fred Wakeland's place. "You take the road out here," he said, pointing toward the bank, "and then you go out . . . Oh, just a minute, I'll show you where he lives."

He jumped in his yellow Studebaker and led the way to the Wakeland home. He stopped in front of the home, told me that was the place, then turned around and headed back.

He was a total stranger. I didn't know then who he was and I don't know now. But he made me feel good about the whole situation. I didn't need to ask myself any longer whether Troy people were friendly. It was just a little but it meant a lot.

Whoever you are, sir, thank you.

People coming into the *Tribune* office have really been murdering the word "Tribune" and I'm guilty of some of the same. Some call it the "Tri-I-bune," some the "Tri-BUNE," and some the "TRI-bune." I finally became confused myself and consulted Webster on the matter. He tells me that the emphasis should be on the first syllable, with the "i" pronounced as in kick.

By the way, comment on the first issue of *The Troy Tribune* was very good on the whole. One criticism we heard was that there were not enough personal items. We realized this very well when the first issue came out, and the same is true of this issue. Until we become better acquainted around town, it will be that way. You can help us a great deal, however, by phoning us or dropping in with your little news items.

Thanks.

"TROJAN THOUGHTS," JULY 15, 1948, VOLUME 1, NO. 4

Wm. Schmitt, owner of the Schmitt Chevrolet garage, pretty well hit the nail on the head, when he said Troy was fortunate in having Congressman Melvin Price here for a short talk the other evening.

After the address by the East St. Louis Democrat there was quite a bit of political talk among the Lions Club members present, and there has been more talk of political affairs since. From this angle alone it was beneficial.

Possibly the majority of people over the United States say, "There are two things which I never discuss: politics and religion."

Usually they have in mind heated arguments when they say this, and if that's the case it's quite possible they are right. A heated argument on either subject usually means nothing is gained.

However, if a good, calm discussion can be carried on, there is a great deal of benefit for everyone. The more people are aware of the political situation, the nearer we will come to the ideal of good government.

Our hats should be off to Carl and Harry Taake, or whoever was responsible for bringing Representative Price to Troy.

Price, by the way, makes a very good impression. He is not one of those "hot air" congressmen. In his informal address here he didn't take the negative attitude which so many on both sides do every election year.

In the few minutes I talked to him after the meeting, he called the Dewey-Warren ticket "a good, strong ticket." Many a Democratic congressman would have started shouting "reactionary" at the mention of the ticket and many a Republican congressman would not have dealt as considerately with the Truman candidacy as he did with the Republican ticket.

Price also mentioned he didn't think too much of the Eisenhower boom. Truman's program is the one which has never been given a fair trial, he indicated. Truman should have a chance to work it out. Price evidently meant with a Democratic congress.

In any event, he thought the Democratic ticket would also be a strong ticket. "Two strong tickets, that's what we want," Price said.

Price is a member of the very important Atomic Energy committee of the House and Senate. Members of this committee include such top-notch legislators as Senator Vandenberg and Senator Hickenlooper.

At the Lions Club meeting Harold Schmidt asked Price what was the chance of Troy getting house-to-house city delivery of mail. Price said the Post Office department must be certain the local receipts are regularly over $10,000 for the year.

Postmaster J. Wheeler Davis reports that in Troy's top year during the war receipts totaled about $7,500.

Shopping in the home town should be taken as a matter of course by everyone. There are many, many benefits which you will derive from shopping at home. That goes for postage stamps and everything.

There were a number of names missed on the last issue of the *Troy Tribune*. This came about as a result of not having the addressing machine set properly. Next time you should get your copy.

However, even next time and the time to come, mistakes will happen. They will be few and far between we trust, but they will be.

If on any issue you do not get your copy, be sure to call us, drop us a card, or stop in, and let us know as soon as possible and then you will get your copy.

"An Open Letter to Austin Lewis, State's Attorney," June 16, 1949

Dear Mr. Lewis:

Several times in the last months I have had articles in the *Tribune* in which I have joined the *St. Louis Post-Dispatch*, the *Collinsville Herald*, and a number of other newspapers in asking that the wide-open gambling which is now so prevalent in Madison County be brought to an abrupt halt.

Occasionally I see a headline or two in which it is reported you have "closed" certain places notorious for their wide-open gambling.

However, when I read in the *Granite City Press-Record* that gambling casinos such as the Hyde Park and 200 Club are preparing to reopen it makes me wince. And when I see the same thing in other places which have been "closed" I sometimes wonder. (Perhaps you shared my feeling of shame when the situation became so bad in Madison County that the Illinois Attorney General finally took action.)

There is many a citizen in Madison County who feels as I do that willful and open violation of the law should be stopped by our state's attorney. Frankly, we can't understand your attitude toward the situation.

To help clear things up, and to give you a chance to defend yourself, I am submitting a few questions. If you could find time to answer them I would sincerely appreciate it. I assure you your answer will be given the fullest publicity.

When you took the oath of office of state's attorney you took an oath to uphold the law. Do you still feel that it is your duty?

Do you recognize that there is wide-open gambling in Madison County which is illegal, or do you attribute this to "myths" which the newspapers create?

Do you believe that gambling laws should be strictly enforced?

Do you believe that you are doing everything possible to enforce these laws? If you say you believe the laws should be enforced, and if you also admit that there is wide-open gambling in the county, then how long must Madison County's citizens wait before there is a genuine house-cleaning and not a mere face-saving token raid?

Perhaps we have you all wrong. If we do, and you soon begin a real house-cleaning, I can assure you I will be in the front seat cheering.

But in the meantime some of us old-fashioned fuddie-duddies who believe laws were meant to be enforced cannot help but open our eyes and wonder at times.

Hoping you can clear this matter up for me and for a great many others, I remain,

Very Sincerely,
Paul Simon

"'CLOSED' HOUSES OF PROSTITUTION AGAIN OPERATING," OCTOBER 20, 1949

The houses of prostitution along Highway 40 known as the Plamor Inn and the Club 40 which were "closed" by the sheriff in cooperation with the state's attorney's office are now operating in full swing again—except that no liquor is being sold over the counter as it formerly was. I know. I was there. Sunday night I stopped at the Plamor Inn and asked for a coke. I was the only person in the place and after serving me the coke, he asked, "Do you want a girl?"

"Not tonight," I answered. I took a few more sips from my coke and then asked, "How much do they run?"

"Depends on what you want. It starts at five dollars."

"Will you be open later in the week?" I asked.

"Yes," he said, taking a puff from his cigarette with a hand which looked as if it were suffering from arthritis. "Anything you want when you come back."

"Thanks," I said as I walked out of the door. . . .

My next stop was the Club 40 where I again ordered a coke and where activity was more in evidence. A good looking young lady served it to me. Then came around in back of the counter, picked some lint from my suit coat, stroked my back, and said, "Say, if you're interested in entertainment I suggest we go out to one of the bedrooms and talk things over. They won't let us make propositions at the bar."

"OK," I said, and we walked into a small room in which was a very small dresser and a single-size bed, the spread neatly covered over it, with a few cigarette burns on the spread. "How much is it?" I asked.

"Five dollars for once and ten dollars for twice. For ten dollars I can give you a nice long party, honey."

"That's a little much for me," I said.

"Listen, honey," she cooed back, "for five dollars I'll give you a good long stay and arrange for some drinks for both of us on that too."

"Will you be here later in the week?" I asked. By this time she seemed set on my staying there and I was wanting to get out of there just in case anyone might identify me.

"No, honey, this is my last night. Won't you give me just a little satisfaction tonight? We'll have a nice long party in the bed and then if you don't have quite enough money we can settle up afterwards."

"I think I'd better come back later in the week," I countered, and headed for the doorway.

At the doorway of one of the many small bedrooms sat a large, heavy-set woman in a yellow-print dress.

I placed my coke bottle on the counter and saw this girl start a conversation with a wild-eyed fellow nearby. I headed for the doorway and some much-needed fresh air.

I walked out of the place with five dollars still in my pocket—and undiseased. Which is probably more than many a fellow can say.

However I also walked out of the place with a still lower opinion of the activities of our county sheriff, Dallas Harrell, and the state's attorney, Austin Lewis.

With five dollars per person and many times ten, and with the mass production which seemed to be going on there, the operators might even afford to pay county officials a little.

"THE ILLINOIS LEGISLATURE: A STUDY IN CORRUPTION,"
BY STATE SENATOR PAUL SIMON AS TOLD TO ALFRED
BALIK, *HARPER'S MAGAZINE*, SEPTEMBER 1964

"State legislatures are, historically, the fountainhead of representative govern-ment in this country."

So spoke the United States Supreme Court in the landmark reapportion-ment opinion of the last June. The reforms that will follow are long overdue. For there is little doubt that these fountainheads of democracy are—as of this writing—polluted almost beyond belief.

This is my considered judgment after ten years of service in the body where Abraham Lincoln once sat. I did not expect moral perfection when I first went to Springfield. In my home district, in southwestern Illinois, criminal elements had seriously infiltrated both major party organizations until Governor Adlai Stevenson's courageous state police raids of 1950 slowed down their inroads. Illicit bookie joints and vice dens operated as freely as grocery stores in one town, and muggings, bombings, and gang killings were common-place. However, this experience and a realistic attitude about soci-ety's shortcomings did not prepare me for the shock of seeing from the inside how the Illinois legislature—the lawmaker and "public conscience" of the nation's fourth-most-populous state—actually works. This is the legislature which last year enacted a redistricting plan so blatantly unrepresentative that the Illinois Supreme Court upheld Governor Otto Kerner's veto of it. As a result, this November all members of our House of Representatives will be elected at large—the first such election, I believe, in American history. At least 236 names will appear on a special ballot almost three feet long, out of which the voter must select all 177 members of the House.

This is only one of a series of breakdowns so frequent and so serious that I feel compelled to speak out about them.

My colleague, Republican Noble W. Lee, who is Dean of the John Marshall Law School in Chicago and has served eleven terms in the House, esti-mates that one-third of the members accept payoffs. In the light of my own observations, I agree. Most of these are recorded as legal fees, public-relations services, or "campaign contributions," though a campaign may be months away. If questioned, the recipient simply denies that the payment had anything to do with legislative activity. This makes it technically legal. A somewhat smaller number of pay-offs are not veiled at all; cold cash passes directly from one hand to the other.

Recently, for example, the spokesman of a professional association visited a legislator, whom I will call Mr. X, to enlist his help with a bill. "Did you bring the money?" Mr. X asked.

"What money?" the visitor asked.

"Money for the committee, of course," Mr. X replied. "It will cost two hundred to five hundred dollars a vote to get the bill out of committee." His caller dropped the subject and left.

Similarly jolted was a representative of the food industry when he sought a powerful Senator's support for a bill.

"Be glad to talk to you," the legislator told him. "For seventy-five hundred dollars I can get you nine votes."

A few legislators go so far as to introduce some bills that are deliberately designed to shake down groups which oppose them and which will pay to have them withdrawn. These bills are called "fetchers," and once their sponsors develop a lucrative field, they guard it jealously.

I learned this, quite by accident, four years ago in the House. I had found that some school districts and municipalities were paying needlessly high bond interest. So I introduced a bill requiring competitive bidding on public bond issues. Shortly afterward a colleague buttonholed me in the hall.

"What are you doing with my bill?" he demanded.

"What bill?"

"That bond bill. I always introduce it, and I do rather well with it." Seeing my surprise, he added, "Look, why don't you kill it? If you do, it could be a good thing for both of us."

I declined, and the bill was assigned for hearing to a committee whose members had never before shown any interest in this subject. Presently they were urging me to schedule a hearing, which is by custom the sponsor's prerogative. When I did so, the Taxpayers Federation, Farm Bureau, and other respected groups endorsed the bill. There was virtually no opposition. Where-upon the eager committee killed the bill by a vote of twenty to nothing, and I could only wonder why.

There are rumors—which obviously I cannot verify—that under-the-table transactions provide an income of $100,000 a session for one prominent Representative when his party is in power. Other leading legislators and their cliques reportedly collect profits well into five figures.

As in many state capitals, there are no controls on lobbyists in Springfield. A weak law requires them to register with the Secretary of State. But they can hand out any amount of money to influence legislators, without disclosing their expenditures. Legislators in turn need not account for campaign contributions or disclose their source. Nor are there any real safeguards against conflicts between the public's and the legislator's private interest.

Pampering the Ponies

Among the chief beneficiaries of these easy-going ways are our state's race-tracks, which enjoy one of the lowest tax rates in the nation—while our tax on a loaf of bread and a pound of hamburger is the highest in the nation. There are no regular lobbyists representing racing and pari-mutuel betting interests in Springfield. But several influential legislators, or members of their families, are stockholders in racetracks. On special guest nights, busloads of sympathetic legislators are driven to the tracks, given a lavish cocktail party and dinner, then escorted to reserved seats and provided with tips on likely winners on the day's card. At one track, important races are named in honor of individual legislators on these gala occasions.

A notable racing enthusiast is the President Pro Tem of the Senate, a dapper, likable suburbanite named Arthur J. Bidwill, whose family has long been registered with the State Racing Commission as track stockholders. Bidwill distributes fistfuls of season passes in the Senate chambers, and when racing bills are heard in committee he testifies for the industry. At one recent hearing, he was the only witness to oppose increasing taxes on winnings. Yet he prevailed.

A few years ago, backers of Sportsman's Park in Cicero decided to stage trotting in addition to regular racing. To get legislative approval they sent ex-convict Irwin "Big Sam" Wiedrick to Springfield with authority to offer nine influential legislators large blocs of stock in an operating affiliate of the track, at the bargain price of ten cents a share. Among those who accepted was a long-time chairman of the legislature's budget-making commission; another was a shrewd, folksy downstate Representative who has served three terms as Speaker. He bought nearly 17,000 shares in his wife's name and was allowed more than a year to pay. Meanwhile, he received $16,900 in "dividends," enabling him to "buy" the stock without any capital outlay whatever.

The Chicago *Sun-Times* recently reported that his return on this investment amounted to $23,000 in 1963. When a reporter queried him about the transaction (he is now running for another office) he replied, "The only mistake I made was that I didn't get more."[1]

Needless to say, Sportsman's Park got its trotting races despite a long history of hoodlum infiltrations. (The Capone syndicate helped found this track, and only last summer a multi-million-dollar bookie ring was uncovered there.)

The privileged position enjoyed by the state's racing interests was impressed on me during my first term when a bill was introduced to reduce by one-third the taxes on two prosperous downstate tracks in which several legislators owned stock. At that time—in the 1950s—Illinois was starved for revenue, and was heading for the kind of financial crisis that soon was to plague Michigan. Though we were already borrowing against future tax receipts, revenue was still inadequate. To meet this crisis the House voted a 50 per cent increase in the sales tax, to a level of 3 per cent. (It now is 3.5 per cent in Illinois, plus an addition 21.5 per cent for municipalities, the second-highest combined total in the nation.) On the same day the leadership proposed a vote, without committee hearing, on the racetrack bonanza. I objected strenuously and several colleagues agreed. Richard Stengel, a highly respected Representative who later ran for the U.S. Senate, called the bill "the biggest steal since I've been in the legislature."

"You just call it a steal because you're not in on it!" a leading fellow Democrat retorted.

There was a motion for an immediate vote. The bill passed and was rushed to then Governor, Republican William G. Stratton, for signature.

Stengel and I, suspecting skullduggery, filed a protest urging the Governor to veto the bill. The response was a unique experience—a resolution of censure against us filed by a House colleague, Carl Preihs. Stengel and I, he said, were "men who lacked integrity" and had "disgraced" the legislature. Legislative leaders who previously had been friendly suddenly became brusque. We were so ostracized that Stengel, in phoning me, quipped, "Hello Measles. This is Smallpox."

Next day the Governor signed the bill—the only non-emergency measure to be acted upon so quickly in that session—and the censure resolution was dropped.

The Indestructible Syndicate

A bipartisan Chicago group known as the "West Side Bloc" consistently—and usually successfully—oppose periodic efforts to clean up elections, streamline Chicago government, and pass major anti-crime legislation.* This coalition includes a few syndicate-backed Chicago aldermen, one State Senator, and several Representatives. Recently, it has been in the news because party leaders, for the coming campaign at least, have denied some Bloc members places on the at-large ballot on the grounds that they are "undesirable."**

The Bloc crops up regularly in sinister headlines in Chicago. Just before my first term, for example, a State Representative named Clem Graver, a known associate of gangsters, was taken for a ride by unidentified men and was never seen again. The legislature, however, did not really investigate his disappearance.

Shortly afterward I witnessed firsthand the mysterious way in which legislation opposed by the syndicate is voted down even though it is favored by a vast majority of Illinois citizens. In session after session, proposals to create a State Crime Commission were defeated. Few legislators opposed the Commission publicly, though there were some who expressed sincere concern that it might be used for political purposes or would waste money; the majority of legislators either endorsed it or remained silent.

Still, the measure repeatedly died while other commissions with less laudable objectives easily won approval. The main opposition pressure, without question, came from criminal elements.

Last spring Commission adherents tried again. Pressure from the press and civic organizations was intensified when a powerful alderman in Chicago, Benjamin Lewis, was found shot to death in his office on the city's West Side. The Chicago City Council chose not to investigate the case or the possible ties between the unknown killers and politics in Lewis' ward. The bill finally passed. But the legislature cut the new agency's proposed budget in half, to $100,000. Then House leaders went on to pick their representatives on the Commission. Breaking a long-standing tradition, they omitted the House sponsor of the bill, Representative Anthony Scariano—a courageous, honest suburban legislator who has aggressively fought organized crime. Instead, they chose one legislator who voted against the bill, another who had abstained (tantamount to a "no"), one who had voted against it in the previous session, and one who had been Chief Deputy Sheriff of populous St. Clair County at a time when it was so wide open that the Kefauver Crime Committee held a special investigation into its affairs. Reporters later asked Scariano whether he believed the West Side Bloc had kept him off his own Commission. "It wasn't the YMCA," he replied.

Almost every major anticrime measure proposed in Springfield in recent years has suffered similar sabotage. In the 1959 session, for example, a bill was introduced to ban a gambling type pinball machine that had been outlawed in all states but Nevada, part of Maryland, and Illinois. Presently, one newspaperman reported seeing jukebox king Frank Zito (a delegate to the syndicate's famous Apalachin "Summit Conference") in a Capitol hallway, an unusual sight even in Springfield. The bill soon ran into trouble—a House committee tried to kill it quietly for lack of a quorum; the Speaker declined to schedule it for a full House vote until 3:00 A.M. on the last day of the session. When the bill nonetheless passed, Governor Stratton inexplicably vetoed it. In 1961, a similar measure was quietly amended to death. Last spring, another version passed—but, like the Crime Commission, only in watered-down form. It does not prevent the *manufacture* of these machines.

Around this time, Chicago Police Superintendent Orlando W. Wilson and other top law-enforcement officials were sponsoring another bill, patterned after a New York law, which would change syndicate gambling from a misdemeanor to a felony. The measure was killed. This time the Republican Majority Leader himself handled the main parliamentary maneuvers with the House Speaker, also a Republican, cooperating. The Chicago *Daily News* commented editorially under the headline, "Syndicate Rolls a Seven."

Bipartisan Gravy Train

Gambling and horse racing are not, of course, the only odd objects of legislators' benevolence. There is, for instance, the influential Republican Senator who owns a finance company. He routinely looks after the small-loan industry, which in Illinois is so loosely regulated that "easy payments" may carry interest charges as high as 36 per cent. Another Senator privately represents the state's largest highway-contracting association, according to a Chicago newspaper. Also among his clients was an engineering firm organized just in time to win a $600,000 state contract for a toll-road survey. Such conflicts of interest are common in both parties, which work together in ways that have little to commend them.

A bond between the parties is an interest in preserving patronage. Illinois has a spoils system second only to Pennsylvania's. There are nearly twenty thousand political state jobs; and local governments, especially Chicago, provide thousands more. "Never mind the issues, how many jobs can you get us?" is the theme song of hosts of precinct workers during campaigns. Legislators often collaborate to satisfy this hunger. The results are sometimes peculiar.

Occasionally, for instance, a Republican legislator turns up on a Democratic payroll. Thus, in 1961, two Republicans who held Democratic spoils jobs in Chicago announced that they were too ill to vote, and a third GOP member voted with the Democrats at our first organizing session. As a result, the Republicans failed to elect a Speaker though they held a one-vote majority in the House.

Cook County, which includes Chicago, elects the large majority of Democratic legislators. Whoever controls the political jobs in Cook County in effect controls the party. That man now is Chicago's Mayor Richard Daley.

When a major bill is considered in the legislature, the floor leader, after getting instructions from Chicago or from the Governor's office, simply announces, "We're for it," or, "We're against it." Only a few Democratic members from downstate—of whom I am one—and a handful of independent Cook County legislators dare to take a different position.

Budget-making in our legislature is handled by a self-perpetuating clique behind closed doors. Millions of dollars—approximately half the state's total revenue—now are frozen in "earmarked" funds guarded by special-interest lobbies. There are right now huge, untouchable surpluses earmarked (but not being fully used) for highways, driver education, county fairs, and the like, while schools, mental health, welfare, and other vital programs lag for lack of money, but the legislature spends freely on certain highway programs. One pet project was a toll-road system costing hundreds of millions of dollars more than a comparable freeway.

The chairman of the Toll Highway Commission, Evan Howell, resigned a lifetime federal judgeship to accept the chairmanship at a lower salary. Subsequently it was revealed that he had founded a "contractors' club" with dues of a thousand dollars—allegedly to assure preferential treatment for members. His expense accounts in less than two years ran to $11,000, including such items as a Lake Shore Drive apartment in Chicago, and $18 a day for newspapers. Clearly an inquiry was in order. But Governor Stratton prevented an investigation with the help of most GOP legislators and two Democrats.

Near the end of the 1955 session this impregnable defense was broken by a weird incident—chairman Howell made a derogatory remark about a legislator in a Springfield bar. Like other legislators, Illinois lawmakers will overlook many things, but never an affront, real or fancied, to the legislature's "dignity."

The next day, amid indignant shouts, an inquiry into Howell's conduct was voted. Only six quick hearings were held, and the committee was not supplied with a lawyer or even a full-time clerk. Nonetheless some of the dismal facts I have cited here were brought out and published in a committee report. Howell was forced to resign, but there was no further probing.

Forgotten Headlines

Such speedy burial was to prove impossible in a situation that developed shortly afterward. This was the case of Orville E. Hodge, popular, play-boyish, and apparently wealthy Republican State Auditor who had used up a two-year appropriation for operating his office in eighteen months. Now he was asking legislators for whom he had done many favors to bail him out by approving a half-million dollar deficiency appropriation to cover his shortage.

If ever a case called for legislative scrutiny, this seemed to be it. Two of us in the House said so, and opposed the appropriation. But, under prodding from Hodge, the request rolled through, plus a new appropriation almost $2 million larger than the previous one.

A few months later the Chicago *Daily News* revealed why Hodge had needed extra money: With the help of an assistant and a cooperative bank, he had stolen $2,500,000 in public funds. He had loaded his payroll with key legislators' friends, used public money for high living, associated closely with hoodlums and gamblers. According to the St. Louis *Post-Dispatch*, he even had entered a partnership in a motel with a rackets boss in the St. Louis area, Frank "Buster" Wortman, and slot machine king Thomas J. Berry. Only masquerading as wealthy, Hodge actually was of fairly ordinary means. These revelations shocked the entire state, and many citizens elsewhere. A thorough investigation and major reforms seemed imminent. Hodge was quickly tried, and convicted of misappropriating a proportion of the total funds. Then he was hurried off to prison without extensive public questioning. Only minor fiscal reforms were enacted, and proposals for a full-scale legislative probe were defeated. In 1963, Hodge was paroled without ever having told his full story.

The case refused to die, however. George Thiem, Pulitzer Prize–winning reporter who had broken the scandal in the newspapers, published a book, *The Hodge Scandal* (St. Martin's Press). In it he quoted a representative of a leading utility company, who described how it had succeeded in persuading the Illinois legislature to pass a bill saving the company $35,000 a year in franchise taxes. The price, said the utility man, was $35,000. And the money was paid to Hodge, whose friends in the legislature took care of the details. One former legislator, for example, admitted that Hodge gave him $2,000 for his "help" on this and other bills. The utility measure, naturally, passed easily.

"We didn't think the fee was excessive," a utility tax consultant told Thiem. "We got what we wanted. The fee was in line with what we were used to paying."

A major scandal like this, of course, makes front-page news. But, by and large, the press does not pay enough attention to the state legislature. Only a handful of papers—most of them in Chicago—even attempt full-scale legislative coverage. All too rarely is even a roll call published statewide showing how legislators vote. Nor is there a complete daily journal of proceedings beyond the mere disposition of bills. Clearly this lack of public scrutiny is an open invitation to mischief which, I fear, is equally present in many states.

Ten years ago, a report of the Committee on American Legislatures of the American Political Science Association said, "Modernization of American state legislatures is considered by many to be the most important piece of unfinished business in the area of government reorganization." From my experience in Illinois and my knowledge of other legislatures, I would consider that an understatement.

Notes

¹*Editor's note*: The "shrewd, folksy" downstate legislator described in the "Pampering the Ponies" section is widely believed to have been Representative Paul Powell of Vienna. This is the same Paul Powell who was discovered upon his death to have been hoarding approximately $800,000 in cash stuffed in shoeboxes in his hotel room closet in Springfield.

*For a fuller discussion of the problem of organized crime in Chicago, see Police Superintendent O. W. Wilson's "How the Police Chief Sees It" in *Harper's*, April 1964.— *The Editors [Harper's]*

**The Republican candidate for Governor, Charles Percy, has declared open war on the West Side Bloc. At a special convention in June he succeeded in purging from the ballot six Republican legislators he had characterized as "dry rot." . . . Hence—whatever the outcome in November—there is at least a faint hope that the tone of the Illinois legislature will improve somewhat.[—*The Editors (Harper's)*]

"Announcing P.S./Washington, a Weekly Column by Congressman Paul Simon, the 24th Congressional District of Illinois," February 2–8, 1975

Each week I'll be sending the news media in the district my comments on various matters pending before Congress. It will be an informal column in which I'll try to avoid the use of phrases and terms too many of us in government use, which often confuse the public.

If from time to time you would like to see me write a column on any specific subject, drop me a note.

I have now been a member of Congress for one month, barely long enough to find my way around. But you might be interested in some of the less-than-headline details that a new member goes through.

Clearly a highlight so far was the annual State of the Union message. I'm old-fashioned enough to get a real thrill at being present at this important annual occasion in the history of the nation.

You have to reassure yourself that you really are there as the House convenes, the Senate walks in, the Cabinet walks in, the diplomatic corps and the President. Presiding are Speaker Carl Albert and Vice President Nelson Rockefeller.

You'd have to be pretty callous not to have a feeling of pride and gratitude as you take part in this ceremony.

Much less dramatic, but of no small significance to new members, is getting office space. It is assigned on the basis of seniority, the oldest member in terms of service having first choice and on down to the freshman members.

There were 84 freshmen without seniority, since some had seniority on office space because of previous service in Congress.

Each of the 84 went to a box and drew a number. The freshman who drew number one, Cong. John Krebs of California, got first choice of space.

I drew number 81!

So when you visit the Simon office it will be on the top floor of the Longworth Building, room 1724. Not as nice as the offices Kenneth Gray had, because of seniority—and worse than some of my freshman colleagues because I drew number 81.

But more important than the office space we occupy is the work that gets done. Our office has been working hard and I hope the end result will be a good one for our district and for the nation.

The most newsworthy move made by the new Congress is to do away with automatic seniority. I support this change. No person should automatically continue to hold office—regardless of ability—simply because he continues to breathe and be reelected.

Cong. Henry Reuss of Wisconsin asked me to make a seconding speech for his nomination as chairman of the key Banking and Currency Committee. I was pleased to do it—and also satisfied to see this able man (only fourth in seniority) win the committee chairmanship decisively.

This change away from automatic seniority has to be a healthy move for the nation's lawmaking process.

The winds of change are clearly present, and I'm pleased to be in the halls of Congress at this time.

Hopefully the end result will not be change simply to have change, but change which can help the nation solve some of our severe problems.

2

American Government and Politics

The selections in chapter 2 deal with Paul Simon's thoughts and observations on the broad gamut of American government and politics at the federal and state levels. He served at both levels and for about the same amount of time, eighteen years in state government and twenty-two years in the national government. During that time he was always busily engaged in the politics and the issues of the day, but he was also always thinking and writing about what was going on around him. He constantly watched the legislative process and tried to discern the larger patterns and lessons that would transcend the heat of the moment. In that sense, in today's social science terms, we would term him a "participant-observer," that is, he was a mover and a player in the legislature and in the executive branch while at the same time being the diligent journalist, observer, and analyst steadily trying to make basic sense of it all and identifying the fundamentals and constants at work around him. He was an especially keen observer on behalf of his constituents and fellow citizens. They could not be there with him daily as he made his way through the legislative labyrinth, but he could take time on the weekend to give them a sense of what his week had been like and to share the lessons he drew from those experiences that would interest the folks back home and have an inevitable impact on their daily lives. For Paul Simon, the legislature was a living laboratory where he was always trying to learn new things, which he could then help teach to his friends and neighbors in Illinois or in the world.

This chapter begins where study of American government should always begin, with the Constitution. Paul was a student of American history, and that included the history and meaning of the Constitution. He was particularly devoted to the Bill of Rights and even more ardently to the First Amendment, the source of protection for those basic freedoms of speech, religion, the press, petition, and assembly. Simon was always trying to balance free speech and a free press with the duties and responsibility of living in an ordered society where rights must necessarily be limited at some times and in some circumstances. This was an equation that Simon was continually attempting to solve. The first two selections in this chapter are devoted to free speech and national security issues, and Simon provides a touching story from his childhood that reflects his enormous respect for his father, Martin Simon, and the lessons about personal courage and standing up for one's beliefs and for the underdog that he learned from his father. Those lessons are also reflected in his thoughts about the proposed flag burning amendment and its implications for patriotism and for the balance of freedom and security concerns.

Paul Simon has rightly been called a liberal in terms of his views and voting record. He certainly embraced that label and did not try to avoid it when he ran for office. At the same time, he was not a doctrinaire ideologue deeply entrenched in his philosophical beliefs and afraid to stray from the party line. He constantly thought about and wrote about the size and scope of the state and federal governments. Simon wanted government to serve the people without at the same time becoming too intrusive in their daily lives and businesses and without trampling on their individual rights. He thought frequently about the imperatives of living in a complex web of mutual relationships, responsibilities, and limits, which are imposed by the government acting on behalf of the people, but he also thought about the protection of individual rights and freedoms in an ordered society. All of these philosophical and practical concerns may have led him to his appointment to the Judiciary Committee in the U.S. Senate, where he was able to grill future judges, most notably Supreme Court justices, about their own views and what kinds of judges they were likely to make, even though he was the only member of the committee without a law degree. He had great respect for the courts and especially the Supreme Court of the United States, and the selections included here indicate his esteem for the judicial branch, an esteem that was well grounded in his knowledge of and regard for the Constitution.

Simon's concern for the size and scope of the government is especially evident in some of the selections included in this chapter regarding the budget, the deficit, and the size of the government. Simon was always concerned about the deficit and the need for government to live within its means. He wanted a broad array of public programs that would serve the very real needs of his constituents; however, he likewise favored setting the tax rate at a level that was necessary to pay for whatever current functions the legislature and the executive branch deemed worth doing. He was an early and avid champion of the Balanced Budget Amendment, and in this he was certainly no doctrinaire liberal; however, in his advocacy for tax revenues equal to expenditures, he would not pass the litmus tests imposed by today's tax-adverse conservatives, either.

Paul Simon was a man of the legislative branch of government, and he spent thirty-six of his forty years in public office engaged in the legislative process. At the same time, he was an advocate for executive power and especially the power of the presidency. We are a government of separation of powers and checks and balances, and that very separation guarantees a constant struggle between the branches of government and especially between the two most political branches. Simon was notably concerned that executive power could be harnessed in service to a well-reasoned foreign policy. He knew that there were definite limits on the legislative branch with regard to the making and conduct of an activist foreign policy, and he defended executive rights there, although he was also acutely aware of the need to limit the executive with vigilant legislative oversight. Working out that balance is still a quest that faces us today, and some of Paul's columns here offer cogent commentary on the principles that should guide us in that quest.

Simon spent almost as much of his adult life in service to state government as in national service. Even when he went to Washington, he maintained close ties to the governmental and political processes back home in Illinois. He wrote frequently about the powers and problems of state and local government and was always freely offering his solutions to the current problems and controversies of Illinois government. Most of those problems are still with us today. His observations on both reapportionment and redistricting and on the state pension and debt situation are just as relevant today as they were when he wrote about them decades ago.

The keys that unlock the doors to the state legislature, the Congress, or the executive branch offices are obtained from the successful pursuit of power in the electoral game. Paul Simon played that game very well. He lost only two major elections in his career, the governor's race in the 1972 Illinois Democratic primary and the race to be the Democratic nominee for president in 1988. He won most of the rest of his races by substantial majorities. The only time he was not tough and aggressive in his campaigns was in the pursuit of the Democratic nomination for governor of Illinois in 1972, when he held back and conserved his resources in anticipation of the presumed harder race against Governor Richard Ogilvie in the fall. He learned from that race and never made that mistake again. He was innately distrustful of the polls and some of the blacker arts of the spinmeisters of his day, but he used them anyway and learned from those who could tell him what they meant for his candidacy. He was always skeptical of the excesses of the media-based marketing experts, especially if they wanted to help him change his image, but at the same time the image he had crafted for himself—the thoughtful, bow-tied traditionalist and reformer—was an image that he protected carefully. The difference in his mind was that the image was also the reality, and there was no artifice in that image. It was who Simon was. He often worried about and wrote about those who would sell their souls in service to their drive for power, and his Lutheran upbringing led him to fear that quality and monitor it constantly in his own motives.

This constant monitoring of the electoral process and the toll it takes on candidates was a continuing theme in his writing. He was notably and consistently critical of the role of money and the grinding need always to be raising campaign funds that marks modern American politics. Paul was a reformer and thought that the way we finance campaigns was one of those ever-present challenges that threatened American mass democracy. He would have been appalled at the recent U.S. Supreme Court decision in the *Citizens United* case. He thought Congress had the right and responsibility to try to fix campaign finance limits and to require full disclosure of who is financing our campaigns. He thought campaign funding and the pursuit of personal wealth through the political process often went hand-in-hand and were the sure routes to individual and collective corruption. He wrote about these themes in some of the selections included here, and his observations are even more apt now than they were when he wrote them. The only thing that has changed is that the price tag has gone up and the ability to regulate has diminished.

Paul Simon was no fan of what we popularly call "negative campaigning" and attack advertising during his era in American politics, and that trend, too, has only grown in twenty-first-century America. Paul felt that the mass media have a right and an obligation to hold candidates to high standards. He wanted an assertive and well-informed media that could stand toe-to-toe with the candidates. He wanted elections to turn on a rational public discourse and a reasoned discussion of the issues and challenges that faced the state and nation. He saw public policy in all its complexity and wanted people to understand that the choices they faced were not easy ones. He wanted the politicians to admit that the decisions they made were challenging ones that required them to weigh the options carefully and to decide difficult issues on close calls. Ideological shibboleths and bumper sticker mottoes were not helpful in teaching civics. He thought thirty-second campaign ads were particularly unsuited to the task of educating the public, and he believed in campaigns and elections as exercises in public education and the attainment of civic virtue. Thus, his comments about the electoral system and the role of the media in magnifying some of the worst elements of that system are timely today, since our campaigns have not been elevated or ennobled since Simon wrote about them.

THE CONSTITUTION

"DEFENDING THE CONSTITUTION: A CONSTANT VIGIL," P.S./WASHINGTON, JUNE 28–JULY 4, 1987

One of the greatest lessons I've learned in life is that when you believe in something, stand up for it. Don't let public pressure change your stance.

That lesson was demonstrated most vividly to me by my father who took a public stand against internment of 110,000 Japanese-Americans during World War II. The public outcry was strong against Americans of Japanese heritage following Japan's attack on Pearl Harbor.

We lived on the West Coast where that sentiment was particularly intense. My father, a Lutheran minister, went on a local radio station in Eugene, Oregon, to explain why he thought President Franklin Roosevelt's action ordering the internment was wrong.

We had an old print shop in a building in the back of our house. I can still remember standing in front of the cutter while my father explained why it was wrong for the American government to deny Japanese-Americans their constitutional rights by taking them from their homes and putting them in camps.

There was a small furor in the community and I can remember being embarrassed by it with my friends. My father was on an extremely unpopular side of things. I felt like I had leprosy and, at that point in my life, I wished my father had not done it.

But now as I look back, it's one of the things I'm proudest of my father for. It must have taken a great deal of courage for my father to do that.

It was a great lesson for me. If you believe something, stand up. If there had been a few more Americans to say "this is wrong" maybe we would not have perpetrated this horrible deed against so many Japanese-Americans.

There is another reason to remember the internment. We are celebrating the 200th anniversary of our Constitution, a document that has survived dramatic changes of many kinds since 1787. But the shameful internment in 1942 demonstrates why we can't take the Constitution for granted.

The tragedy of the relocation for the Japanese-Americans was more than the horrid living conditions of the camps, lost property and the irony of many of their sons dead and maimed fighting for the United States. The Japanese-Americans suffered psychological stress, embarrassment and humiliation.

And the relocation confronted the rest of us with the fact that we had paid only lip service to the cherished tradition of equality and constitutional protection. We must never let it happen again.

"Simon on Flag Issue: Why I'll Fight to Defend the Constitution," P.S./Washington, June 24–30, 1990

I'm deeply offended when I read about someone burning a flag. I would be deeply offended if I read about someone burning a Bible. I once saw people in Ku Klux Klan sheets and I cannot describe the sense of disgust I felt. But every time people do something that offends me I should not rush to amend the nation's most basic document, our Bill of Rights.

This has become an issue because the Supreme Court, in a 5–4 decision, struck down a law I supported to prohibit flag burning. I disagree with that decision. If it is constitutional to write a law against burning our money, it should be constitutional to write a law to prohibit flag burning.

The all-time champion of freedom of speech on the Supreme Court, Justice Hugo Black, a quarter-century ago wrote in a court decision: "It passes my belief that anything in the federal Constitution bars a state from making the deliberate burning of the American flag an offense."

But because of the recent 5–4 decision, there has been a race by too many in public life to amend the Bill of Rights for the first time in more than 200 years.

How many people in our country were arrested last year for burning the flag? Four. Are we going to rush to amend the Bill of Rights because four people in a nation of 250 million burned flags?

What protects the flag is not the law, but the loyalty we feel to this nation and what that flag represents. At our home near the small, rural community of Makanda, Illinois, we have a flag flying. We're proud of that flag.

Perhaps I'm a little old-fashioned, but when I served in the Army, I got a thrill out of marching in a unit behind a flag. The flag and the freedom it represents are important to me.

So I am outraged when someone burns a flag. But I am also outraged when someone wants to change our Constitution because it's politically popular to do.

When I took my oath of office, I swore to only one oath: "To uphold and defend the Constitution from all enemies, foreign and domestic." The oath was not "so long as it's politically popular to defend the Constitution from all enemies, foreign and domestic."

My guess is that if a flag constitutional amendment passes, we will probably still find four people in this huge nation who are extremist enough to burn a flag. So what is accomplished by a constitutional amendment? Nothing, other than a few votes garnered for those who want to appear as patriots. Yes, I am outraged by flag burners. And I'm outraged by people who think I'm unpatriotic for defending the Constitution.

I'm also outraged by people who steal from savings and loans. I'm outraged that millions of young people don't have a quality education. I am outraged that we have homeless people. I am outraged that millions of Americans cannot afford decent health care.

These are things Congress and the President can act upon, to make this a better country. These are things that test our real loyalty, our sense of national community. Instead of dealing with these problems, some use the flag amendment to gain approval by an action that weakens our country's basic document.

In Central and Eastern Europe we are thrilled to see freedom emerge. Most of these nations, once under the dominance of communists, look to our Constitution and our Bill of Rights as shining examples of freedom. Let us not compromise that document in a moment of public hysteria. Isolated attacks on the symbol of our liberty cannot justify a general attack on liberty itself.

ON THE SIZE AND ROLE OF GOVERNMENT

"THE SIZE OF THE FEDERAL GOVERNMENT,"
P.S./WASHINGTON, AUGUST 15–21, 1976

My friends at Station WMCL in McLeansboro recently had an editorial calling for a reduction in the size of the federal government by passing "a law to prevent the government from filling vacancies due to retirement, resignation or termination. Through attrition the number on the federal payroll will get smaller each year." That sounds good, and there are agencies in which I'd like to apply that procedure.

But do we want to reduce the number of coal mine inspectors? Do we want to reduce Social Security personnel, slowing those checks even more? Do we want to reduce the number of FBI agents? Do we want to reduce our Army that drastically?

I think not.

The editorial is based on the assumption that the federal government has grown tremendously. You may be surprised at the actual figures. In 1961 there were five million federal employees, and in May of this year (the latest figures available) there were five million federal employees.

Some agencies have grown, others have declined. Under President Nixon an amazing 80 new agencies were created, though in fairness, most of those assumed functions which the federal government already exercised.

By comparison with the relative stability of the federal government, state and local governments had five and one-half million employees in 1960 and by 1975 that figure had more than doubled to 11.7 million. Much of that growth has taken place in our schools.

If you subtract the Department of Defense and the Postal Service from the number of federal employees, the balance is just over one million federal employees, and that figure has been fairly constant. And considering the fact that there are 220 million Americans, that is not an outlandish figure.

There are some imbalances and some excesses. I tried to get rid of one useless agency, the Postal Rate Commission, but narrowly lost. Sen. Gary Hart of Colorado recently pointed out that 3,200,000 Americans work for the Department of Defense, but just 179 work for the Arms Control and Disarmament Agency—about one-third the number that work in the American Battle Monuments Commission. The great growth in federal expenditures has been in programs like Social Security, programs which I believe most Americans think are sound.

Where there are abuses, where we can cut back, we should.

But we cannot simply freeze all employment.

We should be prudent in our employment policies. There is always room for improvement, but the situation is probably a little better than you thought.

"GOVERNMENT REGULATION," P.S./WASHINGTON, FEBRUARY 18–24, 1979

There is an understandable mood against government regulation in Congress and Main Street, U.S.A. There are so many ridiculous illustrations of nit-picking things that government regulators do—each of us can find examples—and these are aggravating.

But before we go overboard on stripping government regulators of all their power, it is important to note another side also. Our air and water are cleaner today than ten years ago, thanks to air and water pollution regulations. That means a healthier population and longer life for the average citizen. Perhaps the most graphic example of both the problems and the opportunities is OSHA, the Occupational Safety and Health Administration within the Department of Labor.

There is no question that many OSHA inspectors have been impractical, suggesting that a fire extinguisher had to be raised or lowered a few inches, giving complicated details about using a ladder, or advising farmers that manure on a concrete barn floor could be slippery.

The new administrator, Eula Bingham, has eliminated more than 1,000 of those regulations, properly terming them useless.

But the other side of the story is that OSHA has done some good. When Congress relaxed OSHA's authority over certain industries, the number of accidental deaths in those industries more than doubled in one year, going from 962 to 1,926.

OSHA now offers special help to small businesses who request them to come in, suggesting ways plants can be safer. Since OSHA went into effect in 1972 the number of industrial injuries in Illinois has dropped by 16 percent. In Michigan they have dropped by 45 percent. Those are impressive statistics.

Each member of Congress gets a host of examples of needless regulations every month. Regulations often go far beyond the intent of a law that Congress passes. And sometimes those who are supposed to make the law and regulations work seem bent on making the government process as difficult as possible for people, rather than as easy as possible.

But granting all of that, we should be careful what we deregulate as well as what we regulate. Partial deregulation of the airline industry has been a great thing. Dropping more than 1,000 OSHA regulations has been good.

But there continue to be good and reasonable laws and regulations that our society needs.

"Air Bags and Government's Role," P.S./Washington, January 13–19, 1991

My wife and I decided that our 1980 Chevrolet, with well over 100,000 miles on it, should be traded in for a new American-made car. I travel a great deal, usually not in my car, but I have become safety conscious because of the accidents and tragedies I have seen.

Whether it is greater safety at railroad crossings, or making O'Hare Airport in the Chicago area more safe, these are issues I've spent a great deal of time on.

I use my car seat belt, not only because of the statistical evidence that using seat belts saves lives, but I had a friend die in an accident because he was not wearing a seat belt. And I recall what a Jackson County emergency ambulance service driver told me, "I've never taken a dead body out of a car when the person was wearing a seat belt."

But the latest automobile safety improvement beyond seat belts is air bags. Again, the statistics are clear, and if you doubt the statistics gathered by the federal government, just listen to what the insurance people have to say. They are interested in saving lives—and money.

Because of that knowledge, when Jeanne and I went to buy a new car we decided that we would get one with an air bag on the driver's side and one on the passenger's side.

To my amazement, the only cars that have them are the Lincoln and the Mercedes.

I told the automobile sales people with whom I talked that I would be willing to pay an extra $500 or $1,000 if I could have an air bag on both sides. "Sorry," I was told by everyone. "We don't do that."

The good news is that by 1994, nearly all cars will be available with air bags on both the driver and passenger sides.

Chrysler, to its credit, was first to have air bags on the driver's side in all its American-made cars. But if it's clear that air bags would save thousands of lives—and it is—why should we be selling any new cars in the United States, whether they're made here or abroad, that do not have at least two air bags? All this brings up the fundamental question of how far government should go in our lives.

The first question is whether an action will actually save lives or accomplish something worthwhile. In many cases, lawmakers have less-than-obvious choices. In this one, the evidence is decisive.

The second question is whether a theoretical answer can actually be enforced. There are areas in our personal lives where enforcement becomes difficult, if not impossible. But in the regulation of cars, enforcement is relatively easy.

A third question is one of cost. I have read different estimates on what air bags add to the manufacturer's cost on a car. But it is probably around $200 per air bag. Is it worth it to add that burden on the public? My answer is yes, though people I respect differ with me. But when you look at the lives that can be saved, I find the evidence compelling.

This type of decision, with the same three criteria, faces legislators whether they sit on a city council, county board, state legislature, or in the U.S. Congress. Should we have fluoridation of our public water? Should we encourage states to prohibit alcoholic drinking among those under 21? Should a county have zoning? The questions go on and on.

In some cases, I decide that government should provide leadership, and in some cases I decide against it. But where government should act is one of those fundamental questions that legislators face over and over, and your insights and practical suggestions on these issues can help us make better decisions.

CONGRESS: THE DUTIES OF A CONGRESSMAN

"YOUR CONGRESSIONAL OFFICE," P.S./WASHINGTON, APRIL 20–26, 1975

What goes on in a Congressional office? You know that I attend committee meetings and then vote on the floor of the House. But what else goes on? There are three offices in the district: Carbondale, West Frankfort, and Mount Vernon. The main office is in Washington.

I asked our Washington office to keep track of the number of letters we answered this past week: 987. In addition there is some mail in the district offices. Some weeks the mail will be heavier than that figure of 987, some weeks lighter.

We also try to serve people who call the office or stop by, though generally a letter is a more effective way to reach the office because we have exactly what your views are, or what you want. The address is simply: Paul Simon, House of Representatives, Washington D.C. 20515.

If you do want to call and the line is busy, call back again. We have five lines into the Washington office and they frequently are all busy. Also, you can usually save yourself a phone bill by calling one of the district offices. They will relay the information to us in Washington.

Perhaps half of the people who write or contact us do so to express their views on matters which face the country, and the other half with some type of problem they face: social security, black lung, military and many others.

In addition to handling these things, the staff keeps me reasonably on schedule, telling me when committee meetings are scheduled, working in meetings with people from Southern Illinois who visit Washington, and trying to save time for me to read the mail and prepare for bills which are coming up.

Two members of the staff are called "legislative assistants," and they do research on bills, and help me with drafting proposals which I will introduce in Congress. The picture the public many times has is of people with soft jobs who work few hours, living the life of ease in Washington, D.C.

The fact is that the staff works hard, puts in more than 40 hours a week (with no extra pay for overtime), genuinely tries to be of help to people who need our help—and often work on weekends and holidays. On one recent holiday I would guess that about half the Congressional staff personnel for all the Congressmen were hard at work—and none of them got any extra pay for it.

Without a dedicated staff no Congressman could do a good job, and the people in my district and other districts can be grateful for what staffs do.

"Congress: Reality Better Than Image," P.S./Washington, October 9–15, 1977

If you are looking for good news that does not make the headlines—and unfortunately good news tends to bore people—the magazine *U.S. News and World Report* had some good news in it the other day.

The person who heads the magazine's congressional staff, Thomas J. Foley, reflected on his 20 years of reporting on Congress and came up with these six conclusions:

(1) Congress is more democratic (with a small "d") than it used to be. Twenty years ago a handful of men held all the power in Congress.

(2) Seniority is less all-powerful than it once was. Ability plays more of a role in leadership.

(3) There is less secrecy in lawmaking.

(4) Congress's ethical restrictions have been significantly beefed up.

(5) Congress is more responsible in fiscal matters.

(6) Congress works harder.

Foley does not suggest that there is no room for improvement. Obviously there is.

But the nation's citizens could read a host of newspapers, listen to all of the radio and television broadcasts, and read the major news magazines and come away with precisely the opposite opinion of that expressed by Foley.

Read about Korean payoffs and other wrongs and you come to the conclusion that things are really going in the wrong direction in Washington. The quiet, steady improvements that have been made are not particularly newsworthy.

No changes in our rules or in the laws will ever be a substitute for an alert citizenry electing responsible, capable men and women to public office.

But some changes in our procedures still are needed:

(1) Detailed income disclosure should be required of members of Congress, their spouses and minor children. Present disclosure requirements are better than they were but are still not adequate.

(2) A change in rules is needed so that members serve on not more than one committee. To have to be in two committees at the same time (while sessions are going on in the Capitol) does not make sense.

(3) We should change the rules to encourage greater attendance during sessions when amendments are considered. Now an amendment may carry by a vote of 14–11, in a House with 435 members. This change has to be tied in with the previous point, so that our schedules do not demand that we be in two or three places at the same time.

Even without these changes, the people of the nation have more cause for pride in Congress than they realize. That is self-serving, coming from a member of Congress. But the people in my district ought to know that I am proud to serve here, and though there are days of discouragement, there is also some satisfaction in knowing that the reality is better than the image.

"Travel More, Not Less," P.S./Washington, April 27–May 3, 1980

One of the subjects most poorly covered by the media on the Washington scene is Congressional foreign travel. The Washington press corps does an excellent job in a number of subject areas, but foreign travel coverage rates poorly because:

1. The assumption that foreign travel is an abuse of public privilege is near the surface of most stories. Where there is abuse of public travel it obviously should be pointed out, but most congressional foreign travel is not abused.

2. The great public disservice by Members of Congress is not traveling enough, voting on issues important to the future of this nation and other nations with little background for those decisions. I have yet to see a news article or editorial criticizing any Member of Congress for not traveling, yet that is by far the greater abuse. Would we have had the problems in Vietnam, Afghanistan, and Iran if more Members had traveled and understood these areas better?

3. The imbalance of travel is not noted.

Two incidents brought this last point to my attention. Visiting in Washington recently with an official of Togo, I asked him when the last Member of Congress visited his country, and he replied: 1964.

Visiting with the Ambassador from Uruguay I asked him how many Members of Congress have visited that important South American country in his five years as Ambassador here. His response: one (Rep. Larry McDonald of Georgia).

The last published compilation of congressional travel I have been able to get is for 1978.

During that year not one Member of Congress visited Afghanistan, Pakistan and Grenada—three countries that have become important in foreign policy.

Strategically important countries like Libya, Somalia, East Germany, Poland, Honduras and the Dominican Republic each had one visitor.

Members of Congress should not do the work of the State Department, but Congress has a major voice in shaping the outlines of our foreign policy and recent history suggests that too often we blunder, not because we are poorly motivated, but because we are poorly informed.

The media compounds this problem by failing to point out the irresponsibility of not traveling. Frequently I have had colleagues tell me they would really like to travel to understand a situation better but they are afraid to because of the criticism they will get back home. There is literally no fear of criticism for not traveling.

I also believe the Foreign Affairs Committee of the House and Senate each year should send a list of countries to House and Senate Members suggesting that a trip to this country or that country would be in the national interest. Some countries are over-traveled, some under-traveled.

In 1978, there were 123 congressional visits to Great Britain, 94 to Japan, 77 to Switzerland, 67 to China, and 63 to West Germany. But Nigeria and Algeria—both major sources of energy for the U.S.—had no visitors.

Nor did these countries: Albania, Andorra, Angola, Bahrain, Bangladesh, Barbados, Belize, Benin, Bhutan, Bolivia, Brunei, Bulgaria, Burundi,

Cameroon, Cape Verde, Cayman Islands, Central African Empire, Chad, Comoros, Congo, Djibouti, Equatorial Guinea, Ethiopia, Falkland Islands, Fiji, Gabon, Ghana, Gibraltar, Gilbert Islands, Grenada, Guinea-Bissau, Iceland, Kampuchea, Lesotho, Liechtenstein, Madagascar, Malawi, Maldives, Malta, Mauritius, Mongolia, Montserrat, Nauru, Nepal, New Hebrides, New Zealand, Niger, Oman, Paraguay, Pitcairn, Qatar, Rwanda, St. Helena, San Marino, Sao Tomé, Seychelles, Sierra Leone, Solomon Islands, Sri Lanka, Surinam, Swaziland, Togo, Tonga, Trinidad-Tobago, Turks and Caicos Islands, Tuvalu, Uganda, and Uruguay. (Joe Johnson of my staff pulled together this information.)

How many of those countries have not been visited in five years? In ten years? In how many of those countries are we "missing the boat" and hurting our economy and our security because we simply lack fundamental knowledge? More than 99 percent of the travel expenditures of the federal government are made by the executive branch. The legislative branch, which has a major policy role, too often acts on impulse rather than knowledge.

That is not a good way to establish policy.

THE PRESIDENCY

"THE PRESIDENCY: HOW STRONG SHOULD IT BE?," P.S./WASHINGTON, SEPTEMBER 28–OCTOBER 4, 1975

During debate on the floor some weeks ago, one of the Republican leaders, Congressman John Anderson of Illinois, commented: "The trouble with you Democrats is that you look at the White House and see Richard Nixon sitting there. He is no longer President and there is a certain amount of fundamental trust the nation must give the chief executive if we are to govern effectively."

That paraphrases his remarks, but I believe it does so accurately. There is much truth to what he said. One of the fundamental struggles taking place is resolving the relationship between Congress and the presidency. The topic of debate may be oil or foreign aid or the defense budget, but the more fundamental struggle keeps emerging. We have gone through a period in which Congress did not have an adequate voice in the nation's policy. Vietnam and Watergate have caused us to reexamine that course.

And so we have placed restrictions—proper restrictions—on the warmaking powers of the President as well as other powers. Perhaps as good an example as any is the Food for Peace program (Public Law 480) in which a better balance also has been achieved. Congress appears likely to enact a permanent change, requiring that 70 percent of the food aid sent abroad must go to the most needy nations. We do not specify which of the needy nations should receive the aid, nor precisely how the administration should make its decisions on the other 30 percent.

Here the fundamental policy is determined by Congress, with the President's signature, but the details of carrying it out are left to the executive branch. In the complex military aid to Turkey question, however, I have the feeling that because of some administrative inadequacies Congress is making decisions which really ought to be left to the executive branch. The Greek-Turkey-Cyprus situation demands a flexibility of response that Congress is not equipped to handle.

No session of Congress and no President will come up with any final answer on the balance of power between the two branches of government. The proper middle course to be followed is much easier to determine with the reading of history than when you are in the middle of the storm of events making the decisions. But my impression is that we are now leaning a little too heavily on the Congressional side of the decision process. And I am not alone in that conclusion. A *New York Times* article by James N. Naughton quotes Congressman Les AuCoin of Oregon:

"A committee of 435 cannot run the country—and an intensely political committee of 435 egos surely cannot. No one dislikes the policies of the last seven years of GOP administrations more than I do. But the way to change that is to recapture the White House rather than attempt to make Congress something which inherently it cannot be. Sooner or later the Democrats will again control the White House. We will have won a hollow victory if we have structurally weakened what is still the best instrument for leadership in this country."

"CONGRESS OR THE WHITE HOUSE: WHO SETS FOREIGN POLICY?," P.S./WASHINGTON, AUGUST 24–30, 1986

During debate on both the Contra controversy and South Africa sanctions, a fundamental question arose: How far should Congress go in getting involved in foreign policy?

There is a general feeling—one that I share—that it is sound policy to let the President supply the details and the general outline of foreign policy, so long as it is within the guidelines which Congress believes are sound. That is a good theory. But you get into very practical problems when you start looking at specifics. Here are some general areas where the majority of the members of Congress of both political parties disagree with the President:

- We believe that we should be pushing much harder than we have for verifiable arms control agreements with the Soviets.
- We believe that foreign aid should be provided to other countries where people are in great need, but that greater restraint should be used in providing weapons to other countries. A limited weapons policy permitting nations to defend themselves makes sense, but the shift in emphasis from economic assistance to weapons assistance is unsound.
- We believe the administration's refusal to do anything more than preach pious sermons to the South African government alienates us from the other African nations, puts us on the side of those who will inevitably lose in South Africa, plays into the hands of those who are pushing communism, and—most important of all—it does not put this nation on the side of justice.

If we believe the President and his administration are wrong in these areas, then we have to do some nudging, sometimes gently and sometimes not so gently.

And that's what we have been doing.

On military aid to the Contras on the border of Nicaragua, the President has had the support of the majority of Congress—thanks in part to some arm-twisting—but a sizable minority of us in both political parties disagree with him. We believe the $100 million we are providing the Contras (plus indirect costs of more than $400 million) results in needless deaths and long-term harm to the policy goals of the United States. And so we resist that policy, so far without success. But there is a danger in congressional action in these and other foreign policy fields.

Congress can only act with a heavy hand. We have to get a majority of votes for any policy position and that requires changing a few words here, modifying policy there, and then passing something that is not necessarily a good policy weapon. Sometimes foreign policy has to be carried out quietly and with great skill and finesse. Congress has little ability to do anything quietly or with great skill and finesse. The danger is that we will get into the habit of making a great variety of detailed policy decisions.

I recall when Gerald Ford was president there was debate in the House on some foreign policy question. Then-Congressman John Anderson stood up and said, "The trouble with you Democrats is that you look at the White

House and believe Richard Nixon is still there." There was some truth to what he said.

Both sides should avoid getting into bad habits that cause problems not only for this administration but for future administrations. Part of the answer should be greater consultation by the President with Congress in establishing policy. I have served under three presidents—Gerald Ford, Jimmy Carter and Ronald Reagan—and there is significantly less genuine policy consultation under this administration than under the previous two.

A little give and take by both sides can serve current policy well. It can also serve the future well.

ON MAKING NOMINATIONS TO THE SUPREME COURT

"THE SUPREME COURT: AN EASY TARGET," P.S./WASHINGTON, JULY 10–16, 1977

Throughout the history of this nation the U.S. Supreme Court has been one of the favorite targets of all of us, for no one agrees with all the decisions handed down by the courts.

And historically some great mistakes have been made. It is possible, for example, that there would not have been a Civil War had the U.S. Supreme Court ruled differently more than 100 years ago in the case of the run-away slave, Dred Scott.

But in much of the criticism of the Court (including editorials in some of the finest newspapers) there is a failure to understand that the purpose of the Supreme Court is not to determine what is good and wise and humane and sensible. These are the functions (or at least should be) of the legislative and executive branches of government.

The function of the Supreme Court is to determine what is constitutional and what is not, what the law says and what it does not say.

If Congress passes a law that every house in the nation should be painted purple, and the President signs the bill, the function of the Court is not to determine whether it is wise to follow that course, but whether Congress and the President are within the constraints of the Constitution in taking that action.

The decision by the Court sustaining the right of the state and federal governments to decide whether or not these governments will pay for abortion is an illustration in point. Most of the criticisms I have read and heard should be directed at the legislative and executive branches of government rather than the Court.

The Court did not decide the wisdom of paying for abortions, only whether the Constitution requires federal and state governments to pay for them. And the Court properly—in my opinion—decided that this is a matter for the other two branches to determine; it is not a constitutional question.

I regularly receive letters which ask why the Court "stands up for murderers, kidnappers, communists, and those who stir up trouble."

The Court, in these cases, stands up for constitutional rights—and if a murderer or a Communist can be denied those constitutional rights, some day you and I might be denied them too.

The recent decision that a small Nazi group must have the right to march in a Chicago suburb and express its opinions is an unpopular Court decision, but a right decision.

The Nazis stand for everything I abhor: racism and totalitarianism among other things. Every member of the Court abhors their stands also.

But that is not the question. The question is whether someone with an extremely unpopular view has the right in a free society to stand up and express that view. The Court rules that they have that right. And because of that Court ruling, you and I are a little more secure in our freedom also.

For those Nazis in reality pose no real threat to the nation. They are a handful of emotionally immature people who should have been permitted to have their event in the first place and not have received all of this publicity. The best way to spread the news about something like this is to try to suppress it. And while the Nazis pose no threat to us, denying people the right of free speech would pose a threat to everything we believe in.

The Court makes some mistakes. It is composed of human beings.

But through the decades it has been a great defender of our freedom.

"Advise and Consent: What Does It Mean?," P.S./Washington, August 3–9, 1986

"The President was elected by all the people in the nation. You should go along with his choices for judge." That message is from an Illinois citizen, and it's partially right and partially wrong.

Generally a senator should go along with the President's appointments. I have. Of several hundred presidential appointees I have voted against six. Why vote against these six?

Just as the President has a constitutional responsibility, so do those of us in the Senate. We are to "advise and consent" to the people the President names, not rubber stamp them.

When the framers of the Constitution discussed naming federal judges, at first they proposed the entire Congress—House and Senate—name the judges. They gradually realized that would be unworkable, so they changed it so the Senate would name the judges.

It stayed that way until the final drafting session, and then it was changed so the President would name the judges but "by and with the advice and consent of the Senate."

From earliest times, that power has been used by the Senate, but used with prudence. For example, George Washington's nominee for chief justice of the Supreme Court was rejected by the Senate. In the cases of judges there is a particular reason for the Senate to look carefully. Those appointed will serve a lifetime. When the President appoints an ambassador to Australia or a secretary of commerce, that person serves as long as the President wants him or her to serve. But in the case of a federal judge, that appointment is for the life of the judge.

I voted for a federal judge in Texas when the majority of my party voted against him. He had made a mistake—legal but unethical—some years before but otherwise his record was outstanding. So I voted with the President. In a few other cases I have not voted with the President. But when I have voted against the President's nominees, I have felt that a strong case was evident that a mistake was being made.

The Senate is voting on two of the most important appointments a President can make: Chief Justice of the U.S. Supreme Court and a new member of the Supreme Court. I am on the Judiciary Committee that, as I write this, is holding hearings on these nominees, William Rehnquist and Antonin Scalia. I have avoided making a commitment on either man prior to the votes. Both have visited with me, and I have listened to days of testimony before our committee. When the dust settles I shall cast my votes.

Regardless of the political affiliation of the President, each of us in the Senate has the solemn and constitutional responsibility to cast these votes with care.

Those who wrote our Constitution clearly wanted that.

"No on Rehnquist, Yes on Scalia,"
P.S./Washington, August 17–23, 1986

The Senate Judiciary Committee has approved two nominations for the United States Supreme Court—William Rehnquist as chief justice and

Antonin Scalia as associate justice—few votes that I cast on the committee will equal their importance. The full Senate will take up the nominations in September. I entered the hearings inclined to confirm both nominees. But after the evidence was presented and weighed, I decided to vote against one of the nominees, Mr. Rehnquist.

I asked myself two basic questions: Will this nominee fulfill the responsibilities well and will this nominee be better than someone else the President might name? In reaching these decisions, at the Supreme Court level consideration of political philosophy is not only in order, it is required if the Senate is to take our responsibilities seriously.

William Rehnquist wrote in the *Harvard Law Record* in 1959:

"Until the Senate restores its practice of thoroughly informing itself on the judicial philosophy of a Supreme Court nominee before voting to confirm him, it will have a hard time convincing doubters that it could make effective use of any additional part in the selection process."

The future Supreme Court justice was correct.

In the case of Justice Rehnquist, he clearly has the capability to continue as a top legal scholar, and I have no question about his ability to administer the Court as its chief justice.

I have serious reservations about his ability to fulfill the role of the symbol of justice for all of our people. His record on civil rights and civil liberties going back long before his years on the Court is not strong. His vision of the law alienates large numbers of Americans.

When I ask myself the question, Will this nominee be better than someone else the President might name?, the reality is that any member of the Court can fulfill the role of chief justice as the symbol of justice for all the people better than Justice Rehnquist can.

I am opposing his nomination, recognizing the strong probability that he will be approved. If that happens, I hope he will understand the added symbolic responsibilities of his new role.

In the case of Judge Scalia I again recognize his ability. He is more rigid on some issues, such as affirmative action, than I would like, but he shows flashes of open-mindedness. If he should be turned down, I have no reason to believe that the President will nominate anyone who would serve better as an associate justice.

I voted for Judge Scalia.

"STATEMENT OF PAUL SIMON: SENATE JUDICIARY COMMITTEE," SEPTEMBER 4, 2001

I'm pleased you are having this hearing on the historic role played by the Senate and the President in judicial nominations.

At the founding of our nation, the idea was that the Senate could be a sort of informal cabinet for the President, advising him regularly on a host of matters. It soon became apparent that that hope was unrealistic. When the Senate reached the point of confirming nominations from the President, the Senate invited George Washington to join them for consideration of the nominees, but Washington wisely declined, stating that the Senate should feel free to accept or reject nominees without any pressure from the President.

By tradition the President does seek the advice—under "advice and consent"—of Senators or ranking House members for district judgeships. The Constitution is being followed. At the appellate level it is sometimes followed. Because I served on this committee I had conversations with the White House on a few of these appointments. But at the most important level, the Supreme Court, it is rarely followed today. We are a long way from a Supreme Court contest in which President James Garfield wrote that a nomination he made "will settle the question whether the President is the registering clerk of the Senate or the Executive of the United States."

Two days after George W. Bush took the oath of the presidency, he met with six Democrats—Senator John Glenn, Carter press secretary Jody Powell, Walter Mondale's chief of staff Richard Moe, former Congressman Bill Gray, former Democratic National Committee chair Robert Strauss, and myself—on how he could reach out to Democrats. I stressed that when it comes to nominations for the U.S. Supreme Court he should take his time, consult with members of this committee of both political parties, and with others, because that legacy will live long after his presidency.

On the lower courts, it is important that you get the opinion of the American Bar Association. Even with that screening, occasionally a marginal nominee would appear before us, where I said to myself, "I hope nothing too complicated comes before this judge." I stopped only two nominations that I recall, one a nominee who made racially insensitive remarks and the other a nominee who refused to resign from a club which discriminated, a practice I am pleased to say the committee now follows.

Beyond that, unless views expressed by a lower court nominee are extreme or there is evident lack of ability or question about integrity, I believe the nominee should be approved. Let me illustrate. When Clarence Thomas came before this committee for chairmanship of the Equal Employment Opportunities Commission, I voted against him because he did not believe in the mission of the agency. When he came before us as a nominee for the appellate court, I voted for him but said at the time if he should be nominated to the U.S. Supreme Court I would probably vote against him because of his philosophy. That I did.

On Supreme Court nominations, whatever is considered by the President properly should be considered by the Senate. And while it is true that sometimes nominees follow an unexpected pattern, in the large majority of cases the background of the nominee is an accurate gauge of the future decisions that Justice will make. In one of the worst decisions the Supreme Court ever made, the Korematsu decision, approving President Franklin Roosevelt's 1942 order to suddenly relocate 115,000 Japanese Americans—not a one of whom had committed a crime—one of the three Court dissenters was a nominee of President Herbert Hoover and among the six in the majority were Justices Hugo Black and William Douglas, usually champions of civil liberties. And one of the few people within the administration to speak out against the President's actions was J. Edgar Hoover, later not so sensitive to our basic liberties. But that unexpected pattern is unusual.

The best recent example of how a nomination should be handled was President Gerald Ford's nomination of John Paul Stevens. The President asked Attorney General Ed Levi to scour the landscape for a quality justice. Senators were consulted as were many others. The President did not act hastily. No President should. Nor should the Senate. While it is not ideal, the Supreme Court can operate with eight members, and whatever problems that presents it is much better than approving someone like Woodrow Wilson's appointment of Justice James McReynolds, the clear winner of the award as the worst justice ever to serve on that high body.

During my twelve years on the Senate Judiciary Committee, no President ever talked to me about a possible Supreme Court nominee prior to the nomination. A president should do that. That's what the Constitution calls for. The President does not need to follow the advice of the Senate, nor the Senate of the President. The Senate favored naming Aaron Burr as Ambassador to France and sent James Monroe to talk to the President about it. George Washington refused saying he had "made it an invariable rule never to suggest to a high and responsible office a man whose integrity" he questioned. The President was right, the Senate was wrong.

Three suggestions:

1. *Again, you should take into consideration philosophy for a Supreme Court nominee.* When Earl Butz came before the Senate as the nominee for Secretary of Agriculture, Senator Hubert Humphrey said to him: "I am worried about your economic philosophy. . . . Your bonds and stocks are to your credit. . . . You have earned everything that you have. You can put all that in escrow, but I don't think you can put your philosophy into escrow." If that is a consideration for a Secretary of Agriculture, how infinitely more true is it of a life-time member of the United States Supreme Court.

2. *Practical political experience should be at least a minor consideration.* Linda Greenhouse recently had an article in the *New York Times* in which she mentioned that only one member of the Supreme Court, Justice Sandra Day O'Connor, has ever held elective office, having served in the state legislature. Greater elected office experience would be of help to this court.

3. *A broad look for nominees of the Supreme Court should include non-lawyers and members of the opposite party.* Justice Hugo Black favored having one or two members of the Court who are not lawyers. Someone who became a Supreme Court scholar like Irving Dilliard of the *St. Louis Post-Dispatch* would have made a superb Supreme Court justice. Let me add that at the age of 72 I am not talking about myself. As to political party, in the last century, Presidents Taft, Wilson, Harding, Hoover, FDR, Truman, Eisenhower and Nixon all nominated at least one justice of the other party.

One final footnote. In the history of the Senate, it has rejected one-fifth of the nominees to the Supreme Court. In the nineteenth century it rejected one-fourth—reason enough for the President and the Senate to work together.

STATE GOVERNMENT

"FOR AN OPEN MEETINGS ACT," SIDELIGHTS FROM SPRINGFIELD, BY STATE REPRESENTATIVE PAUL SIMON, FEBRUARY 17, 1955

"Eternal vigilance is the price of liberty."

We hear that so often that sometimes we forget that it has meaning for us today also. One area where I believe that is the case is in the area of "freedom of information." Democracy is built on the idea that if the people have the information, they can and ultimately will make the right decision.

But if you take the information away, you take away the basis for a democratic decision—and you weaken democracy. Unfortunately all of that is not too far from us.

In Congress there is a growing tendency to have "executive" or secret sessions of committees, and for departments and boards to have fewer press conferences and give out less information.

In some cases there is an excuse . . . National security sometimes can require it at a national level. But all too often even then "security" can be a cover-up for not giving out information the public should have.

At the state, county and local level, there is the same danger of secret meetings—but even less excuse for them. Last week I introduced in the Illinois House of Representatives a "Right to Know" bill similar to one in California. It would require that almost all meetings of state, county and local government bodies be open to the public.

If it should carry, it would give the public more information about the action of government bodies—and possibly prevent some of the "deals" made behind closed doors.

In a democracy the public is entitled to know not only what the decision is, but also "how" that decision was reached and "why" that decision was reached.

Then an informed public has a better chance to make a proper decision at the next election. And the public has a chance to influence the decision government bodies are making.

"FOR OPEN PRIMARIES," SIDELIGHTS FROM SPRINGFIELD, BY STATE REPRESENTATIVE PAUL SIMON, MAY 15, 1957

If you voted in the last primary election, your county clerk has you listed in the official records as having voted either Democratic or Republican.

There are many people—and I'm among them—who feel it is just a little foreign to our ideals of a secret ballot to have to declare your political affiliation in order to vote. I am very open about my party preference as are many other people. But there are those who are reluctant to declare their political affiliation. As a result they don't vote in the primary.

Representative William Horsley of Springfield was the chief sponsor of a bill which two weeks ago was defeated rather decisively—a bill which would have made possible a secret primary vote. The measure received 39 votes. To pass the House of Representatives 89 votes are needed. So the proposal was 50 votes short. Perhaps even more significant is that it received 10 votes more than it did the last session. The House is somewhat larger than it was the last session. But the percentage of the vote clearly indicates that the measure is gaining ground.

Very briefly, the Horsley proposal was that in a primary you could call for a Democratic ballot, a Republican ballot, or a ballot on which both parties are listed. If you chose the ballot with both parties on it you could vote in either party's primary (but not both)—and no one would know by your ballot what party preference you may have.

Opponents of the measure use these basic arguments: (1) If anyone isn't willing to state his political affiliation, he has no right to tell that party who the nominee should be. (2) It would give Democrats a chance to nominate the weak Republicans and Republicans a chance to nominate the weak Democrats. This would mean the end of responsible, two-party government. (3) A largely unspoken reason for opposition is that an incumbent office-holder does not look with warmth on changes in a system that helped get him into office.

Another reason for opposition advanced during the debate was that we should leave education to the educators, labor unions to the labor leaders, and politics to the politicians. Representative Ed Derwinski of Chicago then got up and said he thought the gentleman who made those statements had best summarized his reasons for supporting the measure. Derwinski pointed out that the purpose of a primary election is to serve the people and not the politicians.

I think there are three solid reasons for supporting a secret primary: (1) It is in line with the historic principle of having our voting secret. (2) Anyone active in politics will tell you that in many ways the primary is more important than the general election. Making people go on record either as Democrats or Republicans causes many to stay away from the polls. The result is a small minority of people are able to swing the power in the primary. (3) The experience of other states does not support the charge that the two-party system is weakened by a secret primary. Massachusetts, for example, has distinguished Republicans like Governor Christian Herter and Senator Saltonstall and outstanding Democrats like Senator John Kennedy. The experience of Massachusetts does not indicate that the secret ballot weakens the structure of government.

Next session the proposal probably will be in again. And it will receive a few more votes. Someday you'll be voting a secret ballot in the primary—if you live long enough.

"Facing Reapportionment Problems," Press Release from Illinois State Senator Paul Simon, January 17, 1965

Unquestionably the most ticklish matter which the Illinois legislature must tackle during the coming months is that of reapportionment. Both the House and Senate must be redistricted, and there is a possibility the national House of Representatives districts may have to be changed also.

This is more difficult than tackling issues, because it involves personalities. In reality we have to vote for districts which eliminate some of our colleagues and in some cases pit one against the other. This is never easy. The questions I am asked most often concern the Senate. Let me try to answer some of these briefly.

Why did the Supreme Court rule that state senates must be according to population?

The federal Constitution says that the citizen's vote shall in no way be diminished. It would be illegal, they argue, to say that Negroes shall have one-half a vote and white men one vote. It is equally unfair to give people in one county one-half a vote and in another one vote.

Doesn't this violate our traditions?

No. The large majority of states started with both houses based on population. We gradually grew away from this tradition. Illinois is one of the states which originally had both houses based on a population basis. This was true—in theory—until the 1954 vote on our state constitution. The federal Constitution made an exception to this theory for the U.S. Senate.

Why is there fear of this then in Illinois?

The fear in Illinois grows out of the Cook County vs. Downstate feeling. Cook County has 51 percent of the state's population. This could put Cook County in charge of both houses. Unlike most states, Illinois has a patronage base for its politics and through control of patronage, the head of the party in Cook County has considerable control of the vote by Cook County legislators. Whether the party leader is a Democrat or a Republican, there is always fear when a large group of votes is controlled.

Will Cook County control both houses?

I doubt it. In one of the Supreme Court's rulings they permitted one house of the Colorado legislature to be controlled by 45 percent of the population. The Court felt this was reasonably close to the "one man, one vote" principle. I would guess that a legislature giving a slight edge in one house to Cook County and a slight edge in the other to Downstate would be constitutional.

How real is the Cook County vs. Downstate fight?

Not as real as most people imagine. In more than 10 years in the legislature I have never seen a vote which was divided strictly Cook County vs. Downstate. In those ten years I have heard more than 30,000 roll calls. A second factor which should be kept in mind is that with each reapportionment and shake-up come a few more independent legislators in each party, both from Downstate and Cook County. In my opinion this is all to the good.

A third factor which should be kept in mind is that a Cook County suburban legislator (outside Chicago) tends to vote like his Downstate colleagues. And the great growth in Cook County is not in the city but in the suburbs. All of this means that those who fear the worst out of the reapportionment of this session may be in for a pleasant surprise.

"OMBUDSMAN," FROM THE STATEHOUSE, BY LIEUTENANT GOVERNOR PAUL SIMON, FEBRUARY 10, 1969

During the election campaign of 1968, I made a pledge repeated many times to serve as a trouble-shooter and a complaint department for the citizens of the state. The term used to describe such an official is "ombudsman," a Swedish word describing someone who investigates complaints for citizens.

I have been Lieutenant Governor for only a month, and already it is clear that there is a need for such an official—someone who can, in a sense, be a lobbyist for people who have no lobbyist.

The first duty of this office is in the legislative field, and to serve as acting governor whenever the governor leaves the state; but as much as time permits we will try to handle citizen complaints.

We have received a great variety of complaints—some legitimate which we have been able to do something about, and some with little basis. What kinds of things are we doing?

The recent heavy rains brought floods to many areas of the state. One woman sent us a telegram saying that the local governments were fighting back and forth about who had what jurisdiction to meet the emergency needs—and no one was doing anything. We got on the phone on the matter and in about an hour and a half had things worked out, with the different governmental units agreeing to specific assignments.

Some requests are in connection with license problems and public aid. Some are from communities which face grave economic problems. Some are from suburban areas with growing pains.

A group of Puerto Rican leaders in Chicago contacted me and wanted to meet on school problems which they face. There are about 300,000

Spanish-speaking citizens in Cook County, and problems in their areas have occasionally erupted in violence.

I met with them and heard perhaps 20 requests for action, some of which we will be able to do something about, some of which we will not. But perhaps as important as anything, these people talked with the number two man in state government and felt that someone was genuinely interested in their problems.

The Kerner Commission Report says that riots are caused in part by people feeling an inability to reach anyone in government. They come to regard government as some kind of beast not really interested.

In deep Southern Illinois counties face special difficulties, and I am working with legislators of both parties on them. Many small communities are barely holding their own or are dying—and perhaps because of my residence in a small town—I think this represents a loss to the state in many ways.

Governor Richard Ogilvie has indicated both in public and in private that he supports this effort to try to meet citizens' problems. Right now the stack of letters is growing, but as fast as our small staff can do it, we are trying to help citizens with their problems.

"INCOME DISCLOSURE: THE TIME HAS COME," FROM THE STATEHOUSE, BY LIEUTENANT GOVERNOR PAUL SIMON, SEPTEMBER 29, 1971

If what has happened in Illinois politics this year doesn't make it proof-positive that we need strict income disclosure laws for all state elected officials and their key appointees, I don't know what else it would take. For the sake of public confidence—if for no other reason than that—we must act.

There is time in the legislative session convening in October to pass a meaningful income disclosure law. A bill—not as strong as it should be but an improvement—passed the Illinois Senate earlier and it is still alive in the House of Representatives.

If we fail to pass a strong measure, all of us who hold office will continue to suffer in the eyes of the public. A nationally recognized polling agency disclosed a few years ago that 63 percent of the nation's voters believe that most elected public officials are in office mainly to fill their pockets. If such a poll were taken in Illinois today, that percentage would be even higher. We face a crisis in confidence.

If political leaders refuse to meet this crisis head-on, we jeopardize our system of government. And disclosure of income in detail, as well as disclosure of economic assets and liabilities, is the only way to meet it head-on.

It is also the only way to meet the complex problem of conflict of interest. Put matters on the table in public view and then the citizenry can make reasoned judgments, whether we are serving ourselves, or serving the public.

Individual citizens must do something more than just read the headlines if legislators are to vote for a meaningful disclosure law yet this year. Here is what you can do: (1) Write letters to your State Senator and State Representative. Tell them you feel the time has come for income disclosure by public officials in Illinois. (2) Write a letter to the editor of your newspaper expressing your views on the subject. (3) Call radio "talk" shows and let the moderator hear what you have to say on the matter.

I have disclosed all of my income and the sources of that income during my 17 years of public life. My wife and children are part of that disclosure. My administrative assistants, along with their wives and minor children, publish their income annually. Disclosure of income hasn't hurt any of us. And it lets the public make informed judgments about our motivation in dealing with the issues which come before us.

AMERICAN CAMPAIGNS AND ELECTIONS: CAMPAIGN FINANCE, NEGATIVE CAMPAIGNING

"A THREAT FROM THE FAR RIGHT," P.S./WASHINGTON, JULY 26–AUGUST 1, 1981

Last week four right-wing groups announced that they would spend $200,000 to try to defeat 27 Democratic congressmen. I was one of the 27.

I do not fear their presence in our area. Southern Illinois residents will make up their own minds come Election Day. I do, however, resent their arrogance, their belief that they can tell people in our area how to vote. I believe that most Southern Illinoisans share my resentment.

The following is a statement I released to the media after these groups announced their intentions:

Under three administrations now—two Republican and one Democratic— I have supported the President when I felt he was right and opposed him when I believed he was wrong.

Now, through some front organizations, a group of wealthy, right-wing extremists are threatening me. If I do not vote the way they want on the President's tax cut, they say they will try to defeat me in the next election.

I came to Washington to represent the people of my district and the best interests of the nation, not to become a rubber stamp for any President or any political party, and certainly not for these self-appointed policy dictators. And I do not react well to threats.

While I deplore their tactics—the crudest I have seen in my years in politics—I welcome their money into Southern Illinois. Their money may help our economy a little, and if and when the Reagan budget takes full effect, our economy will need it.

But they will not dictate to the Republicans, Democrats, and independent-minded people of Southern Illinois simply by spending thousands of dollars to campaign against me. If these people want to run against me and run against the people of Southern Illinois, let them come into the 24th District. We in Southern Illinois are not afraid of them or their tactics. The people of Southern Illinois have good sense and will recognize these tactics for what they are.

It is clear that they are hiding behind their front organizations to try to become wealthier at the public's expense. They know I will not help them in that goal.

I favor a modest tax cut. But almost all economists from the chairman of the Federal Reserve Board on down tell us to proceed with extreme caution, that a tax cut the size the President is asking for can create significant inflation problems. And my sense is that the people of Southern Illinois want a balanced budget and lower interest rates, and they know that a big tax cut makes those goals even more distant.

Southern Illinoisans can make their own decisions on issues and on candidates.

"THE SOARING COSTS OF U.S. ELECTIONS,"
P.S./WASHINGTON, DECEMBER 26, 1981–JANUARY 1, 1982

"Congress for Sale" screams the cover of *The New Republic*. "The best Congress money can buy" is the over-worked line in at least a dozen articles I have read.

The reality is that our present system of financing congressional campaigns—as well as races like that for Governor of Illinois—is a national embarrassment.

Faced with a win of less than 1 percent in 1980, and thereby becoming the target of several groups, I spent far more in 1982 than I have spent in any previous election year: $413,477. But that compares to $746,092 and $648,925 in the congressional race just north of part of the 22nd congressional district. And it compares to more than $2 million in one race in Massachusetts. I'm sure that most targeted incumbents spent more than I did. The system of financing campaigns is bad, not in the way that most articles suggest, but in a more subtle though equally harmful way.

There may be some members of Congress who vote for or against a bill specifically because of a campaign contribution, consciously saying to themselves, "I'm going to vote this way because I received a campaign contribution." But that, I believe, is rare. What is true is that those who make campaign contributions have much greater access to policymakers, and access spells votes.

Part of it is simply that a candidate feels a sense of gratitude toward those who contribute to the campaign. It is true for me; it is true for all candidates. And you listen especially carefully to people toward whom you feel a sense of gratitude.

The difficulty there is that too often those who have money then have access, and those with limited income do not. It is one of the reasons I schedule "Open Office Hours" around Southern Illinois, to make sure that anyone who wants to see me can do so.

But that approach is hardly an answer to a national problem. The political system should not be structured in a way that grants the powerful much easier access to policymakers than those with limited resources or those in great need. In the U.S. in the 1982 congressional races $320 million was spent—and in the last British parliamentary election $3 million.

There is also the problem of wealthy candidates spending huge sums to almost literally buy public office. Many of the finest members of the House and Senate are millionaires. But it is not good to have a growing percentage of policymakers who, through their independent wealth, are remote from the economic problems ordinary people face. Answers are not easy, but there are answers.

They are not likely to surface until there is much wider recognition of the inherent evils of the present system of financing campaigns.

"Today's Biggest Scandal," P.S./Washington, November 17–23, 1985

One of the foremost academic observers in the United States has put it bluntly: "We can no longer conduct rational defense and economic policy because of the influence of political contributions."

A former member of Congress has talked about the "psychological mortgage" that members of the Senate and House have as a result of campaign contributions. Both are correct.

The truth is that spending in political campaigns is far beyond the point of healthy. We are increasingly putting the decision-making process up for sale.

My campaign for the U.S. Senate cost $5.3 million. My opponent spent substantially more. Both figures are a source of concern, but both my opponent and I had little choice under today's system. In North Carolina—with half the population of Illinois—the two Senate candidates spent twice as much as we did in Illinois.

It is not that members of the Senate and House are directly for sale, but the present system means that the big contributors have greater access to policymakers, and all members know when they vote certain ways it will help their campaign treasuries, and if they vote the opposite, it will hurt. The public loses in the process. What can be done?

We used to have the same contribution system for the presidential elections that we currently have for the Senate and House. Presidential candidates had to spend huge amounts of time raising money. They still do until the convention nominates a candidate, but now once that convention has taken place there is public funding—paid with funding from a small box that you voluntarily check off on your income tax form. Sen. Charles Mathias, a Republican from Maryland, and I have introduced a bill calling for the same procedure for Senate elections that we use in the presidential races, starting in 1988.

It would substantially reduce the amount spent in campaigns. Both candidates would have the same amount to spend. And like the presidential campaign, after the primary there could be no personal or political action committee contributions. The public would be the big winner for public policy would be less influenced by who spends the big bucks. Sen. Mathias chairs the Rules Committee that has jurisdiction. That increases the possibility that something can be passed. But odds are against it. Obviously, some of the special interests that are so dominant on the Washington scene would suffer; they oppose it. Many members of the House and Senate oppose it because there is a tendency to believe, "Whatever system got me elected must be good." The biggest national scandal today is the way public policy is distorted by campaign contributions. We ought to change it.

"Campaign Finance Reform," NPR Commentary, February 26, 2002

The news that both political parties are scrambling frantically for "soft money" before it may become illegal at the end of the year is welcome in the sense that they believe the measure that passed the House will be approved by the Senate and signed into law by the President.

We need campaign finance reform and this is one step—but only one step—in the proper direction. Even with this, it is still true that our laws are much looser than democracies of western Europe and Canada. One recent Senate candidate spent more money in his campaign than the British did in their entire election last year. Experience suggests that even the current reform will need further change in 10 or 12 years as people find ways around the law.

Early in our nation's history Thomas Jefferson and Alexander Hamilton had great philosophical divisions, Jefferson suggesting that all votes should count equally, but Hamilton wanted only those who owned property to be able to vote, not the rest of the population. Hamilton wanted the wealthy to have greater say in our government and Jefferson opposed that idea. As a grade school student I learned how proud we could be that Jefferson prevailed.

But guess what? Even with this current reform, Hamilton is prevailing because people of wealth have much more influence through our system of financing campaigns. The contributions that can be legally made—even with this new law—come overwhelmingly from those in the top 1 percent of the income bracket.

One simple reform would help: Require radio and television stations to provide several free two-minute time periods to major candidates. In the last two elections roughly 98 percent of the U.S. House incumbents who ran for reelection made it. Many deserved to be reelected—but not 98 percent of them. Reform will come one step at a time—and free air time in the slots the nation gives to radio and television stations would be another step in giving the elections more to the people, not the big pocketbooks.

AMERICAN CAMPAIGNS AND ELECTIONS: THE ROLE OF
NEWSPAPERS AND OTHER MEDIA IN THE ELECTORAL SYSTEM

"IMPROVING STATEHOUSE COVERAGE," *COLUMBIA JOURNALISM REVIEW*, SEPTEMBER–OCTOBER 1973

In eighteen years in state government—fourteen in Illinois' legislature, four as its lieutenant governor—I have seen press coverage of the legislature gradually improve and, not coincidentally, the caliber of legislators improve as well. But having said that, I must add that there is much more room for improvements. Some points to consider.

1. *The quality of press coverage is related to quantity; not enough reporters are assigned to cover state government.* Some 2,200 newsmen are accredited to cover Congress. In Springfield, excluding reporters for the two local papers, eight reporters cover state government fulltime. (That number is swelled during legislative sessions.) If someone said that only eight reporters were covering Pakistan, you would be amazed; the Illinois governmental budget is almost ten times that of Pakistan.

By far the best coverage is in the newspapers. One of the finest reporters on the Springfield scene, however, is a radio reporter, Bill Miller, who syndicates material for several stations. Largely because of his leadership and aggressiveness, radio coverage in Illinois is superior to television coverage. TV stations have been assigning reporters to state government more frequently than they formerly did, largely for spot news. Because WGN-TV sends Steve Schnickel to the capital and WLS-TV sends Hugh Hill, these two Chicagoans can ask penetrating questions at press conferences in Chicago. Others could also be mentioned.

The quantity and quality of coverage varies from state to state. Massachusetts has much more coverage of state government than Illinois, both in space and time allotted and in numbers of reporters assigned. This is at least partly because Boston is the capital—though it is worth noting that Massachusetts, whose population is half that of Illinois, can claim more man hours devoted by newsmen to state government. Coverage in both of these states is vastly superior to that in most others.

2. *Editors must help destroy the attitude on the part of reporters that an assignment to Springfield (or any other capital) is an assignment to purgatory.* When Illinois legislators decided in 1837 on the new location for the state capital, one farsighted legislator voted for a small community in Lawrence County called Purgatory. There are times when that seems appropriate.

Too often good reporters view the state capital as an unhappy stopping place on the way to Washington or some other assignment. A good example is Tom Littlewood of the Chicago *Sun-Times*, one of the best reporters ever on the state scene. After some years, he happily moved on to Washington. I don't blame him, but state government suffered a loss.

Our United Press International news team is so changeable that often those covering state government are all novices. Reporters can stay too long and become too much a part of the scene, but covering state government is not like writing about an automobile accident; you do not produce instant, good reporters of the state scene. UPI now has three good young reporters covering the capital. I hope they stay long enough to provide leadership.

We can reduce the "purgatory complex" problem in four ways:

- Increase compensation for the reporter covering state government. A pay scale often reveals what assignments are considered important.
- Make space available for state government news. It is discouraging for a reporter to send in a good story that never sees the light of day. Reporters should be encouraged to produce quality stories and know that when they do, the stories will appear.
- When the periodic "push and shove" for steps up the journalistic ladder do occur, don't forget the reporter who works hard at the state capital. If he knows he will be considered for something more than an expletive, his attitude toward the state assignment may be less negative.
- We need more journalism programs like the one recently launched at Sangamon State University, where student reporters can work fulltime covering state government under the supervision of an experienced reporter. Whether these students eventually receive state capital assignments or not, in future years their stories and editorials will be enriched by this background.

3. *Writing an editorial on state government is like pitching a baseball: There should be follow-through.* By "follow-through" I do not mean simply another editorial on the same subject. If a newspaper or station editorialized that the House Judiciary Committee should approve House Bill 1, then there should be an editorial the day after the committee meeting stating that the bill passed or did not pass, with a list of the House members who voted in the public interest and those who did not.

In the past year in Illinois I have seen only one editorial that had this kind of follow-through, in Chicago *Today*. My judgment may be too sweeping, but I doubt that a researcher could find six editorials in Illinois newspapers this past year which pinpointed responsibility in this way. The only newspaper that I have seen anywhere in the nation that does a good job on this is the St. Louis *Post-Dispatch*; there may be others.

Any medium that adopts this policy will increase its impact on the legislative scene immediately and immensely. I can hear an editorial writer say, "What does the legislator at the other end of the state care what we say?" He does care. Some people from his district will see it or hear it; editors from his part of the state may reprint it; and one of these days he will be running for reelection and he will have an opponent who may use it. Even if none of these things were applicable, readers and listeners are entitled to know how legislators voted on a matter considered important enough to comment on.

4. *A greater sense of balance and perspective is needed in news coverage.* If two bills are introduced in the legislatures the same day, one to assist 50,000 Spanish-speaking students of Puerto Rican or Mexican background and the other a bill to outlaw pay toilets, I can tell you which will receive the more prominent space and the most radio, TV, and newspaper comment!

After Daniel Walker, who walked the state of Illinois from end to end, defeated Richard Ogilvie for Governor, Ogilvie told Dick Icen of the Lindsay-Schaub newspapers that "the next successful candidate for Governor will cross the state swinging from limb to limb." Ogilvie is not alone in lamenting the attention to gimmicks.

A matter I came across recently while working on a book, *The Politics of World Hunger*, illustrates the point. Every four years the United Nations Committee on Trade and Development meets. This is an attempt by the poorer nations to balance some of the arbitrary trade and fiscal policies of the major powers, often adopted without consultation with or real concern for the weaker nations. Last year the Committee meeting took place in Chile. While it discussed how the world's poor can receive a greater share of the earth's goods, a baseball strike occurred in the U.S. My estimate is that the baseball strike received at least 1,000 times as much space as the UNCTAD Conference, with only a few newspapers an exception to that.

I do not suggest that a baseball strike or the issue of pay toilets should not receive attention. But the news media, by their use of space and time, not only reflect audience interests; they also are telling people what is important in the judgment of professional newsmen.

5. *Newsmen should not seize the most extreme statement as necessarily the most newsworthy.* One legislative leader, in discussing a statement about to be issued, said, "To comment sensibly on a bill does not make news. We've got to say something nutty or it won't print." Though not a journalist, he understood a reality that faces people in state government.

James Reston referred to this weakness in the Feb. 25 *New York Times* when he wrote about a speech by Vice President Spiro Agnew in Minneapolis:

"It is interesting that Mr. Agnew is now speaking in such moderate tones and it is equally interesting that the national press virtually ignores him when he does lower his voice."

Martin Linsky, a former Republican leader of the Massachusetts House, told me, "Every official in our state knows that to get ink or to get air time you have to exaggerate. You can't say a bill is a bad bill and logically spell out the reasons. You have to say it 'would cause the death of local government' and then you'll see your name in print."

In my 1972 primary contest for the Democratic nomination for Governor, I felt I could not join my opponent in promising sweeping reductions in taxes. I did say that I supported the philosophy of the *Serrano v. Priest* school decisions (which he opposed) and that I favored a reduction in the real estate tax although it would mean an increase in the income tax. The Republican Governor charged that my suggestion would mean a 25 per cent increase in the income tax. My Democratic opponent said it would mean a 300 per cent increase in the income tax. The more extreme—though completely unfounded—statement made most of the headlines.

Every five years an editor or newsman covering government should re-read the Joseph McCarthy story. McCarthy used the media through reckless charges and extreme statements. Too often in state government I have seen minor league McCarthys receive attention they do not deserve.

6. *There is too much responding to immediate events and not enough long-range evaluations.* Newsmen and those of us in government share this danger. A reporter wants to please the editor, who wants to please the publisher. Produce. Produce. Produce. And elevated officials are so preoccupied doing favors, reflecting on what a vote or statement might mean in the next election, that a short span of a decade hardly receives consideration.

Where are we going? What are we really doing? Where should we be going? I don't see enough of that kind of writing.

In the academic world there is the encouragement for a periodic sabbatical. A modification of that should be used more frequently in journalism. An editor or news director should occasionally say to a reporter, "Take a month and look at the big picture. Where is this state going in the field of education? For one month just read, reflect, and interview on that subject." Or it could be about the destiny of a city, or a state's financial status, or the problems of race in a community. Politicians often should do more thinking and less talking. Reporters often should do more thinking and less writing.

7. *More needs to be done to reduce emotional issues so rational judgments can be made.* A classic interview occurred in Michigan during the 1972 elections, when a TV reporter asked a man standing in an unemployment line, "What is the most important issue in the campaign?" He immediately responded, "Busing." That same interview could take place in Illinois and many other states in the U.S. as well.

When the President of the United States denounces busing and when many "leaders" of both parties in a state do the same, it is difficult to maintain a rational stand and survive politically. Most officials who publically condemn busing privately couldn't care less; they are simply seizing it as a convenient political weapon. I do not believe that busing is the answer in every community, but a reasonable person must acknowledge that in some communities it is. Because the issue is so emotion-laden, the media have a special responsibility not only to interview the militants and the more respectable leaders who follow them but to devote some attention to school superintendents and school districts where, quietly, but effectively, busing is one of several tools used to improve educational opportunities for all.

Or take the gun issue. Candidates for office can denounce restrictions on guns in one breath and denounce crime two minutes later, and receive applause from both the crowd and the media. The media have done a better job on this issue than on busing. The Chicago *Tribune*, for example, had an excellent series on the gun problem, but it did not adequately pin down public officials. When public officials take irresponsible stands, the public should be told the realities in clear, firm language.

Legislators and state officials who show courage in standing for positions one believes to be right should receive specific editorial commendation in which their names are mentioned. Those who show lack of vision and spinelessness should be named during displays of editorial wrath. More will take unpopular stands and stand against the crowd if there is editorial encouragement.

8. *Editorials need to ask state leaders to experiment.* The major justification for states, other than the accident of history, is that they can try new ideas. We don't need to make national mistakes. We should have fifty laboratories for attacking the problems of our society. The harsh reality is that little experimenting is done today or has been done by states for more than half a century. The creative role has passed to the federal government, and part of the blame can rest with the media.

With the exception of George Norris' unicameral experiment in Nebraska, there has been no major experimental leadership by any state since Robert La Follette served as governor of Wisconsin. Some profess that anything novel could not pass the legislature (not true, if there is a strong governor) and some say that states do not have the funds to experiment. The latter charge has never been true, since 2 to 6 per cent of most state budgets—more than enough for noble trials—could be used with appreciable flexibility. With federal revenue-sharing arrangements (which I believe are unwise), the states have even less excuse.

What kind of experiments? There is talk about public financing of campaigns; let's try it in a state or two, rather than having federal mistakes. More people are discussing a guaranteed job for all citizens; some state should try it in two or three counties. What is its impact and what is its cost? A whole series of experiments could be suggested.

The governor who tries this must have courage, but we may hope that a La Follette–type flame smolders in the breast of some governor who wants to be more than a custodian of his state—a flame that one or two editorials might fan. If he tries it, his political future may be in danger. If he does not try it, the muscles of the federal system atrophy.

No state owes a greater debt to the media than does Illinois, where evidence of an unhappy tradition of corruption in both political parties is being exposed almost daily. With the help of the media, that tradition of corruption will change. Both as a citizen and as a former official, I am grateful to many reporters, editors, and news directors for good work. But it is a gratitude balanced by the knowledge that even greater opportunities are presented to the media today in every state.

This article was reprinted, with permission, from *Columbia Journalism Review* (www.cjr.org).

"A Flawed System for Electing Presidents," P.S./Washington, September 30–October 6, 1979

The political pot is boiling.

And much too early.

The British have election contests which last approximately three or four weeks. In Canada the election contest carries on for about two months.

But even before the 1978 election was held, we had candidates for the 1980 presidential nomination. Candidates get tired and the public grows weary. And by the time bleary-eyed candidates weather more than a year of campaigning, and the public suffers through the same, there is a dulling of the nerves that take place, and those who vote in our elections for the candidates who have survived are few compared to most democracies.

The most fundamental question remains: Does this process produce our finest possible leadership? I mean no disrespect for the nominees which both parties have produced in recent years when I suggest that the process is flawed.

There should be a willingness—even an eagerness—to serve as President on the part of those who seek office. But there should not be so much eagerness that a reflective person will not put himself or herself through that kind of lengthy abuse for "the prize." The person who wins should possess something substantially more than an emotional craving to hold office.

I recall when a then-senator, Walter Mondale, ruled himself out of the 1976 presidential race because he did not want to spend a year living in motels, racing frantically from state to state, looking pleasant but ducking issues rather than pondering them. I admired his decision even as I regretted it. The media must share part of the blame for our problems.

Every presidential candidate knows that putting on a feathered head-dress in South Dakota will get much more national publicity than a substantial discussion of the nation's education needs; every presidential candidate knows that rarely do reporters press on issues in more than a superficial way, and if they do persist, the stories of substance are buried or not used and are likely to replace in prominence a crowd count, or the fact that the campaign train hit a cow, or the crowning of the Jones County Blackberry Queen.

The TV shot on the 6 o'clock news will last 20 seconds to a minute, and the cameras will pick up a good line written into the speech by a New York advertising agency, rather than the substance of the address which is complicated.

The party structure is partly to blame. We have "reformed" ourselves too much. What appeared to be reform went too far and resulted in irresponsibility. That is true in Congress, and it is true about party conventions.

We should have more serious weighing of the issues and less circus. We need to respond to national need, not national polls. Unlike most democracies, our legislative branch has almost nothing to do with whom the parties nominate. In part that is the system; in part it is because members of Congress are expert practitioners in the art of ducking. And while many members will complain about the party nominee of either party, few are willing to stand up and be counted. As I write this I am somewhat in a "down" mood, and so is the nation. Not hopelessly so. But the public is yearning for firm, tough, dedicated leadership.

Maybe it is Jimmy Carter or Ted Kennedy; maybe it is John Connally or John Anderson or Ronald Reagan. But I have the sinking feeling that if the right leadership emerges, it will almost be despite our excessively lengthy and chaotic election system.

"MODERN-DAY WITCH HUNTING,"
P.S./WASHINGTON, JANUARY 9–15, 1983

Periodically someone on the Washington scene takes some action which is described in editorial comment as "a witch hunt." It is a reference to an unhappy period in our history when a few women were accused of "solemn compaction or conversing with the Devil" or "giving entertainment to Satan"—descriptions in the law which could result in death in the early Colonies.

The "witches" were people who had mental problems, or some defect in character or personality which caused others to attack them. It also became a sadistic form of entertainment for the colonists, in somewhat the same way that boxing is today, where we cheer as we legally permit two people to batter each other's brains. We end up battering our sensibilities also, as did the colonists.

But there is another more common form of "witch hunt" that concerns me that entertains the public but does a great disservice to our system of government. It is the negative political campaign. I am not referring to my most recent opponent, who generally ran a constructive campaign. But within our area and in other parts of the nation I once again saw election efforts conducted by people in both political parties that were overwhelmingly negative.

Like the ancient attacks on the witches, those who made the attacks took defects—actual or imagined or created—and twisted and turned votes or events in such a way as to make modern-day witches of their opponents.

The victim of this approach to politics is not simply the political opponent, it is also the public which watches this entertainment spectacle without realizing what is happening to them, and it is also democracy itself which is diverted from a discussion of community, state or national affairs to an exchange of wild charges. That does great harm to our system of government.

The Democratic and Republican leadership from the national level to the local level ought to be drafting a code of ethics which office-seekers would be urged to sign to require, among other things, that candidates spend the bulk of their time and expenditures on promoting what they would do, rather than in charges against their opponents.

And if such an atmosphere for candidates could be created, perhaps then the other negative groups, such as the National Conservative Political Action Committee (NCPAC), could be forced into ethical conduct also.

Political campaigns should be sensible discussions of public policy, where candidates agree on some matters and disagree strongly on others.

But abusing people as we once did in attacking "witches" is not only an irresponsible assault on individuals, it is in fact an attack on our system of government and should be recognized as such.

3

Guidance on Continuing Problems and Issues

EDITOR'S NOTE

Paul Simon was a person of broad and diverse interests. He was deeply concerned about a wide variety of public policy issues, and he delved into a number of causes during his long career. In contrast, the legislative process, especially the Congress of the United States, rewards specialization and focus. Political scientists who study Congress note that the committee system almost forces members to focus on the narrow range of matters that come before the handful of committees a legislator will serve on during his or her career. They build up experience and knowledge in those narrow fields and wield much more clout than the ordinary member in the fields dictated by their committee assignment. Simon's assignments, especially to the Science and Technology and the Education and Labor Committees in the House and to the Foreign Relations and the Labor and Human Resources Committees in the Senate, were strategic in that matter because they reflected his deep and long-standing interests in foreign policy, education, and the labor movement. He was especially concerned about American educational practices, for example, and his service in the House gave him a platform to advocate for better training for teachers, a longer school day, higher academic standards, and the teaching of foreign languages at an early age. Simon was also committed to the public funding of education and especially to student loans and grants as a way to make mass education more widely available to all. The G.I. Bill was one of his models, and it provided the example for his favorite argument about the need to fund students' educations and thus create a higher level of economic prosperity for the nation. Paul was a strong advocate for Pell Grants and the direct student loan program, and he fought hard for those in the legislative scrum. He was highly critical of the banks being able to play the role of middleman and making a tidy profit off student loans, which were all guaranteed by the full faith and credit of the U.S. government. That fight was not finally settled until the passage of the Affordable Health Care Act of 2010 under President Obama when the direct student loan program was added to the health care reform act. However, the continuation of the national direct student loan program was just a sidelight to the major fight, which was for a national health care plan that would cover all or part of the 49 million or so Americans who were previously uncovered by any kind of governmental or private health insurance plan. Paul Simon was clearly and unequivocally in favor of the Clinton administration's attempts to pass a national health care plan in 1993–94 and would probably have been an advocate for the plan that did ultimately pass in President Obama's first term. One cannot read the selections on health care and student loans included in this chapter without gaining a strong impression of Simon's commitments and values in these fields, and those writings provide some very clear signals for how he might have voted on these controversies.

Even today, the fight over the health care act continues as the insurance companies and various business and conservative groups try to get rid of the health care reforms and as the banks seek a revision of that act that would put them back in exclusive control of the student loan business. The fight for total repeal of the health care act, with all the powerful interests arrayed against the plan, would unravel that earlier legislation with regard to the student loan program as well as reverse field on the larger matter of the health care plan advocated by the Obama administration. So, some fights are almost never entirely over in an American political system that rewards financial muscle and the ability to hire expensive lobbyists and to make substantial campaign donations to grateful candidates who become compliant members of Congress.

The list of topics in chapter 3 includes a litany of the problems and political struggles of the last three decades of the twentieth century. These include equal rights for women, for the physically and mentally impaired, and for various minority communities. Paul was always on the side of expanding rights and extending the blessings and privileges of American citizenship to the broadest base possible. This also included immigrants. He was a believer in the transforming power of the American dream and was inclusive in his outlook on who should be the beneficiaries of life in this free and egalitarian nation. It is inconceivable that Paul Simon would have been on the side of intolerance shown to our current immigrant populations, including those who are here illegally. He would have wanted to find a pathway for them to become citizens and would have been a proponent of the current "Dream Act," which would provide for certain sanctions to be applied to the illegal immigrants and then for a way to bring them into full citizenship and into the mainstream of the American economy and society. He had a special burden for children all over the world and would have been an advocate for those immigrant children born in this country to be accepted into full citizenship with no discrimination or diminution of their rights.

Paul was also very interested in television and the role it could play in the education of our youth; however, he was aghast at the wasted resource it had become and especially by its fixation on violence to which young people were exposed by hours and hours of daily viewing. Simon thought the industry should police itself, and if it did not, the government should step in and regulate. He believed consumers should demand more and better of television, and that was one of the causes he pursued throughout his legislative career. No one in Congress knew more about these subjects or advocated more ardently for them than Paul Simon.

Paul was not especially well versed in popular culture. He barely knew one movie star from another and knew even less about most popular television shows. His interest in TV extended mostly to the MacNeil-Lehrer news program on PBS and to Sunday afternoon football. Nevertheless, he believed that television, the movies, and other channels of popular culture could profoundly influence mass behavior, and he thought the media and the popular entertainment industry should be mindful of their power and of their opportunity to help shape mass civic education.

One of Paul Simon's earliest causes was the protection and distribution of clean water to the nation and to the world's common people, especially the children. Paul pursued this objective through his congressional platform and through his writings. He wrote a well-reviewed book on the subject, which then became a cover story for the Sunday supplement *Parade Magazine* in 1998. The book and the article then received national and international attention and led to invitations from all over the nation and the globe for Simon to come and talk about water and its importance to the modern world. This also dovetailed with his interest in foreign policy, particularly the Middle East and Africa, where the constant need for more potable water and the plague of water-borne illnesses, especially among children, sap the strength of the people and drive some of the more aggressive behavior of many governments. Near the end of his life, Paul and his second wife, Patti Derge Simon, took a trip to Jordan and Israel to attend a water resources conference; it was the last overseas trip he took before his death in December 2003.

In spite of the need to specialize, Paul Simon had eclectic interests, and he pursued them whether it advanced his legislative career or not. In fact, sometimes his critics thought that his assorted interests were followed to the detriment of his legislative agenda and that this kept him from having the kind of impact on the making of the laws that other more focused members were able to have.

Simon's interests in the issues of his day cover the other major selections in this chapter: guns and gun violence, poverty and hunger in the world, the challenges of energy and the environment, the role of the military, and the challenges posed by crime and incarceration in a nation that locks up more people than any other nation on earth. These were not always popular issues, and the policy stances he took were often unpopular and out of step with the majority of his constituents. Nevertheless, he believed firmly that he should follow his conscience and then try to explain himself to his constituents and to the public at large. These weekly columns and the other forms of writing he did served that need to explain and educate. Most of his constituents understood what he was doing and respected his opinions and values in general while perhaps at the same time disagreeing with many of the particulars. He continued to make his case and to explain his views even after he left Congress and became a member of the faculty at Southern Illinois University Carbondale. As the director of the public policy institute that bore his name, he was the peripatetic professor not only lecturing to his students in the classroom but also traveling the nation and the world at the invitation of a steady stream of groups and organizations who wanted to hear from him and to understand what his views were because they sensed that he was a leader who cared deeply about all people and about improving the lives of ordinary citizens. The fights he fought are not over, and the controversies he engaged in are still with us today. Paul's counsel is still cogent and still just as relevant to the current public dialogue as it was in the days he sat down at the old Royal typewriter and pecked out these columns each week.

"Where Government Can Help,"
P.S./Washington, February 17–23, 1980

There are areas where government should not expand its services, but there are areas where government should, and Mr. and Mrs. Robert Throgmorton of 200 E. Patrick in Marion provide an example of where government should be helping more.

Robert Throgmorton was in construction work, never getting rich but getting by, until he suffered a severe heart attack two years ago.

His wife is suffering from crippling arthritis, plus a hernia below the rib cage. Doctors have advised the Throgmortons that unless she receives some additional injections and medication, she will end up in a wheelchair or flat on her back for the rest of her life. In addition, she has cataracts on both eyes and will go blind if she does not have operations.

He has been advised that he should have heart tracings (EKG) regularly. The problem is that the Throgmortons are already overwhelmed with hospital and doctor and pharmacy bills.

They can't afford the injections and medication that Mrs. Throgmorton needs, even though part of it may be paid by Medicare.

They can't afford the EKG heart tests which the doctors say are absolutely essential for him, even though part will be paid by Medicare.

They live in a house trailer and try to be good citizens. They receive a total of $493 a month, a combination of social security and $62.50 a month for his pension as an ironworker and another small pension of $14.50 a month. Ordinarily, that would be enough for a retired couple, but not enough for a retired couple deep in medical problems.

Because the Throgmortons are proud people, probably not too many people—even their neighbors—understand their problems.

Illinois Public Aid says they receive too much income to be eligible for financial help, though I'm trying to get Public Aid to reconsider. They agreed to let me write about them so that others might be helped. There are answers. Most nations in Western Europe, and some elsewhere, help people like the Throgmortons.

Right now those over 65 years of age are over 10 percent of our population, but they pay 28 percent of the hospital, medical, dental and pharmaceutical bills.

Senator Gary Hart and I have introduced legislation which takes care of the three most pressing medical needs in our country: help for those who are pregnant mothers and children through the age of six, those over 65, and those cases where medical bills exceed 20 percent of a family's income. On two of these three counts, the Throgmortons would be helped.

I really believe the American people want to help people in situations like the Throgmortons. But these problems are somehow hidden. It becomes a matter of shame for the Throgmortons, rather than for our society. We don't need to go the full route of government control of the medical field—as some advocate—but something is fundamentally wrong when we don't respond to the needs of people like the Throgmortons.

"Hot Topic on Town Meeting Circuit," P.S./Washington, February 18–24, 1990

At town meetings in Illinois, the one topic that comes up most frequently is health care. And the message people are delivering is clear: We have to do better.

Twenty years ago that message came from a handful of people. Today, even Lee Iacocca, president of Chrysler, says we should adopt the Canadian health insurance plan. I've had at least a dozen business executives in Illinois tell me something similar in the last few months.

People who are uninsured, or who have insurance that does not meet their bills, and a host of others who fall through the cracks are sending the same message: We have to do better.

The *Chicago Tribune* did a poll in Canada, and another in the United States, asking a simple question. Are you satisfied with the health delivery system in your country? In Canada, 56 percent responded favorably—not a high figure, but not bad. In the United States 9 percent responded favorably, and that 9 percent response means change is going to come.

Precisely where we are going, no one knows. A commission headed by Senator Jay Rockefeller of West Virginia is to report to Congress soon on recommendations for long-term health care. Only two major industrial nations do not take care of their parents and grandparents if they need long-term health care: South Africa and the United States. Can we do better? Of course we can. Roughly 38 million Americans have no health insurance coverage at all.

When it is announced that an automobile plant is shutting down, what those workers lose is not only their weekly income; they also lose their health insurance coverage, and that can mean financial devastation.

Many Americans have insurance, but their insurance does not cover their needs. If I ask someone, "Do you have health insurance?" that person will know the answer. If I follow up and ask, "How much health insurance do you have?" most people do not know the answer.

Businesses are seeing their health insurance claims climb. One executive I talked to in the Peoria area budgeted $800,000 for his firm's health insurance costs. The bill came in at $1.4 million. Total employer health care costs were equal to 1.2 percent of payroll in 1960 but had risen to 5.2 percent by 1986. Where do all of these problems lead us? Within the next five to 10 years we will see a major overhauling of the health delivery system in our nation. We need it.

Between now and that time, professionals in the field of health delivery should get together with citizens to discuss what the right answers are. Between now and that time, we also can take care of our most pressing needs, like long-term health care.

What we do not need is an unplanned lunge into something dramatically different.

We can do better, but let's make sure that the changes we create really do improve things.

"Americans Back Basics of Clinton Health Plan," P.S./Washington, May 1–7, 1994

This nation needs a health care plan that covers all Americans.

Confusion is being spread about the President's health care plan, but the *Wall Street Journal/NBC News* poll is accurate, in my opinion, when it finds that when people are asked whether they favor the President's plan, they are not certain; they are confused. But when the same people are asked about the specifics of the plan, they are overwhelmingly for it.

I hear horror stories about the Canadian plan (which is not what the President is recommending), but it is interesting that not a single member of the Canadian parliament, from the far right to the far left, has introduced a bill to repeal their health program.

It is also interesting that Canada finds so many Americans crossing over the border to get health care. According to some Canadian officials, this is far more than the number of Canadians coming into the United States for care.

An argument I hear about the Clinton plan is that it will create a huge bureaucracy. There are two responses to that:

First, if you exempt the armed forces, there are 200,000 more people working for health insurance companies than for the federal government. Bureaucracy is not unknown to the insurance industry.

Second, federal employees have an "alliance" (a cooperative buying group) that gives federal employees the choice of more than 300 insurance plans, basically the same way the Clinton proposal will work. What is the cost of administering this program? One-eighth of 1 percent of the total cost of insurance.

I run into far too many people with health financing problems, and it could happen to you. If you have a child with cancer or diabetes, suddenly you could find your insurance dropped—or priced so high you cannot afford it.

The Clinton plan provides three basics: everyone has insurance coverage; you can choose your own physician; and there is cost control. All three will benefit almost all Americans.

But won't it hurt small businesses? Sixty-two percent of small businesses now cover their employees—but they pay an average of 35 percent more for coverage than does a big company like General Motors. Under this plan they will save that 35 percent. And they will save on premiums from cost control.

From the 38 percent of small businesses not now covering their employees, they will generally pay 3.5 percent of wages. So if the average salary for the business is $5 per hour, that will cost the business 17.5 cents per hour. Before the last increase in the minimum wage from $3.80 to $4.25, there was much talk that it would put many small companies out of business. It did not.

For health coverage, it will take only a fraction of the increase in the minimum wage, and offer small businesses one great plus: They will not lose employees to other companies because the others offer health insurance.

On my last trip to Illinois, like every other one, I had people come up to me with stories of desperation, people who need health insurance coverage.

The United States is the only developed nation in the world that does not offer health coverage for all its citizens. That should embarrass us. Yes, it is controversial, as Social Security was when it passed. But we did the right thing when we passed Social Security, and I hope we will do the right thing again and pass the President's health proposal.

"AMERICANS MUST SPEAK OUT ON HEALTH CARE REFORM," P.S./WASHINGTON, AUGUST 21–27, 1994

There is much confusion surrounding the issue of health care, most of it caused by those who make money from the present system and do not want it changed. Here are some facts to keep in mind:

- The United States and South Africa are the only two western, in-dustrialized nations that do not provide health coverage for all their citizens.
- Those who say covering 95 percent of our citizens (from the present 83 percent) by the year 2000 would be adequate miss the simple real-ity that 12.5 million Americans would then still be without coverage and that is not tolerable. Nor is a wait like that excusable.
- Those who favor universal coverage are as varied as the AFL-CIO, the American Association of Retired Persons and the American Medical Association. Ordinarily that unusual combination would carry the day, but the opposition—primarily part of the insurance industry—has been much more vocal and has caused confusion. And the confusion has silenced the millions of Americans who are without protection.
- Under universal coverage, such as proposed by the Senate Committee on Labor and Human Resources, those who are now covered and like the health protection they have, can keep it. But if they lose their jobs, they will have protection. And their neighbors who do not have coverage will be protected.
- People will have at least as much choice of physicians as they have now. Many Americans will have more choice.
- Eighty percent of those who are not covered by health insurance are working Americans or their dependents. The non-working poor are covered through Medicaid, though often inadequately covered.

Will health care coverage for all Americans cost something? Yes, par-ticularly if you are a smoker. Is it going to cost something if we don't do it? It will cost more in dollars and in human misery. What about small busi-nesses? Sixty-two percent of them cover their employees now, and they will end up saving money on their health insurance. For those who do not cover their employees now, there will be some additional cost, but less than the last increase in the minimum wage law.

All of this is written as the Senate and House prepare to take up health care on the floor, and the picture can change. But rarely is there a struggle as dramatic as this one and as clear-cut, where the public interest is in seeing that 38 million Americans without health insurance receive protection, but those who profit in one way or another from the present system fight it. If the decision is made to protect the American people, there will be a number of not-so-small side benefits:

- People who fear moving to another job because they might lose health insurance would no longer have to worry.
- American manufacturers (like automobile companies) will find themselves more competitive with the Japanese, Germans, Swedes and French because U.S. companies who now cover their employees will no longer be forced to pick up part of the tab for those who do not. One manufacturer told me that he expects their medical costs to drop by about one-third over a short period of years.
- People on welfare who fear taking a low-wage job, such as at McDonald's, because they will lose their medical coverage, will be able to work and lift themselves out of poverty.

The American people overwhelmingly favor protecting all of our citizens. Whether special-interest politics will prevent that is the question we will answer in the next few weeks.

"Profiteers' Victory over the Public in Health Reform May Be Short-Lived," P.S./Washington, September 18–24, 1994

As I type this, the health care legislation that has been so much discussed appears to be taking its last breaths, and it is doubtful that it will be revived before the next session of Congress.

That means that 38 million Americans will continue to have no health care coverage and for those of you who have it, there is no certainty that if you change or lose your job you will still have health care.

For the nation's economy this news is equally bad: In 1980 the nation spent 1 of every 11 dollars on health care; this year it is 1 of 7, and by the year 2000 it will be 1 of 5. No other nation comes anywhere near those high figures—and the other western industrial nations have health protection for all their citizens, at much less cost.

A respected pollster, Peter Hart, told the *New York Times*: "The worst of the process worked. Yes, there was a dialogue, but it was so influenced by the special interest groups that the public didn't get a true and honest debate. What they learned is everything they had to fear—and very little about what they could hope for."

Those who profit from the present system prevailed; and the public interest group did not.

The insurance companies—not all of them—who thought they might lose a few dollars in profit, and the tobacco companies who fought vigorously, may have won a temporary victory, but the insurance companies particularly may have forced a situation where they won a battle but will end up out-smarting themselves and losing a great deal.

If some version of the Clinton plan had prevailed, responsible insurance companies and insurance agents could have continued to do well. Yes, they would have had to spell out their policies more clearly, but that would be more than offset by the additional customers they could get among the 38 million uninsured.

Now there will be growing recognition that even with a president pushing a reform program, big money prevailed over the public interest at the national level—and there will be much more support for a single-payer system on a state-by-state basis, similar to the program that Canada has. That leaves the insurance companies out completely.

There is much propaganda in the United States about how terrible the Canadian system is. If the Canadian system were so terrible, it is amazing that not one member of the Canadian parliament wants to repeal it.

A 1989 poll of public opinion in the United States and Canada found that 3 percent of Canadians would like the U.S. system but 61 percent of Americans would prefer the Canadian system.

There have been problems with the Canadian system. At one point in Ontario there were waiting lists for surgery but that was corrected. Canada has no co-payment—a small fee to be paid by each patient—and my Canadian friends say that has been a mistake, that it causes overutilization.

But most of the other charges against the Canadian system are pure myth. Yes, the United States is ahead in research and I want us to stay ahead. But we can do that and still do much better by all of our people. Here are some of the myths and realities:

"Canadians come to the United States for health care." Some do. That is particularly true where we have specialties on heart care or that type of thing—but the costs are picked up by the Canadian system. But far more Americans go into Canada to try to take advantage of their system than the Canadians who come here. Fewer than 1 percent of the hospital beds in border U.S. cities are occupied by Canadian citizens. But Canadian parliamentarians are considering legislation to prevent so many Americans from coming into Canada to take advantage of their system.

"It sounds great, but if I need serious surgery, I would have a better chance of getting it in the United States than in Canada."

Think again! Look at these statistics: heart and/or lung transplants—per hundred thousand in the U.S. and Canada, virtually identical; liver transplants—6.8 per hundred thousand in the U.S., 7.1 in Canada. More bone marrow transplants in Canada, and the list goes on.

The infant mortality rate is one-third higher in the United States than in Canada. The average lifespan is two years greater in Canada than in the U.S.

"Physicians don't like the Canadian system."

The average physician does not make as much money in Canada as in the United States, but even with that, only 240 Canadian doctors either came or tried to come to the United States in 1992 and the numbers are declining.

Canadian doctors like a system that pays them promptly without a hassle, with more than 96 percent of the claims paid within four weeks.

A 1993 survey by the *New England Journal of Medicine* found Canadian physicians 50 percent more likely to be satisfied with their system than U.S. doctors are with ours. *The Toronto Globe and Mail* reported a 1992 poll of Canadian physicians and found 63 percent satisfied with their system. One percent of the doctors called Canada's system of health care poor and 83 percent described it as good or excellent. Eighty-five percent of the doctors agreed with the statement that the Canadian health care system is better than the United States'.

All of this means that the greedy among those who fought health care reform in our nation may have been too greedy for their own economic health.

The battle may now shift to the states, where the public interest may prevail over the profiteers.

"ROBIN WILLIAMS, CHRISTOPHER REEVE, AND THE U.S. HEALTH CARE MUDDLE," P.S./WASHINGTON, JANUARY 28–FEBRUARY 3, 1996

A few years ago when I sought reelection to the Senate, the actor Christopher Reeve was good enough to be the draw for a fundraiser I had in New York City, and afterwards we had dinner together.

So though my knowledge of show business is slim, I have followed his career with some interest. And I joined the nation in a collective groan of regret when I read about his accident on a horse that paralyzed him. Recently I saw this item in the *Washington Post*:

"Actor Robin Williams has pledged to pay Christopher Reeve's medical bills when the paralyzed actor's health insurance runs out later this year. . . . Reeve's ongoing treatment is expected to cost about $400,000 a year. Williams and Reeve made a pact more than 20 years ago, when both were attending Juilliard, that if either made it in show biz, he'd help the other in time of crisis."

I applaud what Robin Williams is doing.

But something is wrong with our system when Robin Williams has to do that. And what about the millions of Americans who have no Robin Williams to help them? There are now 41 million Americans with no health insurance. If those same people lived in Italy or Denmark or Great Britain or Canada or Japan or any other West European industrial nation, their health costs would be covered.

On December 14th, the Centers for Disease Control and Prevention in Atlanta released a study that shows infant deaths for women with incomes above the poverty line in the United States are 8.3 per 1,000 births. But for women below the poverty line it is 13.5 per 1,000 births.

Because we are insensitive to both poverty and to health care needs, these needless deaths are occurring. Today, as I type this, I read a newspaper story that talks about "the disaster of President Clinton's proposing a health care plan." The disaster was not that he proposed a plan; the disaster was that we did not pass one. If Christopher Reeve lived in Canada, Robin Williams would not have to pay these costs. And the average lifespan in Canada is greater than it is in the United States.

In a poll taken a few years ago, Canadian citizens were asked if they were satisfied with their health care system. Fifty-six percent responded favorably, not a high percentage, but not bad. Then the pollsters asked if they would prefer the U.S. health delivery system. Three percent said they would prefer our system! Those who profit from the present U.S. system spread largely untrue stories about the flaws in the Canadian system. When I talk to my friends who are Canadian parliamentarians, they do suggest some modifications that they would like to make.

But I have yet to talk to a single Canadian citizen who does not prefer their system to ours. Three cheers for Robin Williams! But three Bronx cheers—boos—for our short-sightedness in not protecting all of our citizens.

"A Patient We Can Cure," Commentary, *Chicago Sun-Times*, August 29, 2000

What is moving this nation slowly—much too slowly—to guaranteeing health care delivery to all Americans is a combination of three things:
- 44 million Americans without health insurance coverage.
- HMOs where a bookkeeping clerk determines how much care is given.
- The complexity and ineptness of our insurance-medical-hospital system.

That last point came into my home via yesterday's mail. My wife died in February but I still am getting bills, the latest for lab fees on Dec. 10. In a form letter dated Aug. 21 my insurance carrier writes that they will not cover $49 in lab fees that I knew nothing about, and I should pay the $49. Why do I get this notice for the first time 8½ months after her lab visit?

I wade through my medical and hospital bills and the statements from the insurance company with difficulty, and I can only imagine the frustrations that someone with a fifth-grade education faces trying to decipher things.

Physicians complain—with justification—that between insurance company papers to fill out and government forms under Medicare and Medicaid, paperwork is taking far too much time from the actual practices of medicine.

The overworked phrase—managed care—can save consumers, insurance companies and the government money when humanely and prudently administered. But too often a clerk who probably has to go through 100 forms an hour routinely and sometimes recklessly makes decisions on medical care.

A basic protection that patients should have is the right to sue the HMO for its medical mistakes. We can sue physicians and hospitals; why not HMOs? Would that send our health insurance costs up a little? Probably. Would it be worth it? For the patient and medical provider, yes.

Adding to our other woes, one insurance policy will cover one thing, another something else. A few years ago I helped a man in suburban Cook County get a lung transplant, something not clearly spelled out in his health insurance policy. In the process I learned that as of that time about half the insurance policies covered a lung transplant and half did not. My guess is that hardly any readers of this column have any idea whether their insurance policy covers a lung transplant. Reading an insurance policy rarely helps. It only adds to the confusion.

Finally, I hope we will move to doing what other developed nations do: provide health protection for all of our citizens.

People complain about Medicare, and there are legitimate concerns and deficiencies. But I know that not a single member of Congress has introduced a bill to get rid of Medicare. Why should that medical protection be there only for those of us over 65?

I hear horror stories about the Canadian health care system, almost all of them distortions. The Canadian system does have flaws, but not a single member of Canada's parliament has introduced a measure to get rid of it. The same can be said of the British system.

People who defend the status quo warn them about the evils of "socialized medicine," by which they mean government-sponsored programs to protect everyone. I do not hear them complain about "socialized highways." There are areas where government leadership is needed to protect people.

"Socialized schools" is another example. We do have government-sponsored schools, and few thoughtful people would want to get rid of them. But people who do not like them have the option of parochial or other privately launched schools, or home schooling.

That should be our model. People of seriously limited income should be able to get health protection, and even someone with above average income should be so protected. If people want to pay privately for additional health services, they should have that right.

Between now and Nov. 7, candidates of both parties will launch carefully crafted balloons on health care. If we hold their feet to the fire, they should understand that the American people want practical government guarantees of good health care delivery.

EDUCATION AND LITERACY

"CAMPUS DISORDERS: WHAT'S THE ANSWER?," FROM THE STATEHOUSE, BY LIEUTENANT GOVERNOR PAUL SIMON, APRIL 2, 1969

According to the dictionary, the word "campus" originally meant: "An open space or field, as for martial exercises." There is still more truth to that than most people find comfortable.

What has happened on some of the campuses throughout the nation is obviously not good. The campus must be a place where the mental processes should prevail, not threats or violence.

No responsible person can defend some of the excesses which have marked a few campuses. But before we panic, several things should be kept in mind:

1. The huge majority of students are acting responsibly. This is true even of the most highly publicized campus in the nation, San Francisco State. Too many people are drawing conclusions from headlines that the whole student population of the nation has gone berserk.

2. Difficulties on campus are not new. When I went to college there was occasional violence with students of a rival college after a football game.

Five years ago there was a rash of panty raids on campuses. In 1823, Thomas Jefferson wrote about the University of Virginia: "The insubordination of youth is now the greatest obstacle to their education."

3. While there have been exceptions, generally college administrators in Illinois have handled the situation effectively. At Southern Illinois University, for example, students who broke into the president's office were promptly expelled and prosecuted.

There are reasons for hope even in the most difficult situations. One factor which I believe will moderate the total situation will be the end of the Vietnam War, which hopefully is not too far off.

Two years ago I wrote a paper for the Illinois State Historical Society on riots in Illinois history. In doing it, I came across factual support for an often stated but seldom analyzed concept: When there is violence abroad, there is a tendency toward violence at home.

Almost all of the major domestic disturbances in the United States during the first half of this century occurred around the years of World Wars I and II.

The second sign of hope in all of this is that the U.S. students today are much more concerned about the needs of society than they were when I went to college.

I vividly recall picking up the morning newspaper in my dormitory at Dana College in Nebraska and reading about the Communist take-over of Czechoslovakia. I rushed over to the college canteen to talk to someone about this tragedy—and literally no one was interested.

That would no longer be true on any college campus. We should view the headlines we read with a little balance, not defending irresponsible conduct, but not giving up on the nation's young people. The answers to the campus problems must be largely given by college administrators, and in no case should there be hasty answers written by lawmakers in an emotionally charged atmosphere.

"BAD NEWS ON THE EDUCATION FRONT," P.S./WASHINGTON, FEBRUARY 7–13, 1982

A recent issue of the *Chronicle of Higher Education* had separate articles which together constitute a bundle of bad news—news that does not erupt in headlines but which portrays a condition which should be of concern to all Americans:

- The nation's university libraries have purchased 3 percent fewer books a year for the last five years.
- The inflation-adjusted revenue of U.S. colleges and universities dropped 2.4 percent between fiscal years 1979 and 1980.

The item from Canada on students from the poorer nations reflects what is also happening in the United States. Students from the poor countries of the world are finding it increasingly difficult to attend college in the United States because of costs. And where do many of them now go? To the Soviet Union, which is boosting its aid to foreign students at the very time the United States is cutting back. The Soviets seemingly recognize an opportunity in this situation.

The library figure is a troubling one. It's one indication, among others, that as our colleges and universities undergo further financial squeezing, quality will suffer. No one notices when there are fewer books purchased. But we later notice the effects of this kind of erosion of our country's knowledge base. And the loss of revenue for schools—reflected in the library example—means that other non-visible features of college education will quietly suffer; ultimately, the nation suffers. Money alone will not produce quality education. We have ample evidence of that. But if it is true that the America of tomorrow is largely shaped in the classrooms, lecture halls and college labs of today, then it should also be apparent that we cannot build a better, stronger nation by spending less and less on education. Yet that's our present course, and the request before Congress is one that would greatly accelerate that trend.

"Good News from Oilton, Oklahoma,"
P.S./Washington, May 2–8, 1982

It is in the nature of public office that you generally hear from people who have problems. But now and then there is an exception.

Congressman Mike Synar of Oklahoma gave me a letter from a woman who lives in Oilton, Oklahoma, who asked that he give it to whomever is responsible for the student assistance program. She writes:

"I wanted to personally thank the government agency that is responsible for federal grants to aid students in their pursuit of a higher education.

"It has made my son's goal of completing a higher education a lot easier. For the past five years Russell has attended Oklahoma State University, thanks to the grants and a lot of hard work on his part. He works 24 hours on the weekends, a job he has held since he was 17. He will graduate this year in the school of accounting. He has maintained a B overall average and has been on the Dean's Honor Roll five times.

"You have helped, along with Almighty God, to create a more productive employee and a higher wage earner. In return he will pay higher taxes for the government and there will be a better future for him, and for me, and his wife and our family, as well as a source of pride.

"God bless our country, where with a capable mind and determination, the American dream is still alive and doing well.

"So you see gentlemen, the money is not being wasted, only 'loaned' for a better future."

That letter illustrates something that is easy to lose sight of: that solid, constructive, positive things are happening.

It is in the nature of news that bad news tends to dominate.

Yes, there are some students who have abused their opportunities, and where there is abuse it most certainly should be stopped.

But for every student who misuses public funds, there is a host of hard-working students who are struggling to get by, barely making it through college, who will contribute to a better country following their college years. Last year Japan graduated twice as many electrical engineers as did the United States. It is one small indication of the competitive world we face.

There are those who now tell us to cut back on college opportunity for young people. If their advice is followed, more than two million students will be denied loans and grants in the 1983–84 school year. That is a course which will hurt these people and their families, and it is a course which will hurt the nation.

Our number one resource is our people. That resource should be developed as fully as possible.

"THE KEY TO A STRONG INDUSTRIAL BASE," P.S./WASHINGTON, AUGUST 15–21, 1982

Brains, more than brawn, must be stressed if Southern Illinois and the United States are to experience the industrial growth we need.

We have streets that need to be repaired, sewer systems to be built and other work which will require muscle.

But increasingly a region and a nation that want to move ahead must prepare themselves for a much more complex world. We must continue to position ourselves on the cutting edge of modern industrial technology.

What does that mean, in practical terms?

For Golconda and Vandalia and Cairo and Harrisburg and all the communities in Southern Illinois that want progress, it means continued and greater stress on education. Are there ways we can improve the educational product? Of course there are—and if we are serious about the future we should be looking at them.

And what is true for communities in Southern Illinois is also true for the nation.

Last year Japan (which has half our population) graduated twice as many electrical engineers as we did, and in total numbers of all types of engineers graduated 73,500 compared to 62,900 in the United States—and many of those who graduated in the United States were from other countries. Who do you think will be ahead industrially 10 years from now, Japan or the United States? The answer comes at least in part from the educational base.

That is why proposals to cut back on educational opportunity and educational emphasis in this nation are so shortsighted.

In the next 20 years market conditions and opportunity will change dramatically. We cannot prepare people for technologies not yet developed, but we can teach people the basics: how to read and write effectively, the fundamentals of mathematics and science.

Our competitors—Japan, West Germany, the Soviet Union among others—are putting increasing resources into an educational base for the future, and we must do the same.

How?

1. Take a look at the elementary and high school programs wherever we live. Are we offering the science and math courses we should? Are we offering foreign languages? Are we encouraging good teachers to stay, both with adequate pay and by saying "thank you"?

2. Are we encouraging people who live in our community who cannot read and write to acquire those skills? We have millions of Americans in that category which hurts them, hurts our society and hurts our economy. Are we using the local school system or library or churches to promote these basic skills? Are we encouraging those who have been out of school many years to acquire new skills, to broaden their vocational and cultural horizons?

3. Community colleges now teach a majority of the nation's college freshmen. These colleges also help with adult education. They can also give vision to a community and an area. Are they? Are we encouraging and supporting community colleges as we should?

4. Four-year colleges and university programs and the students who attend them need support. Unless the nation reverses its present downward slide in higher education support, the number of colleges in the nation soon will decline. The nation must ask itself if that is where we want to go. And the schools themselves—such as Southern Illinois University, McKendree College, Greenville College and our community colleges—must also ask if they are serving the larger community interest as effectively as they should.

Stressing education may not seem like the key to a strengthened industrial base, but the lesson of the last three decades is that it is. What has been true of the past 30 years will be even more true of the next 30 years.

"Strength through Education," P.S./Washington, February 18, 1985

The United States must remain strong. All Americans agree on that.

The question is *how* we remain strong. The budget presented to Congress by the [Reagan] Administration suggests that one of the ways we remain strong is to spend 13 percent more on the defense budget, and cut back on funding for education. That is a course that will result in a temporary increase in military strength, but ultimately will weaken our nation militarily, economically, and culturally.

In Japan, West Germany, Sweden, the Soviet Union, and other countries they are putting more emphasis on education and if we intend to compete in the future it is a mistake to launch a program that will deny the opportunity for a quality education to many Americans.

We have to be tougher on ourselves in education, and most of the answers for that rest with the state and local government. We have too many "soft" courses, too few academic standards and demands. We pay much more attention to standards for podiatrists who work on our feet than for teachers who work on our children. State and local governments primarily make those decisions.

But at the federal level we make major higher education decisions on access and quality.

The Administration has suggested that no family with income of more than $32,500 should be eligible for any college loan or $25,000 for grant or work programs, and that the total amount of loans and grants available to anyone going to college could not exceed $4,000, less than half the cost of most four-year colleges.

What would happen if that proposal were to succeed?

It would result in three things, all bad:

1. Hundreds of thousands (perhaps more than a million) young people would have to drop out of college. Do we build a better America that way? Hardly. Our military needs better trained people, not more poorly trained personnel. Last year Japan graduated twice as many electrical engineers as we did; Japan has half our population. Who will be ahead in the field of electronics 10 years from now? We know, because we shape our future through education. Dropping huge numbers of young people from college opportunity will needlessly limit our potential.

2. If the proposal were to be accepted, a recent trend that is not good would be accelerated: the economic segregation of American higher education. Increasingly those who go to non-public colleges and universities are from upper income families; those who go to public institutions are from families with more limited income. We ought to avoid building a class system in any way. Elite schools exclusively for the well-to-do should not be a part of the American scene.

3. The proposal would cause a drop in the quality of U.S. higher education at the very time we need to raise quality. If the federal government were to follow the Administration plan, schools would be forced to spend money on student aid instead of faculty salaries, books in the library, and courses important to the nation (like studying the Japanese language) where there are not many students. There would be no immediate, visible effect. There would still be a college faculty, but with faces changing. The library would still look the same when you walk past it. And there would be no student riots or great commotion when you drop some courses. But in an increasingly competitive world the net result would be that quality goes down.

Education cannot be immune from the search for ways to save money. But great caution must be exercised or we will be building a frail future.

"U.S. Rates 'F' in Literacy," P.S./Washington, June 2–8, 1985

There is a little-known aspect of the Nicaraguan situation from which we can learn, both for foreign and domestic policy.

President Reagan has expressed concern about the Cuban military presence in Nicaragua, and while I do not view a few thousand Cuban troops there as a threat to our country, I would feel better if they were not there.

I am more concerned about another Cuban presence in Nicaragua, both because of its long-range implications for Nicaragua and for what it says about the United States.

Among the realities the new leadership of Nicaragua recognized at the time of the revolution were these three:

1. Nicaragua had a major problem with illiteracy in its population.
2. Cuba faced a similar situation when Fidel Castro took over and he dramatically improved Cuba's illiteracy rate.
3. The United States, despite many pluses in education, still has a high illiteracy rate and has done virtually nothing about it.

Faced with these three realities, and already having a Marxist tinge that made Cuba's government attractive to them, Nicaragua's new leaders called on Cuba to help with their illiteracy problem.

The result has been a reduction in Nicaraguan illiteracy from 52 percent of the population in 1979 to 12 percent since the Somoza dictatorship fell.

Another not-so-incidental result is that there have been 2,000 Cuban literacy workers covering the countryside in tiny Nicaragua. Those literacy workers are probably going to have a much greater influence on the long-range political course of Nicaragua than the Cuban troops ever will.

To my knowledge, there is no country on the face of the earth that has asked the United States for help in solving literacy problems because we have so many of our own.

We rank 49th among the 158 nations that belong to the United Nations in literacy levels.

We have 5 percent of the world's population, one-third of the world's economic power—and we are 49th in our literacy levels! We have 23 million Americans who can read a stop sign, but cannot address an envelope, cannot fill out an employment form—and worst of all—cannot help their children with their school work.

If the figures compiled by the U.S. Department of Education are accurate, they forecast a terrible trend.

In addition, there are many who can address an envelope but cannot read a book or magazine article or a newspaper. About one-third of the adults in America cannot read and understand these words I am writing now.

What are we doing about this drag on the nation's culture and economy?

Almost nothing. People who cannot read and write are hiding it, out of embarrassment. The rest of us are ignoring it. Last year, I got $5 million placed in the library bill to help libraries assist on this problem—especially by encouraging neighborhood libraries to double as tutoring centers for these adults—but that is only a token of what needs to be done. Every dollar we spend to teach people how to read and write will be repaid several hundred times in added tax revenue, in addition to an otherwise enriched and better society.

Most important, we need a national commitment to solve this problem. And solve it we can. If we do, other nations will not have to look to Cuba as an example of moving on the literacy problem. They can look to us.

(Readers interested in learning more about this problem may want to read the book *Illiteracy*.)

"FROM GUNS TO BUTTER AND BLACKBOARDS," P.S./WASHINGTON, MAY 21–27, 1989

Not all news from Washington these days is bad. Let me tell you about a battle I lost, but one that will be won next year or the following year if I read my figures correctly. We spent less than 2 percent of our federal budget on education, if school lunch programs are excluded from that total.

The education problem this nation faces is not as dramatic as the savings and loan crisis, but in the long run is infinitely more important. If we don't do a better job educating all Americans, our nation is destined for sluggish economic growth and a quality of life for many that is far below what it should be.

I introduced an amendment on the Senate floor to take 1 percent of the defense budget, $3 billion, and put it into education programs. That would mean more than a 10 percent increase in education funding, permitting us to do some of the things that are really essential for our nation.

Leaders of both parties had reached an agreement with President Bush on the budget, and so they opposed my amendment. I understand that. Not only did I have the opposition of the leaders of both parties, but obviously also the opposition of the defense industry.

And the education community did nothing to fight for my amendment because they felt—accurately—that my amendment didn't have a chance to pass. I knew that too.

But instead of being left with only six or eight votes supporting my position, which many anticipated, my amendment went down to defeat 64–31.

What makes it of interest is that my supporters came from both political parties, and from people who would be classified as both conservatives and liberals. Despite all the pressure, there was a broad base of support for my amendment.

I favor a strong defense. But a nation has to be strong educationally if it is to remain strong militarily. And we have had ample evidence of waste in the military. We could find that 1 percent without doing any harm to our defense. Military experts are loaded with examples of where we could find that $3 billion.

It makes no sense for the United States to spend three times as much per capita for the defense of Western Europe as do our friends in Western Europe. That made sense in 1950, perhaps in 1960, but it certainly does not in 1989.

Our most serious economic competitor, Japan, has a 2 percent school dropout rate. Ours is 28 percent. The dropout rate in much of urban America is dramatically higher than 28 percent. We can and must do better.

About 30 million adult Americans cannot read this column, but we do almost nothing about this. Those who have the problem hide it, and the rest of us ignore it.

I could go on.

The educational needs in this country are severe. We have to face that reality and adjust the spending priorities of the federal budget. Those 30 senators who went against the prevailing tide and pressure to support my amendment said so. I am grateful to them.

They are Sens. Adams, Baucus, Bingaman, Boren, Boschwitz, Bradley, Bryan, Bumpers, Burdick, Conrad, DeConcini, Dixon, Grassley, Harkin, Hatfield, Hollings, Kerry, Kohl, Leahy, Levin, Matsunaga, Metzenbaum, Mikulski, Pell, Pressler, Reid, Robb, Rockefeller, Specter and Wirth.

"LONGER SCHOOL DAYS WOULD BOOST U.S. STANDARD OF LIVING," P.S./WASHINGTON, OCTOBER 9–15, 1994

Without fanfare, the United States Congress has adopted a small amendment to the Elementary and Secondary Education Act that could have a far-ranging impact on our nation.

A few weeks ago the Senate adopted an amendment I proposed—co-sponsored by a bipartisan group of senators including Claiborne Pell, Robert Byrd, Herb Kohl, Jim Jeffords, John Chafee and Carol Moseley-Braun—authorizing that $100 million a year be given to schools that move from our present 180 school days a year to 210 days a year. The dollars were reduced in conference with the House of Representatives to $72 million, not a large amount in a nation of 45 million elementary and high school students, but enough to start us on the road to improvement. It is enough to get school boards and school administrators across the nation talking about our problem.

In Japan, students go to school 243 days a year, in Germany 240, and in most other industrial nations numbers that are greater than ours. Can we learn as much in 180 days as they do in 240 or 243? Obviously not.

Why do young people in our nation attend school only180 days? In theory, so that they can go out and harvest the crops. Even in small-town, rural America—where I live—that is not true for most young people. Our world has changed, but our educational system has not changed.

The schools that move to 210 days in order to qualify for the extra federal dollars will find that their students learn more, and do better, whether they go on to college or not.

Increasing attendance from 180 days to 210, still far behind Japan and Germany, is the equivalent of adding two additional school years of study by the 12th grade.

The few who will lead on this, and see their students do better on the average than other American students, will soon be followed, I believe, by many other schools who recognize the improvement such a change will bring.

This is not the federal government forcing any local schools to do anything, but it is a message from the federal government that if we want our young people to compete with the rest of the world, we will have to be better prepared.

Increasingly, we will compete with others either with better prepared personnel, or lower wages.

The answer to what we should do is obvious, but we're not doing much about it. This legislation is a start.

Some months ago, in one of the committees on which I serve, we heard the story of a U.S. corporation trying to decide where to locate a small manufacturing plant. Their choices: Mexico, the United States or Germany. Mexico had the advantage of the lowest wages, the United States of better prepared workers than Mexico and lower wages than Germany, and Germany—with better trained workers and an average hourly manufacturing wage now $6 higher than the United States. They chose Germany because the workers are better prepared.

Recently, I visited Motorola headquarters, located in Illinois. Motorola is adding workers at its Libertyville, Ill., plant and they require that applicants be at least high school graduates. Motorola then tests them but finds only 1 in 10 applicants meets its minimum requirements.

Motorola also has plants in Scotland, Germany, Japan, Singapore and Taiwan. In those countries they do not even give the tests, because they find the educational background of the workers has prepared them adequately.

The lesson for us should be clear. We're going to have to do much better. A 210-day school year is not the sole answer, but would be a step toward doing better.

"Appropriations for Literacy," NPR Commentary, August 18, 1997

As taxpayers, all of us applaud when sensible things are done to save money. But sometimes what appear to be savings can cost money in the long run.

The House and Senate Appropriation Committees in Washington are funding most of the literacy efforts at the current level. People who cannot read and write harm themselves economically and culturally, and harm the nation. So keeping the literacy funding at the current level, in view of the overall budget crunch, is not great news, but not bad news.

However, a small—small by federal standards—appropriation for literacy, that has no one with any power to lobby it, has been eliminated. That is $4.7 million for prison literacy programs.

Drug use and other problems cause much of the crime in our nation, but one of the causes is that some of those involved in criminal activities see only extremely limited alternatives for themselves.

Eighty-two percent of those in our prisons and jails are high school dropouts, and a majority of these are labeled "functionally illiterate," meaning that they cannot read a newspaper or fill out an employment form. If these prisoners were to stay in penitentiaries the rest of their lives, perhaps not having literacy training for them would make sense. But almost all of them will eventually walk our streets again, and if we want them to avoid their past criminal behavior, we should be providing constructive alternatives. People who cannot read and write have a hard time getting a job. Show me an area anywhere—white, black or Hispanic—with high unemployment rates and I will show you an area with high crime rates.

Two years ago, Congress voted to cut out assistance for college courses for people in prison, a shortsighted vote that had political appeal. But it ignored the fact that on the average the more education a prisoner receives, the less likely he or she is to return to ways of crime and to return to prison. I hope someone in the House or Senate will amend this appropriation and restore the $4.7 million prison literacy program. The amount is one four-hundred-thousandths of 1 percent of the budget.

Anti-crime programs are not just building expensive prisons, but also doing low-cost things to prevent crimes. Revenge may be emotionally satisfying but it is not as good as rehabilitation.

"More Money for Students," NPR Commentary, July 1, 2003

The combination of fiscal policies of the state and federal governments on higher education will cause long-term harm to the nation. This did not happen during the term of one President or in one state administration around the nation.

The federal commission which studies student finances reported that over a ten-year period, two million students with the ability to handle college work did not attend because of the financial squeeze. That means a huge loss to the nation in productivity in the years to come—and a loss in income. A state-by-state analysis of average income shows that the states with the highest percentage of college graduates have the highest average income, to no one's surprise. Cut back on college funding and you cut back on future income.

In Federal Fiscal Year 1949, we spent 9 percent of our federal budget on education, almost all of it on higher education. Now about 2 percent of the federal budget goes for education. There is one other huge shift. In 1949 three-fourths of the money for students going to college was in the form of grants, one-fourth loans. Today it is the reverse, three-fourths loans, one-fourth grants. That too often determines what career a student chooses, because students understandably want to pay back those loans as soon as possible. And sometimes it determines whether they buy a house or start a family.

Adding to the difficulty is that state governments are in a squeeze and higher education is one of the easy targets for money. At one point higher education was almost a "sacred cow"; you could not cut it. Then during the Vietnam War, when we had a misguided national policy of drafting only those who did not go to college, campus violence erupted, and cutting university budgets became politically popular. The result? States are cutting university budgets, tuition is being raised, and eventually the states and nation are short-changed economically.

Which would benefit the nation more? Tax cuts, or more money for students to go to college?

The popular answer is tax cuts. The right answer is aid to students.

CIVIL RIGHTS

"Equal Treatment for Women," P.S./Washington, July 6–12, 1975

As an old football fan, I enjoyed the chance to have as witnesses before a subcommittee on which I serve seven of the top football coaches in the nation, including Darrel Royal of the University of Texas, Tom Osborne of the University of Nebraska and Bob Blackman of the University of Illinois.

The topic of their testimony and our question: the rights of women in the field of education. They are concerned that new regulations proposed by the federal government will hurt the present athletic programs at universities.

The problem is much bigger than athletic programs. And whether you are for or against the Equal Rights Amendment, is it clear that women have not had an equal opportunity in many fields.

The income figures show it—income figures that will not be changed overnight, but that should gradually change. Here is a county-by-county breakdown of average full-time working male and female incomes, age 16 and over, in my district:

County	Male	Female
Alexander	$5,406	$2,791
Bond	6,692	2,680
Clinton	7,132	3,258
Franklin	6,794	3,282
Gallatin	6,232	2,743
Hamilton	5,234	2,779
Hardin	5,676	2,211
Jackson	5,819	2,855
Jefferson	6,621	3,191
Johnson	6,217	3,658
Marion	6,596	3,225
Massac	6,537	2,911
Monroe	7,998	3,498
Perry	6,916	3,217
Pope	5,495	2,327
Pulaski	5,363	2,495
Randolph	7,347	3,196
Saline	6,887	3,098
Union	5,949	3,549
Washington	6,300	2,948
White	6,634	2,632
Williamson	6,955	3,511

These are 1970 figures, now five years old. Obviously all income has gone up since then, because of inflation if nothing else. Presumably the gap between male and female workers has closed somewhat, though it is safe to say the gap remains substantial.

Right now, with the law and court decisions saying that discrimination in wages is illegal, the federal agencies are putting forward rulings on how we handle various situations, including the field of education.

Here are a few educational statistics which show the problem:

- More than 75 percent of the well qualified students who do not go to college are women.
- At the university level, women average $1,500 less than men teachers.
- Ohio State spends 1,300 times more for men's athletics than women's.

Many other statistics could be added. How can we encourage fairer treatment for women without hurting existing programs such as athletics?

The aim should be not to tear down what is good, but to improve the opportunities for those who have not shared fully. That's one of the problems we are wrestling with in Washington these days.

"WIRETAPPING: A BASIC STRUGGLE CONTINUES," P.S./WASHINGTON, MAY 23–29, 1976

The attempt to maintain a free society involves, among other things, a delicate balance between liberty and security, and that balance is at stake in a little-noticed new report on wiretapping given to the President.

The people who prepared the report divided on the question of whether there should be more or less wiretapping of the telephones of American citizens.

Most people agree that freedom has its limitations. Justice Oliver Wendell Holmes said that freedom of speech does not include the right to go into a theater and shout "Fire!" when there is no fire.

Justice Hugo Black believed that there should be literally no restrictions on freedom of press, and if a newspaper or radio or television station charged you falsely with the crime of murder, you should not be able to sue for libel. No other justices shared that opinion, fortunately.

But where do you draw the line between the right of government to protect citizens and the responsibility of government to protect freedom? Most of us recognize that a certain amount of self-discipline is essential for democracy to function. We generally don't see how far we can go in the abuse of freedom or how far we can go in excessive use of police force. Common sense and good taste restrain us, and those two factors are as important to the success of our form of government as the three branches of our government.

When the Bill of Rights was attached to our Constitution, no one had a telephone. Today in the wiretapping issue the courts, the police, and citizens are faced with a dilemma for which there is no clear-cut constitutional answer. But two factors should weigh heavily as we make this decision:

First, if there is doubt, generally it is wise to resolve that doubt on the side of freedom. The most casual study of history suggests that freedom is elusive, and once you lose it, the chances are not great that you will regain it.

Second, while there is no mention of the telephone in the Constitution, the Constitution says that no one can enter your house without a specific search warrant. If police enter your house without a search warrant and find a warm body with a knife in its chest and your fingerprints on the knife, that cannot be used as evidence against you.

If those who wrote the Constitution went to that extreme to protect the sanctity of your home from government intervention, the spirit of that constitutional principle suggests to me that Thomas Jefferson and James Madison and the others would not have tolerated the government listening to your telephone conversations.

If you want to condemn the President or your congressman, the governor or the mayor, you should have the right to do that over your telephone without worry that some governmental agency is either listening to or recording your conversation.

There are a thousand-and-one ways to reduce crime without endangering liberty. Let's do those things. Crime can be reduced, but it should be carefully, effectively done.

The Bicentennial year is an occasion to reaffirm our freedoms, not erode them.

"THE FIGHT FOR HUMAN RIGHTS," P.S./WASHINGTON, AUGUST 7–13, 1977

It is one of those brief, embarrassing moments.

Some of us who have been named to check on compliance with the international Helsinki Accord were meeting with a man who had suffered greatly and fled the Soviet Union. I noticed something in his coat lapel but I was just far enough away from him that I could not make it out. With a smile I asked him, "It that a Jimmy Carter peanut in your coat lapel?"

"No," he replied gravely. "It is a bit of barbed wire. Those of us who have been held in Soviet Union prisons and have been able to get to the West often wear this, to remind others as well as ourselves of what we once faced, and what others still face."

We had been discussing with him the stance of President Carter on the human rights issue. There are those who say we should be silent. "Embarrassment causes anger, and anger is something we should not encourage between nations," they argue. "The Soviets and other Communist nations are gradually giving their people a little more freedom. We should encourage more of that by being silent and not rocking the boat."

Others argue that freedom is what we stand for and we should not hesitate to say so. If that embarrasses someone, so be it. No one can predict the response of nations anyway, they argue, so stand up for what you believe in, regardless of what anyone thinks.

What is clear is that President Carter—more than any President since John F. Kennedy—has been stressing our belief in human rights.

If we use some common sense as we make clear what we stand for, I believe that is a good thing. Too often in recent years we have played the role of the international bully who plays power games with local dictators, ignoring the hopes and dreams for freedom of the people in those nations.

The United States is not a piece of ground. It is that, true, but much more. We believe in freedom, the right of people to determine their own destiny. And we should say so. But we ought to do it with some sensitivity. We should not be pious about it; it should not be said with a "we are better than you are" attitude; we should state our beliefs acknowledging that we have some major defects in the human rights field in our own country.

And our actions should match our words. We cannot say we believe in human rights all over the face of the earth, and then do nothing to help hungry people get food. Sermons about human rights from an overfed and sometimes unresponsive Uncle Sam do not win converts.

We should also not expect others to erect wooden images of our system. Each country will develop differently. And we did not get where we are overnight.

When nations move even a little toward freedom, we ought to commend them for their movement, rather than denouncing them for the ground not yet covered.

We also ought to try to be consistent, though that will not be easy.

Most important, we should recognize that the diplomatic battles for freedom—unlike military battles—will not be won when a flag goes up somewhere or with any massive surrenders. The struggle toward freedom cannot be measured by a speech in the Soviet Union or a Pravda editorial.

And it will not be measured in miles but in inches.

To win that inch-by-inch struggle for freedom will take patience.

Not during the lifetime of the Carter Administration, nor in your lifetime or mine are we likely to see many dramatic breakthroughs for freedom. One will occur now and then—as in India a few months ago—but that will be rare.

The battles will be won not by those who shout the loudest but by those with patience, who know what they believe in, and say it and live it in a low-key way—but firmly.

I hope we have that patience.

"THE PROPER ROLE FOR AFFIRMATIVE ACTION," P.S./WASHINGTON, APRIL 15–21, 1995

"Affirmative action" is not-so-suddenly becoming a major topic of discussion.

Affirmative action is like religion or education: A good thing, but it can be abused.

Affirmative action means opportunity and fairness. It does not mean quotas. It does not mean hiring unqualified people.

Some believe that affirmative action hurts minorities and women and those with disabilities, because when people secure jobs there will be some who say, "He (or she) only got that because of being a minority." Or a woman or being disabled. They believe that it is demeaning for people of ability.

The distinguished African American writer Shelby Steele properly suggests that we are troubled by "race fatigue" and "racial anxiety." He opposes affirmative action and wrongly—in my opinion—calls the opportunities that result "entitlements."

No one is entitled to a job or an opportunity because of race or gender or ethnic background.

I accept the idea that diversity in our society needs encouragement and is good for us.

If, for example, someone employs 500 people—and they all happen to be white males—it still may not be possible to prove discrimination. One answer for that situation is to go through the lengthy legal process of proving discrimination.

A better answer is affirmative action, where that employer understands that his business should not compromise quality, but opportunity should be given to those who don't fall into the usual personnel pattern. Employing people on the basis of ability is just good business, and affirmative action encourages good business.

My office is an example. If I were to hire everyone from Chicago or from Southern Illinois, the people of Illinois would regard that as strange. I look for diversity in geography, and it does not compromise quality. I don't lower my standards when I choose to hire someone from central Illinois.

In the same way, I have consciously made sure that in my employ there are African Americans, Latinos, Asian Americans and people with disabilities. Anyone who knows my office operation knows that we have not compromised quality to do this.

Has this harmed the people of Illinois? To the contrary, it has helped them and it has helped me.

To move away from affirmative action, back to a situation where discrimination has to be proven to bring about change, invites clogging the courts with endless litigation, and denying opportunity to many.

A federal judge in Texas ruled that the University of Texas law school can set a general goal (not a rigid quota) of admitting 10 percent Mexican Americans and 5 percent African Americans, but if the school lowers its standards to reach those goals, that is unconstitutional.

That strikes many legal scholars as sound.

Interestingly, if that same school gives preference for admission to children of alumni—who are overwhelmingly white—no one objects to that. But if steps are taken to diversify the student body, some of the same alumni object.

Complicating all of this is the fact that many Americans are out of work. The opportunity for people of limited skills to have a job is declining, and will continue to decline.

The person in that situation rarely says, "I'm not working because I don't have the skills that are needed." It is often easier to say, "I don't have a job because a black (or a woman or a white or someone else) got the job I should have." And so tensions rise.

The answer is not to get rid of affirmative action, but to work on jobs programs for those of limited skills, expand education opportunities for all and increase efforts to give training (including reading and writing) to those who are unemployed.

We should diversify opportunity, and at the same time see that everyone has the basic tools to function effectively.

IMMIGRATION

"AMERICA THE MELTING POT," P.S./WASHINGTON, JANUARY 11–17, 1987

"We're getting too many Asians in our country," someone said to me after a recent town meeting. Not too many years ago I heard the same thing about Cubans. Whatever the group, throughout our history there have always been complaints about "others" coming in.

Benjamin Franklin, usually wise but sometimes—like all of us—badly mistaken, in 1751 complained about German immigration which "will shortly be so numerous as to Germanize us." He complained that these new immigrants "swarm into our settlements, and, by herding together, establish their language and manners to the exclusion of ours."

More than a century ago Boston Mayor Theodore Lyman called the Irish "a race that will never be infused into our own, but on the contrary will always remain distinct and hostile."

No mayor of Boston would say that today!

In early Illinois history there were many complaints about the German and Irish immigrants. Today no one needs to be told what the German and Irish immigrants have contributed to our country. And Asian-Americans have done, and will do, the same, as is the case with Cuban-Americans.

This does not mean that we can simply open our doors. The number of immigrants has to be limited. If we were to open our doors with no limits, we would be flooded with people, unable to meet their needs, and we would do great harm to our economy.

The biggest immigration problem has been illegal immigration. Until passage of the new immigration law, we have the impossible situation of making it illegal for workers (primarily from Mexico) to come into this country to work, but it was perfectly legal for employers to hire them.

By this contradiction in our laws we created a magnet, and that has caused problems and has caused many people in this country illegally to be almost defenseless against an employer who wanted to exploit and abuse them. If the employees complained, they would be deported.

Each new wave of immigrants has turned out eventually to be a great asset to the nation.

That will continue to be the case. Yes, often the parents will have a real struggle to get by. But usually their children and grandchildren mesh into the American scene well and have much less of a struggle.

Arkansas has on its license plates: "Land of Opportunity."

That continues to be what most people around the world think when they consider the United States. And it is true. Your neighbor who can barely speak English may have sons and daughters who will be university presidents and senators and civic leaders. That is the history of our nation.

It's a proud history.

"Immigration Law Isn't a Cure-All," P.S./Washington, April 5–11, 1987

As the federal government gets ready to implement a new immigration law, there are other things we can do to ease our immigration problems.

In a recent speech I suggested seven steps to help:

1. *We must work with Mexico to improve the economy of our neighbor to the South.*

Some observers have noted with considerable accuracy that the United States is bounded by two countries, one we do not regard as a foreign country, and one we ignore.

Ignoring Mexico's problems is folly. It invites political extremism next to our borders. It avoids the reality that a less prosperous Mexico makes more likely a less prosperous United States. And it ignores the population facts that would cause great stress between our two countries. The right answer is to work cooperatively with Mexico now to encourage so much that is good in that country.

2. *In Central America, the United States should listen to our southern neighbors who are virtually unanimous in publicly saying our policies in that area are short-sighted, hurting the cause of democracy, and an encouragement to extreme elements.*

Our friends are right, and our policy is wrong. And that flawed policy has caused more than half a million Central Americans to enter our country as undocumented workers. That number could grow dramatically.

When foreign policy is built upon passion rather than reason, it is usually wrong. The people of Nicaragua may not be in love with the Sandinistas, but the evidence is strong the Contras are less popular.

Those who would attempt to topple the Sandinistas through supply of weapons to the Contras usually have a view of the developing world about 20 years old. They see a wave of new leaders in developing nations moving toward Marxism. That was true two or three decades ago, but most of these leaders have become disillusioned with that dream and are much more pragmatic today. If we show with our concern and our example that a free system can provide answers, they will move toward freedom. We should encourage free institutions, economic development and peace in Central America. To the extent that we ignore any one of the three, we aggravate U.S. immigration problems.

3. Civil libertarians, immigration and law enforcement officials and concerned citizens should discuss what can be done to solve the problem of an identification card.

Almost all nations have one, and every study on the enforcement of immigration collides with this problem. Many Americans believe the idea of having an identification card smacks of a police state. Are there ways to solve the problem perhaps through the issuance of a voluntary identification card for those who want it? I don't have the answer. All I know is that every study on the immigration problem runs into this dilemma.

4. We should step up efforts to find an inexpensive way to convert salt water to fresh water.

The question is not whether that inexpensive method will be found, but when. If 1 percent of the present defense budget was devoted to research, the contribution to the security of this nation and to the enrichment of humanity would be beyond measure. It would be a great help to the economy of Mexico, relieving the pressure to emigrate dramatically. A breakthrough is not imminent, but what is now a non-priority should become one.

5. A sensible jobs program that, in a fairly sweeping way, overhauls our present welfare and unemployment compensation system is needed for both those born in the United States and for our new citizens.

We are not going to let people starve within our borders, so we face the choice of paying people to be productive or non-productive. That should not be a difficult choice. Legislation I have introduced to guarantee a job to all who want to work would move us in the right direction, assisting not only the less fortunate, but making the nation more productive.

6. Efforts to assist immigrants to acquire English language proficiency need to be strengthened.

The zealots who banned teaching German in schools during World War I were as wrong as the anti–foreign language Know-Nothings of the 1850s or those who passed legislation prohibiting Chinese translations in our courts. But immigrants who cannot speak or read or write English are at a greater handicap than they would have been a century ago. Assimilation is retarded. If the same effort that is now put into fear-filled campaigns against the non-English speaking were directed toward more English classes and further educational and skill development, everyone would benefit. And the answer is not simplistic solutions like dropping bilingual education. Bilingual education is needed for many students as a bridge until competence and confidence is developed in English skills. Our failure to do more is harmful to immigrants and harmful to the development of a more productive nation, guided by informed citizens.

7. *Finally we must recognize the different cultural backgrounds others bring to our shore provide an opportunity for cultural enrichment.*

Immigration presents both problems and opportunities. But the simple gesture of friendship, both to our new neighbors and to the nations from which they came, will bring rewards beyond calculation.

"ON ANTI-IMMIGRATION SENTIMENT," NPR COMMENTARY, SEPTEMBER 17, 1997

Periodically, the United States goes through a cycle of anti-immigrant sentiment. More than a century ago, we had a political party that elected several statewide officials in a few states that become known as the Know-Nothing party. Part of their platform was to stop all immigration into the United States.

Illegal immigration should be discouraged through our laws, and the best way to do that is to put stiff penalties on employers who knowingly hire them. The magnet for illegal immigration is jobs. Former Senator Alan Simpson, a Republican from Wyoming, tried to put some teeth in the law on this, but he achieved only partial success. Many members of Congress who made great political speeches about "too many foreigners" coming into this nation didn't have the backbone to vote against a few constituents who followed unhealthy employment practices.

What percentage of our population was born outside our country? 9.6 percent. How does this compare to 50 years ago? About the same. Sixty years ago, it was 11.6 percent. Seventy years ago, it was 13.2 percent. Eighty years ago, it was 14.7 percent.

A smaller percentage of those who were born outside of the nation are on welfare than native-born Americans. They contribute to this nation as physicians and scientists, engineers and inventors and teachers, and in a host of other ways. We have been enriched immensely by these new residents. And the daughter or son of the immigrant who may be sweeping your floors may well serve in the United States Senate in the future. A few years ago, 11 of the 12 valedictorians in Boston's high schools were Asian-Americans. Are we better off as a nation because they are here? You bet we are.

My favorite story is of a woman I met on the northwest side of Chicago who told me, "Ve've got to do someting about all dose foreigners from coming into dis country." We let her in and now she wants to stop others from coming in.

There are things we should do. Be tough on those who come in illegally. Have English classes available for those who cannot speak English.

But the story of our country is a nation enriched and aided by immigration. It has always been somewhat controversial, but it has almost always helped us.

HUNGER

"A Hungry World," *The Edge Magazine*, May 1968 (based on an address to the Dallas/Seattle Luther League Convention, 1967)

"A man was once on his way from birth to death on the road of life. Like most of our fellow human beings who live outside of a few wealthy nations, he was desperately poor and hungry. He was stripped of decent clothing and left half dead. It so happened that a Lutheran minister was going down that road and when he saw him he piously said that next Thanksgiving they would have a collection for him. But doing anything more significant would involve getting into politics. And he didn't want to dirty his hands in that way. So he walked by on the other side. So likewise a Luther Leaguer when he came to the place and saw the desperate man, said how thankful he was that he had plenty. 'I would stop and help him, but I'm on my way to a Luther League convention in Seattle. And then comes school, so much of life is ahead of me that I really can't worry about him. Besides that, he ought to help himself!' so the Luther Leaguer walked by on the other side. But a Chinese communist when he saw him . . ." and you know the rest of the story. I don't like that version and neither do you.

My small town of Troy is perhaps typical of the areas that most of you come from. My town of Troy has 1800 people; we're all white, all Gentile and tragically proud of both. We live close to our public schools and whenever a speaker doesn't show up for an assembly, someone gets on the phone and calls my wife or myself. A couple of years ago I spoke to the seventh graders about what a State Senator does and afterwards we had a question and answer period and towards the end of the question and answer period, a little fellow in the back of the room raised his hand and said, "Do you think Negroes are ever going to move to Troy?" And I said, "I hope so." But I could see on the faces of those seventh graders, as I gave that answer, that they were learning reading, writing and arithmetic, but they were not learning something infinitely more important: to have respect for all people. If I had a choice of what my two children are to learn, either reading, writing and arithmetic, or respect for all people, either as a Christian or as an American, it would have to be the latter.

I just returned from a trip through the Middle East and part of Europe. In the Middle East I saw again what always haunts you. You see all the young people and older people, one eye blind or both eyes blind. When you were born they spent a couple of pennies for silver nitrate to protect your eyes. But over there they have a great deal of eye disease and they don't have a couple of pennies to protect their eyes. In the United States, 25 children out of 1,000 born die before they're a year old. In some countries of the world 200 die, the first year, out of every 1,000 born. There are 200 million more illiterate people in the world today than there were six years ago. Sixty percent of the people of the world have an annual income of less than $100.00 per year.

One hundred thirty-two million young people in India today are never going to get any education; 80 percent of the income is spent on food. We spend in the United States an average of 18 percent of our budget on food. One of the most fascinating evenings I've ever spent was in the Prime Minister's residence in New Delhi where the then Prime Minister Nehru was the host. Mrs. Gandhi, who now is the Prime Minister and then was the President of the Congress party, had just come from a small village in India and she was trying to explain to these people that they belonged to a country called India. They understood nothing about democracy and Communism and things we talked about. But there is an explosive new factor in the world that they do understand, and this is a greater explosion than the population explosion or any other explosions we talk about. That is an explosion of awareness in the developing world. Because in that small village they know there are people who eat until they are filled. They know that there are people who teach their children to read and write. And they want some of these things for their children as they should want them. If the free world (and this means, largely Christian) leadership doesn't come up with the answers, they're going to go to the ones who have promises and, of course, that's the Communists with their promises.

The basic appeal of Communism today is to the desperate, hungry people of the world. Only 10 nations in the world today produce more food than they consume. And one startling, awesome fact is that food production in the world is increasing at the rate of 1 percent annually, and the population is increasing at the rate of 2 percent annually.

Newsweek magazine this year had a public service ad and I'm going to read part of it to you. They said, "Is this a good year to be born, 1967?" and their answer, "Perhaps in most parts of the USA, but not in 118 other nations in the world. There the odds are that a child will not receive any medical attention at his birth or in his entire life. If he survives to school age, the odds are two to one that he will never get any schooling. If he does go to school the odds are three to one that he will never complete elementary school. It is almost certain that he will go to work at age 12. He will work to eat, to eat badly and not enough. His life will probably end at age 40. His only hope is that you and other responsible citizens everywhere can help his country adopt a political ideology, a freedom and a sound economy which will produce shoes for his feet, education for his mind, food for his stomach, medicine for his fever. He could grow up with high hopes for the future, or with a rifle in his hand pointed at your son."

President Johnson, in a couple of sentences in the State of the Union message to the nation earlier this year, said something that was almost completely overlooked. He said, "Next to the pursuit of peace, the really greatest challenge to the human family is the race between food supply and population increase. That race tonight is being lost. The time for rhetoric has clearly past. The time for concerted action is clearly here; we must get on with the job." In February the State Department issued a statement saying that we're on the verge of massive starvation in our world. The President's Science Advisory Commission issued a massive three-volume report saying that the most pressing problem facing our world is the imminent starvation which faces the huge majority of people. I saw a small item on it in the *New York Times* and a couple of other newspapers. It was largely unnoticed.

There is a new book on the stands right now called *Famine 1975: America's Decision Who Will Survive*. The books says it's going to be so bad in less than 10 years that our nation is probably going to have to decide which nations will live and which nations will starve to death. By the year 1980, that's a little more than 10 years away, there will be an additional one billion to 1.2 billion people on the face of the earth. Five out of six of these people will be born in food-deficient countries, countries that are already desperate for food. Between now and the year 2000 there will be six billion people.

I would like to praise three small groups: The Mennonites, the Quakers or Friends, and the Seventh Day Adventists. They have done infinitely more than the Lutherans, the Catholics, the Presbyterians, and all the rest of us in helping the poor beyond our borders. Now I don't know that these three small churches have any more of an admonition to "love thy neighbor" than we who are Lutherans. I don't know the exact figure. But I think it's very clear that Luther Leaguers attending the convention in Seattle and in Dallas are spending more money attending these two conventions than all the Lutherans in the USA spent this year in helping starving people beyond our borders. I'm not suggesting that you shouldn't attend a Luther League convention. I am suggesting maybe we have things a little out of balance. My guess is that Lutheran churches in the United States probably spend more money on inside plumbing than we spend on helping the poor beyond our borders. My church in Troy just built a new edifice. Our new church cost us $185,000. If I were to go to the next congressional meeting and spend, let's say, $185,000 on feeding starving people in India, I'm afraid they'd think something was wrong with me. And yet maybe this is the kind of thing we ought to be doing if we really want to call ourselves Christians.

Let me just suggest briefly a couple of things you could do. Remember that the issue is complex. But that shouldn't stop you from doing your duty. You girls who work in the kitchen toss things together (I've seen my wife do it). It looks infinitely complex to me. I can't understand it, and yet somehow she comes out with cookies or whatever it happens to be. She digs in and does it. And our duty is to dig into these issues and do it. What is most basically needed is a change in attitude that we have to be concerned. If you, for example, would write to your congressman this week and say, "Let's adopt a long range policy of helping starving people," my guess is that would be the first letter of this type he'd received in the last six months or a year. And he receives many letters saying, "Let's not throw away money beyond our border." It's somehow ironic that we have a long-range strategy of getting the man to the moon but we have no long-range strategy of getting food to starving people.

If you are going to be a farmer, take a look at our agricultural policy. If you're going to be a scientist, how about doing some experimentation on how you can make the jungle areas of Brazil and Africa produce food. If you're going to be a pastor, let's not just be in isolation from the problems of the world, but lead your parish in these problems. And some of you, I hope, will get interested in politics, and not just follow public opinion but lead public opinion. Whatever you're going to be, use that profession, including that of being a housewife and a mother, to help fellow human beings wherever they are.

GAMBLING AND TAXES

"WILL A STATE LOTTERY ANSWER OUR PROBLEM?," FROM THE STATEHOUSE, BY LIEUTENANT GOVERNOR PAUL SIMON, MARCH 19, 1969

Recently the *Rockford Morning-Star* editorially condemned the idea of a state lottery in Illinois to solve our financial problems. But that newspaper's opinion is hardly universal. Even at a meeting of educational leaders the question was raised, "Isn't a state lottery the answer to our problems of finance?" There are two answers to that question.

1. Under the present state constitution, we cannot have a state lottery.
2. In the two states which have a state lottery, New York and New Hampshire, experience shows that a state lottery is anything but satisfactory from the viewpoint of revenue.

Virtually every state at one point in history had legalized lotteries. They were taken for granted in Illinois and most states. When Lincoln was a member of the Illinois General Assembly lotteries frequently were authorized to raise money for various projects.

Lotteries were not only a part of the state scene but were carried on in the colonies prior to the United States becoming a nation. The first legalized lottery in what is now the United States was in the colony of Virginia to erect a Lutheran church there.

But in Illinois and other states, the lotteries proved to be too tempting a prize for some public officials and others operating the lotteries. The lotteries became so obviously corrupt that when new state constitutions were written, lotteries were prohibited.

There soon will be a state constitutional convention in Illinois which could authorize lotteries. But a lottery for the next two years is unconstitutional. Even if it were possible, the experience in New Hampshire and New York should make any reasonable person pause.

In neither state has there been a problem with corruption so far, but income has been far below expectations. New Hampshire is now considering dropping the lottery and New York each month has a lower and lower income from the lottery. In both states income is only the proverbial "drop in the bucket" compared to needs.

It is a natural temptation to look for some easy answer to our state's financial problems. Unfortunately responsible answers are not easy.

"On Gambling," NPR Commentary, January 21, 2003

Governor Rod Blagojevich bucked national trends to become chief executive of Illinois, and there may be moments when he wonders why he ran for the office. A person of ability, he faces serious problems; the most weighty is: "Where do I get enough money to eliminate the deficit and still move the state ahead?" He should not want to simply be a caretaker as Governor. That is not the heritage he should leave.

One of the temptations is to help solve the financial problems by authorizing an expansion of gambling. It is an easy way out, and a bad way out.

It is true that people spend their money voluntarily in casinos. However, it is also true that with every casino come an increase in gambling addiction, an increase in embezzlements, an increase in family problems, and a suicide rate higher for gamblers than for those addicted to alcohol or drugs.

Gambling is the only addiction actively promoted by the government. If you saw signs urging you to smoke cigarettes or drink more whiskey, sponsored by the government, you would rightfully be offended. But when our government accommodates—and promotes—legalized gambling it is doing virtually the same thing.

Government should not be encouraging activities that prey on our weaknesses.

In addition, the industry is tainted by a history of corruption. Former Governor Edwin Edwards of Louisiana is in prison for taking gambling bribes. One former governor of Illinois served time in prison for gambling-connected abuses. Legislators in several states have been indicted or convicted of gambling industry related bribes.

Occasionally someone unable to control the gambling habit makes the news with illegal conduct. Much more frequently the addict steals from his or her family and we never hear about it. I spoke out against the national spread of this disease several years ago and after that people I knew contacted me saying, "Our friends don't know about this, but you can't believe the agony we have gone through because one member of our family has a gambling addiction."

My mother belonged to a Lutheran church which has a parochial school. One of the substitute teachers—unknown to her family—had become an addict and money the family thought was going to pay bills went to a casino. One day the family came home and found a note saying they could find her, parked in a car, at the nearby shopping mall. She had committed suicide.

Governor Blagojevich cannot make a popular decision on revenue. But make it a sound decision, Governor, not one that takes advantage of our weaknesses.

GUNS AND THE NRA

"THE NRA'S IRRESPONSIBLE 'VICTORY,'"
P.S./WASHINGTON, SEPTEMBER 25–OCTOBER 1, 1988

The runaway winner for the most irresponsible letter on a legislative matter so far this year—and the competition is fierce—is the National Rifle Association. And the NRA won, even though it tarnished its reputation with members of Congress for the campaign it conducted.

Sarah Brady, wife of presidential Press Secretary Jim Brady, has been promoting legislation to require a seven-day waiting period for someone buying a handgun so that police could check out whether that individual is a convicted felon or has a history of mental problems. That's all the bill does. Police organizations around the nation strongly favor it.

The man who runs my Springfield office, Joe Bob Pierce, has a gun collection. He's a member of the Electrical Workers union, a former Baptist minister and a Mason. Joe is a good all-around person who happens to enjoy collecting guns. I asked Joe if there was anything wrong with this legislation and he assured me there was no reason for any hunter or gun collector or anyone who is going to use a gun responsibly to oppose it.

But look at the arguments put out by the National Rifle Association:

NRA: The bill would cost "billions of your tax dollars."

The Congressional Budget Office says the bill would cost the federal government nothing.

NRA: It would "impose back-door registration on American gun owners."

Not true. The bill requires records be destroyed within 30 days.

NRA: It would be the "first step in banning all guns in America."

I don't know a single senator or House member who favors that.

The final sentence of the inflammatory letter: "Don't let the U.S. Congress impose total gun control on America."

After reading this misleading letter, a great many gun owners around the nation understandably wrote to stop the Brady bill.

Unfortunately, the NRA frightened enough members of Congress so that the suggestion for a one-week delay in purchasing handguns was defeated in the House, 228 to 182.

It was a victory for irresponsibility.

This measure would not have stopped all crime. But it would have helped a little. Over and over we have instances—like the shooting of Jim Brady and Ronald Reagan—where a handgun is purchased to kill or maim but a waiting period would give law enforcement authorities time to check out the buyer. In John Hinckley's case, law enforcement officials believe the background check would have revealed a previous criminal offense and stopped the gun sale.

My friends at the NRA, who once supported a waiting period, would be wise to remember this fact about the law in any field. Change will come. If reasonable change is resisted, then unreasonable changes may occur.

The police organizations are right.

Sarah Brady is right.

The National Rifle Association is wrong.

Unfortunately, in too many instances, dead wrong.

"An Incomprehensible, Irresponsible, Baffling Boondoggle for the NRA," P.S./Washington, July 14–20, 1996

Buried in the annual Defense Department authorization bill is an outrageous gift of $77 million that will benefit something called the Corporation for the Promotion of Rifle Practice and Firearms Safety.

This corporation is the new "private" incarnation of the old National Rifle Association–backed Civilian Marksmanship Program. This program was intended to make sure people could shoot straight in case they entered the military. In recent years, however, it has simply funneled cash, weapons and ammunition to private gun clubs, thanks to the power of the NRA. Until a federal judge ruled it unconstitutional in 1979, gun clubs which participated in this program were required to be NRA members.

Under public pressure to eliminate this useless and wasteful program, Congress "privatized" the program last year.

In fact, the corporation is private in name only. When the corporation becomes fully operational in October of this year it will be *given* by the Army:

- 176,218 rifles the Army views as outmoded, but valued at $53,271,002.
- Computers, vehicles, office equipment and other related items valued by the Army at $8,800,000.
- 146 million rounds of ammunition valued by the Army at $9,682,656.
- $5,332,000 in cash.

That totals $77,085,658.

Our friends in the National Rifle Association strongly back this measure and it appears to be a boondoggle for them.

What the Army should do with outmoded weapons is to destroy them. Our government has a theoretical policy that it does not sell federally owned weapons to the public. The Civilian Marksmanship Program violates this policy, and the new corporation would continue to violate it.

Why we should be subsidizing rifle practice—which is the theory behind this—baffles me. Hardly any of those who will use the weapons will enter into the armed forces. The Defense Department did not request this. I had never fired a rifle or handgun before entering the Army, and with minimal training I became a fair-to-good marksman.

Sen. Frank Lautenberg of New Jersey and I tried to eliminate this incomprehensible expenditure from the bill; we got only 29 votes for our amendment. The NRA still has power.

We should be reducing the numbers of weapons in our society, not increasing them. A government policy of destroying weapons and not selling outmoded guns to the public is sound.

While rifles are not the primary weapons for crime—pistols are—some of those 176,000 weapons will get into the hands of people who should not have them. If 1 percent reaches someone who is irresponsible, that is 1,760 weapons.

Let me in advance extend my sympathy to the families of people who will be killed by these weapons; they will be needless victims of this folly.

"Gun Dealer Requirements," NPR Commentary, December 17, 1997

The statistics are everywhere: Violent crimes in this country are still high compared to other nations, but they are declining in number. There is no single cause for this and no one knows with certainty what is helping. But probably helping are more police walking in neighborhoods, and more police personnel; stopping law violations when they first occur no matter how small, so that offenders do not think they can get away with crime; outlawing of certain weapons that are known as "semi-automatic" weapons that no hunter would use—one of which advertised in gun magazines that it was fingerprint proof, and it is hard to understand why any responsible citizens would want a fingerprint proof weapon.

But one almost unknown factor is the tightening of requirements to become a gun dealer. Until three years ago we had more federally licensed gun dealers than we had service stations. Only you didn't see most of them, because they did not have stores but sold guns from their kitchen or basement or the trunk of their car. It cost only $10 a year for a federal license to sell guns, less than the cost of an Illinois automobile license. And you did not have to provide fingerprints or a photograph. One media outlet sent in the name of a dog and got a federal license to sell guns for the dog.

Three years ago the law changed. Fingerprints and photographs were required. The fee of a three-year license went up to $200. We required that gun dealers abide by state laws and local ordinances. What has happened? The number of federally licensed gun dealers has dropped by more than half, from 286,000 in 1993 to 124,000 today.

Not only has that reduced the number of dealers, it has made possible checks of criminal records of dealer applicants, and permits the Bureau of Alcohol, Tobacco and Firearms to check on those who have licenses. Twenty-six hundred dealers have voluntarily given up their license when questioned, and more than 300 have had their license revoked.

Responsible citizens can still buy a gun with ease. But making it harder for the questionable operators has helped everyone interested in a stable society.

"Gun Violence," NPR Commentary, February 24, 1998

If you live in Sydney, Australia, you are as likely to become a victim of burglary as if you live in Los Angeles, but you are 20 times more likely to be murdered in Los Angeles than in Sydney.

Those statistics are from a recent joint U.S.-Australian study released recently by the Earl Warren Legal Institute of the University of California.

London in 1992 had 20,000 more burglaries and robberies than in New York, but seven people were killed in London in connection with those crimes, but in New York City 378 people were killed by the smaller number of the same crimes.

You are more likely to become the victim of an assault in Canada and New Zealand, per 100,000 people, than in the United States, but you are more than four times as likely to be murdered in the United States than in those nations.

Why these huge disparities? According to the University of California study the principal reason is guns. We're much more tolerant of who can get a gun, and of the types of weapons available than most countries.

Almost one-third of the murders by gun in the United States start with an argument. If one of the participants in a heated argument did not have a gun, probably someone would emerge with a black eye or other bruises, but not death.

Our violent crime rate has declined slightly the last three years as we have instituted some changes in police procedures and removed some people from the chance to legally own guns, as well as removed some of the most obnoxious weapons from legal sales. The TEC-9, for example, that has been involved in many murders advertised in gun magazines that it was "resistant to fingerprints." Why does any responsible citizen want a gun that is fingerprint proof?

Responsible citizens and hunters should continue to be able to have guns. But a look at the comparative statistics of the United States and other nations suggest that greater tightening of our laws is in order.

"ON THE NRA," NPR COMMENTARY, FEBRUARY 7, 2000

I disagree with the National Rifle Association on just about everything. I favor giving responsible citizens the opportunity to have weapons, but we have far too many guns in our society, particularly handguns. What has cut the crime rate in recent years is not completely clear, but part of it is the restrictions on having guns that we now place on convicted felons and people who have a history of mental problems—and clamping down on those who have the right to get a federal license to sell guns. Since the fingerprint requirement for dealers went into effect, their number has been reduced by more than one-third. All of these changes the National Rifle Association opposed—including outlawing certain weapons, such as the TEC-9, which is advertised in gun magazines that it was resistant to fingerprints. Why would a responsible citizen want a gun that is fingerprint proof?

But one point the National Rifle Association makes is valid: We should enforce the laws that we now have on the books. People who are knowledgeable tell me that too often prosecutors are not pursuing those who clearly violate the law on possession and sale of weapons, but overburdened prosecutors sometimes believe that gun offenses are too minor to pursue. In one case in the central part of the state I understand that a convicted felon and gang member working through a front man illegally sold a gun that later killed a police officer, and yet the convicted felon has not been prosecuted up to this point.

It is generally believed that what deters crime is not the severity of the punishment but its sureness and swiftness. When people who have a background of criminal activity see that their illegal actions of whatever nature are not prosecuted, that invites more and more criminal action.

I join President Clinton in favoring the registration of handguns. If we require the registration of automobiles because of their potential danger, why not handguns? The National Rifle Association opposes the proposal. In my opinion, they are wrong on this, but they are right when they say we should enforce the laws that we now have on the books.

"THE OIL DEPLETION ALLOWANCE,"
P.S./WASHINGTON, MARCH 16–22, 1975

One of the most controversial measures which has been before the Congress this session is the proposal to eliminate the oil depletion allowance. It is also one which affects my district directly because of the sizeable amount of oil production in our area.

Basically the oil depletion allowance has given a tax break of $3 billion each year to the oil companies to encourage production. But 84 percent of that amount has gone to 10 companies, while approximately 20,000 producers—the small "wildcatters"—get 16 percent.

It's important to note that those small operators find more than 80 percent of the new oil in this nation. They have been performing the important function we need and they ought to be encouraged.

Congressman Charles Wilson of Texas headed a movement to protect the small wildcatter who does not operate filling stations or have refineries, and I was happy to join him in that fight. Interestingly, the large oil companies opposed the Wilson amendment.

Their stand was that the Wilson amendment put them at a competitive disadvantage to the small companies. My feeling is that the major companies need a little of that competition.

The smaller companies have a harder time securing capital, buying equipment in times of shortages—and when an oil field is developed, the majors move into the territory around the discovery and take advantage of the economic daring of the wildcatter.

The Wilson amendment lost 197–216. It would have exempted up to 3,000 barrels of production a day. I spoke in behalf of his amendment.

When the proposal to tie the small producers and the majors together came before us, I voted to eliminate the oil depletion allowance which has encouraged the small operator—but has also been a bonanza to the big oil companies. I would have felt much better voting for the amendment had the Wilson provision been included. The measure is now in the Senate, where I am hopeful something similar to the Wilson amendment will be adopted.

The small businessman—whether in the field of oil or any other—needs encouragement. The large operator generally does not need special tax breaks.

"The Energy Crisis Is Real," P.S./Washington, June 19–25, 1977

After Watergate and Vietnam, and other scandals which have hit the nation, people understandably mistrust what they hear from government leaders, and one of those areas of disbelief is the energy situation. What makes that disbelief and concern deepen on energy is the general feeling that the public has been "ripped off" (a phrase our children have given us) by the big oil companies. There has been abuse by the government; there has been abuse by the big oil companies.

But don't fool yourself: the energy crisis is real. Testifying before a subcommittee on which I serve, Federal Energy Administration (FEA) Administrator John F. O'Leary among other things told us two facts, one of which I thought should have been a major news item in the next day's newspapers:

First, last year there was a demand for 13 trillion cubic feet of natural gas, and we discovered sources for two trillion cubic feet, despite a sizeable increase in drilling.

Second, by 1985, half the houses in the nation now being heated by natural gas will have to be heated in some other way.

Those two statistics tell a part of the problem we face. And to pretend the problem does not exist, or to avoid taking some decisive action on it, is short-sighted.

How will this affect you (in addition to the immediate natural gas problem)? Here are some things which I'm guessing will be part of your future:

1. From next year on, the new car you buy is more likely to be a smaller car.

2. The price of gasoline, oil, natural gas and all other forms of heat is going to go up.

3. If you rent, your landlord eventually will have to put insulation in your home if it does not have insulation now. That will save the nation energy, and save you money.

4. If you own your home or other real estate, you will have a harder and harder time selling any housing property if it is not insulated. The government eventually will force this to happen, but for most people the market for houses will force insulation before the government does.

5. Within five years inexpensive bike trails will be built along many of our streets and highways; within ten years in some of the larger cities you will have to pay a toll to drive on the streets during the hours of heavy traffic.

6. You will see some major changes in the next 15 years in the way we heat our homes, the way we provide light, and the way we transport ourselves.

Things you and I can't imagine right now will make these areas change in the future as much as the arrival of television has changed our entertainment. These are guesses, some of which may look a little foolish 10 years from now.

But two things are certain: The energy crisis is real. And that will change our lives.

"An Energy Lesson from Cyprus,"
P.S./Washington, September 4–10, 1977

Life is full of ironies and some of those are visible on the rooftops of newly built homes for refugees in Cyprus.

I was in Cyprus recently, at President Carter's request, as part of a small delegation attending the funeral of their President, Archbishop Makarios.

Senator Charles Mathias of Maryland, Congressman John Buchanan of Alabama and I spent an afternoon visiting places where the United States has been spending some of its Agency for International Development (AID) money. What interested us most were the solar heating units on the homes of refugees.

The units are primarily used for hot water heating, which is one of the major users of energy in Cyprus, the United States or any other country.

An electric hot water heater in an American home, on the average, will use slightly more electricity during the course of a year than will an air conditioner. A water heater uses 15 percent of all the energy consumed in the home.

Those solar units on the Cyprus refugee homes cost approximately $240 each. The United States has helped in the resettlement and housing of the refugees (as we should) and on the average we assume about 54 percent of the cost of refugee housing—including the solar heating units. The ironies are these:

- While in the United States we complain loud and long about an energy shortage and the need to find alternative forms of energy, a poorer nation is doing much more about it, in large part through U.S. help.
- The United States pays 54 percent of the cost of those solar units, but try getting FHA approval for a loan for a house that included solar heating in the United States!
- Or getting a solar heating unit that costs anywhere close to $240 in the United States. Part of the reason for this is of course cheaper labor in Cyprus, but most is the fact that the companies there have seen the need, the demand has been created, and they have produced in quantity inexpensive, effective solar heating units.

Those solar units in Cyprus—or anywhere—are built so that electricity or some other form of energy can supplement the sun's heating ability. Whatever the sun does not do, electricity or oil or gas does.

At least half the homes in Cyprus appear to have solar heating while in the United States probably fewer than 1 percent have solar heating. Both these statistics are guesses on my part, but conservative guesses.

It is true that Cyprus has more sun that most parts of the United States, but it is equally true that solar energy can be put to good use in the coldest portions of our nation. We can learn from others. We have talked much about the energy crunch. Cyprus has acted.

"REDUCE RELIANCE ON FOREIGN OIL," P.S./WASHINGTON, DECEMBER 9–15, 1979

Is there a possibility that oil prices could be brought down a little?

There is, and it is both in our economic interest and in our political interest that we move in that direction. To the extent that Iran has awakened us to our excessive dependence on foreign oil, the tragedies of that situation could be helpful in forcing us to move to a more sensible policy. How can it be done?

It will take two steps: (1) We must reduce the imports of foreign oil. (2) We must form a government entity to get bids from foreign producers. My friends at the *Southern Illinoisan* of Carbondale call the latter idea "pie in the sky." A long-time co-worker in the field of journalism, Karl Monroe of the *Collinsville Herald*, sees it as a boondoggle that would not work.

I respectfully disagree.

What we do now—and no one can deny this—is hand a blank check to OPEC. And the higher that price of oil goes, the more money the major oil companies make. The refineries in the U.S., under this proposal, would simply notify the government corporation of the amount of their oil needs. The government corporation would then buy from abroad, through secret bids, rather than the oil companies buying directly from abroad, sometimes from themselves. Former Secretary of Energy James Schlesinger says we would save money by doing it this way.

Other nations have successfully brought their prices down somewhat by this mechanism. Is there any reason the United States cannot do the same?

This would be particularly helpful if we combined it with a reduction in imports, a powerful weapon the President has which has been virtually unused. If we reduced imports by 5 percent, we would have to reduce domestic consumption 2½ percent. If we reduced imports 10 percent, we would have to reduce domestic consumption 5 percent. And so on.

As an excellent article in *U.S. News and World Report* of November 26th points out: "The lower the demand, the less able OPEC is to enforce high prices . . . Most of the 13 OPEC members have embarked on huge spending programs and these depend upon high oil sales."

And right now our stocks of crude oil are at an all-time high of 355 million barrels. That gives us a slight cushion. Can we actually reduce oil consumption? Yes, if we are willing to.

Long-range there are things like coal gasification and major solar energy projects which can help us. But there are many things which can happen fairly soon. For example:

- Electric units are still using 1.5 million barrels of oil daily. That is equivalent to 20 percent of our imports. We can literally overnight reduce that figure substantially through the use of the grid system which this nation has, and within months save more through conversion to coal.
- Solar hot water heating units could be encouraged. Hot water units consume 15 percent of home energy. Many countries have moved far ahead of the U.S. in the numbers of solar hot water units.
- 38 percent of energy used goes for heating and air conditioning buildings. We can do much more to encourage insulation. Portland, Oregon, has passed an ordinance which says that after 5 years no home can be sold which is not insulated. Other cities and states could be urged to do the same, provided they also set up a method for loans for insulation for people who cannot afford to pay for it. We need a national effort for insulation.
- A host of other possibilities could be listed, and if all else fails and we face a real need for further reductions, gasoline rationing or a heavy gasoline tax with reductions in other taxes (like social security) at the same time would reduce oil consumption.

Our problems are not insoluble. We need some imagination. We need some courage.

"Preserving Mother Nature's Gifts,"
P.S./Washington, August 31–September 6, 1986

An advantage of being in the Senate with its six-year term, over being in the House with its two-year term, is that for the first time in well over a decade my wife and I took a two-week vacation in an election year. I was able to get in some work during the two weeks and some stops that I had been planning for some time, but primarily we relaxed.

I came away again with the overwhelming feeling of how grateful we should be for living in a land with such a variety of geographical splendor. We should make sure we preserve that splendor for our children and generations to come.

One of the stops we made was at the Northern Cascades National Park in the state of Washington. A two-hour trip on a boat up Lake Chelan, through magnificent mountains to Holden Village, is awe-inspiring—an overused phrase but an accurate one in this case.

But it is not just that one park. The mountains, the ocean, the streams, the trees, the wildlife, wherever they are—all tremendous gifts God has given us, and we have the obligation to preserve them, not the right to demolish them.

While the scenery in Illinois is not as dramatic as in a few spots in this nation, there are magnificent places most Illinois citizens have never seen: Galena and Jo Daviess County in northwestern Illinois; the drive along the Mississippi in several spots but particularly in the Alton-Grafton area and from Hamilton to Nauvoo; the Garden of the Gods in deep Southern Illinois. And I am missing 100 scenic spots for each one I mention.

But we cannot take for granted that the great places of natural beauty will be preserved. Every time we heedlessly toss out a beer can or a soft drink can, every time we toss out a cigarette which has not been completely put out—all the thoughtless acts we perform that put in jeopardy our heritage are a disservice to ourselves, and to the future. It is also true of the less obvious.

We are gradually eroding the topsoil of the nation's farms, a threat to the future economy of the nation and to the world's ability to live. The biggest immediate threat to agriculture is the plight of the farmer struggling to survive economically. The biggest long-term threat is the shortage of topsoil. Beautiful national parks, clean air, clean streams, substantial and deep topsoil are not an inevitable part of our future. At the Northern Cascades National Park I heard someone say—commenting about the deer and other wildlife of the park—"We are their guests. We should act like good guests should." That is an attitude more of us have to acquire.

If we give our children cleaner air, cleaner streams, richer topsoil and better national parks, we will have shown that we appreciate our heritage. Unfortunately, so far the record is a mixed one. In some areas we have made progress. In too many areas much remains to be done.

"Preparing for the Next Energy Crisis," P.S./Washington, January 18–24, 1987

There is a small cloud on the horizon to which we are paying little attention.

The OPEC nations appear to be getting together a little on oil production. How much cooperation there will be among them we don't know. But there is at least the possibility that they will get together once again and we will soon find ourselves in the same mess we had in the mid-1970s. We also seem to quickly forget conservation measures adopted during the shortage years as soon as oil prices fall and supplies increase. Recent reports show U.S. oil imports last year rose to their highest level since 1980. U.S. imports were up 22 percent in 1986, the American Petroleum Institute reported.

What are we doing to prepare for another energy crisis?
Nothing.
You mean there are no plans to deal with such an emergency?
None.

But, some will argue, we have a strategic petroleum reserve we have been building up, a huge storage of oil that we could use in an emergency.

That would make sense, and help some, but the administration wants to get rid of the strategic oil reserves that we have. The world's most important economic power, the United States, has no long-term coordinated energy policy. If tomorrow there would be a sudden cutoff in oil from Saudi Arabia, our biggest supplier, we are not prepared to do more than stumble through, groping for answers.

We should be doing more planning and more research. How can we more effectively and more widely use gasoline produced from corn? How can we encourage more conservation? How can we more effectively use the vast coal resources of our nation? What should we be doing to plan for the day when our present nuclear energy facilities start aging again and need to be replaced? A host of questions should be concerning us.

But we are driving along each day assuming that today's abundance of oil and gasoline will continue without interruption. It will not, and we had better prepare ourselves.

Last year, I cosponsored a bill offered by Sen. Lloyd Bentsen of Texas to help address the problem. Under the bill, any year that imported oil accounted for more than one-half of our energy usage, the President would have to come up with a policy to make us less reliant on imported oil. I don't have all the answers as to what should be done, but one thing is certain: It is folly to assume that a tomorrow that is less abundant in oil and gasoline will never come.

"AMTRAK NEEDS MORE FINANCIAL SUPPORT, NOT LESS," *DAILY HERALD*, JANUARY 3, 2001

Government policies are not always based on pressing needs, but sometimes also on what we want in our society. So we have high school football teams and bands because we sense they somehow add to the richness of a school and a community.

Passenger rail service combines genuine needs with a touch of nostalgia and that vague feeling that this is something our nation should have. And a fair, if not overpowering, case can be made for its support on the basis of needs.

Commuter rail passenger service reduces automobile traffic and air pollution, saves time for those using cars by keeping other cars off the highways, and permits customers who ride the rails to their jobs to use their time more effectively, adding in a small way to the nation's productivity.

Our long-distance passenger service, called Amtrak, has some of the same benefits but in most instances is more costly to the government per passenger mile than commuter service. And Amtrak is in greater immediate jeopardy as government subsidies shrink.

Amtrak officials too often assure members of Congress that if they can just have a little more subsidy for a year or two, or for purchasing major equipment, that "soon" Amtrak will be self-supporting. Judging by the experience in other countries, that day will never come.

With the exception of New Zealand and three lines in Japan, all passenger services in the world are subsidized. And it is worth it. The United States should not become the only industrial nation in the world without good rail passenger service. Opponents argue that it is not a "national" passenger service because seven states do not have the service: Alaska, Hawaii, Maine, New Hampshire, Oklahoma, South Dakota, and Wyoming.

Alaska and Hawaii are understandable exceptions. If the other states demonstrate great interest and demand, they will be considered. When I served in the Senate, I supported many measures that did not benefit Illinois directly, but you operate on the assumption that we're "one nation, under God, indivisible," and what benefits another state, indirectly will help Illinois.

The railroads also pay real estate taxes for the land they use. Highways do not. Airports do not. When I see speed trains in Japan, Spain, France, Sweden and other nations, my instincts tell me we are making a mistake by not developing the same, though we may be inching in that direction. Former Congressman George Sangmeister of the Joliet area sponsored legislation for the study of five high-speed train routes in the nation, and I served as the chief sponsor in the Senate. They have now been designated, and we are crawling toward implementation at the same time we are inconsistently weakening Amtrak.

Airline passengers benefit from rail passenger service indirectly because if air fares go too high, there is the potential of a shift to Amtrak.

The key is to find a sensible balance: Not too much subsidy or the Amtrak executives will have no incentive to improve service and operate efficiently, but not so little subsidy that service deteriorates further. When we see Southern Illinois University students board the trains in Carbondale in large numbers, as University of Illinois students do at Champaign also, no one needs to tell us that the students are safer than on the highways. We know it.

Great Britain has partially deregulated its rail service and has a unique way of assuring some efficiency. The railroads are fined for not being on time, heavy fines. Because subsidies have been low, Amtrak has cut back on service and issued bonds to meet basic capital needs. In 1999, Amtrak paid $98 million in interest on those bonds and $58 million on the principal, compounding its problems.

There may be a sliver of light. Chairing Amtrak has been Gov. Tommy Thompson of Wisconsin and his right-hand person on the board is former Massachusetts Gov. Michael Dukakis. Thompson has just been named to the Cabinet by the president-elect. While his new position has no jurisdiction over transportation, he is unlikely to be suddenly silent about Amtrak's needs. And Dukakis will have some influence with Democrats in the House and Senate. The early months of the Bush administration probably will determine Amtrak's fate.

TEACHING FOREIGN LANGUAGE

"A Treaty We May Be Violating: Declining Foreign Language Study," P.S./Washington, March 13–19, 1977

A little-noted provision in the document which the United States and 34 other nations signed almost two years ago at Helsinki commits the United States to encouraging the studies of foreign languages and cultures.

But compared to five years ago, ten years ago, or twenty years ago, fewer —not more—Americans are studying foreign languages. We properly point out when the Soviets or others violate human rights provisions of the Helsinki agreement, but we also have an obligation to live up to provisions of that agreement.

One statistic intrigues me, one which does not make sense for us as a nation economically, culturally, or militarily: There are more teachers of English in the Soviet Union than there are students of Russian in the United States. There are other interesting straws in the wind, which show that we are not paying attention to other nations and cultures as we should:

- For almost two years I taught at Sangamon State University at Springfield, Illinois, in many ways an excellent university. But that university does not teach one single foreign language course. I don't believe that ten years ago or fifty years ago there would have existed an institution of higher learning in the nation which did not teach foreign languages.
- Fewer and fewer colleges and universities demand a foreign language as a requirement. Only about 10 percent of the schools now require it.
- The Foreign Service of the United States no longer requires any foreign language background before you can enter. When you talk to State Department officials, they say they would like to get people with language skills, but because so few Americans have studied foreign language they were forced to drop this requirement.
- Fewer and fewer American students spend any of their college years abroad, about half as many today as in 1973.
- Up-to-date statistics are hard to get, but the figures for the percentage of high school students studying foreign languages for a few years tells a story: 1965, 31 percent; 1968, 30 percent; 1970, 28 percent; and 1974, 24 percent.

What difference does all of this make? My concern in not the few sentences in the Helsinki document, sentences which no one is likely to pay much attention to, but that this may show a lack of concern, a turning inward by our citizens, that cannot be good. If, prior to the tragedy of Vietnam, we had a few hundred more Americans who spoke Vietnamese and were in contact with the people there, it's possible we could have avoided the devastation of that war.

Why do our friends from Germany and Japan and Sweden sometimes sell more products in other nations than we do? Sometimes the answer is fairly simple: they speak the language of the buying country and we do not.

We are living in a world that grows smaller and smaller. We in Southern Illinois or Washington, D.C. are closer today to any point on the globe than our northern colonies were to our southern colonies when our nation was founded. If we are to build a world of peace and stability, people will have to talk to one another. That means that some of those beyond our borders will have to learn English, and some of us will have to learn their languages.

We will be enriched—both culturally and economically—if we do.

"'OFFICIAL' OR NOT, ENGLISH IS NATION'S LANGUAGE," P.S./WASHINGTON, MARCH 26–APRIL 2, 1989

Periodically one issue arises that has superficial appeal: Make English the official language of the United States. (A few go even further and want to make "American" the official language.)

The reality is that English *is* the official language of our country. Anyone who lives in the United States and wants to participate in any meaningful way in our economy or in our political process has to learn English. Exactly what it would mean to declare English the official language I don't know—and neither do its sponsors.

When I appeared in a debate with the person promoting this idea in California, I asked: "Does this mean there could be no court interpreters for someone in a California trial who speaks only Chinese? Does this mean that we would prohibit New Mexico from printing documents in both English and Spanish?" And on and on. No, these things were not meant.

It is unclear precisely what is meant, other than the same vague anti-foreign feeling that has been part of our country since its earliest days. Many believe that today we have the highest percentage of our population speaking English than at anytime in our history.

But that misses a basic point. Years ago, you could come into this country and easily get a job swinging an ax or a sledgehammer, and if you spoke Swedish or Italian or Polish instead of English, that was no great obstacle to getting a job.

Today, we are a vastly different society. To get most jobs you have to fill out an application form, impossible to do if you don't read English. If you are a custodian in a plant or a school, your employers want you to be able to read and understand the instructions for using cleaning compounds and chemicals.

Farming is no longer relatively simple chores. Farming today means operating milking machines and computers, in addition to the more routine duties. In the world of 1989 and beyond, acquiring an adequate education is increasingly important. And almost as essential is being able to speak and read and write English. The way to really deal with the problem for those who do not have this skill is not to advocate making English the official language, but providing classes for those who do not speak English.

And one of the ironies of the campaign to make English the official language is that many of those who back it are the same people who vote against funding classes to teach people how to speak English. In Los Angeles there are about 35,000 on the waiting list to get into classes to acquire English skills and approximately 83,000 in California.

There were 4,749 on waiting lists last year to get into these adult education classes in Illinois. New York City has a waiting list of 10,000. Yes, learning the English language is important in our nation with so many immigrants.

But the way to handle the problem is not pious-sounding proclamations that English is our official language. The way to deal with the problem is to provide funding for classes so that those who do not speak English can learn it.

"BEEF UP THE COUNTRY'S FOREIGN LANGUAGE SKILLS," COMMENTARY, *WASHINGTON POST*, OCTOBER 23, 2001

In the wake of the Sept. 11 terrorist attacks, FBI Director Robert Mueller put out an urgent call for Arabic and Farsi translators, going so far as to post an 800 number for applicants. His announcement once again exposed our nation's appalling deficiencies in foreign language expertise. This is not a new problem.

Almost 20 years ago, with many of my Senate colleagues and under the leadership of Sen. David Boren, now President of the University of

Oklahoma, I supported the creation of the National Security Education Program, which addresses critical national security deficiencies in language and cultural expertise. Nearly three decades ago William Casey, then head of the CIA, told me of the nation's urgent foreign language situation. This past August, the University of Maryland's National Foreign Language Center warned in a major study of language and national security that "the United States . . . faces a critical shortage of linguistically competent professionals across federal agencies and departments responsible for national security."

Clearly, the urgency of the FBI's needs just scratches the surface of our international deficiencies. Americans are proficient in almost none of the languages of Southwest and Central Asia, nor do opportunities to learn these languages exist. Yet today some 80 federal agencies need proficiency in nearly 100 foreign languages to deal with threats from terrorism, narcotrafficking and communicable diseases—and to advance our commercial and economic interests. While the demand is great, the supply remains almost nonexistent. Only 8 percent of American college students study another language—a proportion that has not changed in 25 years.

Now is the time to renew and expand our federal investment in the National Security Education Program (NSEP), as well as in other language programs. NSEP participants work throughout the federal government and provide expertise in the languages and cultures of more than 50 nations. The program is currently working with the FBI to provide the agency with Arabic and Farsi-speaking participants as translators and analysts to help in the short-term crisis. Former senators Gary Hart and Warren Rudman, in their "Road Map for National Security" report, called upon Congress to expand it. Yet NSEP has not received the financial support it needs.

Similarly, several long-established foreign language programs are suffering from benign neglect. Institutions such as the Pentagon's Defense Language Institute and the State Department's Foreign Service Institute need recognition and funds if they are to provide sufficient language instruction for federal employees. Department of Education programs, such as Title VI of the Higher Education Act and the Fulbright-Hays exchange programs, also require renewed federal attention to strengthen our nation's language infrastructure.

In every national crisis from the Cold War through Vietnam, Desert Storm, Bosnia and Kosovo, our nation has lamented its foreign language shortfalls. But then the crisis "goes away" and we return to business as usual. One of the messages of Sept. 11 is that business as usual is no longer an acceptable option.

"Television Violence: Cause for Concern," P.S./Washington, October 3–9, 1976

Does watching violence on television make our children more violent? "Yes" is the overwhelming answer of social scientists who have studied the problem. Common sense has told us all along that viewing violence on television is not good for our children. Now there are a number of scientific studies that tell us our "common sense" is accurate.

One of those studies, directed by Leonard D. Eron of the psychology department of the University of Illinois, looked at the behavior of 875 boys and girls from third grade until a year after high school graduation.

What Dr. Eron found is that boys, not aggressive at age eight, but who watched violent TV programs, are significantly more aggressive at age 19 than those boys, aggressive at age eight, who watched mostly nonviolent TV programs. He concluded: "One of the best predictors of how aggressive a boy will be at age 19 is the violence of television he prefers at age 8."

For girls the results of Dr. Eron's study are different. Since females have usually been victims rather than perpetrators of violence on TV, girls identified with the victim and became more nonaggressive. But new studies show that girls now get aggression scores as high as boys, and it may be due to the increasing aggressiveness of women shown on TV. (Now we have programs such as *Wonder Woman* and *The Bionic Woman* to show how women can "win" with physical strength.)

No one questions that the problem of juvenile crime has increased dramatically in the last decade. Deaths by violence in this age group rose 16 percent from 1963–73. Arrests of juveniles for violent crimes increased by 247 percent from 1960–73.

While they were growing up—from the ages of 5 to 15—these young people probably watched more than 100,000 violent episodes on television. They saw more than 13,000 persons killed. And they spent more time being "taught" about crime on television than they spent being taught in a classroom.

According to another recent study, the so-called "Family Hour" instituted by the major networks this past season has not changed the fact that eight out of ten TV programs contain violent behavior. Our children are still getting high doses of switch-blade knives, kicks in the groin and "Saturday night specials."

It may never be possible to prove beyond a doubt that watching "play-acting" violence contributes to real-life violence. But Jesse Steinfeld, when he was the U.S. Surgeon General, looking at the results of a study he had commissioned on TV violence, said: "There comes a time when the data are sufficient to justify action. That time has come." He said that in 1972.

My colleague, Rep. Tom Railsback of Moline, Illinois, has introduced a resolution expressing the sense of Congress that those responsible for TV programming consider the harmful effects of TV violence on our society. I support him on this.

I have opposed censorship and I fought the civil liberties battles during my years in the Illinois legislature and as lieutenant governor. I will continue to support our fundamental civil liberties.

But I don't believe it is an infringement of those liberties to recognize that excessive violence on television is not healthy for this nation—and that the licensed airwaves of the U.S. need not be available for such violence.

"Real Life Imitates TV Violence," P.S./Washington, June 23, 1985

I walked into a motel room recently after a long day of running around Illinois, turned on the television, and suddenly I saw a man being cut in half by a chain saw, in vivid color.

It was not real, of course, but it looked real. I couldn't help but wonder what watching that does to young minds still being formed, particularly young people who may have emotional problems.

A few days ago, I visited with a friend I've known since he was a college student. Now married, he has two small children. His wife mentioned that after their two children watch a violent television show (and most cartoon programs are loaded with violence) their conduct becomes more aggressive. Violence on television has risen more than 100 percent since 1980. From January to April, prime-time television averaged 13.8 acts of violence per hour.

The average child between the ages of 2 and 11 views television 27.3 hours each week. By the time a person is 16, he or she has watched over 20,000 hours of television—including 200,000 acts of violence, 50,000 of which are murders.

Children's cartoons show an attempted murder every six minutes, on the average.

Not surprisingly, that mammoth display of violence has an influence on the lives of people, and that influence is not good. I have been reading through various studies and the evidence is overwhelming: viewing too much violence can cause violence, particularly in those who have emotional problems. Violence is imitated.

As the National Institute of Mental Health concludes: "Violence on television does lead to aggressive behavior by children and teenagers who watch the programs."

The Surgeon General of the United States came to a similar conclusion.

And studies show that even people who do not act violently after watching TV violence end up with much greater fear of violence than those who watch only a small amount of television. I will be meeting soon with representatives of the three major television networks to see if something can be done voluntarily. The networks could improve things substantially.

I also will be introducing legislation to require a 10-second warning at the beginning of shows or commercials that contain excessive violence: Warning to Parents. Viewing this program may be dangerous to the mental health of your children.

A group called the National Coalition on Television Violence headed by a respected psychiatrist at the University of Illinois School of Medicine, Dr. Thomas Radecki, is working in a solid way on this problem. Their address is P.O. Box 12038, Washington D.C. 20005. They can provide you with information on those who sponsor programs heavy with violence. Sponsors of such programs should hear from the public.

We do not want censorship in a democracy. But somehow we have to deal with this problem in a meaningful way.

"Media Have to Take Some Responsibility for Violence," *Daily Herald*, January 10, 2001

A coalition of seven groups involved in book publishing, including the prestigious Association of American Publishers, has issued a warning about government screening of the media for violence. "Censorship is not the answer to violence in society," their statement says.

So far, so good. I agree with that. But then, perhaps at the behest of the television and movie industry, they start getting on thin ice. They find that the "causes of violence in society lie beyond violent portrayals by the media."

They assert that parents should shape their children's media choices. They state that existing research does not find a connection between media violence and violence in our society. And if the public felt it would do harm, it wouldn't sell.

That is a fine collection of half-truths that weaken their basic argument against censorship. I am a member of the American Civil Liberties Union, and I oppose government censorship. When I served in the U.S. Senate,

I voted against the government mandate of the v-chip because I felt it would be ineffective, but primarily because it involved government in determining content.

But the well-intentioned group that issued the statement should consider these realities:

1. There is no single cause of violence in our society, but television entertainment (and movie and video games) that glamorize violence do harm. The television industry for three years did studies at my request, conducted by five of the nation's top universities, and the studies showed that on entertainment TV, 72 percent of the violent incidents show no adverse effect of the person committing the violence, and only 4 percent have an anti-violence theme. The lesson for children is clear: Violence pays.

Getting the industry to clean up its act is not a substitute for gun-control laws, getting jobs for people in high unemployment areas, aggressive drug treatment and education programs, and other answers that we know will work. But television violence is part of the problem—something many in the industry are reluctant to acknowledge.

A 30-second commercial can sell soap or perfume or a car. Twenty-five minutes of glorifying violence can sell violence. Should we then have no violence on television? On the news there is violence, but exchanges in the Middle East, for example, do not glorify violence. They give us the grimness. Widows cry. And if you were to make a movie about the Civil War, it would contain violence, but it should not make it appealing.

2. Of course, parents should pay more attention to what their children watch. But most homes have more than one television set, and parents would be rare indeed if they monitored what is watched when their children visit the neighbors. And most importantly, the Nielsen rating shows that in the poorer neighborhoods—which are already high in crime—children watch about twice as much TV as the national average. Saying it is the duty of parents to monitor TV is partially correct. But the industry also should act responsibly.

3. Their assertion that research denies a connection between entertainment and actual violence is simply false. Contrary to their contention, the research on this link is overwhelming. They should check with the National Institute of Mental Health or the American Academy of Pediatrics. That there is some relationship to violence in our society is clear. How much is a matter of dispute.

4. The argument that "if people thought it was harmful, it wouldn't sell" is paper thin. Try that logic on cigarettes. Media people properly denounce

officeholders who just follow the polls to make decisions. That is no way to govern. But TV executives who simply follow the dollar, no matter what sleazy direction it leads and no matter how much harm is done, are prostituting themselves as much as poll-following candidates and public officials are.

For a democracy to function effectively, self-restraint is needed. For the media, the answer is self-restraint, not censorship. If the seven organizations that issued the statement against censorship also had called on sensible self-restraints by the industry leaders, they would have done a much greater public service and would have done more to reduce the threat of censorship.

CULTURE, ART, AND THE MOVIES

"ART INFLUENCES BEHAVIOR," P.S./WASHINGTON, MARCH 11–17, 1979

I confess I am not much of a television buff. I watch the news when I can, watch a football game when I can, watch the Sunday interview programs when I can, but that's about it. My teen-age children are constantly embarrassed how stupid their father is about who the big stars are and what the important shows are and what the popular songs are.

But I did see portions of the two *Roots* series and part of the *Holocaust* story. They were important for this nation and for other nations. The reason they were important is best summarized in an interview novelist John Gardner had with Don Edwards and Carol Polsgrove in *Atlantic* recently: "When you see movie after movie which celebrates violence, you are going to have a violent society; there's no question about it . . . Art leads, it does not follow."

The combination of fact and fiction which appeared in those television series provided many Americans the chance to understand in much more human terms some of the problems others have faced, and why brutality and lack of sensitivity toward the problems of others must not be permitted to be a dominant part of our national scene.

In Germany, *Holocaust* showed to record-breaking audiences even though shown on public television. From the comments I have read, it was a moving experience for many Germans who lived through that period, and for many younger Germans who did not realize the enormity of the crimes committed. Art, in the form of this television series, provided a special type of leadership in Germany no political office-holder could possibly provide.

There was violence in these series, it is true, but they did not make heroes out of the violent. Art does lead, but where it is leading is less certain. And I have the uneasy feeling we may be encouraging the wrong forms of art.

When a book about running appears and catches on, the nation increases its running habits and strength.

When a book about a certain type of diet appears and sells well, the nation grows slender and healthier. When Barbara Tuchman writes about fourteenth century history, and writes fascinatingly, there is renewed interest in history. But rock bands draw much larger crowds than symphony concerts, *Playboy* more readers than *Harper's*, *Gunsmoke* more viewers than *Meet the Press*. The freedom to choose our form of art is essential. And the biases I show in those last few sentences should never be permitted to force choices by law.

But perhaps we should learn to expect a little more of ourselves and encourage writers and artists and television producers who are willing to appeal to the best in each of us.

Recently I learned of a principal in a Maryland school who commended a teacher for the exceptionally fine work she had been doing this year with her students. "It is easy to do good work when you have a group of students with a much above the average IQ," she responded. The principal assured her that was not the case. The teacher argued, pointing out that in the sheet of information she had on each student in a small corner was written a number such as 118, 124, 133. She quickly figured out that those numbers stood for IQ. "They're locker numbers," the principal told her. She had an average class but because she saw them as having above average potential, they did above average things.

Somehow in the movies we see, the books and magazines we read, the music we listen to, the records we buy, and the art objects we acquire, we should be expecting a little more excellence of ourselves and of others. The television shows I mentioned are not alone in showing that quality can have appeal; *60 Minutes* is another example. Others could be mentioned.

I know that John Gardner—formerly from Southern Illinois—is right when he says that art leads. But where we are permitting ourselves to be led is less clear.

"Mr. Smith Goes to Washington, Again,"
P.S./Washington, September 24–30, 1989

One of the constant questions which confronts those of us in government at all levels is: How far should government go? When should we act and when should we refrain from acting?

I have just experienced a good example of this dilemma. Someone whose talents I have long respected stopped by my office. Actor Jimmy Stewart, who once starred in the film classic *Mr. Smith Goes to Washington*, came to Washington, asking for something he believes deeply the federal government should control.

It may seem trivial to most people, but to actors and directors from whom Congress is hearing these days, it is deeply important.

The subject: Colorization of old black and white films. Those who produced those black and white films, or acted in them, believe that changing them is like dabbling with a painting produced by a great artist.

As someone who sees movies rarely but usually enjoys them when I do, my extremely limited artistic sense tells me that I agree with Jimmy Stewart and the others on one point: I want to see *Casablanca* and *Gaslight* and the other great black and white films as they were, not through some color process that is often painfully poor.

But having agreed with the advocates up to that point, the next question is whether the federal government should intervene. My inclination is to say that with all of the problems the federal government has, this is not a small, added burden we should take on. There are issues so complex that the public rarely forms any opinion. There are issues that frankly bore the public.

But colorization of films is one we all can relate to. However, I have received only a handful of letters on this, from a state with almost 12 million people. I can only conclude that this is not a matter of concern to any but a select few. I hope there is some way of solving this problem without federal government intervention.

"Cultural Chasms That Divide Us," ### P.S./Washington, January 29–February 4, 1995

Madeleine Doubek, political editor of the *Daily Herald*, the widely circulated newspaper based in the northern and western Chicago suburbs, noted that at a recent news conference I answered a reporter's question by saying: "We have to reach . . . across the borders of race and religion and ethnic background and economic barriers. We have to communicate to people in the suburbs that they have something at stake in the fate of those who are less fortunate in our society." She called me and asked whether that implied racism and classism in the suburbs, and I responded that it did. I do not suggest that those evils are a monopoly of the suburbs. Prejudice rears its ugly head in the central cities, and in the rural areas, as well as in the suburbs.

But there has been a flight from the problems of the cities, a flight to better schools and less crime. Sometimes those two understandable causes have also been confused with flight from African Americans and Latinos.

But whatever the cause, the result is a growing gulf between urban America and suburban America, and that's not good for anyone. We don't want this nation to develop into a Bosnia or a Northern Ireland. The harm that comes from the deepening divisions in our society should be obvious. What can we do about it? More specifically, what can suburbanites and all of us do about it? Let me suggest a few things:

1. *Religious institutions play a powerful role in American life.* Ask the question at the appropriate meeting, or the right people, what your church or temple is doing to bring greater understanding across the barriers that divide us. I would be interested in hearing of specific actions that are planned or are being taken.

2. *Rotary Clubs, business and professional women's groups, teachers' associations and other civic and business-related groups can sponsor programs that help to create greater sensitivity.* The myths that are believed about another race or religion or ethnic group often can be demolished in this type of setting. When business and professional people understand that it is good economics not to discriminate, everyone wins.

3. *Individuals can make sure that their children are exposed to people of differing cultural backgrounds in a positive way.* Too few white families have ever had an African American or Latino or Asian American family to their homes for dinner. The same can be said across too many ethnic and religious barriers. What seems like a small thing for your family to do can be immensely important for the future of your children, and the future of your community and our nation and our world. I spoke at three events honoring Martin Luther King Jr.'s birthday this year, and what disturbed me about two of the three is that I spoke only to African Americans. Dr. King wanted us to reach out to one another, understand one another, and replace hatred and prejudice with love and understanding. That message is needed in the suburbs, but also in our cities and rural areas.

"One nation, indivisible" we recite when we say the pledge of allegiance to our flag. Do we mean it? Are we willing to do concrete things to make it a reality?

"SUPERFICIALITY LINGERS WHILE SUBSTANCE FLEES," COMMENTARY, *CHICAGO SUN-TIMES*, SEPTEMBER 19, 2000

What causes something a journalist writes or a public figure says to evoke a response, while other subjects of a much greater importance do not? We can learn about our culture in the feedback we receive.

More than a decade ago, on NBC's "Saturday Night Live," the announcer proclaimed: "And now our host for this evening: Paul Simon." Both the singer and I walked out and had a pre-planned mini-argument about which one the program wanted as host. He won, of course.

For two weeks afterward everywhere I went people approached me saying, "I saw you on 'Saturday Night Live.'" I've appeared on all the Sunday morning network news shows, and rarely did anyone comment on that, though if a clip from the show made the evening news there would be a little response. Even today, when I appear on a college campus, someone usually mentions that "Saturday Night Live" program.

Because our culture is entertainment-prone, rather than news-prone, the presidential candidates are appearing on the Oprah Winfrey, David Letterman and other shows as well as the straight news and opinion programs. And to the extent that the Winfrey-Letterman type of appearance generates interest in public affairs, that is healthy.

I occasionally do a brief commentary for the 10 National Public Radio stations in Illinois. Three years ago I made an observation that caused more reaction than any NPR commentary I've had on much weightier subjects. It still gets reprinted. I said: "I applaud most of the new technology that brings sweeping changes to our offices, and through computers, provides me information in minutes that in the pre-computer age would take months to accumulate. I love it when I am in a remote village in Portugal, and I can get cash out of a machine in 60 seconds with an ATM card from a bank or credit union here in the United States. I don't understand how it works, but I know that it does, and it is a great convenience.

"But when I place a phone call to an office and a recorded voice on the other end tells me: 'Thanks for calling our company. If you know the extension of the person you are calling, please dial that now.' Well I don't know the extension or even the name of the person to whom I want to talk. I just want some information.

"The recorded voice continues: 'If you want the design department, dial one. If you want to reserve time to discuss making a bid, dial two.' And so the voice continues through the first nine numbers. But none of the nine is exactly what I want. So out of frustration, I take a chance on something that sounds like it might be close. And then the line is busy. I have wasted what seems like two minutes. I sympathize with Napoleon, who told one of his officers: 'You may ask for anything you like except time.'

"I feel like sending a bill to the company. I make a mental note that if I ever have enough money to buy stock, don't invest in this company. It has to spend too much for public relations to calm people whose time they have wasted.

"There ought to be a special award for businesses and law offices and physicians' offices and schools and hospitals and assorted other entities that have a real live human being answering the phone and asking in a pleasant voice: 'May I help you?' I feel like responding, 'You already have.'

"So here's a toast to the various business and professional phone listings that have a warm, human body who talks to us: May your diminishing tribe survive, and perhaps, even grow some day. Your service to humanity is huge compared to the minor miracle of cloning sheep."

Why the large response on this and not on something crucial like the looming world crisis on water? Because we identify with that telephone problem. The water issue has not touched us yet. Why the Oprah Winfrey-David Letterman fascination rather than with "Meet the Press"? Because they both ask questions with which more people identify. A "Meet the Press" question on Kosovo is somehow less interesting than what a candidate eats for breakfast.

That's not good, but it's reality.

"Seventy-Two Phone Books," NPR Commentary, April 8, 2003

I recently called to change an airline reservation, and had to listen to several recorded voices before I finally got to talk to a live human being and not a machine that gave me several bad choices for information. When a genuine woman came on the line, I told her that even if she could not help me, it was a pleasure to talk to someone rather than a recording.

For reasons I do not know, a life insurance payment I sent did not arrive at the company office and I received a mail notice that my life insurance coverage would soon expire. I called the company and received only run-arounds. When that happened I understood why the company had made the newspapers with financial problems. I finally ended up sending two more checks, to make sure I had not lost my life insurance. So far none of the three checks has been mailed back to me and I will soon examine my bank statement to see if they cashed one or two or three or none. The recorded messages did not give me the option of talking to a living person.

Helen Deniston of Southern Illinois wanted extra phone books so she could have one at each phone in her home. She talked to the recorded voice and when she explained what she wanted the recorded voice responded, "We will send you 70 phone books." In amazement and annoyance she responded, "I certainly do not want 70 phone books!" Then she hung up, hoping the listening device on the machine was working. She received the extra phone books she requested and a year later, while she was traveling, her neighbor called and said, "You have a porch full of phone books." She did. Seventy-two of them.

There are times when this mechanism comes in handy. When I call my pharmacist after business hours I can leave a refill order. There may be other examples, but I can't think of any right now. What I do know is that generally businesses that try to please their customers do well—and most of us are not pleased with these bodiless voices that give us choices we don't want. I am opposed to capital punishment, except for the person who devised this obnoxious system.

"Portraying a Positive Picture," NPR Commentary, June 17, 2003

One of the practical difficulties we face in free society is that overwhelmingly the bad news makes the news. Yes, there are a few encouraging news items that seep through the process, but the dark clouds of negativism overwhelm each day's news, whether on television, radio or the newspapers.

To add to the disheartening picture, test surveys show that while the public says it wants more positive news, what they watch and read and listen to—and remember—is the negative news, and that is then blown up in the minds of too many people as an accurate portrayal of today's society. Two illustrations give the picture.

I traveled to Israel three weeks ago and moderated a two-person panel composed of the Israeli Water Commissioner and the Palestinian Water Commissioner. Much to almost everyone's surprise, they agreed on most issues. There were two or three reporters present, but so far as I know the encounter did not make the news. If one of them had shouted obscenities at the other, there would have been a story.

The danger in this is that we generalize on what we hear, and if the only things we read and see and hear are the extreme statements, we draw the conclusion that "they"—our enemy or potential enemy—have extreme views and it is unlikely that we can achieve a peaceful, stable, normal relationship with "them." Distorted news results in distorted conclusions.

Within our country, the portrayal of young African-American males on television and in the movies is generally negative. Juries that watch those television shows and movies are sensitized toward the belief that these young men tend to be trouble-makers. Some are. But the top scholar who wants to become a physician or engineer or journalist is much less likely to see his type of responsible citizenship portrayed on the screen.

No law can change these negative images that people around the world get of others, but sensitive reporters and publishers and producers can improve things if they will be a little less eager for that dollar, and a little more responsive to building and understanding and portraying an accurate picture.

ASSISTANCE TO THE HANDICAPPED

"Broken Bones—and Public Policy,"
P.S./Washington, June 1–7, 1975

Breaking a bone and wearing a cast is hardly a matter which would seem to affect public policy, but surprisingly it does.

Recently I broke a bone in my foot, and for the first time in my life I am wearing a cast. Walking with crutches always looked easy to me—until I suddenly find myself awkwardly using crutches, walking back and forth from my office building to the Capitol, where the House of Representatives meets.

And now I am aware that barriers like steps in public buildings present real handicaps for people on crutches, or in wheelchairs, or people with walking disabilities. A few years ago when I served as a member of the state Senate, I co-sponsored measures with Sen. John Graham, a Republican, and Rep. Harold Katz, a Democrat, which called for removing barriers of steps in new public buildings erected in Illinois. The measures passed and became law and now I see their importance—more than I did a few weeks ago, or when I helped pass them.

There are a few advantages to wearing a cast: you only wear one sock a day, you develop some strength in muscles previously little used, but the main benefit is developing some sympathy and understanding for people who face these physical barriers everywhere.

Southern Illinois University at Carbondale has done a remarkable job in making its facilities easy to enter and use for wheelchair students, or those otherwise physically handicapped. Some other schools and cities have done a good job, too. And what we do with buildings, we ought to do in other ways for handicapped people—for all of us are at times handicapped in some way.

You will find my voting record in the Education & Labor Committee here in Washington one of support for measures which provide special assistance to people who face handicaps. It is the humanitarian thing to do—and it also happens to be the sensible thing to do. If we want people to be assets to society rather than liabilities, we have to train them for useful work which matches their handicap. Some of the finest workers—and biggest taxpayers—I have known have been people with severe physical handicaps.

In a few weeks the cast will be off my leg. Climbing stairs will once again not be such a chore. But I hope I will retain an increased appreciation for those who bear their handicaps throughout life.

"A Mayor, an Aide, and a Congressman,"
P.S./Washington, December 27, 1980–January 2, 1981

What do the Mayor of Chester, Stanley Macieiski, Maryln McAdam, a key staff person in the House of Representatives, and Congressman Tony Coelho of California, one of the most promising members of the House, have in common?

All three have handicaps that would cause many employers not to hire them or to give them a chance—and unfortunately there are many of their counterparts around the nation who have not been given a chance.

The Mayor of Chester, Stanley Macieiski, fought in World War II and lost both legs in battle, then became a prisoner of war. Today he walks around on two artificial limbs so capably that few have any idea of his handicap.

Even more significant, Stanley Macieiski has not lost a day of work because of illness since the day he first started work after his discharge from the service. And some people have the idea that handicapped people are not reliable!

Maryln McAdam was hit by polio when she was two years old and has to move about in a wheelchair. Fortunately the schools of Pana, Illinois, permitted wheelchair attendance (as some schools did not in those days) and Maryln went through grade and high school in Pana, then attended the University of Illinois and Southern Illinois University. Now she is an important staff member of the subcommittee of the House of Representatives which works on higher education.

Coming to Washington was not as easy for Maryln as it is for most people because of housing problems. Most homes and apartments which are for rent are not built to accommodate wheelchairs, and Maryln had to delay acceptance of her Washington position a number of weeks because of the housing situation. Fortunately for the nation, she finally found housing and is serving all of us.

Tony Coelho is one of the future leaders of Congress—though that's an understated assessment, for he already is one of the leaders. There are those in Congress who talk a good game; there are those in Congress who know how to get a job done. Tony Coelho falls in the second category.

Tony also happens to be the first person with epilepsy to ever serve in Congress. When he learned he had epilepsy, Tony was dropped as a student at a Jesuit seminary; he lost his driver's license and the chance to get many jobs; and he was turned down for job after job. Then he started the climb up—and it's been up ever since for Tony Coelho. There are a host of places where Tony could not get a job because of epilepsy, but fortunately the people in California where he lives don't feel that way, and the nation has benefited.

Tony, Stanley and Maryln are three good examples for all of us in two respects: First, they should inspire us to realize what each of us can do. Second, those of us who are employers should recognize that those with handicaps are often among the finest of workers.

THE MILITARY, THE DRAFT, A YEAR OF PUBLIC SERVICE

"MILITARY SALES MUSHROOM," P.S./WASHINGTON, MARCH 9–15, 1975

A little known fact of importance to United States citizens and the nations of the world is the growing sales of military hardware from this nation to other nations. From fiscal year 1970 to fiscal year 1974, direct military assistance in terms of our gifts of military equipment have stayed fairly constant: just under $3 billion to approximately 51 nations.

But military sales have mushroomed more than 900 percent during this same period, from less than $1 billion in 1970 to more than $8 billion in 1974. As far as I can determine, 69 nations have been sold our guns and tanks and planes and other weapons. What's wrong with that? There are several things that ought to concern us with these direct military aid and growing military sales figures.

First, the great need of the world is for food and clothing and housing. If we think we are helping to build a world of peace and stability by shipping weapons all over, we're fooling ourselves and jeopardizing our future.

Second, while it helps temporarily in the balance of payments problems which the United States faces and does offer employment opportunity, the economic impact of military sales is limited—and long-run it does not help. Long-run it is not helpful because it does nothing to raise the standard of living of the recipient nations. If their standard of living can be lifted, then they can buy from the United States, and we can build a healthy, long-range trade partnership.

Third, we end up selling to people who will fight one another. Are we so eager to make a few dollars that we want to become the key to killing large numbers of people?

Fourth, it hampers U.S. foreign policy; we say that we sympathize with Israel and then sell Saudi Arabia millions of dollars in weapons, and help train Saudi troops. What sense does that make? Right now India is angry with us because we are providing military aid to her rival, Pakistan. Wouldn't we be better off refraining from furnishing weapons to either side, and provide food and technical know-how to lift their standard of living instead?

Finally, there is always the danger that weapons sold or given will be used against us. We have had enough experience in this that we should not want to burn our fingers again, but we seem to learn slowly. I am not opposed to all sales. Netherlands, for example, is not a threat to anyone, and our $17 million in sales to her last year should not bother us. But most sales are not that innocent. But if we won't sell to these 69 countries, won't France or the Soviet Union or some other country?

They may, but we should lead the way in trying to reach an agreement with all weapons-exporting countries to limit sales abroad. Our leadership should be toward agreements, not weapon sales. We have economic problems in the United States, but they are not so bad that we should adopt irrational military sales policies that will hurt us in the long-run.

"A Year of Service," P.S./Washington, March 9–15, 1980

One of the questions which most concerns our citizens is whether we will have selective service registration. My guess is that [the current bill providing for selective service registration] will pass, that there will be no draft for three to five years, but that a series of things we are now headed for will eventually cause us to adopt a plan which will require all young people at the age of 18 to devote one year of service to their country or their community.

That will include a choice of service in the military, in the Peace Corps or Vista, or working for a mental hospital, library, park district or some other non-profit agency as a full-time volunteer. Those who choose to serve in the military for this one year will receive special financial education benefits. What will move us in that direction will be a combination of two things which will cause shortages of personnel in the military: fewer people in that age bracket, and an improved economy which will discourage volunteers.

I will vote for the current registration proposal for several reasons:

1. It will save some time—estimates on this vary—in the event of a genuine national emergency. If the time saved is only 13 days, as some suggest, that could be a crucial 13 days.

2. At the present time we are excessively dependent on the poor and unskilled to fill our defense needs. That presents problems of ability to use complex equipment and it causes a serious injustice. It means that if the military is needed for an emergency, the poor will shed their blood disproportionately.

3. So long as the children of the poor are the only ones who may be fighting somewhere, it becomes easier for military and national leaders to move those troops into a confrontation situation. If the children of middle and upper income Americans also might be used in a combat situation, we are much less likely to use our troops.

To be even more specific, if the children of members of the House and Senate and the Cabinet are among those who might face combat, the nation's leaders are going to look with a little more care and caution before committing us to involvement.

4. Most defense expenditures are symbols which are never used. Faced with a choice of a symbol like registration, which does convey national will, or more nuclear warheads which could destroy civilization, I much prefer the non-lethal symbol. It is also a symbol which is not likely to escalate the arms race as the MX or some other symbols will. Neither registration nor the draft will solve all of the problems our military has. The primary personnel problem is in the mid-career sector where we are losing pilots and physicians and technical experts who for a variety of reasons do not find military life attractive. But registration—including the option to register as a conscientious objector—probably will become a reality.

Editor's note: The draft was discontinued in 1973 when we went to the All-Volunteer Force (AVF). Periodically, the U.S. Congress debates the issue of whether to bring back the draft, and this column was written at one of those times. Paul Simon was a consistent advocate for a year of public service that would be served by all young people, with military service being one option.

"HOMOSEXUALITY AND MILITARY SERVICE,"
P.S./WASHINGTON, MARCH 5–11, 1995

"How can you support having homosexuals in the armed forces?" a visibly angry woman asked me after a town meeting recently. "Don't you believe in the Bible?" I confess I am not much impressed by people who hate in the name of religion. But let me answer her question partially, since I do not claim to be a theologian.

When I was a boy, my father never had to call me aside and say, "Paul, you ought to be interested in girls." I came by it very naturally. He had to give me other warnings!

Just as my interest in girls came naturally, that is not natural for a small percentage of men. There is evidence that there is a genetic basis for this difference among men, although the scientific research is less complete for women. Regardless of the reasons for this difference, there are several issues that woman with the angry question should address.

If there is a military emergency and we have a draft, would you exempt anyone who says he is gay? The percentage of those claiming to be gay would suddenly escalate! Because you mentioned the biblical basis for your beliefs, since the 10 Commandments mention adultery and not homosexuality, and adultery is condemned at least 40 times more than homosexuality in the Bible, should we keep anyone out of the service who has committed adultery? My recollection of my Army days is that would thin our ranks appreciably.

Or should we judge people by their conduct, not their genes? That makes sense to me.

When I was in the Army—long ago—I served in intelligence and we screened people for security clearances. Those who were gay were not kicked out of the Army—that's a recent phenomenon—but they could not get security clearances because we judged that they could be blackmailed, certainly a proper judgment in the early 1950s. But during those days, and during all of our previous wars, we had an armed service to be proud of, and it was inclusive.

There is also the problem of where you stop the practice of discrimination. If people cannot serve in the armed forces, what about the police force or fire department? Once you start the practice of discrimination, where do you stop? I would finally ask that woman who is so righteously angry: What would you do if your son or daughter came home and told you that he or she is gay? My guess is that even that hard heart would melt. And become more understanding.

"Required Service,"
NPR Commentary, November 6, 2001

Senator John McCain, a Republican, and Senator Evan Bayh, a Democrat, want to increase the domestic service group called Americorps from 50,000 to 250,000—a good idea, but I would go even further.

Starting at a date perhaps five years off, so that we could carefully prepare for it, I favor a year's required service by all young people following graduation from high school or at the age of 18. They would have choices. If they entered the military, they would receive extra pay, but if not they could go into Peace Corps, or Americorps; work for a local park district or a mental hospital; become a teacher's aid or a Red Cross worker. The two years that many young Mormons volunteer for overseas duty would count, as would work for a domestic charitable organization like the Salvation Army.

Pay would be minimal, but after that year of service each youthful worker would be eligible for additional financial aid for college. The net result would be a more mature college student body, and a nation that would gradually become more sensitive to society's problems.

For those who choose military duty—and more than now serve would get that experience—they would find themselves working with a real cross-section of our population. My Army basic training benefitted me that way, in addition to the military knowledge it provided. Having more people in the armed forces would also mean that in the future more decision-makers in the White House and House and Senate would understand that we have a great military, but military leaders can make stupid mistakes just as people in every other field do. I have observed that those who have not served, whether in the presidency or in Congress, too often are reluctant to second-guess a military recommendation. My instinct is that if Bill Clinton had served in the military he could have understood that having the United States take an unenlightened stand against outlawing the manufacture and use of land mines makes no sense militarily or in any other way. Adding to the weight of the voice of a few military leaders was Clinton's not having served and he did not want to look weak, or have his non-service record revived.

Someday I hope we will have a year of required service of some kind. The nation will become richer when we have it.

CRIME AND PRISONS

"Sure, Swift Criminal Justice,"
P.S./Washington, November 22–28, 1981

Are there more effective ways of dealing with crime?

In a recent column, Jack Germond and Jules Witcover tell a fascinating story about Norfolk County, Massachusetts, where under the leadership of Richard G. Sterns they are doing something practical about crime. One of the realities in all larger counties is that prosecutors get overworked and often turn to plea bargaining as an easy way to dispose of their criminal case backloads. So in the Norfolk County experiment they have done this:

- A prosecutor handles no more than eight cases. They've hired enough people to reduce the load to make that possible. That has resulted in a reduction of from 220 days to 73 days between the commission of a crime and the court verdict.
- They do not allow plea bargaining on the "lead charge."
- Prosecutors always recommend a jail sentence. The only negotiation can be over which jail and for how long.

The result has been that 94 percent of those charged are convicted, and 91 percent have been sent to prison. Since 20 percent of the criminals in this country commit 80 percent of the crimes, insisting on prison and insisting on sure, swift sentences is a practical way of telegraphing a message to those inclined toward crime that crime does not pay—to use an overworked but perhaps not entirely accurate phrase—and to let them know early in their careers.

Most crimes are committed by people between the ages of 17 and 24. We must let them, and the community, know in no uncertain terms that swift justice will prevail, that after a fair trial those prison doors will lock.

"Missing Children," P.S./Washington, July 18–24, 1982

Etan Patz, six years old, left home to catch the school bus on May 25, 1979—and no one has ever heard from him since. That happened in the State of New York. I read about it and noticed his parents' statement that federal laws were inadequate to help in the search for missing children.

I asked Maryln McAdam of my staff to check it out and discovered that the FBI automatically keeps data on your car if it is missing, but information about your missing child is not similarly collected or kept unless there is evidence of kidnapping or violence.

So I introduced a proposed Missing Children Act in the House which would do two things: Put missing children on the national computer and enter information about the more than 1,000 bodies of children and adults each year which now are never identified. The cost of using the existing National Crime Information Center computer for this added purpose would be almost nothing and the benefits of the new service would be great.

Data on unidentified bodies should have been put on the computer a long time ago. When an unidentified body is found (as one was in Carbondale recently) that fact is reported to the state police and that is it. But if we had a national computer file, we might very well find that the deceased individual was listed as being missing from Maine or Montana or somewhere else.

It is important that families know when their relatives are dead, and sometimes it is important for criminal investigations. During recent hearings on the Missing Children Act one parent, John Walsh, described the torment of not knowing where to turn for news that could aid in the search for a missing son or daughter—in his case, a young boy who was later found murdered. Some states voluntarily exchange this kind of information by mail at intervals of six months or longer and those months of waiting are hard to endure, he said. We should be making that kind of information instantly available to anguished parents and law enforcement officials and we're not able to routinely do that now. Of the missing children, most are runaways and show up within 24 hours somewhere. Fortunately. But approximately 50,000 young people—no one knows the figure exactly—are not runaways and we do too little to try to protect them.

Some are taken by persons who yearn to have a child; some are taken for purposes of sexual exploitation; the causes and reasons vary, but the problems for the families are overwhelming and so is their grief. To put these missing children on a national computer will not solve the problem but it could help solve some of the cases.

If a family in Illinois reports a child missing and suddenly a child appears in Florida under somewhat suspicious conditions in a family to whom it does not appear to belong, a national computer check would be a simple matter.

Since I have introduced this legislation—and Sen. Paula Hawkins, a Republican from Florida, has done the same in the Senate—I have met many parents of missing children. The agony and the uncertainty they go through is something I had only third-hand knowledge of prior to introducing this legislation. Sen. Hawkins and I have experienced difficulty in getting action because the legislative process sometimes moves painfully slow. But President Reagan has indicated support for our measure, and we have strong support from people in both parties.

I believe that soon the children of the nation will have a little more protection. It is long overdue.

"Practical Steps on Crime and Violence," P.S./Washington, September 14–20, 1986

What can be done about the problem of crime and violence in our society?

There are three immediate steps, among others, that would help: First, get the television networks to reduce the rising rate of violence on television that clearly has an impact on many people; second, fewer speeches and more sensible action on the drug problem; third, change our laws—state laws in particular—that permit people to walk the streets after being convicted of crimes of violence while they appeal.

On the last point, here is a good example of what has been happening. Walter Otis Lane, 27, was returned to the Cook County Jail at the end of July. He had been convicted of rape and sentenced to 11 years in prison. He appealed his conviction and while on appeal he was permitted to go free. While he was free, he was accused of another rape and abducting a Blue Island, Ill., bank director and his wife, forcing them to withdraw $15,000 from the Heritage County Bank and Trust in Blue Island, and then he was charged with shooting the couple to death.

He was caught after allegedly robbing a citizen from Elmwood Park, Ill. I do not suggest that those who are found guilty of a violent crime should not have the right to appeal. They should. But they should not have the right to walk our streets in freedom after conviction, while they are on appeal.

On the drug issue, some action will probably emerge from Congress, but whether the administration and Congress take the really key step is not clear. At one point the major source of illegal drugs was Turkey. This country, working with the Turkish government, has virtually eliminated that source of trouble. Now, according to the *New York Times*, 85 percent of the hard drugs can be traced to crops in Peru and Bolivia. We should be working with those two governments to eliminate the source of our problem. That is basic.

The second key element on the drug problem is an effective education program among young people. They must learn to understand more clearly that not only are drugs bad, but permitting their friends to get into trouble with drugs is a betrayal of friendship.

The third source of violence is right in our homes—that television set. The television industry is permitting more and more violence, and the evidence from study after study is that it is a serious cause for concern. University of California and University of Pennsylvania studies released within the last few weeks have reinforced previous studies on the same subject. The studies show clearly: Television violence causes some of the violence in our society.

I have introduced legislation to permit the networks to get together with cable and the independents and the TV programmers to establish guidelines on violence. The United States does not have to have the most violent TV in the world.

When I met some months ago with TV network executives they said they could not establish standards because of antitrust laws. Now when I try to change the law so that they would not violate the antitrust laws, at least one network is vocal in its opposition to the bill.

The problem is that violence pays off for the television industry. But it and the American public should understand those profits are costly to our society. If the television industry continues to resist sensible steps, Congress should have the courage to defy them.

"On the Prison Population in the U.S.,"
NPR Commentary, October 29, 2003

In the early 1800s, a French citizen, Alexis de Tocqueville, visited the United States because we had such enlightened policies on dealing with prisoners. No one would make that mistake today, for we are known, as Henry Kissinger has pointed out, for our harsh treatment of those committing crimes.

More than two million Americans are in prisons, a higher percentage of our population than any other nation. We are 4 percent of the world population and we have 25 percent of its prisoners. Chesa Boudin, a Rhodes Scholar, wrote in a recent article in the *Nation* magazine about having both parents incarcerated from his age of 14 months, and the great difficulties he had of visiting them regularly. More than 55 percent of male prisoners are parents and 60 percent of female prisoners are. As he points out in this article, we are punishing an "increasing number of children for their parents' crimes."

There are six basic changes needed in dealing with criminals:

1. Make prisons places where people can be rehabilitated. There is far too little of that now, and it only makes it more likely that crimes will be committed again.

2. Give judges great discretion in sentencing. Mandatory minimum sentences sound good—and they may get votes for policy-makers—but a careful examination of their results is disheartening.

3. Many sentences should be for shorter periods. England and Canada, for example, have much shorter average sentences for burglary, and that means a better chance to rehabilitate the prisoner.

4. Make prisons friendlier sites for family visits, giving the person incarcerated incentives for improving himself or herself, and also giving the prisoner hope.

5. The limited experience on minor drug offenses is that drug treatment is much more effective than prison, and costs much less.

6. Prisoners who have mental health problems should receive needed medical attention. That is approximately one out of five in our prisons and jails. Most of them are not receiving that needed medical care now.

Such a six-point program would reduce the crime rate of those released from court jurisdiction, and make ours a safer and more productive—and more humane—society.

We should be tough on crime, but also smart on crime.

4

Foreign and Defense Policy

EDITOR'S NOTE

In the U.S. Senate, Paul Simon was a natural fit for the Foreign Relations Committee, and he spent ten of his twelve years in the Senate on that committee. Evidence of his early interest in foreign policy was already available when he took trips to the Middle East while he was still in the Illinois General Assembly, and he wrote his impressions of that area as a trip report to his Illinois constituents as soon as he returned home. Many of them must have been quite startled to learn that their state representative thought they ought to be paying careful attention to Israel, Egypt, Jordan, and Syria, but Simon made his case. As several of the articles in this chapter indicate, Paul Simon could make a cogent argument that American citizens need a broader outlook on the rest of the world and should realize how other nations continually impinge on our own fortunes. That argument still needs to be made today. Unless we are in a shooting war with some country, most Americans pay very scant attention to events in other regions and know very little about other nations and cultures. This parochialism is not conducive to the informed citizenship required of our status as the last superpower, a status we attained after the demise of the Soviet Union. The American people are buffeted each day by economic and social winds that originate offshore, and we are often puzzled by the actions and attitudes of the people in other countries, some of whom are our friends and some of whom are our adversaries. If we are going to play the superpower role from anything like a rational policy position, we must pay more attention to the increasingly interdependent world of which we are a part. Simon's writings will help us to do just that.

Simon was a strong advocate for what would today be called "soft power" (Nye). That is, he believed in the power of America's ideas and ideals. He was deeply committed to the values expressed in our founding documents such as the Declaration of Independence and the Constitution. He believed that these were timeless values that expressed the best aspirations of not only the American people but also most of the rest of the world. He thought the most powerful and compelling ideals we project to the rest of the world depend on us living up to our commitments to freedom, democracy, and the rule of law at home and making the opportunity necessary to achieving the American Dream equally available to all. He thought we should lead by example rather than by trying to cram our values down the throats of other nations who often have a vastly different cultural and historic background from what we enjoy in the United States. The quality of our life at home was much more important than the superiority of our military forces projected around the globe.

This does not mean that Simon was a pacifist or that he was against all wars or military action. He was a veteran of the U.S. Army who served in Germany early in the 1950s, and he was proud of that service. He was as patriotic as the next public official and turned up regularly for all the Memorial Day and Fourth of July parades. He also proudly flew the flag outside his residence in Makanda. Simon was, however, against wars and military confrontations that did not make sense from a coldly calculated national interest perspective. In the modern parlance of foreign policy doctrine, he was a Realist and not an Idealist (Morgenthau). He did not favor wars fought in pursuit of ideological goals or for the nebulous belief that our way was better than their way. As one of the selections included in this chapter indicates, he was deeply opposed to the U.S.-led invasion of Iraq in March 2003, which was just nine months before he died. He would have agreed with then state senator Barack Obama's declaration against the Iraq invasion when Obama said that he was not against all wars but against "dumb wars." In fact, Simon's daughter, Sheila, endorsed Obama for the Senate when he ran in 2004, confident that she was standing in her father's tradition in doing so. The echoes of that conflict over Iraq and the related but separate conflict over our role in Afghanistan still roil Congress and the American presidency today.

One of the prime exhibits of Paul Simon's foreign policy views was his clear and unequivocal opposition to American policy toward Cuba. Paul was absolutely convinced that the policy was counterproductive for the American and the Cuban people. He thought it was based on illogical and irrational ideological views held by a narrow group of people—mostly the Cuban refugee community concentrated in south Florida. Paul led a delegation of academics and public officials to Cuba in February 2001. These academics included Southern Illinois University's experts in agriculture, aquaculture, engineering, law, health care, history, and political science. At every stop, those in the delegation were greeted by enthusiastic members of their counterpart communities who wanted more exchanges of people, research, and ideas across the narrow straits that divide Cuba from the American mainland. Simon came back from Cuba convinced more than ever that such cultural and educational exchanges would benefit both countries and that the American embargo only isolated Cuba and the United States to their mutual detriment and exacerbated the old Cold War tensions that were outmoded and no longer served anything but ideological ends. Simon argued that the embargo acted as the all-purpose excuse the Cuban leadership always used to explain and justify its failures and that lifting it would take away that timeworn excuse. Again, provide for people-to-people exchanges and depend on the power of our ideals to carry our message.

The Obama administration has eased some of the more narrow restrictions from the Bush era, and the flow of people and money across the straits has increased markedly in the past two years; however, the embargo remains in place officially. More important, punitive legislation, like the Helms-Burton Act, greatly restricts the ability of American companies to try to open the Cuban market to American products and know-how. Paul Simon campaigned energetically against the embargo and the Helms-Burton Act up until the final months of his life. Some of his writings on this issue are included in this chapter. The conflict over our policies toward Cuba still exists and drives an American foreign policy to satisfy the ideological commitments and electoral interests of a very small but intense minority of Americans.

Paul Simon's writings covering a long list of other foreign hot spots are also included in this chapter. The Middle East was an enduring interest, even a passion, for Paul. He visited there regularly and was always worried that a new and massive war would break out there and inevitably draw America into its vortex. He also folded his interest in water policy into his views on that region. He noted that the last several generations have fought wars partially over natural resources and especially over oil. He predicted that the next generation would be tempted to fight over the control of water, a particularly precious commodity in the arid Middle East.

Simon was a strong supporter of the nation of Israel. That is where his natural sympathies lay, and it was hard for him to shake loose from those commitments and find it possible to criticize Israeli policy. But, several of his articles show that he was able to make that leap to the more uncomfortable but ultimately more balanced view that both sides had a right to their grievances and that both sides had committed grave injustices toward the other. Simon ultimately wanted to be an honest broker and wanted to play a helpful role in our government's policy toward the nations of the Middle East. No other conflict and trouble spot is more important than the Middle East in the world today, and American foreign and defense policy toward Israel and its neighbors is still contentious and deeply divisive.

Other trouble spots that attracted Simon's attention included Africa, South and Central America, Vietnam, and Korea. In the latter two cases, the United States has already fought wars there, and Simon urged the nation to move on toward normalized diplomatic relations and to try to integrate the former enemies into the world community and global economy. This step has taken place in Vietnam with the Carter administration extending diplomatic recognition to Vietnam and with its admission into the World Trade Organization and the development of a growing economy. North Korea remains isolated and a problem for itself and for the world. Its reclusive regime remains unpredictable and repressive. Paul Simon actually went to North Korea when he was in the Senate and tried to fashion an agreement that would begin to open up its borders and economy; however, he was disappointed in the results. This did not deter his faith in the power of ideas and cultural and intellectual exchanges to ultimately prevail over even the most repressive regime. American foreign policy continues to try to ascertain the best and most effective balance between the hard power of our unparalleled military might and the attraction of our commitment to freedom, democracy, and prosperity for the greater good of the most people possible.

THE MIDDLE EAST

"ISRAEL: AN EXCITING PLACE THESE DAYS," STATEMENT RELEASED BY STATE SENATOR PAUL SIMON, SEPTEMBER 21, 1967

If you want to visit Israel, you could hardly pick a more fascinating time than now. There is a buoyancy in their air which comes to those who are threatened, expect the worse, and experience an unexpected victory.

The mood of Israel prior to the Six Days' War is perhaps best illustrated by the physician who told me he had many requests for prescriptions of poison from mothers who asked it for themselves and their families, in the event of an Arab victory. Whether well-founded or not, they expected the worst if the Arabs won, and did not want to repeat their experiences under the Nazis.

So the victory meant that the quickly built trenches of defense, seen all over Israel, were not used; that casualties were lighter than anyone hoped for; and the nation breathes more easily—at least temporarily.

The hope among the Israeli leadership is that the Arab nations will recognize Israel's existence as a nation. If that can happen, Israel is not only willing but eager to settle the questions of payments to the refugees and help in their resettlement. Israel believes that if she and the Arab countries could sit down and discuss their mutual problems—water among the major ones—these could be solved.

This was my third visit to Israel. On other occasions I also visited her Arab neighbors but that is still not recommended for Americans at this point, though I would guess this will change soon. From what I sense of this situation in Israel, and from earlier talks with Arab leaders, the real key to any kind of reconciliation rests with President Nasser of Egypt. I have reason to believe—despite their public statements—that both Lebanon and Jordan would be willing to make peace with Israel. Both have much to gain by doing so.

But in each country there is fear of taking the lead because of the sizable internal refugee population. Lebanon and Jordan can follow on this issue, but their governments would probably topple quickly if they took the lead.

Nasser is the only Arab leader of sufficient personal strength to be able to get on Radio Cairo and make a statement denouncing Israel (to satisfy his past position) and then adding, "But we have to be realistic in this situation. The only way we can get our territory back, get the Suez Canal open, and get Egypt moving ahead is to recognize the realities of the present situation." He would then tell his nation that he has reluctantly entered into negotiations with Israel.

Lebanon and Jordan could then follow. Israel's other neighbor, Syria, might not follow at the present time, but it is not that important in the present scheme of things. Other Arab nations such as Tunisia would quickly follow Egypt's lead in recognition.

If something of this nature does not eventually take place—and it is not likely to take place soon—then the Middle East will remain a festering sore on the international scene.

The recognition by Egypt and other Arab nations would probably follow only after pressure exerted by both the United States and the Soviet Union, and there is some evidence to suggest that the Soviet Union would be willing to join us in this. They are unhappy with picking up the tab for the losing cause in the Middle East and are aware that an explosion anywhere in the world today could be impossible to stop.

However, any such move by Egypt and the Arab nations is probably at least two years off. In the meantime, hopefully, they will prepare their people for such an eventuality.

Editor's note: This statement was issued upon the return of state senator Paul Simon from a trip he took to Israel immediately after the Six Days' War between Israel and its Arab neighbors, especially Egypt, Jordan, and Syria. While Simon was a strong supporter of Israel, he was also always committed to seeking peace between Israel and the surrounding Arab countries and consistently favored peace over war.

"TWO MEDITERRANEAN TROUBLE SPOTS,"
P.S./WASHINGTON, AUGUST 21–27, 1977

There are two points of potential explosion in the Mediterranean area, and I have reluctantly concluded that we have to look for peace there inch by inch, rather than in one giant stride. Those two points of high tension are divided Cyprus, and Israel and her Arab neighbors.

In both cases United Nations troops now maintain an uneasy peace. Following the death of the President of Cyprus, Archbishop Makarios, I was asked by President Carter to join the small U.S. delegation headed by Chief Justice Warren Burger which attended the funeral.

We flew over and directly back, and were in Cyprus less than two days.

But even that short trip makes clear that any dramatic movement toward stability is unlikely. The new President of Cyprus—with whom we met briefly—governs with a shaky coalition, and governs only one portion of the island. More than 60 nations were represented at the Makarios funeral, but one was not: Turkey. That tells much of the story. The feelings between Greek Cypriots and Turkish Cypriots are intense.

Unlike the divisions between West Germany and East Germany, where the border guards are tense but the people yearn to join one another, the UN guards between the Turkish sector and the Greek sector are much more relaxed, but the tensions remain between the people of the two sides.

The nation which must provide leadership toward the reconciliation is Turkey, but because the political situation in Turkey, like in Cyprus, is shaky, substantial movement toward reconciliation is unlikely.

However, small positive actions can be taken. Threads of peace can become strings which can become ropes which can become cables for the bridge of peace. And all is not as gloomy as initial impressions might suggest.

For example, despite the division of the capital city of Nicosia, the Turks on the north are providing water for the Greek portion of the city. And the Greeks to the south are providing electricity for the Turks in the north. That is no small matter of cooperation. If diplomats of our country and other countries can encourage—and, yes, pressure—the two sides to take further steps toward cooperation, maybe one of these years Cyprus can once again become a united country with two rich ethnic groups, rather than two hostile camps.

In Israel, the election of Prime Minister Menachem Begin has changed the prospects for dramatic breakthroughs, and the unsuccessful trip of Sec. of State Cyrus Vance simply confirmed what many of us feared, that peace will come slowly—if at all—to Israel and her Arab neighbors. Congressman Stephen Solarz of New York probably knows the new Prime Minister of Israel better than any other member of Congress or anyone in the administration. In the midst of the sweetness and light of the Begin-Carter talks, Solarz—who respects Begin—said that he did not see much chance for a decisively successful meeting at Geneva.

"Begin is more flexible in style than his predecessor, Prime Minister Rabin," Solarz commented, "but less flexible in substance. He is not going to change a lifetime of beliefs now that he has become prime minister." The Vance trip makes the Solarz comment sound prophetic.

Since all of the immediate nations are interested in stability, but mutually acceptable peace terms are not likely to be found, the United States and the countries involved must look for "small things" which can de-escalate emotions and slowly build the structure of peace.

In the meantime, we can hope and pray that the region does not explode.

"Middle East Problems Affect Us All,"
P.S./Washington, December 4–10, 1977

"Why should the United States be so concerned about peace in the Middle East?" a few people in my district have asked me. Their letters suggest that we ought to pay attention to the problems we have in the United States—and they are right in that—and forget remote places like the Middle East. It is an understandable attitude, particularly after our experience in Vietnam, but it is unfortunately an extremely short-sighted one. It is a little like suggesting that if there is a fire down the street we should ignore it and let it burn because it hasn't reached our house.

Yet. And just as fires spread, so do wars.

Little wars become big wars, and living in a world where nations have enough nuclear warheads to theoretically destroy every person on the face of the earth 22 times, we can no longer risk little wars that might mushroom into big wars. And I don't really believe that there are many people so hardhearted that they believe we should just let people go ahead and kill each other while we remain indifferent. There are other reasons for concern also.

Saudi Arabia is the earth's richest source of oil. If war erupted in the Middle East tomorrow and that oil supply were destroyed—which it easily could be—the price of gas and oil and fertilizer in the United States would make any past gas price hikes look like nothing. And inflation would be upon us in a big way. The attitude of isolation also ignores economic realities. The Middle East—like the rest of the world—keeps the U.S. economy going.

In Egypt, for example, I discovered to my surprise that one of the American products they import is frozen chicken. We produce better chicken, more efficiently than any other nation. I saw coal from Southern Illinois at an Egyptian steel plant. Soybeans and soybean oil were there, some of it probably from Southern Illinois. And I am sure there are other products from my district in Egypt. What we sell to Egypt creates jobs in Southern Illinois. And Egypt is just one country in the Middle East.

Perhaps more important than all of these factors is one which some unfortunately do not consider important: unless people all over the face of the earth have some hope for food and education and shelter, there is not too much chance that your children and my children are going to spend their lives in a world of peace. In one miserably poor section of Cairo I saw water coming out of a pipe, and a long line of people waiting to get water. That pipe with its one outlet provides water for 18,000 people in this section of Cairo.

Should it surprise anyone that diseases—particularly diseases of the skin—are common in that area? And should it surprise anyone that people who live in misery are ripe for extremists and radicals? If I lived there, I would probably become a radical, too.

How many of the world's flu epidemics, just as one example, festered and grew and spread from places like that? And just as disease does not recognize national boundaries, so the plague of hatred and misery that deplorable conditions breed crosses national boundaries quickly. Those who say we should forget the rest of the world may believe they are serving themselves by such statements.

If fact, they are doing a disservice both to themselves and the nation.

"Passion and Self-Interest in Foreign Policy,"
P.S./Washington, April 2–8, 1978

One of the practical difficulties in being a member of Congress is that you are so flooded with facts and figures, problems and proposals, meetings and speeches that you have little time to think, to ask yourself basic questions about the meaning of it all. One of the ways I try to gain a little perspective is to make sure that one of the books I am reading is at least 10 years old. It is a habit I adopted a few years ago, and it has enriched my reading tremendously.

I am frequently surprised how timely something written decades or centuries ago can be. After reading the latest reports from the Middle East, I turned to a book of Sigmund Freud's writings and came across these observations of Freud, written as World War I engulfed Europe: "Nations still obey their immediate passions far more readily than their interests . . . They parade their interests as their justification for satisfying their passion."

Did the PLO raid into Israel satisfy the PLO interest or their passion? Did Israel's response satisfy the Israeli interest or passion? And how much was there a mixture of both on both sides? Beyond the immediate problems posed by the latest actions, it seems fairly clear to this observer (and I am a long-time Israel supporter) that some modification in Israeli policy is needed to serve their own security and self-interest in order to establish a firm base for peace in the Middle East. But will Israeli domestic passions permit that?

President Sadat clearly went against prevailing Arab passions to serve Arab self-interest in his dramatic attempt to bring about peace. The question now is whether Prime Minister Begin can go against some of the passions within his party (and within himself) in behalf of Israeli self-interest. But pointing a finger at other nations who act on the basis of passion rather than self-interest is too easy. We are guilty of the same.

In a little-noted speech on the floor of the Senate the other day, Senator Edward Kennedy called attention to the desperate need for food in Laos and asked for a reversal of United States policy so that we could offer to make food available. What holds us back from responding affirmatively? It is clearly not in our self-interest to let people starve. It is not in our self-interest to deepen and intensify whatever feelings of hostility the people of Laos may have toward the United States. Refusing to offer food is not going to make the leaders of that nation any more likely to react in a positive way to American overtures in the future. Refusing to offer food does nothing to help United States farmers and their price problems. What our present policy does is one thing and one thing only: it satisfies our passions. We know of

Laos's involvement in the Vietnam War, though we neglect to acknowledge that it was mostly as a victim rather than as a participant. We know that Laos today has Communist leaders, though we neglect to acknowledge that our actions in that area may have brought that about.

What has happened in that region of Asia has wounded our pride, and instead of reacting with compassion, we react with passion, and that is not in our long-run self-interest. Sigmund Freud wrote his words 63 years ago. We can still profit by reflecting on them today.

"Wanted: Another Sensible, Courageous Arab Leader," P.S./Washington, April 1–7, 1979

One of the ironies of the present situation in the Middle East is that if President Sadat of Egypt had won the Sinai and the other treaty concessions from Israel after a war in which tens of thousands of Egyptians and Israelis had been slain, he would be the hero of the Arab world today. But because he achieved his victory though peaceful means, he is pictured by many Arab leaders as a traitor to their cause. And the more the other Arab leaders denounce Sadat, the smaller they become in world esteem. I have met many fine leaders in Jordan, Saudi Arabia, Syria and Lebanon. And while I understand the various political and emotional constraints which appear to restrict their options, we need another leader of vision and compassion and courage in the Middle East.

Lebanese silence I understand most of all. They barely survive as a nation today. But the leader of the Lebanese community in the United States did the right thing recently in calling for Middle Eastern leaders to back the Sadat-Begin-Carter peace offensive.

Jordan's King Hussein has occupied what once was thought to be a shaky and temporary throne with considerable skill. What his private thoughts about the peace offensive may be, I can guess with reasonable accuracy. But any public statements in support of the treaties by him would be taken at great risk, the greatest risks of any national leader other than Lebanon's.

For Jordan has more Palestinians within her borders than any other nation.

Saudi Arabia's King and Crown Prince are frightened by the Soviet threat, and concerned about domestic political intrigue within the royal family. The Saudi oil fields are potentially an easy target for terrorists. But the Saudis have been excessively reluctant to assume Arab leadership, while at the same time criticizing the United States for failing to exercise leadership.

Of all the Middle East rulers who have every logical reason to support the peace effort, the Saudis could do it with the least risk. They lack the will however.

Syria probably would be the principal economic beneficiary of a peaceful, stable Middle East for Syria's rich agricultural land and industrial potential stands in contrast to much of the rest of the Middle East. But President Assad has remained in power by balancing extremists and appealing to a small but growing, stable middle force in the Syrian government and in the business and professional community. For any of these leaders to act in a way which would reconcile the Arab and Israeli worlds and provide real help to the Palestinians, rather than slogans, would take courage. This is what President Sadat has. And that is what the Middle East needs in another country.

Caution and prudence dictate appealing to traditional hatred and emotions, rather than to reason, compassion and common sense. In some cases the leaders themselves appear to be captives of their own hatreds and emotions.

As an officeholder, I understand those who wish to stay in office and do not wish to take risks. But I also recall that tumultuous welcome President Sadat received when he returned to Cairo after that first visit to Jerusalem. That sentiment which erupted in Cairo is present in other countries also. But it must be appealed to.

Where is that Arab leader who will respond to this great need, this yearning for peace? Where is that Arab leader who, like President Sadat, will appeal to the Arab world's self-interest, rather than its passions? Now is when the cause of peace needs that leader.

"UNDERSTANDING THE MOSLEM WORLD,"
P.S./WASHINGTON, DECEMBER 23–29, 1979

The tragedy of Iran points out a deficiency: most of us who are Americans have little knowledge of the Moslem world, and in this season in which we celebrate religious holidays, we need to remind ourselves of our shortcomings.

We have come a long way in the United States towards understanding the beliefs of others in our midst. Protestants and Catholics and Jews get along well. We understand our divisions, and we understand them with respect.

It is hard for us—now—to imagine the fight in Northern Ireland where Christian fights Christian, though not too many years ago in our country the veneer of civilization in this regard was thin. But while we understand the divisions within each branch of the major religious groups in our country, we have little knowledge of the beliefs of those who follow Muhammad or Buddha, as two major examples.

I know so little about Moslem beliefs that I would have a difficult time asking intelligent questions or entering into a meaningful conversation with them about their beliefs. I know there are two generally broad categories, the Shiite Moslems and the Sunni Moslems, but there are many divisions within these categories. And I know virtually nothing about them.

Not only do we not understand the many differences of beliefs, but when we do not understand something, we tend to fear it. It is much easier to believe that the Ayatollah Khomeini represents the Moslem world if we know nothing about it. And if we do not have ties to the Moslem world, so that they also understand us, it is easier for them to believe that we are not speaking for our hostages, but we are fighting the Moslem world and its beliefs.

I remember waking up one morning, almost by reflex turning on the CBS news station in Washington, WTOP, and hearing the words, "Christian mortar fire today hit portions of Beirut in Lebanon." *Christian* mortar fire. Simply putting the words together offended me.

But we do the same thing to the Moslems regularly. When there is some type of mob action in an American city, we do not say that "Christian mobs today did this and that." But we do describe crowds of people in Moslem countries that way. This is a good season of the year to remind ourselves of the need for greater understanding.

If we understand each other better, it is much less likely that our disagreements will become violent.

"Anwar Sadat," P.S./Washington, October 11–17, 1981

Since the assassinations in our own country in the 1960s, nothing has hit the United States with quite the stunning force as the killing of Anwar Sadat. I wish somehow it was possible to convey to Egypt the high regard the people of the United States have for President Sadat.

As I write this it appears that some religious fanatics apparently were responsible. It is one of the realities of life that almost any force for good, as religion is, can also become a force for evil when in misguided hands. All the world grieves for his death, because of his uncommon courage and depth of commitment. Southern Illinois nearly had an added bond of friendship with him because on the three occasions here and abroad when I had a chance to visit with President Sadat, I told him about "Little Egypt," and our communities of Cairo, Thebes and Karnak—cities he also has in Egypt.

I invited him to come and visit our "Little Egypt." I arranged with Southern Illinois University that he would receive an honorary doctorate, and I had Sen. Percy talk with him about visiting Southern Illinois. He always graciously said he would like to do it, and I believe he meant that.

I happened to be in the Middle East when Sadat startled the world with his announcement that he was willing to visit Israel. Two days later I saw him and it was clear he was serious, though much of the world did not take it as a serious gesture at the time. In visiting other Arab nations in the succeeding days I learned that: (1) their leaders thought he would be killed before he went to Israel; (2) they either viewed him as a traitor to their cause, or as the finest national leader the Arab world had ever produced; and (3) they were unanimous in recognizing his courage.

The morning of the day he spoke to the Israeli parliament I crossed into Israel from Jordan. A representative of the government of Israel met me and told me that Prime Minister Menachem Begin had reserved a seat for me in the Knesset (their parliament) that afternoon.

As I drove from the Jordanian border into Jerusalem, I saw something I never expected to see in that emotion-laden area of the world: Egyptian and Israeli flags flying side-by-side. It was an incredible sight, a virtual "miracle" which happened because of the courage and vision of one man. Sadat did one other thing that will help his country and had to impress all Arab leaders. When he returned to Cairo from Jerusalem he drove in an open car through the streets, literally millions of people cheering this man who represented peace and reconciliation.

The Arab leaders who said he would be greeted by hatred and immediate assassination were wrong. Leaders of other countries had to wonder, with a touch of jealousy, how this man could evoke love and admiration when they thought it would be so different. Will some other Arab leaders show the same courage and vision? Will Prime Minister Begin adopt policies to encourage moderation on the part of others? Will Egypt continue to follow the path and direction established by Sadat?

These questions time will answer, but in the meantime we can be grateful for having had the opportunity of watching and admiring a leader of Anwar Sadat's stature.

"Peace: The Middle East's Only Real Security," P.S./Washington, May 28–June 3, 1989

Almost every day there is unpleasant news from Israel about the violence that plagues the Israelis and the Palestinians. Israel has been our friend and ally. Israel is the most free in its practice of any of the Middle East nations. And Israel's borders provide protection for a people brutally persecuted through the centuries.

But Israel cannot long be secure in its borders unless there is peace in the region. That will not be achieved without some general sense that a fair resolution to the Israeli-Palestinian conflict can be worked out in a settlement whose outlines no one now can accurately guess.

How do we move toward such a settlement?

1. All sides must recognize that the status quo is filled with danger for everyone.

The bullets and stones and tear gas of today are reflections of hatred and fear and misunderstanding. The mini-battles of today, tragic as they are, will be supplanted by bloodshed thousands of times greater on all sides if the fear, hatred and misunderstanding continue to mount.

2. All sides must be willing to take small steps toward reconciliation and negotiation.

Sadat-type dramatic strides toward peace are not likely to occur. The major actors on the Middle East scene are generally cautious. The singular exception is a non–Middle East major player, Mikhail Gorbachev. At some point his leadership could take on a significance for Syria, but we are nowhere near that position now. That means that those who seek dramatic breakthroughs are likely to be disappointed, but those of us who are realistic should encourage the small steps that have the potential of being significant steps that vary from getting leaders to socialize with each other at dinner to concessions on the road to peace.

3. Arab leaders should recognize that Prime Minister Yitzhak Shamir of Israel has offered a potentially significant step forward.

He has said he is willing to have elections on the West Bank and in the Gaza Strip, and then will negotiate with those elected unconditionally—a word he uses carefully—for further steps toward a settlement.

4. Yasser Arafat should ask the Palestinians in the Gaza and on the West Bank to stop all violence of any kind immediately, and certainly no less than six weeks before the elections.

The hard-liners in Israel's governing coalition should be given no excuse for calling off the election. Arafat wants more significant steps than this election. None are likely to come. This is a major step for Shamir, one that offends some of the conservatives in his Likud Party.

5. Israel must be willing to accept American or other foreign observers to the election process.

The hatred and misunderstandings are so deep that many in the Arab world will question the validity of the elections. Let foreign observers, that both Arab and Israeli leaders could quietly agree upon, be present. For example, the foreign observers might be from the United States, France and Morocco. I have no question that the election Shamir talks about will be an honest election, but millions in the Middle East doubt that. Let us reassure them.

6. Once the elections have taken place, let the peace process emerge gradually, and let the people of that region make the decisions.

Once people are elected, they will have to meet with each other to determine what their goals are and how the process can evolve. When they meet with their Israeli counterparts, enough time must be spent together to get acquainted, to diminish fear, to learn their shared hopes.

The United States or the Soviet Union or the two of us together cannot dictate what emerges. The people of the Middle East must forge the product. We can help with resources, gently nudge now and then. But there will be no *Pax American* in the Middle East.

Israelis and Arabs must make the decisions and the concessions that bring the only real security the Middle East can have: Peace.

"Remarks by Senator Paul Simon," Amman, Jordan, July 16, 2001

It is a privilege to be back in Jordan again.

I first came here as a young, green journalist in 1957. I remember leaving an interview with King Hussein—the first time I met him—and then that afternoon crossing though the Old Mandelbaum Gate in Jerusalem and being met there by a representative of the Foreign Ministry of Israel who said they had heard on Jordanian radio that I had met with King Hussein. They asked if I would like to meet with Prime Minister David Ben-Gurion that afternoon. It was a remarkable day. I shall never forget it. Since that time I have had the privilege of meeting with King Hussein and other leaders of your Government on several occasions. I have known at least slightly every Israeli Prime Minister since David Ben-Gurion, and I have met with leaders of Egypt, the Sudan, Saudi Arabia, Syria, Lebanon and Chairman Arafat of the Palestinian Authority.

Is the situation in this region discouraging? Yes. Is it hopeless? No.

I happen to be a Christian by background. In this area are Muslims, Jews and Christians as well as adherent of other faiths. We must respect and understand each other. Prejudice grows out of ignorance.

Each of us can take pride in many of the things our ancestors have done, but we must improve on them. And we must look not simply to our ancestors but to our children and grandchildren and generations to come.

I have seen the quality of life in Jordan gradually improve. But Jordan and the Middle East could experience great economic growth which would be of help to this area, and to the people of the world. The people of this region can shift from showing the world how citizens of different backgrounds fight each other to showing how people from different backgrounds can come together and work for common goals. That may sound idealistic and unrealistic to some of you, but I am a person 72 years old who has observed how a small group of leaders can turn a destructive situation into a constructive situation, not only in my country but in many other areas, South Africa being one example.

Every leader in the Middle East who is at all knowledgeable understands that the region is facing some huge water problems. The problems that Jordan faces today and some of your neighbors face today, believe it or not, are minor compared to the difficulties your country will be facing in the future as you project population growth and water use.

It is of more than passing interest that in the middle of December the U.S. intelligence agencies made a report to President Bill Clinton in which they said in fifteen years the great resource problem in the world would not be oil but water. And that nations would be fighting each other over water unless farsighted steps are taken to move toward resolution of the problems. The only nation in this region that will not face increasingly severe water problems is Lebanon.

Even if tomorrow an accord were to be reached between Israel and Palestinians, and between Israel and Syria, unless constructive answers are found to the region's water problems, in ten years the region will be faced with violence over water. Jordan is to be applauded for the steps it is taking now. Your neighbors are also doing some things, but what is needed is a comprehensive plan to take you into the coming decades.

I am here as a former U.S. Senator and not as a representative of my Government but I know the key officials of my Government and I believe that what I am about to suggest is something that will appeal to them.

The late Prime Minister Rabin of Israel, who was a water engineer before he entered the military, said that if we could solve the water problem we could make a Paradise out of the Middle East. That is an exaggeration, but not a great exaggeration. The question we face is how we pull leaders together to approach this problem of water.

With bitterness now so intense, how do we move from where we are to where we could go? I believe in Jordan. Jordan could be the key player in pulling things together on water. If King Abd'ullah and the Jordanian leadership were to call on Israel, the Palestinian Authority, Syria and perhaps other countries from this region to develop a comprehensive program for water for the Middle East, I am convinced that we could get several Governments, including my own, to make substantial financial commitments to support such an endeavor.

Any comprehensive plan must address both supply and demand. In the short term Jordan can continue to minimize the water shortage through conservation, such as efforts being successfully promoted by Jordan's Ministry of Water and USAID's WEPIA program—vitally important now—but this is not a substitute for an umbrella regional plan whose urgency we must understand. The initial regional meeting has to be with top Government leaders, not engineers and technicians. There must be the dream and then put people to work to make the dream become a reality.

And one of the things that you will discover—that I have discovered in a variety of national and international settings—is that when you pull people together working on a constructive concrete goal such as seeing that the region has the life-sustaining essential of water, it can be exciting and productive far beyond the issue of water. If people learn to work together on one issue they can learn to work together on other issues. And there is no issue more urgent long-term than the issue of water. Can we guarantee success? Obviously not. But if we do not make constructive efforts along this line we can guarantee failure.

We have to learn to reach out to one another across all the artificial barriers that divide us. The issue of water is one that should unite us.

Let me add that I have been in the business of Government long enough to know that this can too easily be an item in the newspapers or on radio or television tomorrow and then quickly forgotten. This calls for leadership. Jordan can provide the leadership. It would be an exciting undertaking for you and if your leadership decided to launch such an effort, I pledge to do everything I can to help make it reality with resources from my Government and other Governments.

On a tomb in Umm Qais which I saw Saturday, these words were inscribed in stone: "To you I say, passerby: as you are I was, as I am you will be. Use life as a mortal." The question facing us: Will we use life to recall bitterness and add to our tragedies? Or will we use life to build on hopes and dreams so that future generations will look back on us and say: These were people of uncommon vision who built a better world. I urge you to build practical dreams, and if you seize this moment for leadership on water I will exert every effort to make your dreams become reality.

"REMARKS BY PAUL SIMON," JEWISH NATIONAL FUND, CHICAGO, APRIL 30, 2002

Let me inject a cautious word of optimism into the presently bleak picture in the Middle East. When I first traveled to that area as a young journalist in 1957, no Arab leader would even use the word Israel. Today Egypt and Jordan have diplomatic relations with Israel and an Arab summit has supported a resolution by the Saudi crown prince which would move all the Arab nations in that direction.

But the long-term goal of peace and stability is blocked by the agonizing and frustrating bloodshed that occurs almost daily and could so irritate the region that the long-term noble goal is engulfed in flames.

How can we move on the short-range situation effectively and at the same time not become so enmeshed in the immediate problems that we forget our long-term goals?

As one who has been in that region many times since my first visit there 45 years ago, let one friend of Israel and stability in the area make a few suggestions.

First, to my Palestinian friends:

You are losing the public relations war just as Israel is losing the public relations war, and the suicide bomber approach cannot achieve your goals. It may give some of your people temporary emotional highs but it leads nowhere.

If in place of this bloody course you were to follow the suggestion of *New York Times* columnist Tom Friedman and try the approach of non-violent resistance, as practiced by Gandhi and Martin Luther King, you would appeal to the conscience of Israel and of the world, and real dialogue could grow.

The suicide bomber approach also ignores one simple political reality: When a nation is attacked, its people rally around their leader. That is true for the United States, for Israel, and for the Palestinians. Your attacks have raised the support in Israel for Prime Minister Sharon, and their response has increased Chairman Arafat's support among the Palestinians, but the present course has no sensible exit for either people.

When you suggest, Chairman Arafat, that you cannot control every extreme action by your people, I believe that. But you can appeal for a halt to these actions, in Arabic as well as in English, in firm terms so that your people clearly understand that you mean it, and with words that also make clear that acts like suicide bombers are a threat to the future of a viable Palestinian state, which they are.

When I read on the front-page of the *New York Times* about three young Palestinian boys, one only 14, who are part of a suicide attack, the story, written from Gaza City, mentions that the boys were "armed with knives and homemade bombs that can easily be purchased on the street here." Your police may not be able to stop every suicide bomber, Chairman Arafat, but they can stop the sale of homemade bombs if you clearly direct them to do that.

If you take these small actions—yes, they are small—then meaningful dialogue can take place. I have been exhilarated by groups like "Seeds of Peace" which bring Israeli, Palestinian, Jordanian and Egyptian young people together for a shared camping experience in Maine. I invited four of them to come to speak at Southern Illinois University and when they were finished, there was not a dry eye in the audience. We can do better. On one of my last trips to Israel I had dinner at an Italian restaurant in Jerusalem with a man who has become my friend, who I helped to get out of the Soviet Union, along with his family. I asked him if he had any contact with the Palestinians in Jerusalem, where he lives, and he replied, "No. Only in business. You can't trust them." The next morning I had breakfast with two Palestinians and I asked them the same question in reverse, and I received almost the identical answer about the Israelis. Yet I know all three well enough that if I had them come together for dinner they would have become friends. Such contacts are much rarer today because of the tensions. Voices of moderation are muffled. You in the Palestinian Authority have to help change that atmosphere.

Second, to Israel's Arab neighbors:

I welcome the constructive results of your recent summit meetings. But you need to take more small steps that would also be meaningful. For one, stop paying $25,000 rewards to the families of suicide bombers. The money may be significant to the impoverished, but much more significant is your signal that such people are heroes. It appears to some of us that that gesture is an attempt to placate extremists within your nations. You do not aid stability at home by adding to instability in other countries.

I would add that small movements in the direction of freedom and democracy within your countries in the long run will aid you and stability in the Middle East. One of the reasons—not the only reason—for the close ties between the United States and Israel is that Israel is a democracy with freedom of speech and freedom of its people to publish their views and organize political parties. There are those who say that Arab nations cannot sustain democracies. I remember when they said that about Latin American nations, yet today in Latin America there is only one dictatorship remaining. Jordan is much more free than neighboring Syria. I doubt that we would have the free trade agreement with Jordan today were that not the case. Suppression of extreme ideas sometimes causes their growth. Puncture extreme ideas with truth rather than prison and the ideas eventually perish. Slow but perceptible movement toward greater freedom for your people will aid them and the region.

Third, to my friends in Israel:

The instinct to punch back when someone punches you is both natural and popular but sometimes unwise. If gestures to reduce violence by the Palestinians are taken, then reciprocal, maybe even dramatic steps of self-restraint could be taken. Such measures on your part would be prudent. Your long-term security rests with peace and stability and a normal, working relationship with your neighbors. You have almost such a relationship with Jordan today and that can happen with Palestinians, with whom you have so much in common, and eventually with your other neighbors. Your superb creative juices should be used to find practical but imaginative ways of encouraging greater understanding throughout the region.

Here in the United States, each of us can do more to foster Christian-Jewish-Muslim dialogue. In ways we cannot measure, the ripple effects of that can be felt in the far corners of the earth. And we are all enriched by such dialogue.

However, even if all these steps I have outlined are taken and the temporary problems of refugees and borders are surmounted, there is a long-term time bomb awaiting the region: the shortage of water. Israeli Foreign Minister Shimon Peres has accurately stated that water will be either a catalyst for peace or a catalyst for war.

In chairing efforts to work out differences on a variety of measures enacted by the House and Senate, and in mediating labor-management conflicts, I have learned something international negotiators have also learned: Work on something that parties in a dispute can agree upon, and then it is easier to move onto the more difficult problems. In the process of agreeing in one area, they learn to work together and then find it easier to work on other things.

I do not suggest that agreement on water will be easy, but all the nations of that region—with the exception of Lebanon—know they are facing increasingly severe water problems. Several months ago I went to Syria and Jordan at the request of the State Department to meet with government leaders there to urge their cooperation with Israel and the Palestinians on water. I would love to report that I came back and everyone has agreed to work with one another. That is not the case, because the emotional barriers are too high. But no one I talked with denied the eventual necessity of regional agreements on water.

In Amman, Jordan, population approximately 1 million, people can turn on their tap one day a week, and Jordan's population will increase by approximately one-third in the next decade.

Syria twice in the last 25 years almost went to war with its neighbors, Turkey and Iraq, over water. Damascus, a city of 3 million, did not have a water purification system until 1996. Syria's population will grow from 17 million to 23 million by 2010.

The Palestinian Authority has one of the world's highest birth rates, 5.1 percent a year. It has more severe water problems than any entity in that region, problems which will become much worse if sanity is not brought to the area.

Israel's problems are both quantity and quality. Israel has the highest standards of water quality in the Middle East, but they are not as high as in the United States or Western Europe, and the quality is deteriorating. Adequate supplies and quality water are essential to maintain a reasonably high standard of living, and if that is not maintained Israel will lose population, or at least see diminished growth, either of which could threaten Israel's security. If there are not adequate supplies and quality water available, not only is industrial development threatened, there will be an exodus of industry.

One year ago this month, the top present and past Israeli water leaders met in Herzliya and the proceedings of that conference are both informative and disturbing. One of the participants was Eliezer Cohen, a member of the Knesset. Listen to his first comments: "I arrived at the Knesset in order to deal with constitutional matters. I naively thought that the greatest danger facing Israel in the future would be the weapons of mass destruction belonging to Iraq and Iran, which may yet turn out to be the greatest danger. To my great surprise, however, I discovered that the clear and present danger to the State of Israel . . . is not weapons of mass destruction. The clear and present danger is lack of water."

Israel's two largest aquifers, the underground sources of water, are shrinking and troubled with growing saline penetration. The Sea of Galilee, the main above-ground source of water, is visibly shrinking. Israel's per capita water consumption is approximately 40 percent of that in southern California, which has a similar climate, and Palestinians' per capita water consumption is about one-third of Israel's. Both the Israeli and Palestinian numbers eventually should be permitted to rise. But how?

Complicating all of this is that if a solid peace agreement is reached, between one-third and two-thirds of the present source of Israel's water will likely be shifted to Israel's neighbors. If Syria is given the Golan Heights as four Israeli prime ministers, including Prime Minister Netanyahu, have indicated would be part of a settlement with Syria, unless solid water and sewage considerations are part of the settlement, 100,000 Syrians living on the Golan Heights could cause serious pollution to the Sea of Galilee, a major source of water for Israel. Former Israeli Water Commissioner Meir Ben Meir says that if the affluent from the Golan Heights is not properly handled it will "spell certain doom" for the Sea of Galilee.

What can be done for the water future of Israel and the area?

First, we can focus attention on the problem, as the Jewish National Fund is doing. When people are killing each other, water seems such a distant concern. We need to be looking long-term.

Second, such things as the reservoirs supported by the Jewish National Fund assist both in the short-term and long-term. Short-term answers must also include shipping water from Turkey in the large plastic bags, 5.6 million gallons per bag, that Norway is now using to ship water to Cyprus. It is expensive but necessary.

The long-term answer is desalination, the dream of former Prime Minister Yitzhak Rabin, who was a water engineer before he entered the military. He said, "Israel will be like a Garden of Eden again if we can get water inexpensively from the Mediterranean." Amos Epstein, head of Israel's Water Utility Corporation, strongly favors rapid action on desalination, and Israel has two such plants in the offing. More will be needed. But Mr. Epstein points out, "The timeframe for the establishment of a desalination plant in a proper fashion is 54 months." Saudi Arabia, which has more desalination plants than any other nation, once produced 8 percent of its own food and now is a food exporter. But Saudi Arabia has cheap energy. The Saudi example is important because Israel's Negev desert area is more than half of Israel's land, and houses only 7 percent of Israel's population. Until solar energy is more fully developed, desalinated water will be costly for Israel and for her neighbors, but much less costly than the alternative of war.

Key figures must be asked to provide leadership, and one who understands the situation well is the remarkable president of David Ben-Gurion University in Beersheba, Avishay Braverman. He is a leader whose talents should be called upon.

What can the United States do? In the current administration we have moved, in dealing with the outbreaks of violence, from "hands off" to semi-involvement. That is not good enough. We are the 800-pound gorilla in the world today and we must move with sensitivity but with firmness. The bloodshed must be stopped.

Third, we can get the nations of that region working together on planning something constructive in their mutual water problems. As I told Syrian leaders, "You participated in the Madrid talks and it did you no harm." Getting at least Israel, Jordan, Syria and the Palestinians together—perhaps with the additions of Egypt and Turkey—may not result in agreements, but it might. Even the fact that meaningful dialogue takes place is a step forward. But it will not happen without U.S. leadership.

We should also do more in the U.S. to encourage desalination research, to get the cost of this process reduced. Passage of the pending measure to reauthorize what has become known as the Simon Act for research on desalination is important to the United States and to the Middle East. Senator Dick Durbin is the chief sponsor of that legislation.

Finally, even if water agreements are worked out tomorrow between the Middle East nations, the technical monitoring of the agreements becomes increasingly important. The participants in such a conference will not trust each other's technicians. It is difficult enough to monitor river waters, but following the flow and supply of underground sources is much more difficult. We need international technicians, perhaps based in the World Bank, who can provide neutral but necessary assistance, not only in the Middle East but in other areas of tension around the globe.

The cause of Israel and the cause of peace are inseparable. We need to pursue both. And the sooner we recognize the importance of water, the sooner we will move toward achieving our goals.

WATER CRISIS AND CONFLICTS

"WATER: THE NEXT CRISIS," P.S./WASHINGTON, JUNE 14–20, 1981

We get so absorbed in today's crisis that we sometimes forget that there are some long-range things we should be working on more aggressively. One of these, which will bring tremendous changes for the better, is the development of an inexpensive process for converting salt water to fresh water.

When that happens the deserts of the United States will blossom, as they will in North Africa and elsewhere. And in trouble spots like the Middle East tempers can be reduced at least a little, for almost lost in all of the other stories from the Middle East is the reality that part of the tensions there are caused by water problems.

We are headed for some major water problems, particularly in the West, unless this seawater source is developed. Today's headlines are about oil; 10 years from now the headlines are likely to be about water. Even in relatively water-rich Southern Illinois, we will see more and more farms irrigating; we have a few doing it now. After every dry year we have, there will be more farms joining the ranks.

There are four basic methods of desalting water, and the United States has put a total of $320 million into one of these processes called distillation. There is a general feeling that this process is too expensive to be practical in most situations, and the other three processes are being examined.

This year two demonstration plants for other methods will start in Almagorod, New Mexico and Virginia Beach, Virginia. Tentatively a third project is scheduled for Louisiana in 1983.

Desalting, however, is not some vague thing that might or might not work in the future. It is working now, but is too expensive to be practical in most situations. There are over 1500 desalting plants in operation around the world. And that number will grow rapidly if we can improve the desalting process. That takes research. And research costs money, unfortunately.

Within the United States we now produce 100 million costly gallons of fresh water a day out of salt water. But we consume many billions of gallons of water each day.

All nations have a stake in making progress. The United States is working with Mexico and with Israel on specific projects. And many other nations are doing research. When the day arrives that somewhere a breakthrough is achieved and an inexpensive process is developed for converting salt water to fresh water, it will be one of the most important stories of the century—yet it will probably not be on the front page of most newspapers.

"Are We Running Dry?," *Parade Magazine*, August 23, 1998

"By the gift of water you nourish and sustain all living things." These are the words used in the baptismal rite in Lutheran services. But in our world, increasing numbers of people cannot assume they will be nourished and sustained. Within a few years, a water crisis of catastrophic proportions will explode on us—unless aroused citizens in this and other nations demand of their leadership actions reflecting vision, understanding and courage.

It is no exaggeration to say that the conflict between humanity's growing thirst and the projected supply of usable, potable water could result in the most devastating natural disaster since history has been recorded accurately, unless something happens to stop it.

The world's population of 5.9 billion will double in the next 50 to 90 years, depending on whose estimates you accept. Our renewable water supply, however, is constant. Compounding those grim realities is the fact that per capita water consumption is rising twice as fast as the world's population. You do not have to be an Einstein to understand that we are headed toward a potential calamity.

Wally N'Dow of Gambia, whom the *Los Angeles Times* describes as "the world's foremost specialist on cities," says bluntly: "In the past 50 years, nations have gone to war over oil. In the next 50, we are going to go to war over water. The crisis point is going to be 15 to 20 years from now."

Nations fight over oil, but valuable as it is, there are substitutes for oil. There is no substitute for water. We die quickly without water, and no nation's leaders would hesitate to battle for adequate water supplies. A decade ago, U.S. intelligence services identified 10 potential flashpoints where war could break out over water. I no longer have access to that type of information since leaving the Senate, but I know the number is higher today and will be much higher a decade from now. At least 400 million people live in regions with severe water shortages. By the year 2050, it will be 4 billion.

There are more than 200 river basins in the world that are shared by at least two countries. More than a dozen nations get most of their water from rivers that cross borders of neighboring countries which can be viewed as hostile. Even when nations are on the best of terms, like Canada and the U.S., there are serious disagreements over water-sharing issues. While we and our northern neighbor manage our problems without resorting to arms, who can say what will happen in the Middle East, where there are no water surpluses and where the relationships between countries are stormy?

Although water sufficiency problems are not nearly as severe in the United States as in most nations, three of the fastest-growing states—California, Texas and Florida—feel the squeeze on water supplies and soon will face major difficulties. As of 1996, five of the 10 fastest-growing cities in the U.S. are in those states. It is significant that all three states, like many parts of the globe with serious shortages, have at their doorsteps huge amounts of water that still are too expensive to modify for major consumption purposes: seawater.

California. Like most of the world, California has water in abundance where people are not in abundance. Three-fourths of its snow and rain fall in the northern part of the state, where one-third of the people live. Every official California water plan projects a huge gap between need and supply. California's population will grow from 31 million today to somewhere between 48 million and 60 million in less than 40 years.

Symbolic of California's problems is the story of Owens Lake. Early in this century, Los Angeles–area water authorities understood that they'd face problems as the population grew, so they purchased the third-largest body of water in the state, Owens Lake. Today it is called Owens Dry Lake, because L.A. has sucked it dry. But the story does not end there. When the wind blows on a dry day, particulate matter from the "lake" is sent into the air to the point that, in some places, it is 20 times as high as the maximum safety standards for air pollution. The Environmental Protection Agency rates this area the most polluted in the nation for dust particles. People in the area want Los Angeles to fill the lake again, but city officials say that would require 10 percent of their water, something they cannot afford.

Just last month, the Los Angeles Department of Water and Power finally agreed to begin a project to ensure that the air around the lake meets federal health standards by 2006. The lake will not be refilled, but 10 square miles may be covered with a few inches of water to hold down the dust, according to a *Los Angeles Times* report.

Florida. In some ways, Florida's problems are similar to California's: shortages, despite water at its doorstep (a desalination process is in use, but it's in its infancy); mushrooming population, with a larger rate of growth than California's but a much smaller body of land; and problems with drainage and irrigation.

Florida's developed a plan in 1995 for the state's five water-management districts. The foreword to the plan summarizes the situation: "In many areas of the state, the prospects for new . . . inexpensive, clean sources of water no longer exist." The report notes that here are "both quality and quantity problems." It adds, "Ninety percent of the state's population depends on groundwater, and the groundwater is highly susceptible to contamination from . . . municipal landfills, hazardous waste dumps, septic tanks and agricultural pesticides."

Texas. Part of the problem in Texas, as in many other places, is the huge disparity in rainfall statewide. El Paso normally gets about 8 inches of rain a year, while the portion of the state along the Louisiana border receives 56 inches. Aquifers (underground water sources) are being depleted. From 1930 to 1980, water use increased twice as fast as the population. As has become painfully apparent this year, Texas has a greater likelihood of suffering severe drought than most other states. As of July, rainfall was at least 10 inches below normal in most of the rest of the state. What can be done to solve the water problem? Obviously, it's a complex and difficult issue. Once we muster the political will to focus on it, these broad areas should be addressed.

1. CONSERVATION. Conserving what we have is an immediate step we can take.

2. DESALINATION. Efforts to convert seawater to usable water must be supported, and more must be begun.

3. POLLUTION AND OVERPOPULATION. Both are big contributors to water shortages.

"WATER SHORTAGE A REAL PROBLEM UNLESS WE PLAN," *CHICAGO SUN-TIMES*, APRIL 6, 2000

Here's a bit of non-sensational news that could affect you and your children's future. Reuters reported that former Soviet leader Mikhail Gorbachev told a meeting in the Netherlands that the Middle East could face a war over water in the coming decade if sensible answers are not found quickly. He had just been to the Middle East and met with Jordan's King Abdullah, Israeli Prime Minister Ehud Barak, and Yasser Arafat, president of the Palestinian Authority.

Gorbachev relayed their message: "All the leaders said that if nothing changes, with the next 10 to 15 years there will be a conflict [over water]." What does that have to do with your future? A great deal, because the water crisis toward which we are heading involves much more than the Middle East.

- About 300 million people live in areas of serious to severe water shortage. The World Bank says 25 years from now, *3 billion* will live in these areas.
- In the next 50 to 90 years, the world's population will double or come close to doubling, while our water supply is constant. You don't need to be an Einstein to understand that spells trouble. Nations go to war over oil, but there are substitutes for oil. There is no substitute for water.
- International turmoil over water will harm the United States—at a minimum economically. As nations struggle and their economies dip, ours does, too.
- The United States is fortunate. We are 4 percent of the world population and we have 8 percent of its fresh water. But the Metropolitan Water District of Southern California says that by 2010, it will be able to meet only 43 percent of the water needs of the 16 million people it serves.

Texas, Florida, Nevada, Arizona and a few other states also will face serious problems. How does that affect the Chicago area? Instability in the world has unpredictable spinoffs. Whether your children will be fighting somewhere in the world, or trying to maintain peace, no one knows, but the likelihood is growing. The Chicago area already is under a court order limiting water consumption from Lake Michigan.

Complicating this immensely is that the water-poor areas of the nation, particularly the Southwest, will want some of our water. And if you hope to get a bill passed in the U.S. Senate to help some Illinois project, your senators will have to help the Southwest.

What is needed is long-range planning—now. We can predict with some accuracy where problems will erupt. For example, Egypt gets 98 percent of its water from the Nile. Eighty-five percent of the Nile comes from Ethiopia, which will double its population in the next 20 years. Egypt and Ethiopia are on a collision course—unless we act soon.

What should we do?

Conserve water. That means repairing broken water and sewer pipes in older cities all over the world. It means much greater reuse of water.

Clean our water. The United States has the highest water standards in the world, but in some places that is not high enough. The world's aquifers are being depleted, and as their quantity goes down, the same amount of fertilizer and industrial waste becomes more lethal.

Encourage family planning in developing nations. This should not be controversial. Our laws prohibit any U.S. funding for abortions. Increase family planning, and you decrease abortions. The population projections are grim, but almost all nations see the need for family planning. The reality: More people use more water.

Push research and development of desalinated water. Ninety-seven percent of the world's water is salt water. For the remaining 3 percent, two-thirds is in icebergs and snow. Desalinated water is inexpensive enough to use for household purposes, but 85 percent of water used in the world is for agricultural irrigation and industry.

The United States is the military and economic and research giant in the world. Will we lead on this before crises overwhelm us? The answer may rest in your hands. An election year is a great time to communicate your concern.

"Water Problems Will Be the Cause of War in the Middle East," Commentary, *Chicago Tribune*, October 9, 2001

As the after-shock of Sept. 11 slowly wears off, we ask ourselves what lessons can be learned. Our intelligence operations were massively deficient, but that doesn't explain why terrorists targeted the United States.

The answer to that is complicated. Part is simply the spread of our culture, everything from McDonald's to pornographic videos. They produce both envy and resentment. Twisted minds seize small symbols and exaggerate them.

In an interview with ABC-TV two years ago, Osama bin Laden mentioned two concerns: U.S. actions in Somalia and the Palestinian-Israeli struggle.

He failed to note that the U.S. went to Somalia to stop massive starvation in a Muslim nation. It was the senior George Bush's finest hour, even though that is not where public opinion places it today. When 18 U.S. armed forces personnel died and one soldier could be seen on TV being dragged through the streets, leaders of Congress demanded that we pull our troops out of Somalia. The lesson to terrorists, some of us warned, would be to kill a few Americans and we would collapse. Bin Laden noted in his interview that "the American soldiers are paper tigers. After a few blows, they ran in defeat." Americans must realize that working for a stable world is not risk-free. If we are unwilling to take risks, other nations are also less likely to take risks.

Bin Laden also referred to the Middle East situation, a sensitive topic in the Muslim world. The early (and later abandoned) hands-off policy of this administration did no favor to the Israelis or the Palestinians, nor did it improve our image in the Muslim world.

Here is an example where U.S. intervention could serve some good.

A few weeks ago I went to Jordan and Syria at the request of the State Department to talk to the leaders of those two nations about the possibility of working together with Israel and the Palestinians on that area's increasingly crucial issue of water.

Residents of Amman, the capital of Jordan, can turn their tap water on only one day a week. Syria faces problems almost as severe, and Israel has had to curtail water use dramatically.

Looking at the Mideast population projections, the situation will get much worse. Water is a time bomb and Israeli and Arab leaders know it. No nation there (with the exception of Lebanon) can solve its own water problems. The approach has to be regional. They know that.

I appealed to Jordan and Syria to consider working with Israel and the Palestinians on water, a suggestion that did not receive an enthusiastic welcome, particularly in Syria. If the nations could work together on one issue they know will become much more severe, everyone would benefit. If you could get them cooperating on water it would be at least possible—not guaranteed—that they would work together on other issues.

The Bush administration can take two positive steps:

First, convene a meeting in Geneva or some neutral spots of the nations involved, plus the European Union, to plan long-term water answers. Desalination plants will be a major part of the solution—expensive, but much less costly than one day of war.

Second, whatever agreements are reached should be monitored by an international team of technical experts. Monitoring river flows, and particularly aquifer details, requires expertise. The Bush administration can work with the World Bank to create such a body of experts.

By itself, taking this positive action will not stop future terrorists. But it is one piece in a mosaic toward peace in the Middle East and it can help build a better image of the United States.

IRAQ AND AFGHANISTAN

"Afghanistan Is Not Nicaragua,"
P.S./Washington, February 16–22, 1986

Someone asked me a good question: "Isn't it inconsistent for you to help lead the effort to aid the Freedom Fighters in Afghanistan but to oppose aid to the Contras in Nicaragua?"

My stand may appear to be inconsistent, but if you examine the facts carefully those two positions provide the basis for a consistent and sound policy. Let's look at the facts.

Afghanistan was invaded by a foreign power, the Soviet Union, and there is no question that the huge majority of people in Afghanistan resent and resist that foreign occupation.

In Nicaragua we are supporting a civil war action designed to overthrow the government. There was no invasion. The Sandinistas who run the government are not Boy Scouts and are not universally popular, but apparently more popular than the Contras whom we support. Helping people who are resisting an invasion is very different from getting enmeshed in a civil war.

In the case of Afghanistan the overwhelming opinion of the world, as expressed by the United Nations vote, is opposed to the Soviet occupation. Even two of the communist nations have supported resolutions condemning the Soviets and urging withdrawal. Our limited efforts on behalf of the Afghan refugees and the Freedom Fighters are supported by world opinion.

What we are doing in Nicaragua is supported by virtually no one. Democratic nations of Latin America think we are making a mistake. The CIA publishes a pamphlet on how to assassinate leaders there and mines the Nicaraguan harbor, both violations of international law that embarrass us. When we announced an economic boycott of Nicaragua, even El Salvador (on whose behalf we are theoretically doing this) criticized our actions.

About a year ago the State Department asked me to speak to a group of educators from around the world gathered in Washington. Before I spoke I asked if there were any there from Nicaragua, and two men raised their hands. I asked them to stay for a moment after my remarks and then I asked these two, "What should the United States be doing in Nicaragua?" Both said they did not like the Sandinistas, but added, "but we like the Contras even less. Don't send down your weapons that are killing us. Let us solve our problems ourselves."

Last year 6,000 Nicaraguans—mostly innocent civilians—were killed in the struggle between the Contras and the government troops. What did the United States get out of it? A black eye. We reaffirmed in Latin America an already prevailing opinion that Uncle Sam is a bully and an exploiter, insensitive to local opinion.

In Afghanistan we are sending a message to the Soviets not to invade other countries. That is particularly important when you look at Iran, where instability may reign after the Ayatollah's repressive regime passes from the scene. I want the Soviets to get a message through Afghanistan: no invasions. In Nicaragua we are playing into the hands of the communists, confirming what they say about us.

The Democratic nations of Latin America have offered to negotiate a settlement in Nicaragua that guarantees no foreign troops and equipment in that country—ours or anyone else's. Why not accept that offer to negotiate? Instead we are resisting. Every day we continue our present policy in Nicaragua we add to the propaganda arsenal of the Marxists.

Finally, we should recognize one other reality: if we want to overthrow governments we don't like, that's about two-thirds of the governments on the face of the earth. We have plenty of problems without launching into that. Let's attack hunger and illiteracy and the things that Marxism breeds upon. When there are invasions, let us support the people who resist them. But let's stay out of civil wars.

More than two centuries ago the English philosopher, Thomas Hobbes, wrote: "Prudence in the conduct of peace or war is power." In Nicaragua our country is not being prudent. We are eroding our power.

"Needed: A Clear, Firm, and Open Policy," P.S./Washington, July 31–August 6, 1988

There is a fundamental question the United States has not faced, and because we do not face it our foreign policy has been much more stumbling, and much less effective, than it should be. That question is: Should we try to overthrow governments we do not like?

If we accept that role we will have our hands full. Approximately two-thirds of the governments of the world have either foreign policies with which we disagree strongly or domestic human rights policies which we oppose. Because we have not faced that fundamental question, our policies have caused senseless bloodshed and loss of resources in spots as far-ranging as Nicaragua and Angola. The answer to the question should be a clear, firm, and open policy *not* to try to overthrow governments we do not like, with only one exception: When a nation has been invaded.

In Afghanistan we have provided aid to the rebels because there was a clear-cut violation of the sovereignty of that nation by invading outside forces of the Soviet Union. The message to all countries should be clear: No invasions.

What has our over-involvement in Central America, and specifically in Nicaragua, cost? The loss of well over $1 billion, and infinitely more important, the needless loss of about 6,000 lives a year. And what has it achieved? The Sandinistas have become more repressive, using as an excuse U.S. military support of the Contras.

Now we face the same question in Angola. The United States has cozied up to South Africa and aided the rebel forces of Jonas Savimbi because, we said, Cuban troops are in Angola. The irony is that the Cuban troops have been guarding oil refineries owned by U.S. corporations, protecting them from rebel forces armed by the United States. But now an agreement is near calling for withdrawal of Cuban troops. And what is the position of the United States? We say we will continue to supply arms to the forces trying to overthrow the government, even if Cuban troops are withdrawn.

The original cause will have disappeared, but by force of habit we say we will continue the supply of arms, and by that very statement make it less likely that Cuban troops will be withdrawn and a settlement reached. Because our policy is not clear, in any country where there are problems, local leaders can shout, "It's the CIA." And we have done enough foolish things around the earth that that shout—usually inaccurate—sounds plausible.

The United States' image suffers needlessly as a result. If our policy were clear and unambiguous on not overthrowing governments, and we would use the resources now used on weapons to feed the hungry and provide opportunity to the less fortunate, our political standing in the world would be considerably enhanced.

I want a good intelligence service. I served in the intelligence corps during my Army years. I want the CIA to provide the finest possible information for our government. But I don't want them involved in overthrowing other governments.

And where governments follow policies with which we strongly disagree, as in South Africa, let us use economic and politically creative means—not arms—to change that policy and ask other nations to join us in using our collective muscle to achieve change.

President Carter stressed human rights, and while a few snickered at his sometimes pious-sounding sermons on human rights, the word spread everywhere, and his leadership has had a solid, if not dramatic, effect. In South America today there remain only three dictatorships. In Africa, there is solid, quiet movement toward greater human rights in many nations, almost unnoticed. In contrast, our arms shipments to rebel armies like Savimbi's have profited a few in the arms business in this country—but at the cost of lives and U.S. prestige abroad.

Our political failure is caused by our unwillingness to confront the basic question: Should the United States be involved in overthrowing governments we don't like? The Senate, the House and the two candidates for president should confront that question.

"Now the Really Tough Job: Winning the Peace,"
P.S./Washington, March 10–16, 1991

The war to free Kuwait is over. Now we must win the peace, in some ways a more difficult task than winning the war. Saddam Hussein was a disaster as a military leader, but he managed to convey to many in the Moslem world that he was the true Moslem and Arab leader who was standing up to the Christian/Jewish West. He actually belongs to a secular group, but his speeches took on a religious ring that lacked genuineness to those who knew his background, as too few did.

Anti-U.S. demonstrations took place in most Moslem countries. The United States comes out of the war with problems in that part of the world, with the exception of those Moslem nations that actively supported us. Fortunately, some of these nations are in the immediate area where peace and stability must be created.

A few Arab leaders have hinted publically that after this war a peace accord with Israel should be developed. More Arab leaders have whispered that quietly, and whether they will stand up with courage at the appropriate time, we may soon discover.

I have urged Secretary of State James Baker to approach the situation much as you would a labor-management struggle. First, get the two sides to agree on some things, establishing trust, and then move on to the more difficult issues after an element of understanding has been created. How can that be done? Let me suggest this scenario:

First, encourage Israel and the Arab nations to work together on finding less expensive ways of converting salt water to fresh water. The most explosive long-term problem in the Middle East is water. They all know that.

Egypt, for example, lives on 4 percent of its land. As the population of Egypt mushrooms, Egypt's water supply stays the same. That obviously is a volatile situation.

In my trip to Saudi Arabia, Israel and Egypt in December, the leaders of those countries talked much more about water than about oil.

On water, we should be able to get Israel and all the Arab nations working together.

Second, Israel and the Arab nations have a common interest in agreeing on a system for a verifiable method of eliminating nuclear, chemical and biological weapons from that area of the world.

Third, President Bush should name someone of the stature of former Secretary of State George Shultz as a roving ambassador who will devote full time to the search for peace and reconciliation in the Middle East.

If we can encourage Israel and the Arab nations to work on building trust and reducing fears of each other, then we can move to the more difficult problem of people and territory: the Palestinian question. To jump to the toughest question first probably is not wise. But succeeding will take aggressive leadership by the United States. If we provide leadership for war, but not for peace, we will have dishonored the memory of those courageous people who fought this war.

"Iraq," NPR Commentary, September 30, 2002

The most momentous political decision in my memory will be made soon, whether or not to invade Iraq. Until now we have said to those with nuclear or chemical or biological weapons, if you use them on others there will be massive retaliation. Up to this point that has worked. The current administration apparently has given up on that approach. My reasons for belief that is unwise are:

1. If the United States can launch an attack on another nation, what is to stop other nations from picking on their most favorite targets? We open the world to arms chaos.

2. Saying that we are launching a preemptive strike to stop possible abuse by Saddam Hussein puts us on thin ice. What if the Chicago police said they were going to move in and kill someone widely disliked because they think he might kill someone else? Such Police Department action would be properly denounced. Under international law, a preemptive strike is permitted only if the nation is under the imminent threat of attack. We cannot claim that.

3. If our aim is to stop those with ties to Osama bin Laden, Syria has more ties than Iraq and also has chemical and biological weapons, and a dictator. Should we invade Syria? Should we invade other nations that have chemical and biological weapons?

4. If our aim is to prevent the use of chemical and biological weapons, we are likely to provoke their use by such military action. Invade Saddam Hussein's Iraq and he will use every weapon at his command to defend himself.

5. If our aim is to stop terrorism—almost forgotten in the current debate—we should remember that an invasion of Iraq would be massively unpopular around the world. One million Americans live outside our borders and millions more travel abroad each year. Just as certain as you hear these words, an invasion of Iraq will mean the deaths of some innocent Americans outside our borders.

6. One published report says that there is a Pentagon study showing that 20,000 to 30,000 American casualties would be "acceptable." No mention is made about how many innocent Iraqis might be killed. The Vietnam War became unpopular. But initially it had strong public support—much stronger support than the proposed invasion of Iraq has. And even though the polls show 72 percent of the American public supporting an invasion, those figures will plummet when the casualty figures start coming in.

Finally, the other evening I read a statement by General Douglas MacArthur who said that once a war is started no one can control what will happen. Using our military muscle against this dictator is temporarily popular. Using our head to oppose him with non-military means is the wiser course of action.

"The Prohibitive Costs of War against Iraq" (with former Congressman Paul Findley), unpublished, February 2003

In preparing the nation for a war against Iraq, President Bush charts a course fraught with dangers for humanity and prohibitive costs for the American people. We appeal to him to drop plans for war and substitute humane but tough measures of containment.

Even if weapons of mass destruction exist in Iraq, the inevitable costs of war far exceed any possible benefits. From our long experience as members of the foreign relations committees of Congress and subsequent study we suggest:

The cost in human life and limb will be great no matter how "surgical" the air strikes and other bombardment may be. If past is prologue, the full toll, like the carnage of civilians in the Gulf War, will be kept from public awareness. U.S. casualties may be relatively small, but a great number of human beings—mostly Muslims—will be torn to shreds. Their homes and dreams will be destroyed and vast areas permanently blighted.

Muslims everywhere feel a sense of kinship. Just as Christians and Jews and Hindus do. The agony suffered by Iraqi civilians will outrage millions worldwide, including roughly 1.2 billion other Muslims, about five million of them U.S. citizens. This will widen and deepen the ugly gulf that, thanks partly to government profiling and unofficial but senseless bigotry, already exists between Muslims and the U.S. government.

Innocent U.S. civilians will suffer too. More than one million Americans live and work abroad. An invasion of Iraq will stir anti-American protests so severe throughout the world that some U.S. citizens are certain to be casualties. The action by a U.S. plane destroying an automobile in Yemen that apparently included a terrorist was soon followed by the slaying of U.S. Baptist medical missionaries serving in that country. If the U.S. starts a war, retaliation will be repeated many times.

Preparations for war have already severely damaged America's reputation as a champion of the rule of law. At the President's request, Congress has abandoned our government's longstanding opposition to preemptive acts of war, measures that are strictly prohibited in international law except when a nation is under imminent danger of attack. We see no evidence that Iraq poses an imminent threat to the United States or any nation.

War should be reserved as an act of last resort. The new policy trivializes war by making it an easy instrument of presidential power. No nation can now consider itself fully protected by international law from sudden attack from abroad. Other nations will feel free to engage in preemptive war making, and the world will descend into the law of the jungle.

Years ago, the Soviet Union presented a much greater threat to the United States and to other nations than Iraq does today. At the time, some American leaders called for "preventive war." In 1950, Secretary of the Navy Francis Matthews said in a speech that the United States must be prepared "to pay any price, even the price of instituting a war to compel cooperation for peace." In response, President Harry Truman said, "There is nothing more foolish than to think that war can be stopped by war. You don't prevent anything but peace." The firm but cool decisions of Presidents Truman and Dwight Eisenhower and their successors gave the world stability and a greater chance for peace. We should also consider:

The war's financial cost will be enormous. If military operations begin, they may last for years. Administration officials estimate the immediate cost ranging from $50 billion to $200 billion. History suggests it will be close to the higher figure. This estimate comes at a time when the federal budget deficit is growing and governments at all levels struggle to continue critical social services.

A stated goal of the administration is to keep Saddam Hussein from using weapons of mass destruction, but a U.S. attack may actually provoke him into using them. If cornered, he is apt to fight back with every weapon at his command.

Perhaps the greatest costs will be inflicted on America internally. In our quest for security against terrorist acts by the Iraqi dictator and others, we already sustain heavy costs: the impairment of individual liberty, personal privacy, and due process. If we go to war, these costs will keep rising.

President Bush should cancel war plans, stop war talks, disenthrall himself from his past declarations, and announce that the work of the UN inspectors in Iraq should continue indefinitely and so should firm sanctions against the delivery there of war material. He should recognize that our attempts at imposing broad economic sanctions have backfired in Iraq as they have in Cuba. We must learn from history. Unless all nations join in imposing such sanctions, they hurt only innocent civilians and strengthen the group of dictators. They have actually kept Fidel Castro in power for more than forty years while imposing hardships on the Cuban people. The Iraqi experience is similar.

If the president is serious about toppling Saddam Hussein, he should stop attempting broad sanctions and give close attention to insensitivity to the Muslim world that sometimes breeds anti-American violence.

If, as we fervently hope, the president calls off war plans, some people may accuse him of weakness. If so, he can find comfort in the example of President John F. Kennedy in the wake of the Bay of Pigs invasion in 1961. Kennedy won instant respect by accepting full personal responsibility for the debacle. Then, buoyed by a surprising rise in popularity, he moved confidently to other presidential challenges. We believe the American people will always respect and strongly support a leader who changes course in order to avoid an error in policy.

OTHER NATIONS

"Korea: We Need Patience and Firmness,"
P.S./Washington, August 31–September 6, 1975

People who have somehow attached to themselves the title "foreign observer" (always a more impressive designation than "someone who talks about foreign policy") appear to agree that the two spots which could cause a third world war are the Middle East and Korea.

Along with 10 Congressional colleagues, I visited Korea last month, and I came away with impressions that are not particularly startling, but important to my attitude and my vote.

Korea—like the Middle East—is important beyond the country itself because here there is a meeting of four major powers: China, the Soviet Union, Japan and the United States. Unlike Vietnam and unlike our experience in Korea two decades ago, if a war started now it would be difficult to contain. South Korea is unlike South Vietnam in other ways:

1. The people of South Korea are united as South Vietnam never was in strong opposition to a takeover by North Korea. If war starts here it will not be a civil war, but naked aggression.

2. There are 41,000 U.S. troops in South Korea and major U.S. bases. If a war breaks out, we are immediately involved. We do not have the choice Vietnam presented to us.

3. South Korea is booming economically. There is a substantial middle income group and the results of the prosperity, while not spread evenly, have lifted the level of income of almost all Koreans.

But South Korea has problems, and its biggest problem is a neighbor to the north with sizeable military strength, with troops poised just 25 miles from Seoul, the capital of South Korea. A second problem—one we discussed frankly in our almost four hour meeting with the President of South Korea—is civil liberties. While there is much greater freedom than in Communist North Korea, there are serious deficiencies by U.S. standards.

How can we avoid turning Korea into a war zone once again?

The answer is to continue for a few years our U.S. troop presence and our commitment to use U.S. air and naval power if South Korea is invaded. So long as we keep that commitment solid, it is unlikely North Korea will attack. If Kim Il-Sung, the leader of the North, understands that U.S. naval and air power will be at the side of South Korea if there is an invasion, there is not likely to be a miscalculation on his part. If he misreads our evacuation from Vietnam as a retreat into isolationism—and the withdrawal of troops from the South might signal that to him—then there would be a danger of war.

Two years ago I would have supported withdrawal of some of our troops from Korea and Western Europe—and 3 or 5 years from now I may do it too. But right now the world needs to see some patience and firmness on our part.

What about the problem of freedom in South Korea?

We should continue to let officials there know—as our delegation did—that we are concerned about civil liberties. But we should do it quietly and effectively, and with some sensitivity to their nearness to enemy forces. If we have Soviet troops 25 miles from Washington, we might be doing some things we would not be proud of later (as we did with Japanese Americans in WWII.

We cannot expect nations without our traditions to suddenly share all of our attitudes—nor do we want others to become little models of the U.S. But we can express concern about the jailing of opposition leaders, about our beliefs in freedom. If that message is to be effective it should not be too self-righteous, and it should come as a friend speaking to a friend.

"Panama: The Panama Canal Treaty—It Makes Defense Sense," P.S./Washington, August 28–September 3, 1977

The headline in the Salem (Illinois) *Times-Commoner* reads: "Poll Indicates Salemites Oppose U.S. Giving Away Panama Canal." The sub-head reads: "Carter to Appeal to People for Giveaway Treaty." Salem is the county seat of one of the large counties in my district and if the question is posed as that newspaper did it, to the people in my district or anywhere else, the results will be the same. But let me ask the question differently: "Do you believe this nation should follow the advice of U.S. military leaders on the only practical way to keep the canal open, a treaty with Panama?" My guess is that the answer might be different from the people of Salem.

We are not observing a movie with the villains on one side and the heroes on the other. We are making a fundamental decision about the security of the United States, and I hope enough of my colleagues in the Senate and the House—and enough of the people in the nation—will look at the hard facts, and make a decision based on facts.

Here are a few questions and answers that I hope will be helpful:

What is our main interest in Panama?

It is to keep the canal open. While the canal cannot take the largest ships, it continues to be important to the United States and other nations. *Don't we have a treaty that gives us the right to stay there?*

Yes, there is a treaty, but it is not one we can be proud of. As conservative columnist James J. Kilpatrick wrote the other day, it "is a matter of national shame." Panama was created as a nation (formerly part of Columbia) through a revolution with our indirect help. Fifteen days after the revolution, a French citizen seeking personal enrichment signed a treaty for Panama with the

United States which gave us the Canal Zone. As a form of apology, a few years later the United States paid Columbia $25 million, as a gesture of good will.

Interestingly, "The Great Commoner" William Jennings Bryan, who was born in Salem, Illinois and for whom the newspaper there is named, called our seizure of property in Panama "immoral." While creation of the canal was a great feat, the treaty itself is not one we can be proud of. But even if the treaty were valid, that was more than 70 years ago, and we have to recognize that colonialism is now dead. We cannot take a string of land through the middle of another country and expect that country to like it.

What do our top military leaders believe?

Not only is the new treaty supported by the Joint Chiefs of Staff, but both publicly and privately by all the top U.S. military people in Panama. I went there about one and one-half years ago and met with Lt. Gen. McNair and all the top Army, Navy and Air Force people. I spent enough time with them to get their candid views. They feel that for us to fail to work out a treaty would invite the closing of the canal.

How many nations favor the United States keeping the canal?

None.

The shippers have the most at stake economically. What do they favor?

The organization which represents the largest number of shippers favors a treaty. They recognize that without a treaty there may be no canal.

Doesn't Panama have a military dictatorship?

Yes they do, unfortunately. We have to deal with the facts as they are, not as we would like them to be. But it has been a stable regime. They have had fewer changes of leadership in recent years than we have.

Is there a danger that we would play into the hands of the Communists by having a treaty?

One of the persons I visited in Panama was the top Roman Catholic churchman, Archbishop Marcos McGrath. He said that nothing could play into the hands of the Communists and other extremists more than our failure to have a treaty. It is worth noting that in Panama the Communist elements now oppose the treaty and in the United States some very conservative elements oppose the treaty. It is an interesting partnership. It is also interesting to note that the Republic of Panama does not recognize either the Soviet Union or mainland China, and judging by that flimsy standard we are more of a "Communist" nation than they are.

Why would the canal be in danger if a treaty is not agreed to?

Earth slides now close the canal occasionally. More than 75 percent of the 13,000 people who work on the canal are Panamanians. Any one of them with a hand grenade can close the canal. The territory is tropi-cal, with terrains like Vietnam. If Monday morning quarterbacks here believe we can keep the canal open despite the feelings of the people in Panama, they are living in a dream world. We could try, but it would mean the blood of Americans—including those from Southern Illinois—and Panamanians spilled needlessly. And the chance of success would be slim.

Who supports a treaty?

Among the supporters of a treaty are not only President Carter and for-mer President Ford, but conservatives like Senator Barry Goldwater and columnist William Buckley and liberals like Senator Hubert Humphrey. There are, however, many who conscientiously oppose the treaty, and the vote in Congress probably will be close.

One final word.

Whether we like it or not, the United States is the leader of the free world. If we take a position of refusing to give back their own land to the people of Panama by the year 2000, our effectiveness in leading the world will be hampered.

From any logical viewpoint, we should move ahead as our nation's lead-ers ask. But emotions are strong on this and whether the sensible answer emerges we will know in about six months.

"COMMUNICATING WITH VIETNAM," P.S./WASHINGTON, AUGUST 13–19, 1978

"You don't realize how horrible war is until you think: just a few years ago we were fighting those men who sat in our living room." That was the obser-vation of my 17-year-old daughter Sheila who sat in on a meeting between some Vietnamese and U.S. officials which took place in our home recently. I hope the results of that meeting will be good for our country.

When I served for a five-week period at the President's request at the special United Nations session on disarmament, I made it a point to meet as many people from as many nations as possible. One day Congressman William Lehman of Florida and I had lunch with the Vietnamese delegates and we talked about the relationship between our countries.

Up to that point Vietnam had talked about a commitment they felt they had from President Richard Nixon to provide $3 billion in aid, and their position had been that they would not enter into any type of diplomatic exchange with the United States without payment of that aid.

But at the luncheon which we had with the Vietnamese, for the first time they did not talk about any requirements for aid in order to have a diplomatic exchange. We talked about everything from developing oil in Vietnam by U.S. businesses to selling soybeans from Southern Illinois to Vietnam. (Interestingly, Japan is now aggressively pursuing trade with Vietnam.)

I asked them if we invited them to an informal meeting in Washington with some members of Congress and representatives of our government whether they would be interested in exploring our relationship further. They said they might, that they would have to check with Hanoi. I had to check with our State Department before I could extend the invitation because the Vietnamese are limited to 25 miles from a spot in New York City by U.S. regulation, since we do not recognize their government. The State Department said that a waiver of the regulation would be granted if it was requested.

I then conveyed an invitation to a dinner meeting at our home, which they accepted. Those who met were two officials of the State Department, Representative G. V. Montgomery (Democrat of Mississippi), Millicent Fenwick (Republican of New Jersey), Berkley Bedell (Democrat of Iowa), Stephen Solarz (Democrat of New York), Senator George McGovern of South Dakota and Pham Duong and Cu Dinh Ba, top officials from the Vietnamese mission at the UN.

We had a frank conversation, covering everything from U.S. concerns about those who have been reported as missing in action, to the possibilities of trade and investment. One point of discussion was the report which has been circulating that the Soviets would like to take over the American-built naval base at Cam Ranh Bay and use it as a Soviet naval base. It is obviously in the U.S. interest to avoid that if we can. The Vietnamese indicated strongly that that is not likely to happen, that they want to steer an independent course in international politics, not lining up too closely with either the Soviets or Chinese.

A surprising point was that they would welcome U.S. private investments in Vietnam and that they are eager to discuss purchase of food and technology from us.

English, incidentally, is now taught in most of their schools.

Unstated, but I sense present, is a feeling on the part of the Vietnamese government that they feel caught in a squeeze between the Chinese, Soviets and Cambodians and they would like a friend with a powerful voice who could help stabilize the situation in Southeast Asia.

That would appear to be in our best interest also.

"South Africa 'Miracle,'" P.S./Washington, May 29–June 4, 1994

Seldom is world-shaking news good. But when Nelson Mandela stood to take the oath of office as President of South Africa, that electrified much of the world, for the good.

Almost 10 years ago I made my first trip to South Africa and came away convinced that that nation was headed toward one of the bloodiest civil wars in history, in which millions of people would die. Few then would have disagreed with that analysis.

Significantly, there were voices of reason within South Africa and outside of it, urging a change in policy, but they appeared to be muffled by the much louder voices of the extremists on both sides. Some religious leaders spoke out; university campuses had a few voices of reason in their midst; the United States and other nations had an economic boycott. But the chance for a real change in policy seemed remote.

Two key people—one white and one black—played a decisive role in "the miracle." F. W. de Klerk became president, someone whom many regarded as a caretaker leader until a more dynamic one emerged. But he startled South Africa and the world by freeing Nelson Mandela after 27 years in prison and by calling for the end of the stifling system of segregation in that country called apartheid. And Nelson Rolihlahla Mandela, after 27 years in prison, emerged as a dignified man with one amazing, almost unbelievable trait: not a touch of bitterness.

The rest you know. I had the privilege of being at the inauguration a few days ago, at the request of President Clinton, in a delegation headed by Vice President Al Gore and First Lady Hillary Rodham Clinton. The other senator present was my colleague from Illinois, Carol Moseley-Braun. Those who predicted violence even at the inauguration saw a dignified ceremony with whites and blacks working together. Among others present for the event were three of the guards who kept Nelson Mandela in prison. He invited them.

Nelson Mandela reached out to everyone, including his predecessor, F. W. de Klerk, asking him to serve as a vice president, which he now does. The chasm between blacks and whites in South Africa has been greater than in the United States or in any nation. Yet that chasm is now being bridged. What a great tribute, not only to President Mandela and Vice President de Klerk, but to the people of South Africa.

If in South Africa people can reach across huge barriers to establish a better society, can't it also happen in Bosnia, in Northern Ireland, in

Rwanda, in the Middle East—and even in Chicago, Washington, D.C., and New York City?

We should not view the scene in South Africa as something that simply happens in a distant nation, but as the inspiration to all of us to do better, wherever we live.

"On the Cuban Embargo," NPR Commentary, February 27, 2001

A man from Chicago writes an angry letter, castigating me for advocating trade and exchanges and normalizing relationships with Cuba. He wants to know if I don't realize that the Castro record on human rights is not good, and that opponents to Castro have been killed and imprisoned. The truth is that while Castro has done some good things for the people of Cuba on health care and education he would not receive an award for exceptional leadership for human rights.

But the foreign policy of our nation—or any nation—cannot be built on the basis of revenge, but on how we can shape the future more constructively to live in a world of peace and freedom and justice.

If revenge for past conduct dictated foreign policy, the Israelis would never meet with Chairman Arafat and the Palestinians would never meet with the new Israeli Prime Minister, Ariel Sharon. There are huge barriers to building a stable Mideast situation but both sides know that you cannot build a better future by following a course of revenge.

The aim of the U.S. economic embargo of Cuba has been to topple Fidel Castro. He has been in power 42 years. During the period we have had nine Presidents. Our policy is a failure. Almost everyone will admit that privately but we are unfortunately unwilling to acknowledge that publically with a shift in policy. We are the only nation in the world with the embargo. It hurts Cuba by keeping U.S. tourists away and prevents Cubans from buying U.S. cars, food, medicine and other products. Both sides get hurt. And the small steps we could make toward greater understanding are not being taken.

Cuba's record on basic freedoms is not good—but it is better than China's and North Korea's, both of whom we recognize, as we should. Diplomatic recognition is not a *Good Housekeeping* seal of approval for a nation. It is a way of trying to cooperate at least in some areas. It would not suggest that we approve the Cuban system of government, nor would their recognition of us suggest that they intend to mirror our system. The national interest should determine our course, not an emotional response which caters to our passions.

"Easing the Embargo Grudge against Cuba,"
Chicago Tribune, March 4, 2001

America's policy toward Cuba has never made much sense, and it will take on a tone of complete unreality if our nation adopts a policy modifying the economic boycott toward Iraq to include only weapons and supplies of military significance. If we can do that in the case of Saddam Hussein and Iraq, why not Fidel Castro and Cuba?

For 42 years our aim has been to topple Castro's leadership with an economic boycott. Our policy is a relic of the Cold War when Cuba sided with the Soviets. But the Cold War is over and our policy remains unchanged. I have long opposed the embargo and a recent visit to Cuba—including a six-hour session with Castro—confirmed the stupidity of our course of action.

For example, the embargo is hurting Cubans who take circuitous routes to secure needed U.S. medicines. It also harms the U.S. economically and politically. While there are 1957 Chevrolets and Fords and even Studebakers on the streets of Havana, the new cars are from Japan, South Korea, Germany, France and other nations. Tourist buses I saw were from Sweden and Germany. There are Swiss and Japanese hotels, but no Hiltons, no Hyatt. Our policy is costing us money and jobs.

Gradual economic shifts are taking place in Cuba. Self-employment is now tolerated, as is hiring a small number of employees for a business. Foreign investors can hold up to 100 percent of the ownership of a plant or business, though partnering with Cubans is encouraged.

However, Castro is not running a democracy; I wish he were. But among the dozens of non-democracies I have visited, Cuba is more like Poland and Hungary during the latter days of the Soviet Union. In those two countries then and in Cuba today, citizens appear to be fairly free to criticize government policies, but they do not have the freedom to organize opposition to the government.

When you compare the human-rights record of Cuba to China and North Korea, Cuba's record is markedly better, yet we recognize and encourage trade with China and North Korea and not our neighbor.

And in security matters, do China and North Korea represent a short-term and/or long-term threat to the United States? Maybe. Does Cuba? No.

When the Soviet Union represented a threat some argued that the U.S. should stop travel and trade and academic and professional exchanges there. Others argued that a policy of isolation would hold back change. The embargo supporters did not win and the Soviet Union as we knew it no longer exists. The application of this lesson to Cuba is obvious.

President Bush could easily make small shifts in the embargo policy that would aid both nations.

- Americans should be free to travel to Cuba to learn firsthand the strengths and deficiencies of Cuba's government. With the possible exception of North Korea, we remain the only nation that does not permit its citizens to travel freely to Cuba.
- We should encourage academic exchanges.
- Selling automobiles, food and medicine certainly won't harm the U.S.
- We should let Cuban officials travel freely to the U.S. When the president of Cuba's parliament wanted to visit the U.S. recently to attend a world meeting of parliamentarians, he was not permitted to come, a petty action that made us look ridiculous.

President Bush can and should lead on easing the embargo. If he takes a few small steps toward reality he will be pleasantly surprised at the response and perhaps eventually recognize Cuba as we do China and North Korea. Prior to the Iowa caucuses last year, then-Gov. George W. Bush told an audience there, "I know how to lead. I don't run polls to tell me what to think. The most important, most influential job in America should be the president, not the president's pollster." Wise words. A good test as to how meaningful they will be in relaxing our policy toward Cuba.

THE UNITED NATIONS, DIPLOMACY, AND SOFT POWER

"THE U.N. DISARMAMENT CONFERENCE,"
P.S./WASHINGTON, MAY 28–JUNE 3, 1978

This column is being written in New York City, where I am attending a special five-week session at the United Nations on disarmament as one of the United States delegates. While I have visited the United Nations on other occasions, this is my first opportunity to get a littler greater "feel" for what takes place here. During this five-week period, the only topic officially up for discussion is disarmament, though obviously when the leaders of the world get together, the conversation covers more than that.

This afternoon, for example, Senator Charles Mathias (R-Md.) and I visited with a representative of Zaire, the nation in Africa which is experiencing considerable difficulties. Disarmament was not even mentioned in our conversation. But it is good—and important—to have this opportunity to meet and talk about world problems.

But generally, the arms control matters dominate both public and private discussions, as they should. For, incredibly, the nations of the world (primarily the United States and the Soviet Union) are spending a total of $400 billion a year on armaments, or roughly $1 million a minute.

There are two major things wrong with that:

First, we have so much weaponry stockpiled in the name of security that we have become insecure. The nations of the world theoretically can destroy every person on the face of the earth 22 times with nuclear warheads alone.

Second, the $400 billion spent on armaments does little for the world economy, and it keeps the nations of the world from using at least some of these funds to help the two-thirds of the world's population that is desperately poor.

The people who are gathering here at the U.N. are realists, not "pie-in-the-sky" people. But we all know that if we can somehow by joint agreement gradually reduce the world's heavy expenditure on weapons and the huge world stockpile of deadly (literally) tools, that would be a great plus for every nation on the face of the earth. Because we are realists we expect progress to be slow, but we do expect progress.

This meeting on arms control is the first major international meeting on disarmament to take place since 1932, and it is far more significant than the 1932 meeting, both in terms of urgency and because of the fact that several times as many nations are taking part in these talks.

The simple fact that the meeting is taking place and that there is some sense of urgency is healthy. Despite a 72–15 Gallup poll in favor of the Strategic Arms Limitation Talks (SALT II) agreement, the reality is that few people anywhere are interested in or understand the arms dilemma. It remains remote for most people.

But, in fact, the arms race touches the lives and pocketbooks of all Americans and of people everywhere. We must increase understanding of that.

"Peace Corps Volunteer Offers Help and Hope," P.S./Washington, August 4–10, 1985

If you are worried about the future of this country, a visit with some Peace Corps volunteers will give you a good dose of optimism. A few weeks ago I went to Mauritania and Senegal in Africa to assess what is happening with the drought, desert and hunger problems on that afflicted continent.

In Senegal I visited the little village of Keur Momar Sarr, about a three-hour drive into the desert from the capital city of Dakar. I went there to see what a combination of U.S. aid and the work of one Peace Corps volunteer was doing.

I was told that the Peace Corps volunteer was scheduled to leave but postponed leaving one day because he had heard that a U.S. senator was coming to see the project. There in that far-off village in remote Africa I found Ken Gutsch, son of Kenneth and Carole Gutsch of Oak Lawn, Illinois. He had no idea I was the senator who would be visiting and I had no idea the Peace Corps volunteer would be from Illinois. Ken Gutsch, a 25-year-old beginning University of Illinois law student, was living with a family in this village of perhaps 400 people, speaking their language, working with them to improve their quality of life and hopes for the future.

Water shortage is a major problem in this part of Africa. He and some others were digging a well, hoping to find water. They dug 300 feet, and still did not find water. So he planned how they could save the rain water when it comes in that deep well.

When they were about one-third through digging the well he got word that his best friend would be getting married in Iowa. He borrowed enough money to fly back for the wedding, and while he was in the United States he talked to everyone he could to secure funds to finish that well. He managed to get $2,000 in donations, enough to do the concrete work that is necessary as you dig a deep well.

A combination of efforts built a small storage shed where grain from U.S. contributions and help from other nations comes to assist these people to survive. Ken Gutsch has shown them how to store grain safely.

They have built a community garden—several acres of it—in an area where water is more available two or three miles from this village. He helped them with this. He showed them how to save manure from goats and camels, storing it in piles to use on the garden.

I was with him when he said good-bye to the villagers. It was a moving scene. I shall never forget the grown man who could not hold back his tears as he said farewell to Ken.

Ken Gutsch is going on to law school, but he will never be the same for his rich experience in the Peace Corps. His world has opened immensely. And that small village will never forget Ken Gutsch and the country he represents. During my week in Africa I saw perhaps 50 or 60 Peace Corps volunteers, young people like Ken and one woman 69 years old. They were white and black, Protestant, Catholic and Jewish. But all Americans you can be proud of.

And I am.

"THE UNITED NATIONS AT MIDDLE AGE,"
P.S./WASHINGTON, NOVEMBER 3–9, 1985

The United Nations marked its 40th anniversary the other day with speeches from many of the world's leaders, including the President of the United States. There were editorials both praising the United Nations and questioning its usefulness. What is the truth?

Each of us views truth from a different viewpoint, but my impression is that the United Nations has not lived up to all of our hopes, but it has been helpful in many world trouble spots.

I was named by President Carter to be one of the U.S. representatives to the 1978 U.N. Special Session on Disarmament, and a few years later President Reagan named me as one of the U.S. advisers for a similar arms control session. I have had an opportunity to see the United Nations at work. It's a little like Congress: lumbering, somewhat inefficient, members too often doing the expected rather than the thoughtful.

In at least one respect it's worse than Congress. When we pass laws we know there are people within our nation to enforce those laws. At the United Nations, support for action, more than just talk, too often is weak at best.

In another respect, it's more important than Congress. If a senator from another state and I cannot work out an agreement on some matter, our two states are not going to launch a war against one another. That is not necessarily true at the United Nations. By providing a forum the United Nations has prevented some wars. Not all, but some. It has provided opportunities for nations to work together more, an opportunity too often ignored.

When I was at the United Nations in 1978, I invited the Vietnamese delegation to have lunch with a representative of the State Department and me. That lunch set off a series of events that almost culminated in U.S. recognition of Vietnam—and that probably would have prevented the invasion of Cambodia, and reduced the Soviet presence in Vietnam.

That was an opportunity the United States muffed. In the war between Iran and Iraq, the U.N. secretary general has attempted to bring peace, but to no avail. When our hostages were taken in Iran, the United Nations tried but failed to help. In the Middle East and in Cyprus, the United Nations has had mixed results, helping to prevent some disasters but not bringing peace to either area. When a person reaches age 40, it's a good time for self-evaluation and checkup.

The same is true for the United Nations. How do we make it more of a peace-keeping mechanism and less of a forum for speeches? Particularly, how do we make it less of a forum where speeches are delivered and votes taken that are so completely predictable that they are meaningless? Some of the think-tank groups that contribute much to the nation ought to volunteer to give the United Nations a checkup at the age of 40.

We cannot abandon the United Nations. We ought to improve it.

"Increasing Defense Spending Isn't America's Cure-All," Commentary, *Chicago Tribune*, February 12, 2002

Political oratory by leaders in both parties is fine, sometimes even inspirational, but the real budget priorities are set by the administration and Congress—and I fear we many end up with a federal budget that responds more to the national passion than the national interest.

Secretary of State Colin Powell told the World Economic Forum that the U.S. can battle terrorism around the Earth, but we cannot eliminate it without dealing with "the areas of poverty, despair and hopelessness" that can breed terrorism. He is correct, of course, but the budget doesn't reflect that sense of priority.

President Bush has asked for a $48 billion increase in defense spending, roughly a 12 percent rise, and much more in future years. We all want adequate security for our nation, and I hope that part of that money will go to much-needed improved intelligence, including penetration of terrorist groups. Few would begrudge a 4.1 percent salary increase for those serving in our military. However, we are already spending more on defense than the total of the next eight nations with large defense budgets. And billions continue to be spent on a missile-shield system that so far has proved to be a dud, and most military scientists believe cannot be effective. The latest estimates from the Congressional Budget Office are that the system could cost $238 billion. Everything labeled defense is not necessarily a wise expenditure.

I trust that Congress will examine the defense request carefully, and where there is a real security need, we should provide for that. But security is more than weapons. We discovered that on Sept. 11.

A month after the World Trade Center tragedy, *Newsweek*'s lead article was titled: "Why do they hate us?" Much of the world does not hate us but our frequent insensitivity to the other 96 percent of the world's population too often appears as arrogance, the arrogance of "the rich guy" who ignores the poor.

Under the Marshall Plan, we led the world in assisting those impoverished and devastated by World War II. The first poll, taken after Secretary of State George Marshall and President Harry Truman announced the program, showed only 14 percent of the American people supported it. It was overwhelmingly unpopular. But a Democratic president and a Republican Congress joined forces to pass that measure, which not only appealed to our humanitarian instincts, but ended up being a huge help to our economy as well as that of Western Europe.

Today our nation spends more than the next eight nations combined on defense, but is dead last among the 21 wealthy nations of the world in the percentage of our income that helps the poor beyond our borders. As a percentage of our economy, our aid to the world's poor is at the lowest point since World War II.

At a January meeting of officials from the U.S., Western Europe, the United Nations, and the World Bank, the U.S. vetoed a proposal that all of the wealthy nations of the world would double their developmental assistance—a total of $50 billion for all of these nations combined—or roughly the same amount President Bush is asking as an increase in defense for our country alone. In a commencement speech at Notre Dame last spring, U.N. Secretary General Kofi Annan called the U.S. response to the world's impoverished "shameful." Just as the Marshall Plan resulted in both economic and security advantages to the United States, so a more balanced and generous approach to the world's impoverished ultimately can aid in our economic well-being and help build a stable world less tarnished by terrorism.

In contrast to the $48 billion increase in defense, the administration is asking for an $800 million increase in foreign economic assistance—and Congress is likely to reduce that. The administration's request for foreign aid is less than one-half of 1 percent of the total federal budget.

Simply increasing developmental assistance in not a cure-all, not a substitute for building other bridges of understanding. We have 547,000 international students at American colleges and universities. That helps. But only 1 percent of our students ever study abroad, and two-thirds of them go to Western Europe. In the United States we can go from grade school to getting a Ph.D. without having a year of a foreign language, and that adds to our insularity. I believe we are the only nation in which you can go through elementary school without studying another language and, equally important, acquire a sensitivity to other cultures. Factors like these create an atmosphere that too often makes our leaders hesitate to challenge us to do better on foreign aid.

Yes, we want a strong defense. We are willing to make sacrifices to have it. But security is more than weapons and our leaders need to understand that and tell us that.

5

The Budget and the Deficit

EDITOR'S NOTE

It seems that everywhere we look today there are articles and news reports about the federal budget and the deficit and competing plans for how to handle them. Public opinion polls consistently show that these problems, along with the economy in general, are at the top of the list of the American people's concerns about the future. We went for years in this country with the deficit barely being noticed on the national agenda, and now it is the dominant headline. Governmental shutdown and threatened defaults on our national debt are now openly considered and debated. The two major parties could not be more polarized on the fundamental understanding of the issue and what to do about it. The Democrats insist that some revenue increases are required. They tend to focus the need for additional revenue on the Bush era tax cuts and advocate repealing those tax cuts for the wealthy and returning to the Clinton era tax rates as a way to address the deficit. They point to that period as a halcyon economic era that was achieved under a higher tax rate than that which obtained when the recession of 2008–9 began. The Republicans are just as adamant about the need for spending reductions, and they have offered a whole range of cuts in the federal budget's discretionary spending that would hit virtually all Americans directly in the pocketbook. Harkening back to the supply-side economics theories of the Reagan era, the Republicans claim that budget and tax cuts will actually increase governmental revenue in the long run as the economy expands and creates jobs, despite the fact that the deficit grew dramatically under Reagan and both Bush administrations. The public is deeply divided, siding with the Democrats on the need for increased revenue from the wealthy and siding with the Republicans on the need for reductions in discretionary spending. However, when it comes to reductions in programs and expenditures they benefit from and support, most voters are opposed, and they clearly want to have their cake and have someone else pay for it. The debate goes on continuously.

Concerns over the budget deficit in the state of Illinois are no less prevalent. Illinois faced a structural deficit for the entire first decade of the twenty-first century, and then that deficit became intolerable when the 2008–09 recession took a drastic toll on state income while the increased need for governmental services for the newly unemployed significantly expanded state expenditures. Illinois simply had more programs and personnel than citizens were willing to pay for in that era. One of the most egregious problems stemmed from the Illinois pension system for public employees, which has been identified as one of the most underfunded pension systems in the nation. Predictions about its ultimate insolvency are endemic. Despite a state law requiring an adequate level of annual funding and a requirement in the Illinois Constitution adopted in 1970 guaranteeing pension rights as a contractual obligation of the state, successive legislatures refused to make the state's part of the pension payment and borrowed consistently from those funds to meet current obligations. After years of neglect and abuse, in 2011 the Illinois General Assembly and the governor finally turned their attention to the state's budget problems and what had to be done to correct them. As in the case of the national government, the solutions required a combination of increased revenues and decreased spending, painful for all concerned. The debate over how to recognize that reality has been raucous and divisive.

If any of the major players at the national or state levels had been paying attention, they would have found that Paul Simon had been warning for a political generation that these days of reckoning would come. Anyone who read Simon's columns over the years would have been very familiar with his theme insisting that the nation was on an unsustainable course in its reliance on borrowed money to meet current obligations. As was noted earlier, Simon was a chief proponent of the Balanced Budget Amendment proposal, which he championed long before it was at all popular or had many mainstream advocates. It was an unusually courageous and prescient position for an officeholder who was essentially a liberal Democrat in most of his views.

As early as Simon's service in the state legislature in Illinois, he took the position that people should decide on the bundle of goods and services the general welfare of the state required and then raise the revenues necessary to support those. His "pay as you go" principle was predicated on the necessity for public officials to tell the truth to their constituents and not play shell games with public deficits and debt. He also fundamentally objected to having the current generation pass its financial obligations along to future generations to pay the bills. The fact that the past several generations of public officials, enthusiastically aided and abetted by the public, have done exactly that is what now makes any attempt to finally face financial reality and start paying off the accumulated debt so painful in the current context.

Simon's writings in this chapter amplify his very fixed views on public deficits and debt, Social Security, and pensions for public employees. Some of the figures used in these columns are now somewhat dated, since the totals have escalated and the price for paying the bills has increased exponentially because of the magic of compounded interest. One can now add a new set of zeroes to the deficit data provided here. Paul especially objected to the ever-increasing toll the payment of interest on the national debt took each year on the budget. This was money that could have been spent on worthy programs, like education, student loans and grants, and better health care, which would ensure prosperity and enhance the prospects of the next generation. He was particularly critical of the fact that most of those interest payments went to wealthy investors and to central bankers overseas, where we were mortgaging our future and decreasing our options at home.

As some of the articles included in this chapter indicate, Simon was very much in favor of spending money up front to create jobs and to get the workforce ready to perform the work that a modern economy requires. He was a supporter of welfare, but he also held the firm belief that welfare should be a temporary solution to keep families afloat and that the long-term solution was to get recipients trained and find them a job. He wrote that there is a natural dignity to work that is never available to those on welfare and that people need work to keep their pride and morale intact. He was in favor of creating that work in the public sector if necessary, since there was plenty of work to be done, but he also favored helping create jobs in the private and nonprofit sectors. These views also fit quite well with his emphasis on the long-term salutary effects of education for the individual and for society, and Simon was the instigator of the Illinois Community College system based on legislation that he introduced and championed while he was in the Illinois General Assembly.

Simon took an equally adamant stance against state indebtedness when he was in the Illinois General Assembly. He often voted against the issuance of state bonds for infrastructure improvements, such as building highways, even though those were projects he generally favored. He simply did not like the debt and the accompanying interest payments the bonds entailed. Paul Simon was truly the fiscal conservative in the sense of eschewing governmental debt while he was also the true liberal in his advocacy for a wide range of services, especially for the less fortunate in society. His fundamental position was that we should require each generation to pay the bills it accrues. This stance required a synthesis of both positions, which was very difficult to enact into public policy, and he often lost the legislative battles, such as his fight for the Balanced Budget Amendment, which his somewhat unorthodox reasoning required. Indeed, the difficulty and inherent contradictions in his philosophy were often used against him politically. His inability to articulate exactly how and where he would cut the budget and raise revenues was one of the difficulties he faced in the Democratic primaries when he ran for president in 1988. He made an early victory in Iowa the linchpin of his strategic plan for winning the nomination, but those who voted in the Democratic primaries and who attended the Iowa caucuses did not make the best audience for talking about budget cuts and the Balanced Budget Amendment. When he lost Iowa, although by a very narrow margin, that precipitated a downward spiral in his presidential campaign from which it never recovered. In this respect, Paul could not give up on his basic principles and stand on one side or the other of this great divide where the ground would have been firmer and his stance much easier to explain and defend. In this case, he paid a real political price for his principled stance, although there were other factors—especially his getting a late start and being underfunded and under-organized—that also contributed to his unsuccessful run for the presidency.

In this area, as in many others, Paul Simon was a man ahead of his time. He clearly understood the need for each political generation to take care of the needs of that generation. When the country finally achieved a surplus in the federal budget in the late 1990s, Simon and others urged that we use it to fix some of the future problems with Social Security and pay down some of the accumulated debt. Above all, do not give it back in terms of a general tax cut, Simon pressed, but of course, we know that Congress and the president had other ideas and wanted to take the short-term gain, choosing the politically expedient route instead. If the nation had followed Simon's advice then, we would not now be faced with the heartless budget-cutting that must take place and the unpalatable prospect of paying more taxes for a long time to come. Old people and children, the weakest and least politically articulate members of society, are highly likely to have to pay the retribution that comes from the failures of political leadership and political followership from the past generation. This is a mass lesson in civics education now being experienced by the current generation. Playing by the rules and paying attention to the real world are civic virtues. We need a greater emphasis on civic education in our current society. Paul Simon devoted a significant proportion of his personal and professional life to the basic cause of civic education. The selections included in this volume are a testament to that devotion; perhaps making them more widely available will also advance that cause.

THE NEED FOR A BALANCED BUDGET

"A BALANCED BUDGET AMENDMENT,"
P.S./WASHINGTON, MARCH 30–APRIL 5, 1975

Congressman David Treen, a Republican Congressman from Louisiana, has introduced a constitutional amendment, which I have joined nine other Republicans and two other Democrats in co-sponsoring, which calls for a balanced federal budget.

It would require a balanced budget unless two-thirds of the membership of Congress votes that we have an emergency of such a nature that a budget deficit is necessary.

Now we have such an emergency, but the danger is that when we come out of our present economic difficulties—and we will—that we will continue to drift into the quick-sand of larger and larger deficits.

It is politically so much easier to avoid facing fiscal realities than to face them. And so we issue more and more bonds, and fund pension systems inadequately. State governments of both political parties have learned the lesson and now states are playing the same irresponsible game. What's wrong with a deficit? Many things could be said, but let me mention five:

1. An increasing percentage of our tax dollar is going for interest rather than goods and services. Conservative estimates are that by the end of the next fiscal year the amount spent on interest will be $40 billion of the federal budget—more than on anything other than defense and social security. That's almost $200 from every citizen for interest. It means a family of four

will, on the average, give the federal government $800 for interest. I suggest that we have better uses for our money. That $40 billion for interest is more than the total federal budget as recently as 1942.

2. Imbalanced budgets permit members of Congress and chief executives to live in a land of make-believe. There is no relationship between the money we take in and the money we spend. We just print some more and call them "bonds." Families can't do that without getting into trouble and neither can governments.

3. Deficits are inflationary. How inflationary is a matter of dispute, but there is no question about some inflationary impact.

4. Deficits cause interest rates to go up. When government competes with the private sector for money, the cost of money goes up, and we all pay for that.

5. When government takes too much of the money, less is available in the private sector for business and industrial expansion.

All of this does not mean that a deficit should never take place. Right now we need one.

But the times in which we need one should be rare. And unless something like the Treen constitutional amendment proposal catches fire, I don't see the necessary self-restraint present which will cause a sound financial policy. Secretary of the Treasury William Simon—no relative—has been warning us about this. And he is right.

"MANAGING THE FEDERAL DEBT," P.S./WASHINGTON, JANUARY 30–FEBRUARY 5, 1977

"What can be done about the federal debt?" is a question people often ask.

An answer that is easy to give—but much more difficult to accomplish: reduce unemployment. If we had 3 or 4 percent unemployment instead of 8 percent, the budget probably would be balanced. So long as unemployment remains high, it is not possible to balance the budget without great harm to the nation. What Congress and the President must do now is to somehow get employment up as rapidly as practically possible, and then hold federal expenditures to income once that is achieved. How we achieve that combination is both difficult and complicated. I am on the Budget Committee of the House, which is now wrestling with these economic problems.

And the Budget Committee represents the best immediate hope of moving toward a balanced budget. Our committee will establish, with the approval of the House, the amount the federal government will spend, and determine where it will spend it in broad terms. The details of where money is spent are left to the Appropriations Committee.

A second means of at least reducing the deficit—as well as stimulating the economy—would be to reduce interest rates. How we can reduce interest rates without excessively increasing the money supply is one of the knotty questions some of us are discussing at this point. But the fundamental decisions in this area are up to the Federal Reserve Board, not Congress or the President.

If interest rates were down 2 percent, it would be a great boost to the home construction market, it would cut off perhaps $15 billion from federal interest payments each year, and it would give the stock market a tremendous boost. It would also save most Americans a great deal of money.

Interest on the federal debt has become a major problem. An increasing percentage of your tax dollar now goes for interest rather than for goods and services, and that just does not make sense. During the next fiscal year the federal government will spend about $45 billion on interest. The other day the *Wall Street Journal* pointed out that $45 billion is more than the annual sales of General Motors, more than all government spending by Sweden, and greater than the total earnings of the economies of Greece and New Zealand. Only social security and defense now require more money than the interest we pay on the federal debt.

A third way to put some control on this excessive interest expenditure is a constitutional amendment requiring a balanced budget unless two-thirds of Congress votes to the contrary. That would permit us to have a deficit in times like these, with high unemployment, but would put a brake to loose spending habits in times of prosperity. Such an amendment is not likely to pass, though I favor it and am co-sponsoring it.

But simply introducing it focuses attention on the issue, and keeps our "feet to the fire," making Congress and the public somewhat more aware of the dimensions of the deficit problem.

But for the next two years at least, the major instrument for determining how much the nation's deficit will be, and how much we spend on reducing unemployment, will be the Budget Committee.

Though it is not an assignment in which you can please many people, it is a committee spot of great influence and much sought after by members of Congress. I'm pleased to be on the committee and I'm impressed by the caliber of my colleagues. I hope we can both help to get the nation moving and also get our fiscal house in order.

"Economic Illness Requires Unpopular Cures,"
P.S./Washington, April 16–22, 1978

In one of Shakespeare's plays this conversation takes place between King Henry IV and the Earl of Warwick:

> KING: Then you perceive the body of our kingdom
> How foul it is; what rank diseases grow,
> And with what danger, near the heart of it.
> WARWICK: It is but as a body yet distemper'd;
> Which to his former strength may be restored
> With good advice and little medicine.

Most observers believe that the economic strength of our nation can also be restored with some good advice and the right medicine. But we are deluged with conflicting advice, and the pills from which we must choose are legion. In at least one respect the illness comparison is correct: to recover from an illness usually takes some form of minor sacrifice—rest when you'd rather not, pills you would prefer not to swallow, avoiding certain foods you like, perhaps even surgery. This economic illness is epidemic in nature. All of the major powers are experiencing greater or lesser difficulty, though the United States' recovery is the one essential to recovery for all nations, because of our central position in the world's economy. What sacrifices should we be making? What medicine should we be taking? Here is my partial list:

- Reduce the deficit. The House Budget Committee has already reduced it by about $3 billion over the original estimates for the next fiscal year. Some argue that in a $2.3 trillion economy a deficit of $60 billion is not that significant.

  But that $60 billion (plus "off-budget" federal borrowings) must be compared to total borrowing for all purposes (by individuals, corporations and governments), not to total income. Next year it looks as if federal government borrowing will be about 30 percent of total borrowing, compared to about 12 percent in 1969. That sizable borrowing puts pressure on the money market—and that means higher interest rates, which in turn depresses sizable segments of our economy, including the stock market.

- Reduce the tax cut. The Budget Committee surprised some by suggesting about $5 billion less in tax cuts than the President had proposed. The chairman of the Federal Reserve Board also suggests that tax cuts should begin next January rather than this October, saving another $9 billion. It is sound advice, but whether Congress can resist a tax cut in October in an election year is questionable.

- Plan now to make future tax cuts in such a way that they fight inflation rather than inflame it. Economist Arthur Okun has made some excellent suggestions along this line.
- Develop a farm program that is both anti-inflationary and helps the farmers. It can be done through target prices. The measure which the House defeated the other day would have provided one-third of its benefits to the richest 5 percent of the nation's farmers and would have been highly inflationary.
- Plan more effective jobs programs and tie these programs in with reforms of welfare and unemployment compensation. People ought to have the opportunity to be productive.
- Give the President stand-by wage and price controls.
- Have the Congressional Budget Office place an inflation tag on each bill before Congress, so that we know the costs of any measure both in dollar terms and in its inflationary impact. I have requested such action.

This program is not a popular one in all respects, but a patient who is ill should seek that cure, rather than answers that please.

"CUT TAXES OR REDUCE THE DEFICIT?," P.S./WASHINGTON, JULY 30–AUGUST 5, 1978

One of the questions which Congress must decide is whether to reduce taxes or reduce the federal deficit. The politically appealing answer is to reduce taxes. But if people understand the issues involved I am not at all sure that the politically attractive answer is the one the public would want. Because if we reduce the deficit another $16 billion, rather than cut taxes that amount, there will be two benefits:

1. There will be a reduction in inflationary pressure.
2. The Federal Reserve Board probably will reduce interest rates for the nation.

Congressmen Charles Vanik of Ohio and Jake Pickle of Texas have suggested that rather than doing what has great immediate popular appeal—cutting taxes—we should hold the present level of taxes and reduce inflation.

Unless someone comes up with some powerful argument I have not seen, I agree with them. If the people of the nation understand that our alternatives are cutting taxes or cutting inflation, their preference will be to cut inflation.

No one can promise that the Federal Reserve Board would cut interest rates, but I have discussed this matter with the new chairman and my impression is that if the Vanik-Pickle formula were to be followed, a cut in interest rates is likely.

And if interest rates were reduced, all Americans would benefit through lower interest payments, the federal deficit would be further reduced, home construction would receive a major boost, and the stock market would pick up, making the issuance of common stock a more realistic option for capital formation.

The congressional answer likely will be to increase the national debt and spread some of those borrowings around, and call it a "tax cut." That sounds better than to tell people we borrowed more money which we will have to pay on for decades in the future so that you can get a little more of your money back right now. The tax cut route is inflationary, but popular.

It permits congressmen and senators to go back home and brag how we cut your taxes.

The Vanik-Pickle approach of holding the line on taxes is tougher medicine but it is anti-inflationary. I guess what we are really looking for is some easy, simple, painless method of stopping inflation. And there is none. The sooner we realize that all of us will have to sacrifice together to stop the monster of inflation, the sooner it will be stopped.

The Vanik-Pickle approach will not do it by itself. It is one of a series of steps which might be taken. But soon we must start on some strong, vigorous action on the inflation front.

"Allied Underspending on Defense Means U.S. Overspending," P.S./Washington, March 21–27, 1982

A couple of small statistics have been overlooked in all of the discussion of the defense budget: the United States has 42 percent of the combined national income of the countries in NATO and Japan, but we contribute 57 percent of the defense dollars. By 1987, assuming the adoption of the Reagan figures, we will have 42 percent of the combined national income and we will be picking up 67 percent of the cost.

If we were talking about impoverished nations, that would not be a matter of such great concern. But we are talking about nations which compare favorably with our own in terms of national average income; several are ahead of us.

But since the largest single geographic outlay of U.S. defense dollars is to guard against the possible movement of Soviet troops across central Europe, it is not mean-spirited of us to suggest that our European allies ought to contribute their fair share of the cost. Great Britain comes closer to it than any other nation, but even they are considerably behind us.

We now spend almost 6 percent of our national income for defense; by 1987 it will be closer to 8 percent. Even at 6 percent the only nations to exceed our military expenditure in terms of the percentage of their income are Israel and the Soviet Union.

The second largest single geographical concentration of U.S. defense dollars and attention is in the Persian Gulf area. We are concerned about oil supply. But while it is true that we receive about 40 percent of our oil from the Persian Gulf through the Strait of Hormuz, most of the countries of Western Europe and Japan receive almost all of their oil from sources there. Again, the United States is bearing an unfair share of the burden of protecting that oil supply.

The United States, Japan and Germany all spend about the same percentage of their national income on research. But according to Rep. Les Aspin of Wisconsin, an expert in this area, U.S. military research takes about five times as much of the share of total defense spending in the United States as it does in Germany and about 14 times as much as it does in Japan. The net result is that in research areas which are important commercially and for exports, our friends in Japan and Germany are frequently beating us.

I'm not among those who believe that the United States should pull our troops out of Western Europe and Japan. It's possible that we could reduce our troop strength there by 5–10 percent, maintain a strong and effective presence and not send the wrong signals to the Soviets. In any case, our friends in Japan and Western Europe should be willing to shoulder more of that financial burden than they now do.

It is in the security interest of Europe, Japan and the United States that the U.S. economy be restored to good health. Our economy will not improve appreciably with budget deficits as high as the President has requested; virtually all members of Congress, in both political parties, recognize that. But to get the deficit down, defense cannot experience the kind of uncritical growth the Administration wants. Wasting money in defense makes no more sense than wasting money in any other area. Moving toward a balanced budget is not a luxury in our present economic situation. It is a necessity. An adequate defense is also a necessity.

To achieve the right blend of those two priorities will require a re-evaluation of military expenditures by both the United States and our friends.

"Rescuing the Budget," P.S./Washington, May 9–15, 1982

An angry phone call from a constituent—angry at the Senate this time—asked why Congress did not go along with the President [Reagan] on his budget. He had noticed that the Senate Budget Committee, made up of a majority of Republicans, voted 20–2 to reject the President's budget. In 1981 the President got his program enacted virtually intact. Members of Congress and the public were told it would cure our economic ills. Inflation has come down, largely because of the Federal Reserve Board restraints, plus the oil glut and high unemployment. But in other respects the Administration's economic promise and performance differ substantially. Let's make some comparisons:

The promise: interest rates averaging 8.9 percent starting last October 1. The performance: much higher.

The promise: a growth rate of 7.5 percent in the economy for the first quarter of 1982. The performance: a decline of .4 percent.

The promise: a deficit of $37 billion for Fiscal Year 1982. The performance: the Administration's projection is a deficit of $114 billion.

The promise: a deficit of $23 billion for 1983. The performance: the Administration now projects a "current services" deficit of $182 billion for next year.

The promise: a balanced budget in 1984. The performance: the Administration's current services projection is for a deficit of $216 billion.

The promise: a surplus of $7 billion in 1985. The Administration's new current services forecast of performance: a deficit of $233 billion.

The promise: that upon passage of the tax bill there would be an immediate surge in the economy. The performance: within 90 days, a loss of almost $200 billion on the stock market and $300 billion in the bond market.

The promise: that if the tax bill passed, there would be major new business investment. The performance: business investment is down.

The promise: the "safety net" would protect the truly poor and needy people. The performance: hundreds of thousands of the really helpless in our society have been hurt.

That is the picture which Democrats and Republicans face. We want interest rates down, and that means deficits must come down. We want more sensible spending on defense. We want to stop waste, but we don't want to hurt people who really need help. So Democrats and Republicans in Congress are working on a budget considerably different from the President's. We believe he is sincere, but wrong. We respect him and like him but we recognize serious deficiencies and serious dangers in his fiscal package. My guess is that after some long hours and longer oratory we will end up with a package which Democrats and Republicans can support. There are many of my colleagues who do not share my optimism. If we reach a good budget compromise, I believe interest rates will drop. And we need that badly. If partisan considerations and genuine disagreements prevent our agreeing on a budget, then the nation will be the loser.

"Backbone in Budgeting," P.S./Washington, July 25–31, 1982

While I consider myself to be independent-minded and avoid tagging labels on myself, sometimes I am identified by newspapers as a liberal Democrat. Though my fiscal impulses are conservative, I favor more government involvement in certain areas than some of my friends do. It is an honest disagreement. But where we should not disagree is that whatever we spend we pay for. That is why the tax cut voted last year was so irresponsible—in essence we decided to borrow money to give ourselves a tax cut.

Back in 1960 the people of Illinois voted on a $345 million bond issue for mental institutions and universities. As one who strongly supported a better mental health program and an improved university system for our state, I startled some of my friends when I opposed that bond issue. Now I am startling some people by favoring a constitutional amendment to require a balanced budget, a position I have held since my first days in Congress. There are some interesting parallels between Illinois' experience with indebtedness and the current situation with federal deficit spending. Every organization I know of, with the lone exception of the Farm Bureau, backed the state referendum on the bond issue. So did every newspaper I know of.

In opposing it I made two points: First, that we would be much better off increasing our taxes slightly and meeting the need on a pay-as-you-go basis; that the money would not be spent in one or two years as claimed. Second, that such a bond issue would only be the beginning and the net result ultimately would be costly to the taxpayers in both tax dollars and reduced services.

The measure passed, and the money ended up being spent over seven years, not one or two. And now the State of Illinois has a bonded indebtedness of more than $18 billion, according to a recent *Chicago Tribune* series, and is spending well over $100 million each year on interest alone. Illinois took the easy way out and we are paying for it.

At the federal level we also are spending an increasing percentage of our tax dollar on interest rather than on goods and services because no matter what the economic situation, we spend more than we take in.

The federal government's number one expenditure is Social Security, the number two is defense, and the number three is interest. Everything else is far behind. Our interest expenditure for fiscal year 1983 will be at least $113 billion—just about what the total budget of the federal government was in 1964 when Lyndon Johnson was President.

Is it wise to endlessly go deeper and deeper into debt? Is it wise to each year spend an increasing percentage of money on interest payments which might go to help meet the needs of people? Is it wise for the federal government to compete with the private sector so mightily for borrowed money, sending interest rates up?

Then you get to the bottom line question: Can a Congress and an administration show enough backbone to balance the budget without having a constitutional amendment to force it? I have reluctantly reached the conclusion from some years of observing government that it is not possible.

Some charge that it is totally inconsistent for the same President and Congress who have voted record-breaking deficits to call for a constitutional amendment. And of course the charge rings true. Just as it is true that our year-after-year budgets of more spending than income are inconsistent.

The real question, however, is not whether the proposal is inconsistent (which it is) but whether it is in the national interest. I believe that it is.

I will argue for full employment programs with my friends who oppose them; I will argue for more adequate medical care for those who are just getting by in our society with those who somehow do not see the need; but I believe in paying for these initiatives as we go.

If we who serve in high office—and you who put us there—ask for an added service of government, then let us have the courage to tax ourselves for that service. If we do not have the courage to ask for the taxes, we should not ask for the services. It is that simple.

Yes, there will be years in which there must be deficits, and Congress will have the ability to do that. But that should not happen regularly. The national dialogue ought to be about the needs of this nation and how we effectively meet those needs, but it should involve a realistic assessment of costs. I am tired of the nation slipping into the quicksand of deeper and deeper debt. And somehow out there in the American public is a streak of common sense which agrees.

"Bring Back Pay-as-You-Go Government,"
P.S./Washington, August 19–25, 1984

"How can you be liberal on social policy and conservative on fiscal policy?" I was asked recently. That's a fair question. Perhaps it can be summarized by saying that I believe government must be responsive to the needs of the unemployed, senior citizens, the disabled, people who want to go to college but cannot afford it, and others who need a helping hand—but whatever plans we devise, we should act on a pay-as-you-go basis.

One issue illustrates the problem, and my approach. Evidence was overwhelming that our highways and bridges were gradually deteriorating, causing needless accidents and injuries and deaths, as well as tearing up many automobiles.

There were a few who said the federal government should do nothing about it. "Let the states do it," was their answer. The only problem was that the states weren't doing it, in part because any state that raised gas taxes while neighboring states did not ended up losing gas sales and revenue to neighboring states.

There were others who said that the federal government should do the job, but should simply increase the federal deficit to pay for it. "What's $6 billion more when you already have a $200 billion deficit?" was their bottom line. That would, of course, only add more pressure for interest rates to climb and worsen an already bad long-range economic problem.

The third approach was to face it head-on, and fortunately there were enough Republicans and Democrats willing to do that, so that answer finally prevailed. It called for a five-cent increase in the gas tax, spending $6 billion a year to improve roads on a pay-as-you-go basis. It also put a large number of people to work each year, saving significant amounts in welfare and unemployment compensation costs.

It helped people who needed work.

It restored highways to good condition, aiding our economy and our quality of life.

It saved lives.

And it did it all without increasing federal deficits.

If it would have been possible to get the job done through greater efficiency in the use of funds or other cost-cutting measures I would have preferred that. But reluctantly I came to the same conclusion that a majority in Congress of both parties did, that this step was needed.

Approximately 20 years ago Illinois passed its first big general obligation bond issue. The vote in the Illinois Senate was 55–1. I was the one who voted against it, and I pointed out that while I agreed with the need, that step would simply start a series of state bond issues, costing the state and Illinois taxpayers needless millions in interest.

I was assured I was wrong, that this was a one-time bond issue. "Never again," they said. Unfortunately I was right. There have been hundreds of bond issues since then. The other day I noted that the able Illinois state comptroller, Roland W. Burris, reported that the state now owes $3.14 billion in principal on bond issues, and will pay another $2.2 billion in interest. He broke that down to say that each Illinois citizen now owes $465.16 in state indebtedness.

Local school districts and cities have to issue bonds. But state governments and the federal government should not be doing it. We must bring spending and revenue into line.

You can be part of the solution. When you write to your representatives asking for an additional service, add a second paragraph noting that you are willing to pay taxes for it. If you are unwilling to write that second paragraph, don't write the first one.

"When the U.S. Was Debt-Free," P.S./Washington, January 1985

An anniversary slipped by the other day which should have been more formally noted: On January 8, 1835, the United States government made the final payment on the national debt. The nation was debt-free.

Andrew Jackson was President. Secretary of the Navy, Mahlon Dickerson, predicted inaccurately that the date would go down in American history as a holiday second only to July 4th. Senator Thomas Hart Benton in flowery language said this was a phenomenon "so long unseen on earth, a great nation without a national debt . . . to the astonished vision of a wondering world." The newspapers reported there was "great cheering." How distant that January day of 1835 seems—and not simply because of the passage of time.

With a national debt which now stands at $1.6 trillion, we are not likely to see the retirement of the U.S. debt in my lifetime, nor in the lifetime of anyone reading these words.

Now we are struggling to avoid increasing it too much in the next fiscal year, a pale goal compared to the goal reached in Andrew Jackson's day. While the latter goal is less dramatic, it should be the solid resolve of Democrats and Republicans in the House and Senate and in the administration to stop this headlong rush into fiscal chaos. Contrary to what some political leaders may suggest to you, stopping this snowballing debt is not going to be easy.

But the question is not whether it can be done; obviously it can. The real question is one of will, one of courage. Will the Democrats and Republican in Congress have enough courage to move within the next four years to a balanced budget? Will the administration, no longer faced with reelection problems, face the real problem?

We are now living on a gigantic credit card, spending more than we take in, and we are telling those from whom we borrow: send the bill to our children and our grandchildren.

This fiscal year the national debt will be approximately $210 billion. In fiscal year 1962, when John F. Kennedy was president, many people were concerned about a total federal budget that that year crept past $100 billion. Now the federal budget is over $900 billion and the interest alone on the debt this past fiscal year was $132 billion.

January 8, 1835. That date should remind us that difficult things are attainable. We should honor those who achieved that goal of eliminating the national debt by achieving a more modest goal: moving toward balancing the budget.

And then I hope we can seriously talk about gradually reducing the federal indebtedness.

"BAD BORROWING TOO OFTEN MAKES GOOD POLITICS," P.S./WASHINGTON, AUGUST 2–8, 1987

The other day I picked up the *Los Angeles Times* and on page three was a story about the State of California distributing $1.1 billion in budget surplus and immediately under it was a story: "$2.9 Billion in Bond Issues OKd by [State] Senate."

While the state government of California hands out $1.1 billion to citizens in that state, it proceeds to borrow $2.9 billion.

Why not just borrow $1.8 billion and not waste tremendous resources on interest? There may be some logical answers that escape me, but I read through both articles and cannot find any reason for this seeming inconsistency.

I say "seeming inconsistency" because there is a political consistency to it. To hand out money (or services) and let others pay in the future is politically attractive.

Unfortunately, it is not the state government of California alone that does these short-sighted things. The federal government is the No. 1 example for the nation.

We increase defense spending in the name of security, and we build an economically less secure nation through the deficits we create.

No one should be fooled into believing that makes sense.

We have cut taxes and let deficits soar, not because that is logical but because it is politically attractive. We have decided to let others pay for our folly. Those "others" are our children and grandchildren. A family that gets too deeply into financial problems starts to lose its independence. The same is true for a nation.

We now owe more to other countries than the three next largest debtor nations—Brazil, Argentina, and Mexico—combined. In three years we have moved from being the world's No. 1 creditor nation to being the world's No. 1 debtor nation. And, just as a family loses its independence, we are starting to lose ours.

I believe that the action of the President in taking the tariff off Japanese semi-conductors may be related to the fact that we are heavily dependent on Japan to buy our bonds—bonds which finance our budget deficits. I believe the bonds held by Saudi Arabia may be related to the Administration's decision to flag Kuwaiti ships in that region of the world.

A big and wealthy and powerful nation has through imprudent leadership slipped into economic bondage to nations which govern themselves more effectively economically.

Yes, what the government of California is doing does not make sense.

Unfortunately, the government of the United States of America has provided California with an excellent example of paying more attention to the politics of decision-making than the economics of decision-making.

"Getting the Illinois Budget in Order: Principles and Dollars," *Chicago Tribune*, April 7, 2003

It is easier to make decisions on the sidelines than to occupy a seat of responsibility where you will take public heat when decisions are made. I know.

But everyone from Gov. Rod Blagojevich to the greenest legislator should keep a few fundamentals in mind as they wrestle with the difficult revenue picture: Sound decisions are frequently unpopular. The quality that is most needed—and most missing—in government today is courage.

Education is the key to the future of Illinois and the nation. The income level—whether by county or by state—follows the education level. The higher the level of education, the higher the average income.

To the extent we do not pay attention to adult illiteracy and pre-school education, to the extent we duck the needed changes in grade- and high-school offerings, to the extent we pretend we can shift higher education costs more and more to tuition without reducing educational opportunities for many, to that extent we dim the future for our children and generations to come.

The income gap between those of us who are more fortunate and those less fortunate is greater in our nation than in any of the western European democracies, and it is growing. Long-term that is explosive. The reason for this flaw is the way we finance campaigns, with changes in the law designed to aid the politically generous more than the non-contributing strugglers.

A growing temptation for Illinois and other states is to expand gambling—good for campaign treasuries, politically more acceptable than tax increases. But it comes at the expense of ruined lives.

Having described these fundamentals, what would I work for if I were a decision-maker in Springfield?

Anything worthwhile requires sacrifice. The worst course is drifting. Gov. Blagojevich and the legislators should be builders of the future, not simply custodians of what we have inherited from the past. I would suggest we meet current obligations and invest another $1 billion or $2 billion in education and health care. To get there we should:

- Raise the state income tax for individuals to 4.5 percent. That brings in an additional $4 billion.
- Raise the corporate tax to 6.4 percent. That brings in $322 million.
- Decouple from the federal tax base, so that changes in the federal law do not automatically reduce Illinois revenue. Result: $197 million.
- Increase the gambling tax: $105 million.
- Eliminate the horse racing subsidy: $39 million.

These changes bring in an additional $4.66 billion.

My superficial readings of the budget figures suggest that the actual deficiency is about $3.5 billion, rather than the higher figures talked about. If my guess as a long-time member of budget committees both in Springfield and Washington is correct, the $4.66 billion I recommended would give the state more than $1 billion to dream, to innovate, to prepare a better future for this state and for the nation.

Illinois will not become a better state by simply drifting or without sacrifice. The same is true for the nation. Are we up to facing such tough decisions? We will soon know.

TAXES

"On a State Tax Increase," Sidelights from Springfield, by State Representative Paul Simon, February 1, 1959

You might as well face an uncomfortable fact right now: Your taxes will be increased during the current session of the legislature. That isn't pleasant news to you, I'm sure.

Those of us in the legislature don't like to increase taxes any more than you like to pay them. Not only are we taxpayers ourselves, but we must also "take the heat" for tax increases.

We must take care of the young people in our schools and colleges and the helpless in our welfare institutions—and that means more money.

Our schools are growing at the rate of more than 60,000 students per year. Our colleges will double their enrollment during the coming 12 years. Our welfare institutions have been neglected to a point that in some instances would shock any decent, responsible citizen.

We have the choice of letting things deteriorate—or increasing taxes. Faced with that choice, I think the legislature will increase taxes. I can hear some of you asking, "Can't we economize in government and avoid a tax increase?" We can and should economize in our state government. A great many savings can be made and later in the session I will go into detail on some of the savings which can be made. While these savings are substantial, they will not come anywhere near filling the need.

We will need a minimum of $200 million additional for the budget just to get by and that tentative figure probably will have to be increased. From what source will the money come?

My guess—and it is only a guess—is that Governor Stratton may ask for a one-cent tax increase.

Other possibilities are a state income tax for individuals of about 1 percent; a corporation income tax of 4 percent; a one-cent increase in the gas tax; a broadening of the base of present sales tax plus an increase in several smaller taxes (cigarettes, liquor, etc.); and a state property tax.

Many of us are opposed to any increase in the sales tax or property tax, believing that these two sources are hit heavily right now. They are also taxes which the economists call "regressive." That means that the lower your income, the higher your proportionate share of the taxes. The federal income tax, for example, does just the opposite and is called "progressive."

Illinois has the questionable distinction of having one of the most "regressive" tax structures of any state in the United States. Economists who have studied our tax structure have been very critical, stating that we have great inequities.

Labor unions, the Farm Bureau, and most of the school groups have indicated support of some type of state income tax—but the political platforms of both parties in 1958 stated that they were opposed to an income tax. Governor Stratton has stated his opposition on several occasions.

This makes the passage of a personal income tax unlikely during the current session of the legislature. Where will the money come from then? That's like asking who's going to win the baseball game after the first inning. It's difficult to say right now.

The only safe guess is that there will be a tax increase. Your letters may decide just how it will come.

"A Dangerous Bond Issue Proposal," From the Statehouse, by Lieutenant Governor Paul Simon, May 1, 1969

Illinois faces a serious road situation, and Governor Richard Ogilvie has called for a series of taxes to meet the need.

Because of the headlines about the 2.5 cent requested increase in the gasoline tax, little attention was paid to another feature: a call for a massive bond issue of $250 million per year for a 10-year period to build additional highways. This means at the end of the period an indebtedness of two and one-half billion dollars.

About a decade ago, the President suggested to Congress that there be a national bond issue for the federal highway system, but Senator Albert Gore of Tennessee put up a valiant fight for a pay-as-you-go plan. Fortunately for the nation, Senator Gore won, and the nation is not saddled with paying gasoline taxes for interest.

Interest on an indebtedness of two and one-half billion is $150 million per year, calculated at the rate of 6 percent. This is equivalent to 3.5 cents per gallon tax—solely for interest—if the state gets all the money from the tax (and none goes to local government). Under the present formula, it would take more than 7.5 cents per gallon to pay the interest.

The advantage of such a system is that it gets roads built now, quickly. Because of the rising costs of construction, it gets many of them built more economically. But hopefully serious study will be made of alternatives. The other practical "advantage" is, of course, that the roads get built now and someone else pays for them later on. That has some political pluses, but there is serious question whether this is in the long-range public interest.

Going the route of issuing bonds is a little like walking into quicksand: the more you go into it, the deeper you get, and it's extremely difficult ever to change such a pattern. Make no mistake about it. The proposal to issue bonds is a major change in the Illinois highway concept. It is a road of no return.

If you want your gasoline taxes to go for building roads rather than paying interest, you had better take a good, hard look at the current proposal.

"TIME TO STEM TAX BILL DANCE," P.S./WASHINGTON, SEPTEMBER 13–19, 1981

James Schlesinger served as Budget Director, Secretary of Defense and director of the Central Intelligence Agency under Richard Nixon, in addition to serving President Jimmy Carter as Secretary of Energy. A recent article in the *Washington Post* carried his description of the recent tax cut as an event which is "likely to go down in history as the single most irresponsible fiscal action of modern times."

What I feared when I voted against the tax cut is beginning to happen, and the news could get worse if we don't face reality.

Sometime ago when a White House aide talked to me about the tax cut he assured me, "When it becomes clear that the tax cut is going to pass the stock market will really take off."

It certainly did. As I type this the stock market has dropped 160 points since passage of the bill seemed assured, and the bond market is in equally bad shape. A year ago home mortgages averaged just slightly over 12 percent nationwide—which was bad—and now they average just over 17 percent— which is quite a bit worse.

Savings and loans, tremendously important to the home-buying and construction fields, are losing money and banks which have more than 30 percent of their loans in real estate are also having trouble, though they are not in as bad of shape.

Farmers, who must borrow each year, find their incomes eaten up by interest, particularly when grain prices are down and heavy August rains bring on corn blight and root damage. If there's an early frost in Southern Illinois this fall, the soybean losses in our area will be severe, because wet fields meant that most of the soybeans had to be planted late in the season. High interest just compounds the problems farmers already have.

The President and his leaders right now are searching for answers to correct some of these earlier actions. They realize the huge tax cut was a mistake, but it's hard to get the horse back in the barn after it's out. Washington news organizations have reported that the President is now considering tax increases, recognizing that the nation's economy cannot tolerate the huge deficits which the Administration's tax cut will bring on.

Something has to be done.

If the President comes up with a sensible solution, I will be supporting him.

"Tax Cut Proposals Are Political Pandering," P.S./Washington, August 18–24, 1996

The need for a constitutional amendment to require a balanced budget has been illustrated again by the continued intemperate support of proposals for tax cuts by the leaders of both political parties. On this issue, the public sees things more clearly than the leaders may realize.

I was asked about a tax cut at a town meeting I held almost two years ago just after both parties had announced they were for one. I said I opposed a tax cut until we balance the budget—and to my surprise received applause from the audience. After Bob Dole announced he favored an across-the-board 15 percent tax cut for everyone, the New York Times/CBS poll showed 36 percent of the public thought it was the right thing to do. Then they were asked, if such a tax cut would increase the federal budget deficit, would it be the right thing or the wrong thing to do. The response: 11 percent the right thing, 68 percent the wrong thing.

The public is right. A tax cut will increase the deficit.

People want to build a better future for their children and grandchildren; they want the country's future to be brighter. And they instinctively understand that when political leaders pander and offer us goodies just before an election, the aim is not to build a brighter future for the nation, but to gain a few votes in the next election.

Nothing adds to public cynicism more than this pandering.

President Reagan's proposal for a tax cut in 1981 was quickly countered with an almost-as-bad Democratic proposal. President Reagan assured us that if we followed this attractive route, in three years the budget would be balanced. I voted against both the Republican and Democratic proposals of 1981. The Reagan idea prevailed. Did we have a balanced budget in three years? The deficit went from $78 billion in fiscal year 1981 to a record-breaking $208 billion in fiscal 1983 and stood at a staggering $185 billion in fiscal year 1984.

In 1963 President John F. Kennedy complained about the projected $9 billion in gross interest the federal government would have to pay the next fiscal year. This year the gross interest expenditure will be $344 billion. In his debate with Vice President Richard Nixon, then-Senator Kennedy said: "I believe in the balanced budget, and the only conditions under which I would unbalance the budget would be if there was a grave national emergency or a serious recession." That was sound then and is sound now.

Unfortunately both political parties have strayed from that principle. And the deficits since then have reduced our standard of living and increased our interest rates.

If we could devote that $344 billion to health care and education, we would have an unbelievably more prosperous nation today, with far less crime. And our interest rates (including mortgage payments) would be dramatically lower. Spending taxes on interest buys us nothing. Next time you hear a political leader announce that he or she favors a tax cut, be one of those in the audience who thinks of your children, and do not cheer.

"What to Do with the Budget Surplus," NPR Commentary, January 13, 1998

There is welcome news: Both the bi-partisan Congressional Budget Office and the Clinton administration agree that next year there will be a balanced budget—and members of Congress of both parties are planning ways to cut taxes.

But hold on just a minute before that tax cut! Is the budget really balanced? It is balanced only if you don't count the borrowing from the Social Security Retirement Fund as debt.

There is no question that even with these conditions, balancing the budget is a step forward, achieved because both Presidents George Bush and Bill Clinton took unpopular steps at one point in each of their administrations to make this possible.

But the Social Security Retirement Fund problem will become huge if we do not take prudent steps now to see that future retirees have this guarantee. There is a technical surplus today because many more people are working and paying into Social Security than are retiring. But in the year 2012 that changes, and the retirement system starts running in the red—unless we plan and act now to avoid severe difficulties.

So talk about tax cuts is politically popular, but we would be much wiser to pay a little on the debt, and prepare for the long term future for Social Security.

Uncle Sam has been living on a credit card for 30 years, each year spending more than we take in. We know the problems that causes for an individual, and it causes problems for a nation. Now suddenly we find we have a surplus (if you don't count Social Security debt), and there are siren calls to spend that "surplus."

A much wiser course for someone who has been imprudent with credit cards is to pay back a little debt. And that is true for Uncle Sam. It's not as much fun as spending, but it's a lot better for our children and grandchildren.

"TAX CUTS AND THE BUDGET SURPLUS," NPR COMMENTARY, AUGUST 11, 1999

It is nice in politics to please people, but sometimes those impulses don't serve the public well. Budget officials of the federal government now project a $1 trillion surplus over the next 10 years, not counting Social Security retirement, and by a 50–49 vote in the U.S. Senate Republicans passed a $792 billion tax cut which the President says he will veto. However, not daring to be found on the unpopular side, Democrats are talking about a $300 to $400 billion tax cut.

Before we get too eager about tax cuts we should take a small dose of reality. Why is Federal Reserve Board Chairman Alan Greenspan opposed to the tax cut proposals? Because they are at least mildly inflationary. The traditional definition of inflation is "too many dollars chasing too few goods." These tax cuts add to the dollars, not to productivity.

And the $1 trillion surplus assumes that all discretionary spending on things like education and health care will stay at the present level, not even allow an adjustment for inflation. If you make an adjustment for inflation, that reduces the surplus by $595 billion, roughly 60 percent of the "surplus." There is also no adjustment for emergencies such as hurricanes, floods, and other disasters. For example we are talking about spending roughly an additional $7 billion for the farm problem this year, and that's not counted. The projection assumes there will be no significant downturn in our economy. I hope they're correct on that, but history suggests that cyclical downturns will occur.

One alternative to the tax cut would be to reduce our national debt a little, an anti-inflationary move which would benefit our children and grandchildren and take pressure away from interest rates, encouraging investment.

Alternatively, we could invest a little more in education where in some areas we have glaring deficiencies that harm the future of our nation, or use part of it to provide health care coverage for the 44 million Americans who have no health care coverage.

But whatever our personal preferences, prudence suggests that before we spend that surplus, we should wait to see whether it materializes. We should not start another round of living on a national credit card where we spend more money than we take in.

SOCIAL SECURITY AND PUBLIC PENSIONS

"Our Pension Dilemma," Sidelights from Springfield, by State Senator Paul Simon, June 13, 1965

One of the problems that will not be squarely faced in this legislative session—nor was it in past sessions—is the adequate funding of the various pension systems.

In fairness to Governor Otto Kerner it must be stated that four years ago he initiated efforts which have helped the pension funds substantially, but the fact still remains that most of the pension funds in the state are not in good shape.

And while this does not directly affect every reader of this column, it affects many of your neighbors, for pension funds cover workers in all types of governmental units: policemen, firemen, teachers, custodians, and a host of others. There are 347 pension funds of one kind or another operated under state direction. This covers about 270,000 people.

The specialists in this field—called "actuaries"—tell us that financially these pension systems are a long way from where they should be. Good examples are the teachers' pension funds. There are two systems, one for the city of Chicago and one for the rest of the state. While each system has substantial assets, the actuaries say these reserves are far from adequate.

The term used to describe the difference between what a system has, and what the experts say it should have to be in excellent condition, is "unfunded accrued liability." The unfunded accrued liability for the downstate teachers is more than $475 million and for the Chicago teachers more than $285 million.

In theory the experts would like to see all systems funded up to 100 percent, and some pension systems are. But just as most of us do not carry all the insurance the experts say we should have, so most pension systems probably cannot be expected to be completely funded.

If all pension systems were 70 to 75 percent funded, my feeling is that there would be no cause for concern. But the downstate teachers fund is only 36 percent funded and the Chicago teachers fund is only 30 percent funded. It does not take a financial genius to see that this is not wholesome. On the basis of percentages, a few funds are in even worse shape, although the teachers' pension systems cover the greatest number of employees.

This does not mean that next year, or even five years from now, the state will suddenly decide it must reduce pension payments. But unless concern is shown, in a decade or two we could be heading for trouble.

One of the reasons so little is done is that this is a problem easy to postpone. Usually the party out of power talks about it, while the party in control of the executive machinery, which has to worry about raising money, tends to postpone the obligations. The teachers' pensions are based on the theory that the state matches dollar for dollar what the teachers contribute. But the fact is that the state only partially matches these amounts, and those of us who are concerned are making little headway in changing this situation.

Having sound pension systems is a major responsibility of state government, and one that may affect your neighbor, relative, or friend.

"Pension Systems Face Danger," From the Statehouse, by Lieutenant Governor Paul Simon, November 3, 1971

A somewhat complicated—but extremely important—matter which affects a great many Illinois citizens is the financing of pension systems. Some pension systems funded by the state, or regulated by the state, are not in good financial condition. A good example is the Downstate Teachers' Pension System. This covers all teachers outside the city of Chicago. The Downstate Teachers' Pension System has an "actuarial deficiency" as of June 30, 1970 of $936 million. The audit report for June 30, 1971 will not be available until around the first of the year, but I anticipate the deficit will be over $1 billion.

What does an "actuarial deficiency" mean? This means that the actuaries, the pension experts, say that in theory the system ought to have that much additional money to be completely secure. Very few systems, however, are fully funded.

The breaking point for a system that is in reasonably good shape is one that is 75 percent funded. Some experts will go as low as 65 percent. The Downstate Teachers' Retirement System is funded only at 34 percent.

That means that we can get by this year and next year, but 10 years from now or 15 years from now there will be a great many teachers retiring and someone is going to suddenly say, "What happened to all that money?"

This is how this tremendous deficit was built up: When a teacher pays $1 into the pension system, the state by law is supposed to put in $1.20. This has not been done and it has not been done under both Democratic and Republican administrations.

For the current fiscal year, for example, an additional sum of $14 million was appropriated, but that portion was vetoed by the Governor. This year we paid 64 cents rather than $1.20. That means that we not only lose the difference between 64 cents and $1.20, but we lose the interest on it year after year. Unfortunately, there are other examples besides the teachers' retirement system.

The State Employees' Retirement System had an actuarial deficiency as of June 30, 1970 of $279 million. Yet, despite this deficiency, a little noted memorandum went around to all the payroll clerks in state government saying that the various offices should pay into the pension system not 6.4 percent of salary, as we have been doing, but 4.8 percent of salary. This gets us by this year with spending a little less money but it builds up long-range problems for ourselves.

We mortgage the future not only when we create bonded indebtedness; we also mortgage the future when we don't pay into pension systems as we should.

"Senior Citizens: Their Special Problems," P.S./Washington, September 7–13, 1975

Somehow our nation's sense of values has become warped when we are able to get a man to the moon, but can't get false teeth to thousands of citizens who have built our communities.

Our Congressional district has special problems along this line, because we have 15 percent of our population over 65 compared to the national average of 10 percent.

As you make visits to communities in an area like ours—blessed with great natural assets but not great wealth as a banker measures wealth—frequently you meet people who will apologize for their appearance and add, "I can't afford false teeth." The shame should be on those of us who aren't providing the means to get those false teeth, rather than on those who don't have the money to buy them. But the problem of false teeth is just one of the most visible difficulties those of great experience have. (I sometimes think we forget that we all hope to be old someday.)

Here are some other problems:

- Eye glasses and hearing aids are also not covered by Medicare, along with false teeth. I have a measure before the Ways and Means

Committee which would provide all three, for the cost of one submarine.

- Out-of-hospital drugs are really a problem for many older people. Medicare should pay for half of these costs.
- Our attitudes force many people into nursing homes who should not be there. Far more than other countries, we discourage independence. Nursing homes provide an important service, but it's costly to keep people there. As our population grows older (as it is) we ought to think of better alternatives than more and more and bigger and bigger nursing homes.

Great Britain, by comparison, has 10 nursing home beds for each 1,000 people over 65, while we have more than 50.

A young person who is not active is not healthy—and the same is true for older citizens.

But through social security regulations and in a great variety of other ways, we discourage our older citizens from staying active. Our economy needs their productivity, and our culture needs their ability to enrich the lives of all of us. Statistically, we are the richest nation on the face of the earth, but we are the only one of the wealthy nations which does not make sure that all who have built our society have false teeth.

Those false teeth are a symbol to me. A symbol of not caring enough.

We have the money to be more humanitarian. We just have the wrong priorities.

"GETTING PUBLIC PENSION SYSTEMS INTO SHAPE," P.S./WASHINGTON, NOVEMBER 20–26, 1977

"Is the social security system going broke?" letters we receive sometimes ask. Less frequently others ask whether their state or local pension system is in good shape and can be depended upon.

The answer to the first question is that the social security system is not in perfect shape, but not bad. But to make sure that 10 years from now or 20 years from now the system is not weakened, we must take remedial action now.

Unfortunately the way to get the social security system in better shape is to increase slightly the amount of money going into the fund, and so the House has voted some changes that will amount to an increase of a fraction of 1 percent in social security taxes and an increase from $17,700 of salary covered to $19,900 covered starting in 1978.

However, the Senate and the House have passed somewhat different versions and the final answer may not emerge until sometime next year. But action is needed and it probably will come. The state and local governmental pension system is more complicated and less encouraging.

The state of Illinois, for example, has 474 different public pension systems, some of them in very weak condition. The unfunded liability of these systems now is more than $7 billion, more than triple the unfunded liability of just 10 years ago.

And while the Illinois systems are in worse shape than in most states, some states have even worse financial problems facing them, New York being the prime example.

The simple, easy answer is for state and local governments to voluntarily start moving in the direction Congress has moved on the social security system. These pension funds should be beefed up financially, meeting current obligations and gradually filling the gap that years of neglect have left. The problem with that solution is that it is not likely to happen.

Pension systems are not likely to collapse next year, or the following year, and the nature of politics in the United States is that we concentrate on today's problems and tomorrow's problems—not those of five and 10 and 20 years distance.

A theoretical answer is for Congress to mandate state and local governments to fund their pension systems. Congressmen John Dent of Pennsylvania and John Erlenborn of Illinois have worked on that possibility. It remains a possibility, but there is also a question of whether such action is constitutional. One Supreme Court decision in particular raises serious doubts about the ability of Congress to act in this area.

You will not read any headlines about the discussions of what action should be taken. But a few more federal, state and local officials and concerned citizens had better take a much more serious look at this problem or we will reap a harvest of unfulfilled promises and human misery.

"Two Myths about Social Security," P.S./Washington, June 8–14, 1986

There are two widely held myths about Social Security. The young believe it will not be there when it is their turn to retire. There is also an assumption on the part of many people that much of Social Security money goes for welfare and for administrative costs.

Wrong, I am pleased to report, on both counts.

I sometimes hear from the 25-year-olds who want to get out of Social Security to "invest on my own so I can get a better return" since he or she assumes it will not be there when retirement comes. There are four things to consider:

1. While it may be true that a few would get a better return through prudent or lucky investments, that is not true for most people. And if that person with the wise investments has to end up supporting others who don't have Social Security coverage, he or she will end up being the loser.

2. The financial experts tell us that unless we have a serious inflation problem, 50 years from now the Social Security retirement fund will be in better shape than it is now. Your money is safe.

3. Most who advocate the "let me invest my money my way" course ignore the disability coverage they get through Social Security. Go to your local insurance agent and ask to get the benefits you receive from Social Security on disability, and you will find it extremely expensive. No one thinks a stroke or a heart attack will ever come to that person, but unfortunately it can happen to any of us.

4. Public opinion shows the public believes that only 48 cents out of every dollar paid into Social Security actually reaches Social Security recipients. The reality is that 98.7 cents of every dollar does. The Social Security trust fund is probably as efficiently run a government operation as we have.

No, those who would dismantle Social Security make fine-sounding speeches, but they are not taking positions that stand up under scrutiny.

There are still some things that we should do to improve parts of Social Security—particularly Medicare—but on balance Social Security is a good investment and protection for the people of this country, and that includes young people.

"THE MORAL TEST OF A SOCIETY," P.S./WASHINGTON, AUGUST 9–15, 1987

Neighbors recently found a Greenville, Ill., man near death because he was depriving himself of food and air conditioning to pay nursing home costs for his wife. This 80-year-old man has spent $72,000 over the last two years to keep his wife in a nursing home.

Now he must go on welfare and his wife will become a Medicaid recipient, "how sad for America that it treats its elderly citizens this way," his neighbor writes to me. How sad indeed.

When Social Security passed 50 years ago, the average American lived to be 58. We now live to be 75. One in nine Americans is 65 or older. By the year 2000, one in five will be 65 or older. There will then be more than 6 million over age 85.

Those figures spell a clear need: providing quality long-term care for seniors without crushing their families with debt. Every family's situation is different and in some cases nursing home care is necessary. But in other cases, quality care at home would mean independence and an alternative to nursing homes.

Couples who have lived together for decades find themselves separated by a society and government too insensitive to understand the misery and heartache this separation causes.

For example, an older couple lives together and the wife is getting frail. The husband suffers a stroke and cannot bathe or feed himself. She is not able to assist him. So we now send him to a nursing home, breaking up their home, causing untold misery and major costs. If someone were available to help him, there would be savings in both heartache and dollars.

Congressman Claude Pepper of Florida and I have introduced the Long-Term Home Care Family Protection Act. Our bill encourages more home-based care. An estimated 30 percent of nursing home residents really don't need institutional care if there were better alternatives. Our proposal is also for those who are at home now but cannot afford the care they need.

Our bill provides senior citizens with the long-term nursing, rehabilitation, personal services and medical supplies they need to stay in their homes without becoming a burden on their families. But it would not only help seniors. Other disabled persons and children who have been certified by a physician to require significant help with eating, bathing, dressing or other normal activities would also be eligible.

We would pay for the program by lifting the ceiling ($45,000 in 1988) on income subject to the Medicare payroll tax. Those earning more than that would pay 1.45 percent above that amount into the Medicare account. This change would affect only those 5 percent of workers who earn more than $45,000 in individual income (not family income).

Our proposal does not add to the deficit. In fact, it reduces it slightly.

Costs would be controlled by holding the top monthly payments to 75 percent of the monthly Medicaid rate for skilled nursing home services.

Franklin Roosevelt led the fight for Social Security to free all Americans from the fear of an old age of poverty and dependence. A quarter century later, John F. Kennedy proposed another great step forward: Medicare. Today, we face a new challenge. For Medicare provides virtually no protection for older Americans who need long-term nursing care, either at home or in nursing homes. Someday government will guarantee that people like the gentleman from Greenville don't nearly starve themselves to care for their loved ones.

Hubert Humphrey said it well: "The moral test of government is how that government treats those who are in the dawn of life, the children; those who are in the twilight of life, the elderly; and those who are in the shadows of life—the sick, the needy and the handicapped."

I heard Hubert Humphrey make that statement dozens of times and it always sounded good and right to me. We can and must do better.

"On Social Security," NPR Commentary, March 27, 2001

One of the ideas that emerges periodically is that people who pay into Social Security should be able to invest the funds—or part of them—themselves and not have the federal government's low interest payments adding to the trust fund. It is a great idea—until it is carefully examined.

First, imagine the auditing problems. Administering the current Social Security system costs less than 1 percent of the funds spent. If we have the liberty of investing wherever we want, following that paper trail will require tens of thousands of additional people and endless red tape.

Second, stocks go down as well as up, as we have painfully discovered recently. One of the advocates for this change says that we can take the risk away from investments by having the federal government guarantee them. Really? I would love to have the federal government guarantee my investments, but if we thought we had a bottomless hole with the savings and loan debacle, try guaranteeing investments we sometimes imprudently make.

Third, there is no certainty that stocks will reward people more than the present system. If there is a severe drop in the value of investments, who will support the people who otherwise could depend on Social Security income? The NASDAQ stock exchange fell more than 66 percent from March of 2000 to March of this year. Or look at the Dow Jones industrial average, down from a year ago but relatively risk-free compared to most investments. On December 31, 1964, the Dow Jones industrial average was 874.12. Seventeen years later, on December 3, 1981, it was 875.00. It had gained less than one point in seventeen years. Federal bonds are not glamorous, but they do better than that for seniors and those disabled.

If lawmakers want to have tax incentives for people of middle and lower income to invest in the stock market, I'm for that. But stay away from Social Security. Letting us invest our Social Security payments in the stock market would have us skating on thin ice. It would be a good deal for stockbrokers, but people who want security with their Social Security should not be encouraged to go out on that thin ice.

JOBS AND ECONOMIC DEVELOPMENT

"Needed: Money to Create Jobs,"
P.S./Washington, March 23–29, 1975

"There is a simple, easy answer to every serious problem and it is inevitably wrong," George Bernard Shaw once wrote. Our economic problems fall into that category

We have to get people back to work and get the economy moving again. All of us agree on that, but where we go from there is the matter of controversy.

At least temporarily (and perhaps longer than temporarily) we need to have some public service jobs. Call it WPA or what you want to, the necessity for action is clear. There is disagreement between Congress and the President on where you draw the line as to how many jobs are provided, but all want some.

One of the toughest problems in this situation is where we get the money that is needed for business growth, and the roots of this problem go back a few years.

When we got massively involved in the war in Vietnam, President Johnson made the decision (probably forced by public opinion) that we could have both guns and butter without a significant tax increase. It became the first major war for this nation without some severe economic constraints here at home.

But there were deficits. Big ones. And the government took a good portion of the money available to buy bonds for those deficits, money that ordinarily would have gone into the business field for plant expansion.

That is part of our problem today. Our high interest rates and slow economy did not hit us suddenly, though the oil problem worsened them.

But today's problem is compounded by the fact that for the next fiscal year the federal deficit will be around $70 billion, plus state and local indebtedness, which is growing rapidly. The total soaks up a good portion of the money which the business community needs for expansion, which will create more jobs.

There are economists who believe our economic problems will become more severe because business simply won't have the money needed for expansion. And present indications are not encouraging. What is the answer?

It's much too complicated to go into detail here, but these are among the possibilities.

- Hopefully, the various things being done to simulate the economy may reduce the deficit. If, for example, employment should increase by 1 percent, the deficit is reduced $12 to $15 billion by increased tax revenues; and unemployment compensation costs are reduced $2 to $3 billion. That is a sizable amount, which could then be used for business expansion.

- Interest rates must be lowered significantly. Lowering rates without excessively increasing the money supply is complicated, but it can be done. If it takes place, the stock market will leap ahead, and businesses can grow by selling stock (now not a practical possibility) and by ordinary borrowing. Lower interest rates would also give the housing market a big boost.

- Saving must be encouraged. Assets of banks and savings and loans must continue to grow. There are practical ways of encouraging that growth which I will discuss in the future. But as their assets grow, their ability to loan to individuals and businesses also grows.

Our economic problems are not simple and they are not easily solved. But if we use common sense and recognize that the answers may require sacrifices on the part of all of us, we can meet the need, and emerge a healthier nation.

"THE CAUSES OF CRIME," P.S./WASHINGTON, SEPTEMBER 5–11, 1976

A Centralia businessman sent me a quotation from Boston Police Commissioner Robert J. DiGrazia: "Most of us are not telling the public that there is relatively little the police can do about crime. We are not letting the public in on our era's dirty little secret: that those who commit the crime which worries citizens most—violent street crime—are, for the most part, the products of poverty, unemployment, broken homes, rotten education, drug addiction and alcoholism, and other social and economic ills about which the police can do little, if anything."

He is right.

Too many of us in public offices and out of office try to pretend that if we tried some gimmick, employed a few more police, had tougher police, had tougher courts, the crime problem would be reduced drastically. It might be reduced some by any of these things, but it is still true that the problems the police commissioner talked about are the fundamental problems.

The greatest anti-crime measure we could adopt right now would be to give people who want to work a chance to work. Among young people 16 to 19—the high crime rate age group—the average unemployment rate is 19 percent, and among black youth that age it is 37 percent.

Those unemployment rates do not count students who are not seeking work, or others in that age group who are not looking for employment. When you have that great a number of young people seeking work and unable to find it, the result is not only costly in terms of unemployment compensation and welfare, it is costly also in crime. And while there are a few bright spots in the crime picture—for example, the rate of murder in Washington, D.C., was the lowest it has been in nine years in 1975—the general trend is terribly discouraging.

Here are a few statistics to jolt anyone who believes the crime problem is not serious. I am comparing the 1960 crime rate per 100,000 population with the 1975 rate, the latest year for which statistics are available.

	1960	1975
Murder	4.5	9.6
Forcible rape	9	26
Robbery	60	218
Aggravated assault	85	227
Burglary	502	1,525
Larceny	283	2,804
Auto theft	182	469

Those statistics are grim. And we should not fool ourselves about the answers. Anyone who tells you the answers are easy is not telling you the truth. Because the number of young people in our country is gradually declining, we can expect our crime rate to decline somewhat in the near future. But it will still be excessively high until we tackle the really tough problems that help to cause high crime rates.

"Jobs Can Begin at Home," P.S./Washington, February 6–12, 1977

Last summer as I walked through the grounds of the DuQuoin State Fair I spotted a display of attractive woodwork. To my surprise I found that the items had been made in Southern Illinois by a firm just starting in business. The company: Dodds Woodwork and Supply in DeSoto.

The Simon family living room now has a beautiful coffee table we bought from that firm—a coffee table that would sell anywhere in the nation if people had the chance to see it.

Why does a congressman write a column about a coffee table? Several reasons:

1. The federal government has been spending modest sums for some years on areas like ours, areas that have an income level below the national average and high unemployment rates. But here is a man, Robert J. Dodds, who has taken the Southern Illinois labor we have in abundance, and the woods we have in abundance, and put them together. Dodds employs four people.

2. Too often in an area like ours we view our economic salvation as coming from some huge plant moving in. And now and then it happens, like General Tire coming into Mt. Vernon. But we also ought to look to encouraging business and talent we already have. If Dodds Woodwork and Supply can somehow get the message out, and expand, 10 years from now this business could employ 100 or 200 people.

3. If the conventional resources for expanding his business, such as a loan from a bank, will not permit enough growth, there is a possibility that help might be available from the Small Business Administration or some other government agency in the form of a loan. These loans are not easy to get, but there are many businesses operating in Southern Illinois right now because they did get them.

4. In an area like ours where coal plays such an important role, we sometimes rely too much on coal. We should encourage moves toward healthy coal development, but we need a broader base economically, so that when coal is down our communities are not so devastated. We need more people with the initiative and imagination of Robert J. Dodds.

And there are so many such people in our region. I think of Joe Foster in Golconda who has helped tourism with his Riverview Hotel. Or Wayman Presley's travel business which has brought millions of dollars to our area. Or many others who occur to me as I write this—people who in one way or another are like this DeSoto businessman.

Working as a carpenter for Southern Illinois University, Dodds decided to quit and to launch out on his own. And now his business has grown to the point he is behind on his orders.

He has found an unusual method of putting Southern Illinois hardwoods together in an extremely attractive way.

I asked him to send me a letter telling how he got started. He sent a five-page handwritten letter and at the end noted: "Excuse the long-hand written letter. I could say my secretary is off sick. But the truth is I don't have a secretary." He may not have a secretary, but he has an idea, and he's working hard at it. And that's what helps to make this nation tick. We need to do more to encourage Dodds and his counterparts.

That four-leaf clover we seek, to help improve the economy of our region and the nation, may not be at some corporate headquarters in New York, or Detroit, or Los Angeles, but right at our doorstep.

"Stimulating Youth Employment,"
P.S./Washington, July 31–August 6, 1977

A minimum wage bill is likely to emerge from Congress in the next few months. It would make the new minimum wage for the nation $2.65 an hour, and provides for a gradual increase after that so that at the end of three years someone supporting a family of four on the minimum wage would be above the poverty level. The evidence is strong that this would be good for the nation.

But one provision in the measure faces a stiff fight in the House, a proposal by Congressman Robert Cornell of Wisconsin and myself that there should be a "youth differential," so that young people 18 and under could be paid 85 percent of the minimum wage the first six months on a job. The amendment is supported by Congressmen John Erlenborn and John Anderson, both of Illinois. Why have a youth differential?

What happens when the minimum wage goes up is that youth employment goes down. If people have to pay $2.30 an hour (the current minimum wage) or more to hire someone, there is a tendency to hire the person who has learned good work habits, who has been seasoned a bit by holding a job. The unemployment rate among young people is triple the unemployment rate among adults. That has both short-range and long-range implications that are bad, whether you are talking about problems of crime or talking about the nation's economy needing people with good work habits.

A Brookings Institution study last year noted, "The most reasonable verdict is that teenagers have more to lose than to gain from higher minimum wages: they appear to be forced out of the better jobs, denied full-time work . . . If one of the goals of minimum-wage legislation is to eliminate sweatshop low-wage jobs for teen-agers the law appears to be counterproductive."

A Congressional Budget Office study suggests that when the minimum wage goes up 25 percent, youth unemployment goes up 4 to 6 percent. With the anticipated new minimum wage, that would mean an increase in youth unemployment of 2 to 4 percent.

Practically, that means that if our proposal for a youth differential does not pass, there will be an additional 35,000 to 70,000 young people out of jobs. And right now the youth unemployment rate is listed at 18.6 percent, but it is actually much higher. The amendment we propose would have safeguards against dropping older workers to hire teen-agers at a lower rate.

The experience in other countries and in some of our states is that a special incentive to hire young people can be helpful. My friends in the AFL-CIO oppose our amendment. While I often find myself in agreement with them, this time I think they are wrong. It is interesting that in Great Britain it was the labor unions which recognized the problem of youth unemployment and asked for the youth differential. Neither Congressman Cornell nor I suggest that this alone will solve our problem. We favor programs like the old CCC and others that gave productive jobs to all age groups.

But we believe that youth unemployment is a significant enough factor among our nation's problems that to ignore the impact of a minimum wage change on the nation's teen-agers is to do our country a disservice.

"Jobs Instead of Welfare," P.S./Washington, February 22–28, 1981

We seem to learn the lessons of history slowly, if at all. The other day I asked the Library of Congress for a booklet which describes the WPA projects in Illinois from July 1, 1935 to June 30, 1938. It is fascinating reading.

At that point (as now) the nation had millions of unemployed, but then they decided that as much as possible they would give people the chance to be productive, to enrich society and to do something they could be proud of. They turned the liability of unemployment into a national asset.

During that three-year period in Illinois 28 million square feet of concrete sidewalk was either built or significantly improved; thousands of miles of curbs and gutters were constructed; 1,895 new rural bridges were built and 2,160 were repaired; enough highway repair took place to be the equivalent of eleven highways from Cairo to Wisconsin; 19,197 indoor toilets were built for people who didn't have them; sewer systems were constructed and repaired; almost seven million feet of water system was either added or repaired; libraries were built and library services improved markedly; hundreds of parks and playgrounds were built, along with tennis courts and swimming pools; recreational activities were sponsored for young people and older citizens; 61,000 families who needed special help were given home visits; day care centers were sponsored; thousands of adult Illinois citizens were taught to read and write; art projects were encouraged, resulting in almost

300,000 individual paintings, posters, sculptures, etc.; almost 500 people were put to work bringing up to date historical records; writers were commissioned to do guides (including one of Cairo); theater productions were staged. And the list goes on.

Music was encouraged, and I note that the groups sponsored included the Colp Chorus, which gave 108 performances to 40,115 people; the Herrin Dance Orchestra, which gave 99 performances for 28,640 people; and the Southern Illinois Concert Orchestra of Herrin, which gave performances for 46,498 people. We have a choice of a welfare system which hands people money for doing nothing, or a jobs program which pays people for being productive and enriching all of us. The latter is much the more sensible way to proceed.

The closest thing we have to the WPA is CETA, though frankly it is a pale comparison because (among other things) it is not project oriented. But even that pale comparison is threatened with extinction by people who want to "save money," and they will save it by taking people off of jobs and putting them on welfare.

Our aim must be to give more people the opportunity and encouragement—and sometimes a good push—to get off the welfare rolls.

"Merger Mania," P.S./Washington, January 10–16, 1982

One of the main reasons for high interest rates, and one factor in inflation, is the merger of more and more large businesses.

Instead of investing in research, new jobs, and greater productivity, too many corporations are using their investment dollars to swallow up other businesses—and that contributes nothing to research or jobs, and weakens the free enterprise system because it reduces competition.

I have been among those sympathetic to the problems of the American steel industry, though recognizing that shortsighted leadership had caused many of its problems. But almost the same day in which I received a message of distress from the steel companies, I picked up a newspaper and read that U.S. Steel wants to spend $6.5 billion to buy Marathon Oil. If U.S. Steel can borrow $6.5 billion—sending our interest rates up—why can't it borrow half that amount to build plants that are as modern as those in Japan and Germany?

The first half of 1981 saw mergers involving expenditures of $35.7 billion—a 60 percent increase over 1980. If the second half of 1981 matched the first half, then more than $70 billion was spent in a manner which weakens the U.S. economy.

In 1960, 400 corporations controlled two-thirds of the corporate wealth of our country. By 1980 that was down to 200 corporations and the present trends are trimming that number rapidly. That trend is almost inevitable, unless competition and the watchful eye of government are there to prevent it. And at the present time the attitude of the federal government—for the first time since Warren Harding's presidency or even pre–Theodore Roosevelt days—is that there is nothing to fear from increasing concentration of corporate power.

I do not suggest that bigness in and of itself is bad. General Motors, AT&T, and IBM are examples of businesses, which through top-notch research and development efforts, have developed products and services which this nation and the world want. Their records are not "pure as the driven snow" but they did not grow primarily by buying out others. And each has contributed significantly to the American scene. But what possible good can come to the nation from Mobil buying Montgomery Ward and Marathon Oil?

In 1980 the 700 largest corporations spent $28 billion on research and development and $44 billion on acquisitions and mergers. The 1981 record will be substantially worse.

One other significant statistic: Two-thirds of all new jobs created in the United States in the last decade were generated by businesses with fewer than 100 employees. Yet we are embarked on a policy which by indifference encourages mergers rather than research, and aids large businesses which generate few jobs more than small businesses which generate many. And high interest rates compound all these problems, for the high interest rates are putting many small businesses—including farmers—into bankruptcy or forced sale.

Through action or inaction, present policies are changing the character of American business. It's about time that we face up to that.

"Helping the Homeless," P.S./Washington, March 29–April 4, 1987

It troubles most of us when we are driving or walking through a large city and see homeless, desperate people sleeping on the streets. We instinctively sense that they represent not only troubled people, they also represent something in our society that needs repairing.

The House has passed a bill to encourage state and local governments to do a better job in providing shelter for the homeless, among other things. I have joined Sen. Pete Domenici, a Republican from New Mexico, in introducing legislation to provide more assistance for the mentally ill among the homeless. The estimate is that somewhere between one-fifth and one-half have serious mental problems.

This part of the homeless problem was created from the best of motives. When I served in the Illinois Legislature we put great stress on getting people out of mental hospitals and into the community. That was needed. Nationally the number in state mental hospitals has dropped from 559,000 to 126,000—and for most of these people that represents an improvement.

But there are also those discharged who should not have been. Some who needed more of a helping hand were told to go and make their way in society. They were unable to make the dramatic change from a closely guarded and supervised mental hospital to a world of much greater freedom. But the problem is more than mental illness and shelter.

One of the fine new Senate members is Sen. Harry Reid, a Democrat from Nevada.

He put on old clothes, a baseball hat, and some sunglasses and went and slept with the homeless one night and spent part of the next day with them. No television cameras. No reporters. He just quietly found things out for himself. Sen. Reid discovered the three interests of the homeless, in order of importance, are jobs, food, and shelter. Shelter is the most visible need but the least important to them.

In testifying for the Guaranteed Job Opportunity Program I have introduced, Sen. Reid told about standing at the corner of H and Bonanza streets in Las Vegas with some of the homeless. People would drive up in cars to offer employment; some jobs lasted only an hour or two, some for several days. "They would literally fight for those jobs," Sen. Reid said. When a car stopped people would "run up to the vehicle and try to sell themselves to those in the car."

Academic studies that lasted many months came to the same conclusion that Sen. Reid did in one night and day: *The main cause of homelessness is joblessness.* Shelters and other forms of help are needed temporarily. But if we really want to help homeless people, the long-term answer for many of them is jobs. And jobs can do wonders for the mental health of many people. The Guaranteed Job Opportunity Program, S 777, would provide 32 hours of work a week at the minimum wage—$107 a week or $464 a month—or 10 percent above unemployment compensation, whichever is highest. Only those out of work five weeks or longer would be eligible. People would be screened to find out if they need help in learning how to read and write, or speak English, or develop a marketable skill. Developing themselves would be an essential part of the program.

The unemployed would do things that need to be done in every community, with either business or labor having the right to veto projects. The homeless are only a small percentage of those who would benefit from such a measure.

But they are among the most visible. For each homeless and jobless person you see, there are a thousand less visible who suffer in a less dramatic way. The United States can do better.

6

Culture, History, and Politics

Paul Simon loved history and read voraciously about it and the prominent leaders who shaped our nation and the world. He was always seeking to learn the lessons that can be extracted from history and to discover
what the lives of famous and successful leaders can teach us. These are
recurring themes in his writings, as the selections included in this chapter
illustrate. In his devotion to history and the life stories of great leaders,
Simon was following a great intellectual tradition in American education.
If one reads the biographies of many of the early leaders of this country,
it is evident that they took their reading duties quite seriously and were
convinced that they could learn civic and personal virtue from history
and from the examples of those who came before them. Such themes are
evident in the biographies of such early leaders as Abraham Lincoln, George
Washington, John and Abigail Adams, Thomas Jefferson, and Benjamin
Franklin. Lessons from history and biography also figure prominently in
the upbringing and education of more recent leaders like Harry Truman
and Dwight Eisenhower. Simon followed these models and learned as much
as he could; he also wrote columns avidly recommending that others take
the study of history seriously.

Religion and religious education are also frequent themes in Simon's
writings. As his own autobiography indicates, Simon was raised in a very

religious home and environment, and the lessons from his Lutheran upbringing are evident in most of his work. Robert E. Hartley's biography on Simon also covers his early life quite thoroughly and emphasizes how important religion and religious instruction were to Paul and his brother Arthur's life. Educators and parents of that day, like Martin and Ruth Simon, firmly believed that the shaping of character begins at home and that it is reinforced and deepened by the lessons acquired from early and frequent church attendance. Simon's early life was saturated with those kinds of lessons. The instruction from home and church were also just the right influence for shaping not only personal character and virtue but also civic character and virtue. Thus, what was good for the individual was also, happily, good for the community and ultimately the nation.

For all his strong belief in the salutary role of religion in personal and public life, Paul Simon was also an ardent advocate for the separation of church and state. Most important, he believed that the First Amendment clearly required the government to keep a strict hands-off stance toward churches and religion, and vice versa. He did not believe that the churches, synagogues, and mosques, qua organized religion per se, should be actively involved in the political fights of the day. They should help shape individual character, the norms of society, and the mores of the community, but they should not tell their congregants how to vote or for whom to vote. They should not be involved in raising money and sinking it into political campaigns. He was surprised and hurt when he first encountered criticism from the emerging Christian Right led by such pastors and fundamentalist leaders as Jerry Falwell and Pat Robertson, and he reacted quite negatively toward their stinging criticism of him and his political ideology. He also fired back with pointed refutation and rebuttal of their positions.

Early on in his political life, Simon thought the work and influence of the Lutheran church was quite important for enhancing the civic virtues of its people, and he believed that they would just naturally agree with his brand of Progressive politics if they examined their consciences and studied the Scriptures adequately. In short, what we now call the social gospel was his fundamental position on the important teachings of the New Testament in the Christian Bible. He understood that the early civil rights movement was heavily centered and influenced by the black church, and he had no problem with that influence since he thought the cause was intrinsically right and in line with his own sense of justice. Like many liberals of his day, Simon held the easy assumption that proper Christian values would lead people of goodwill to approximately the same conclusions about politics he held. Later, when the push-back from the Right grew to such power, he became a much more ardent and articulate advocate for the separation of church and state and for the churches and religious groups staying out of politics officially, whatever their own private views and morality may have been. This is a case where Simon's political and religious views evolved to a more complex and nuanced position as he learned more and was over-taken by events.

Simon was a partisan who valued bipartisanship, as several of the selections in this chapter also indicate. He worked with and had high praise for leaders as diverse as Gerald Ford, Bob Dole, Barry Goldwater, Tip O'Neill, and Mayor Bob Butler of Marion, Illinois. He understood that each had played an important role in Congress, the presidency, or in their community, and he appreciated their commitment to public service and their hard work. While all but O'Neill were Republicans, they were also workhorses in the governmental and legislative process and were more interested in results and in getting the job done than in scoring ideological debaters' points. These were the kinds of people Simon could and did work with as they inched incrementally toward the common good and the general welfare. There was a certain bipartisan camaraderie that existed when Simon was a member of Congress that was important to him and important to getting the job done. The word "comity" was used often then to indicate the mutual respect that many members had for the other side of the aisle. It is hard to see much evidence of that kind of bipartisanship and respect for the art of compromise in Congress today. Many critics of the legislative process now treat any compromise as a sellout of moral principles. Their disdain for the inevitable give-and-take of the legislative process reflects the absolutes demanded by zealots. Such zealotry is a bad fit for democracy. Today is an era when deep partisan division has replaced the kind of bipartisanship cooperation valued by Paul Simon. The growing evidence of what he believed to be a pernicious polarization was one of the major reasons he gave for his retirement when he announced it well before the 1996 campaign. That polarization has only grown in the years since Simon left the Senate.

"Politics and Morality" (the first annual Adlai E. Stevenson Memorial Lecture, Unitarian Universalist Church, Urbana, Illinois, October 22, 1965), by State Senator Paul Simon, published in *The Cresset*, January 1967

The Adlai E. Stevenson Memorial Lecture was established by the Board of Trustees of the Unitarian Universalist Church of Urbana-Champaign on August 9, 1965. The theme of the lecture is to be: "Politics and Morality." This lecture has been established in the belief that such a memorial is consistent with the concerns of the late governor, and a proper reminder of his religious and political commitments.

I confess a feeling both of pleasure and inadequacy in this opportunity to present the first annual lecture here honoring the memory and ideals of Adlai E. Stevenson.

It has been only a few months since that pleasant summer day when we were stunned by the news of his death. We are still too close to that event to judge with any finality either the stature of the man or the relevancy of his message. But it is patently clear that Adlai E. Stevenson will be remembered long after many of our presidents are all but forgotten, and that his appeal to reason, cooperation and compassion must help guide our destiny if those things we treasure most are to be preserved for future generations.

During the years when Senator Joseph McCarthy regularly made headlines, when fear threatened to replace faith, when we were in danger of remembering only what we opposed, here was a man on the scene who could make us laugh at ourselves, who helped give us perspective, who gently admonished us to remember those ideals for which our nation has stood.

His very appointment as ambassador to the United Nations raised the prestige of that organization. Whether it was a dramatic confrontation with the Soviets over the Cuban missiles, or a complex resolution about Algeria, each of us had the confidence that at the United Nations was a man who not only represented our nation's best interest, but the world's best interest. When he died it was perhaps appropriate that it should be on foreign soil, for he belonged to all nations as much as he belonged to our nation.

In all of the tributes paid to Adlai E. Stevenson following his death, little mention was made of his contributions as Governor of Illinois. Perhaps his gift to state government is best summed up by a long-time lobbyist on the Springfield scene who told me a few years ago: "In all of my years in

Springfield, no one has ever lifted the whole tone of state government as Governor Stevenson did."

I shall not impose on you a lengthy list of achievements in state government, but let me remind you of an important date in Illinois history that is now all but forgotten: May 12, 1950. On that date the Illinois State Highway Police from the northern part of the state swooped down on two big gambling casinos in my county of Madison, catching the gambling gentry and some public officials with complete surprise. It was the first time in Illinois history that state highway police have been used for that purpose. It brought to an end "the good old days"—as some like to call them—when county and municipal officials could plot with the vermin of society and arrange for this gang or that gang to take over gambling in your county or mine. The state police could not have been used in that raid had not Governor Stevenson, over strenuous objections from many politicians, placed the state police on a merit system. And once that was achieved, it became easier to do some desperately needed housekeeping. It is impossible to gauge the long-range improvement that has brought to many of our communities, but it is tremendous. Instead of endless arguments, token raids, and corrupting influences, many of our local governments are discussing things they should have been long ago: whether they should have a detention home for juveniles, whether they need a park and recreation program. In areas where gambling money flowed freely to the treasuries of both parties, happily we are relatively free from these gifts which were always given only at a terrible price.

May 12, 1950 is but one of the many illustrations that in the area of politics and morality, Governor Stevenson acted when distressingly many in public life neither talk nor act to improve the tone of government.

In discussing "Politics and Morality" there are those who say there is no connection between the two and should be none. With this I heartily disagree. That there sometimes is no connection between the two I recognize. But some type of moral foundation for our political process is both desirable and necessary. Politics is certainly not an arena in which you generally choose between good and evil. I wish it were that simple. We are faced with a dilemma that Abraham Lincoln described in 1848:

> The true rule in determining to embrace, or reject anything is not whether it have any evil in it; but whether it have more of evil than of good. There are few things wholly evil, or wholly good. Almost everything, especially of governmental policy, is an inseparable compound of the two; so that our best judgment of the preponderance between them is continually demanded.

Accepting the truth of that statement, does that leave us rudderless in the seas of politics? I think not. While we may disagree on what the moral imperatives should be, there are certain things so basic that virtually all men of good will can find agreement with them. Let me suggest four rules that may seem obvious:

1. *Government policy should not be for sale to the highest bidder.*

"Corruption" and "freedom" are diametrically opposed terms. The theory of a representative democracy is that men of opposing views come together, freely expressing their views, and in the process the public good is served more often than in any other governmental structure. Corruption means the dominance of a special interest over the public interest. Those who are in the filthy business of buying votes do not spend their money unless they get what they pay for.

The taped conversation of three lobbyists in Springfield presents a good example. The court decision to prohibit the use of those tapes for legal prosecution may be a proper decision. But let no one miss the message of those tapes: too often your government has been for sale in Springfield. I heard no one on the Springfield scene suggest that these tapes were not authentic. What they described was three men spending $200 to $1,000 a vote—a total of $30,000—to kill a bill. The tapes make clear that the people of Illinois, by their indifference and cynicism, have tolerated the crudest type of corruption.

In the last fifty years the neighboring state of Wisconsin has not had a single major scandal in state government while in Illinois we have had scores of them. We need to start asking ourselves: Why? The answer is not simple but answers are available. The most fundamental answer is that the public must start becoming intolerant of the easy dollar that corrodes the very foundation of our society.

When I say that government policy should not be for sale, this means policy changes beyond the crudest prostitution of our policies.

We have not faced up to the question of campaign expenses and contributions, for example. President Theodore Roosevelt wanted us to follow some modification of the British system, where expenditures are tightly limited, and funds come from the government. I strongly favor such a change. A campaign for governor of Illinois, for example, costs more than $1 million for any serious candidate and most of those who contribute this money expect something in return. That "something" is not always in the public interest. Preferential treatment for everything from contracts to ambassadorships will continue within our nation until we face up to the viciousness of our current practices which all too often place government policies and positions up for public auction.

2. *Those governing have a moral obligation to spend public money carefully.*

Government by its nature has certain inefficiencies. This is true of a state, a county, a municipality, a university, and even that strangest of Illinois governmental creatures: a mosquito abatement district.

Those of us who govern should be aware of these inefficiencies and hold them to a minimum.

As an extreme example, in the 1963 session of the Illinois General Assembly, $96,500 was appropriated to study the disease of race horses. When I asked the sponsor how much we were spending on cancer research, he replied he didn't know but felt the appropriations for the already pampered ponies were very important. Another senator got up and said he had been betting on horses he was sure had some diseases, and the legislation passed and became law.

At the federal level a few weeks ago Senator Daniel Brewster of Maryland attempted to limit federal farm support to any individual or corporation first to $25,000 and then $50,000. Both times he was defeated, despite the fact that Senator Brewster had pointed out that one Arkansas corporation had received over $16 million in 1964 under this program that was originally conceived as a help to the small farmer.

Government spending is by itself neither automatically right nor wrong. But when tax funds are used to help race horses rather than people, when tax money is used to sustain an archaic system of party patronage like we have in Illinois, when public funds are spent unnecessarily on interest instead of goods and services, then we must act. Failure to act makes honorable people question not only the unwise expenditure but the necessary expenditure, and worthy causes suffer along with the unworthy.

3. *Government has an obligation to permit the free flow of ideas.*

Founded as we are on the importance of the individual, we must not only respect a man's right to walk down the sidewalk and seek a job, but also the right to express unpopular views. We are not founded on the premise that you can put an idea into jail.

The greatest weakness of the Communist world is its unwillingness to permit the free flow of ideas. Yet there are those in our midst who would have us emulate them.

For example, those who periodically suggest that we must have state censorship of textbooks in Illinois have a misunderstanding of the function of our government, and fail to comprehend our greatest asset. "The melting pot strength" of our country was not, as some believe, simply a breeding process by which the Swede, and the Italian, and the German intermarried. "The melting pot strength" of the United States has been that all of these people brought their ideas, and in this cross-fire of ideas we were able to freely pick what we felt were the finest.

Stopping this free flow of ideas is not only unwise, it is also immoral. Belief in the value of each individual must bring with it the respect for his right to express his views. To do otherwise is to deny him his individuality.

4. Government has an obligation to help the helpless.

To some people the test of morality in government is simply one of honesty. You can vote against measures to help the racial minorities, the hungry, the mentally retarded, and those otherwise oppressed, so long as you don't steal a dollar. While I don't favor corruption, this simple formula is far from adequate in our complex society.

Is it morally right to ignore the fact that we place the Negro into a ghetto? Are our standards of help for the mentally retarded adequate, when often they are treated worse than cattle? The questions continue, and it is unfortunately easier to dig up problems than solutions. But one answer should be apparent: ignoring these problems is wrong.

The controversial play "The Deputy" is not an accurate portrayal of history, but its basic moral is true: people who ignore great need and injustice are responsible for their existence. And sometimes those who cry "welfare state" comfort us more than they disturb us, for they imply we are already doing too much to help the helpless.

Let's look at the facts in just one important area: world hunger. The Food and Agricultural Organization of the United Nations and the Swedish economist Gunnar Myrdal are talking about "mass starvation" in the coming decade. We know that the majority of people alive today are going to die before their time either for lack of food or for lack of protein in their food. Poverty beyond our borders is growing at an astounding rate. More than 60 percent of the people of the world today have a per capita annual income of less than $100.

While this alarming situation exists, we in the United States become richer and richer each year, and spend less and less—both in absolute and relative terms—to help the world's poor. Following World War II the United States spent approximately 2 percent of its gross national product on the Marshall Plan, which turned out ultimately to be an investment in our own prosperity. For fiscal year 1966, when the trouble spots like South Vietnam are excluded, we will spend 1/5 of 1 percent of our gross national product to help the poor beyond our borders. The Christian-Jewish portion of the world comprises less than 20 percent of the world population, yet has about 75 percent of the world's wealth.

While I fully realize the political popularity of being against foreign aid, we must recognize that we are doing less and less to help the growing number of poor, and we continue such a policy at our own peril. The division between the world's "haves" and "have nots" must be bridged. We owe our collective conscience and we owe the future a more realistic measure of response to world poverty.

And this is but one area where we have a moral imperative to do more to help the helpless, to shake loose from our middle class indifference.

Perhaps Adlai Stevenson's hero Abraham Lincoln, more than any other American, embodies the blending of politics and morality to which we look in retrospect with pride. Certainly no American document is such a moving mixture of the two as is his second inaugural address.

The speech which projected Lincoln onto the national stage more than any other was delivered at Cooper Union in 1859. Perhaps there he best summarized the admonition that each of us needs: "Let us have faith that right makes might, and in that faith let us, to the end, dare to do our duty as we understand it."

Adlai Stevenson would expect no less of us.

We should expect no less of ourselves.

Editor's note: This speech, delivered by Senator Simon at the Unitarian Universalist Church in Urbana, was later published in *The Cresset*, a publication of the Lutheran Church, Missouri Synod, in vol. 24, no. 4 (January 1967): 10–12. This article is used by permission from *The Cresset* and Valparaiso University. The following was taken from the website of *The Cresset*: "First published in 1937 by the Lutheran Church Missouri Synod's youth ministry The Walther League, *The Cresset* was founded to introduce culturally isolated German Lutherans into the American mainstream. . . . Valparaiso University [is] an independent Lutheran University in Northeast Indiana . . . [and] *The Cresset* became a publication of the university in 1951."

"A Meaningless Rating," P.S./Washington, May 11–17, 1980

Various organizations give ratings to members of Congress and members of the state legislature, and frequently the ratings are totally meaningless, taking a few votes out of hundreds or thousands, and judging an entire record on those few votes. A perfect example of the problem is a rating by "The Christian Voice" on "moral issues."

Their "moral issues" are items like whether a member voted for or against creating a Department of Education, "no" being the morally correct vote according to them. Another example is a constitutional amendment to "prohibit the busing of children to a school other than the one nearest their home." In this case if you did not vote for this amendment (which would have halted an excellent school program in Carbondale, for example) you are listed as having cast an immoral vote.

My total on their list—out of a possible score of 100—is zero. A Methodist minister in Congress, Rep. Robert Edgar, got 8 percent; Rep. John Buchanan of Alabama, a Baptist minister, got only 29 percent; and Rep. Robert Drinan of Massachusetts, a Catholic priest, got a moral rating of zero. While Rep. Richard Kelly of Florida, the member who has admitted taking $25,000 in the Abscam scandal, got a moral rating of 100 percent.

The people who run "The Christian Voice" have a right to their opinion on creating a Department of Education, for example. But to say that those who don't agree with them are immoral suggests that they may understand little about both Christianity and politics.

The nearest scriptural base for a "rating" that I can recall is in Matthew 25, the judgment day scene, where Christ lists the questions we will be asked: Did you help the hungry? Did you give water to the thirsty? Did you provide clothes to those needing them? Did you take care of the sick? Did you show concern for those in prison?

Did any of the items which "The Christian Voice" uses as a checklist reflect these concerns which Christ mentioned? Somehow they "improved" on that almost 2,000-year-old list so none of the original concerns were reflected.

I was pleased to receive a statement put out by the national presidents of three Lutheran churches: "It is arrogant to assert that one's position on a political issue is 'Christian' and that all others are 'un-Christian,' 'immoral,' or 'sinful.' There is no 'Christian' position; there are Christians who hold positions . . . To describe one group's political position as 'The Christian Voice' . . . is wrongly judgmental. It is also an affront to Jewish and other religious advocates whose religions hold social justice as a social form of love of neighbor."

I respect and understand those who disagree with stands I take. Sometimes I have to struggle within myself before taking a position. But I have little sympathy for those who equate their position with God's position, who in a simplistic and non-scriptural way confuse both theology and politics.

"Prescription for Prayer Not the Answer,"
P.S./Washington, June 20–26, 1982

Judging by my mail, the people in our district favor a constitutional amendment to encourage prayer in the schools, even though almost all the major churches and church organizations oppose such an amendment. But a small item in a magazine caught my eye the other day. It said that almost 60 percent of the people of Sweden seriously question the existence of God, but both prayer and reading of scripture have been part of the Swedish public school scene for more than 100 years. That suggests that those who look to scripture reading or prayer to somehow automatically create a more receptive attitude toward religion could be badly mistaken.

My own inclination is to believe that we cannot expect the schools to do what we fail to do in our homes and in our churches. Those who favor a constitutional amendment generally do not understand what the courts did. The courts have said that no state (such as New York) or school district can require a prescribed prayer on the part of students.

That seems to be eminently sound. It is common sense, for what is an acceptable prayer to a Catholic might not be to a Protestant; what is acceptable to a Christian might not be to a Jew; what is acceptable to a Jew might not be to a Buddhist, whose numbers are substantial in Hawaii.

When I was in the third grade, a Mrs. Woods came to our public school once a week and told Bible stories. We looked forward to that each week. As long as there were no objections, that would still be acceptable. Time set aside for silent prayer is also permitted.

In many communities where virtually everyone is of the same religious persuasion, there is a variety of religious expression which takes place in the public schools.

But where religious preferences differ, the religiously acceptable becomes more and more diluted to the point that it becomes almost meaningless.

There is a second problem that I see with the organized "voluntary" prayer.

It is revealed in a story told to me by my respected colleague, Rep. Dan Glickman of Kansas. Dan happens to be of the Jewish faith and he grew up in Wichita, Kansas, the city he now represents. When Dan was in fourth grade, the school opened each morning with a Christian prayer. Dan, not being a Christian, was excused, and each morning this small fourth-grade boy had to leave the room while the others prayed. "It was an experience I shall never forget," Dan explained to me. "It told me and the others that I was different at an age when you want to be as much like everyone else as possible."

The proposal for a constitutional amendment to encourage prayer in the schools is well motivated. But it is based on a misunderstanding of what the courts have said and it ignores the practical experience of other countries. On top of that, it is not fair to students like Dan Glickman.

This nation needs more attention to religious matters, but constitutional amendments will not provide that.

"The Importance of Separating Church from State," P.S./Washington, July 21–27, 1985

Senator Sam Ervin, the wise old man from North Carolina who died a few months ago, wrote in his autobiography: "If religious freedom is to endure in America, the responsibility for teaching religion to public school children must be left to the homes and churches of our land, where this responsibility rightfully belongs. It must not be assumed by the government through the agency of the public school system."

Why would he say that? Why do most of the organized churches of this country oppose a constitutional amendment to have organized prayer in the schools—either spoken or unspoken?

Neither Sen. Ervin nor the churches oppose prayer. But those who have studied the history of governments know the dangers to both religious freedom and to governments of too much government entanglement with religion.

Government can best encourage religious institutions when it is neutral. An example would be the tax exempt status of non-profit organizations. It applies to the Catholic Church, the Jewish synagogue, the Lutheran church—but it also applies to the Society of Atheists.

Government can assist religious activity when consenting adults voluntarily use the services. We have chaplains in the armed forces and we open the House and Senate with prayer. But those who do not wish to participate in the opening prayer can skip it. Those in the armed forces who do not want to attend chapel can avoid it.

But third-graders ordered to pray, silent or spoken, have no choice. If we believe that by government ordering them to pray we are helping either government or religion, we fool only ourselves. Why did Thomas Jefferson and James Madison and the other founders of our nation feel so strongly about keeping government from fostering religion?

Because they had seen the abuse.

For example, a few decades before our Declaration of Independence, Chief Justice George Jeffreys of England made this statement in a trial of a Presbyterian woman charged with sheltering two men who shared the same religious affiliation.

Chief Justice Jeffreys noted: "There is not one of those lying, sniveling, canting Presbyterians but in one way or another has a hand in the rebellion. Presbytery has all manner of villainy in it. Show me a Presbyterian and I'll show thee a lying knave." In Thomas Jefferson's colony of Virginia, a Quaker was not permitted to live within the state. If he came back three times, he would automatically be executed. Many other abuses of too much government and religion working together could be cited from our nation's earliest days.

In nations that have official religions, where that religious belief is backed by government pressure, their people generally are not as active religiously as are the people in the United States. Both government and religious leaders should think long and carefully before we discard the wisdom of those who founded our country.

"Cloaking Politics in Religion," P.S./Washington, July 6–12, 1986

One of the things I have tried to promote throughout my years in journalism and public life is tolerance, whether it is racial or national or religious or political. So it was a bit startling to pick up Dr. Jerry Falwell's publication, *Liberty Report*, and see a large full-color painting of myself on the cover, scowling a bit, and with the picture the words: "Sen. Paul Simon: A Religious Bigot?"

I turned to the index on the next page and it said to turn to page four for an article, "Sen. Simon Locks Arms with Religious Bigots." So I turned to page four.

In the article Dr. Falwell said that I show "a complete lack of tolerance." Why?

A hearing was held—by a Senate subcommittee on which I serve—on the Office of Juvenile Justice and Delinquency Prevention (OJJDP), which is supposed to establish and maintain programs to prevent juvenile delinquency. Prior to the hearing I had read news accounts describing how OJJDP had approved a grant of $186,710 to a dean of Liberty University, Dr. Falwell's school, and to another consultant for preparing materials for high school students on the Constitution. It is true that I objected to the expenditure, as did the Republican chairman of the subcommittee.

First, the purpose of that government office is to prevent crime among juveniles. Preparing materials on the Constitution for high school students does not precisely fulfill that purpose, much as I applaud studying the Constitution. Nor does it fit what some wanted the office to do in law-related education, teaching young people the importance of obeying the law.

Second, there are plenty of private publishers who can provide materials for schools on the Constitution. We do not need to have the federal government spending taxpayers' money on that, most especially at a time when the director of this agency was doing all he could to disrupt or discontinue the fundamental activities of his agency.

Third, there is no question that Dr. Falwell is a polarizing figure, whether you agree with him or not, and if material is to be prepared for high schools, it should come from sources as broadly respected as possible. Personalities identified with either the far right or the far left should be avoided. One other interesting item in the article is the last paragraph: "Sen. Simon would not return calls from the *Liberty Report* regarding his remarks."

Since I have received no such calls, I asked my staff whether anyone had. They had received no such calls. David Carle, my press secretary, called the publication and asked who wrote the article, and who called, and when they called. No one there could say for sure, nor did they call later with that information as they said they would. I'm sure that Dr. Falwell has many talents, as do those who work for him. Sticking to the truth does not appear to be one of them.

I have made clear my distaste for those who wrap their political views in a thin veneer of religion and pass it off to the public as religion. Perhaps that has offended him.

Maybe he doesn't like Lutherans, Democrats, or bow ties. I'm not sure. But it is not often that I get my face on the cover of a national publication in color. As a matter of fact, this is the first time I can remember that has happened. I have, however, defended the right of religious broadcasters to continue to use the airwaves, and I have defended the right of people with whom I disagree strongly to air their political views.

Maybe this is Jerry Falwell's oblique way of saying thanks.

"Religion and Public Life: Partnership of Convenience or Conviction?," P.S./Washington, February 22–28, 1987

I was a guest lecturer at the University of Notre Dame on the subject of politics and religion. Here, in part, is what I said:

The marriage of politics and religion is one that the political community and religious community must approach with care. The United States has emerged with a working relationship between the religious sphere and the political, each influencing the other, but with neither playing a dominant role in the life of the other. That has proven to be healthy both for religion and for government.

One of the reasons for conflict in church-state relationships is that the nature of making political decisions involves compromises. If that did not happen, democratic government would be ineffective and replaced by some form of dictatorship. Those of us in politics recognize that practical compromises have to take place. Whatever our religious moorings, few of us in political life claim any certainty that we know God's will on a given issue. In political life, compromise that is not a compromise of principle is not a dirty word and is essential to the process.

The religious leader generally believes his or her dogmas come from God, and that makes compromise difficult. You cannot compromise what God has told you to do or believe. And even when religious leaders meet to discuss differences, rarely is the word compromise ever used. When Roman Catholic and Lutheran theologians meet and reach agreement on the centuries-old divisive doctrine of justification, the wire services announce that "an understanding" has been achieved. The word compromise is not used and probably none of the participants would concede either side made any compromise.

When the inflexibility of religious dogma is applied to political life, then practical compromises necessary for progress sometimes cannot follow. Those at the pinnacle of leadership in the major religious bodies understand that. But there is a zeal on the part of some of their followers, and some of the television preachers, that is appreciably less understanding. The desire to be part of a small group holding truth and fighting for it against the forces of evil has appeal to followers, sometimes too much appeal.

To be part of a religious elite that has a monopoly on the ultimate truths is emotionally satisfying, but having been so anointed, it becomes dangerous when these emotionally charged certainties are applied to political life.

The substance of faith gives way to cultural tradition and division, and zealots on each side, applying their faith to political life in an unthinking way, kill in the name of religion. I shall never forget waking up one morning in Washington, automatically turning to an all-news radio station, and the first words I heard were: "Christian mortar fire today hit the Moslem section of Beirut." What a strange phrase: Christian mortar fire. Political compromises are difficult in Lebanon today, complicated by generations of animosity between religious groups. Political compromise becomes more tortuous because it takes on the coloration of a compromise of faith, a compromise of revealed dogma.

We should be cautious in asserting the connection between faith and a specific political action. We should embrace both belief and tolerance.

All of us can learn and grow. Each of us lives our faith inadequately and applies it imperfectly.

We are not just, but we can be searchers for justice.

We are not always understanding, but we can pursue understanding.

We are not always right, but we can seek what is right.

We do not hold the truth, but we can search for the truth.

We do not have peace, but we can come much closer to it.

We do not see the future clearly, but we can improve our vision for a better nation and a better world.

"Religious Zealotry Can Turn Good into Evil," P.S./Washington, February 5–11, 1995

There is much that is good about people who have religious beliefs and practice their religion, however imperfectly we all do it. But religion can be abused when people are too zealous—and can be abused when there is a shell of religion that translates into hostility to others.

Almost all religions, if not all, suggest that we should be concerned about those less fortunate. According to a poll conducted for the Center for the Study of American Religion at Princeton University, those who attend religious services weekly in the United States are significantly more likely to think seriously about their responsibilities to the poor.

Many other examples of the good that religious belief provides our society should be given. But when people are so zealous that they kill people at abortion clinics, or try to impose their beliefs on others, then what is good can become an evil. Many of the most bloody wars have been conducted in the name of religion, usually simply used as a tool by ambitious rulers, but sometimes out of genuine belief by the leaders.

There is also the problem where faith has almost diminished to nothing, except hostility to others who do not share the same religious heritage. My impression is that most of those involved in the violence of the Protestant-Catholic struggle in Northern Ireland are not necessarily people of deep religious commitment, but people who have grown up with one heritage and have learned to hate the other side.

During my years in the Army I was stationed in Germany, and I remember the young German who told me with great pride that no one in his family had married a Roman Catholic for over a century. I asked what church he attended, and he told me that while he was proud of being a Protestant, he didn't attend any church. But he had learned to hate.

Hitler had only nominal Christian ties. He believed little, and practiced nothing in the way of religion, but his religious heritage somehow left him with a hatred of Jews.

In Bosnia, nations with strong Orthodox ties are generally much more sympathetic to the Serbian cause than other nations, not for genuine religious reasons but for heritage reasons. Serbia is largely Orthodox Christian.

Muslim countries believe that the reason Europeans and Americans have not responded more to the plight of the Bosnian Muslims is precisely because they are Muslims. I do not believe that is true for the United States, but unfortunately it contains some truth for the more tradition-bound European nations, even though the actual practice of religion is much less evident in Western Europe than in the United States. The empty shell of Christianity too often only has hostility toward non-Christians.

One of several good things about what we did in Somalia (incorrectly labeled a disaster by those who look at it superficially), in addition to preventing starvation by hundreds of thousands of people, is that a nation labeled by the world as Christian/Jewish, the United States, came to the rescue of a people almost totally Muslim. How would we have looked if the world's most powerful nation had done nothing about massive starvation in a desperate country! But many Muslim nations were permanently surprised that we responded.

The lesson of history is that the genuine practice of religion is wholesome, good for the individual and good for a community and nation. But extreme caution is in order when leaders try to impose their beliefs on others through government.

And the "stop" sign should go up when political leaders who share a heritage call on others to hate or kill those who do not share the same faith.

"Balancing Rites, Rights," Commentary, ## Chicago Sun-Times, July 25, 2000

A small, encouraging story tells of the decline of influence in Egypt of the radical fringe of the Muslim community there. The same thing is occurring in Indonesia and Iran. Balancing that are less favorable news items from other nations, particularly Afghanistan. Frequently the news accounts attribute extreme actions to "Muslim fundamentalists."

Religion can be a powerful force for harm or a powerful force for healing. Clashes on the basis of religion occur when Hindu and Muslim extremists in India assault each other and Roman Catholics and Protestants do the same in Northern Ireland.

But faith communities are also playing constructive roles. The passage of the Civil Rights Act of 1964 which brought down the worst segregation would not have occurred without the courageous stands of religious leaders. South Africa's transition from white domination to a full-blown democracy came in part because of similar courage by faith leaders.

What is the proper role of religion, in our nation and in others? A few guidelines are in order, though no guidelines can apply to every situation:

We should be careful about labeling groups negatively, such as "Muslim fundamentalists." The problem is not Muslim fundamentalists, or Christian fundamentalists or their counterparts in any faith community. The problem erupts when people of any faith group attempt to impose their religious beliefs on others through government. Whatever we advocate should be promoted with tolerance and understanding for those who differ. Zealotry in advocacy can be counterproductive if it is mixed with intolerance.

In the case of civil rights, a majority of the nation's religious leaders felt this was a moral issue and took a strong stand, though in the early 1960s it did not have broad popularity.

Even when a clear majority of religious leaders favor something, there are times when government should proceed with caution. In almost all of the early U.S. colonies, Catholics and Jews were not permitted to hold public office, a stand supported then by most Protestant leaders.

Don't we have "a wall of separation between church and state"? No. That phrase came out of a letter Thomas Jefferson wrote. There is no absolute separation. No one believes that if the local Methodist church is on fire that you can't call out the fire department. No one wants to change the name of St. Louis or St. Paul or San Francisco. Those who wrote our Constitution said that for the first time in the history of nations we would not have an established state religion. They advocated tolerance and free speech.

Then why can't we have prayer in our schools, or post the Ten Commandments? The Supreme Court has ruled that you cannot impose prayer on others. They have also said that posting the Ten Commandments crosses a line of government involvement in religion.

But schools can constitutionally teach about religion. Charles Haynes of the First Amendment Center of Arlington, VA, has developed guidelines for public schools doing that which groups as diverse as the American Civil

Liberties Union and the National Association of Evangelicals have agreed upon. And education need not be valueless. Teaching tolerance, honesty, hard work and other virtues is both helpful and constitutional.

How do you apply church/state principles to tough problems like abortion? Not easily. Moses said he did not believe in divorce, but because of the hardness of heart of his followers he would grant writs of divorce. Officials have to separate their personal beliefs from their role as government leaders. Where the religious community is deeply divided, such as on the question of how to discourage abortion, government should move more cautiously. The crusade of eight decades ago that resulted in Prohibition, advocated by about one-third of the nation's religious leaders, did not turn out to be a success.

We need interaction and dialogue between government and religion. But we do not want government to run our religious institutions and we do not want religious leaders running our government.

LESSONS FROM HISTORY

"AN OLD BOOK TEACHES SOME LESSONS,"
P.S./WASHINGTON, OCTOBER 30–NOVEMBER 5, 1977

How important to a nation are those voices which challenge some of the beliefs and ideas we hold? We know—or should know—that fundamental to the functioning of our form of government is a free flow of ideas. That free flow of ideas sometimes causes confusion, but it also offers strength permitting us to choose from a variety of options, not just those spoon-fed to us by some dictatorship.

The other day my eighth-grade son told me he had to do a report on the relationship between the Soviet Union and China. I started going through books I have on the two countries and suddenly found one I had not looked at in years.

Titled *The Situation in Asia*, and written by Owen Lattimore, it was published in 1949.

Readers who are less than 40 years of age may not recognize that name, and those over 40 may find it has a familiar ring but do not remember why.

Owen Lattimore is the former State Department official and professor at Johns Hopkins University who came under attack from Sen. Joseph

McCarthy. McCarthy by implication called him a Communist and a Soviet agent, but later backed off from that.

Lattimore's great "sin" consisted of telling the nation something that few of us believed then—I was among the disbelievers—that China and the Chinese Communists were not just puppets of the Soviet Union, that if we treated them differently and did not freeze them out of our contacts, that there might well be a break between the Soviets and the Chinese Communists.

He urged us to treat all of the Communist countries as individual entities, not just as puppets of the Soviets. As I glance through his book now, it is clear that so much of what he said was correct, that history is going to judge his views more kindly than it will those of many of his critics. If instead of reacting emotionally and irrationally to Lattimore we had listened carefully to what he had to say, history might well have been considerably different.

Maybe—just maybe—there would not have been a war in Korea. Maybe—just maybe—there would not have been a war in Vietnam. No one knows these answers with any certainty.

What is clear is that instead of listening to him we tolerated officials who tried to silence him, to make a villain out of him. Instead of maintaining contact with the non-Soviet Communist nations, we treated them all as if they were part of the Soviet system, and maintained virtually no contact with countries like Red China, North Korea and North Vietnam.

We cannot rewrite history, or undo what has happened. But the next time someone expresses an unpopular idea, remember first that the expression of all types of ideas is what gives this nation its fundamental strength. And remember also that it might be worth listening to that person. He or she just might be right.

"Lessons from *Holocaust*," P.S./Washington, April 23–29, 1978

The television series *Holocaust* presented a grim reminder to the nation that humanity can stoop to some unbelievable depths. I don't believe what happened in Germany could happen in the United States—but I'm sure the people of Germany didn't believe such a thing possible there either. We can learn some lessons from the *Holocaust* series:

- Stand up for your beliefs. If you see something wrong taking place, don't remain silent.
- Remember what you are *for*, as well as what you are against. This is most difficult in the situation right now in Skokie, Illinois, where Nazis want to march in a heavily Jewish community. Within the

framework of the law and without infringing on freedom of speech, I believe authorities there can deny people the right to march in uniforms or carry a Nazi flag. But if they want to walk through the community handing out hate-filling literature, much as you and I deplore it, we must defend their right to do it. That is a bitter pill to swallow, but by defending the rights of those we disagree with most we defend the rights of everyone.

- Be careful of those who build on fear. Hitler was a master of that.
- Recognize the emotional sickness of those who come with messages which are anti-Jewish, anti-black, anti-Catholic, anti-Italian or anti any other racial, religious or national group. Those who use such approaches need your understanding, not your hatred. But you must recognize that there is a fundamental emotional flaw in such people. Their views are warped, their leadership not to be trusted.
- Nations and individuals drift into indefensible behavior one small step at a time. Major Dorf, the Nazi responsible for massive slaughters in the television series, first wanted a job, then obeyed orders and gradually drifted toward mass murders and ultimately his own suicide. The way to avoid national calamity is clear: don't take those first steps in the wrong direction.
- Don't engage in phrases, jokes or conversations which put down another person's race, religion or national background. They all add to the wrong kind of cultural climate where irresponsible conduct might take place. A good example of this is the Polish "joke," which is not humorous to our Polish friends and should not be funny to us.
- As much as possible expose your family to the opportunity to meet people of other backgrounds so that your children can learn one of the most important lessons of life—that people are people. Television is helping us in this (and hurting us in other ways). People who do not have friends of other cultural backgrounds can be persuaded to fear others. If life comes down to an "us against them" battle, it's clear which side we end up on; but if everyone is "us," life takes on different dimensions.
- Read a little history now and then so that we will not have to repeat the mistakes of the past.

The other evening on a Washington radio call-in program someone asked me about a "Jewish conspiracy," and every once in a while I'll get a letter from someone worrying about blacks or Catholics or some other group that the person writing has been persuaded we must learn to fear and hate. Happily those messages are rare. We are maturing as a people.

A television series like *Holocaust* should keep us moving in the right direction.

"Lessons from the Durants," P.S./Washington, December 6–12, 1981

Two fine historians, Will and Ariel Durant, died within a few days of each other recently; the male member of that duo reached the age of 96, and she, the age of 83. After producing a series of fascinating histories, in 1968 they wrote a short book titled simply *The Lessons of History.*

I thought it was worth re-reading, and it was. To some degree an enterprise like theirs will always be subjective, so no reader is likely to agree with all of their conclusions. But the Durants have earned respect for their work through a firm base of scholarship and through decades of impressive effort. Among other things they conclude:

- "There is no significant example in history . . . of a society maintaining moral life without the aid of religion."
- "Patriotism unchecked by a higher loyalty can be a tool of greed and crime."
- "Normally and generally men are judged by their ability to produce—except in war, when they are ranked according to their ability to destroy."
- "The gap between the wealthiest and the poorest is now greater than at any time since Imperial plutocratic Rome." Athens of the sixth century B.C. had an extreme between poverty and wealth and violence seemed likely. "Moderate elements secured the election of Solon, a businessman of aristocratic lineage. . . . He devaluated the currency, thereby easing the burden of all debtors (though he himself was a creditor); he . . . ended imprisonment for debt . . . he established a graduated income tax that made the rich pay at a rate twelve times that required of the poor; he reorganized the courts . . . he arranged that the sons of those who had died in war for Athens should be brought up and educated at the government's expense. The rich protested that his measures were outright confiscation; the radicals complained that he had not re-divided the land; but within a generation almost all agreed that his reforms had saved Athens from revolution."

- "The fear of capitalism has compelled socialism to widen freedom, and the fear of socialism has compelled capitalism to increase equality. East is West and West is East and soon the twain will meet."
- "If a man is fortunate he will, before he dies, gather up as much as he can of his civilized heritage and transmit it to his children. And to his final breath he will be grateful for this inexhaustible legacy."
- "Nothing is clearer in history than the adoption by successful rebels of the methods they were accustomed to condemn in the forces they deposed."
- "The conservative who resists change is as valuable as the radical who proposes it—perhaps as much more valuable as roots are more vital than grafts. . . . It is good that the old should resist the young, and that the young should prod the old; out of this tension . . . comes a creative tensile strength, a stimulated development."
- "The Englishman does not so much make English civilization as it makes him; if he carries it wherever he goes, and dresses for dinner in Timbuktu, it is not that he is creating his civilization there anew, but that he acknowledges even there its mastery over his soul."

Finally this famous duo of historians observes: "We can learn enough from history to bear reality patiently, and to respect one another's delusions."

Sometimes, in the midst of our day-to-day battles over the issues of the moment, it's good to listen to, and learn from, those who have distilled lessons for us from thousands of years of our own history.

"Can You Legislate Morality?,"
P.S./Washington, August 28–September 3, 1983

This week's observance of the 20th anniversary of Martin Luther King's March on Washington invites many questions about our national character, and one of them is this: Can you legislate morality? "I don't think you can change the hearts of people with laws," many have said.

They are partly right. Morality is a higher standard than the law's standard. But it is not beyond the law's influence. We have seen dramatic evidence over the last two decades that the law does bear upon our actions as citizens, and also upon our opinions. The law changes our conduct, and the change in our conduct often changes our hearts.

Civil rights legislation shows that the law, when properly used, can be a forceful tool for good. Many of these laws were enacted through the exercise of moral authority which Dr. King showed us, climaxing in Washington on August 28, 1963.

These laws have broken down many of the artificial barriers between Americans which had supported unfounded fears we had about each other. There is no question that racial attitudes in the U.S. have changed remarkably during our two decades of experience with the civil rights laws, though we still have a long path to travel. An opinion survey in 1948 found about 80 percent of Southern respondents arguing for segregated bus and train accommodations for whites and blacks. A measure of how far we have come since then are surveys over the last six years showing that about this same proportion of Southerners today favor integrated *schools.*

We are a nation founded on an ambitious set of ideas, and we will always need people like Thomas Jefferson, Abraham Lincoln, Susan B. Anthony, Franklin Roosevelt and Martin Luther King to keep the ideals before us. Each of these leaders blended idealism with a constructive use of government as a tool to honor and implement those goals.

Each came under harsh criticism. But these leaders were the patriots of their eras: Each succeeded in strengthening our democracy and in making it work better. FDR, lambasted by big business, ended up rescuing our free enterprise system, and in the process he helped make more millionaires than any president before him.

Probably no one on the scene today has the same stature of a Martin Luther King to challenge and inspire us to closer adherence to our national ideals. Probably no one on the scene is hated as he was then. But he met hatred with compassion. He met bitterness with dreams. And we are a richer nation today for it.

"The Noble in Each of Us," P.S./Washington, December 29, 1985–January 4, 1986

We have just celebrated holidays that appeal to the best in each of us.

Whether we are Christians celebrating Christmas, Jews celebrating Hanukkah, or people of no religious conviction, we all have our better instincts appealed to during this season.

We consider and help those less fortunate more now than at any other season of the year. And we feel good about it. There is a lesson for political leadership in all of this. Political leaders can appeal to fear, to hatred, to selfishness, to greed—and they can be "successful" making such appeals, if "success" is measured by winning at the ballot box or in the public opinion polls. But political leaders can also be successful in a finer way, by appealing to the noble in all of us.

There is both the noble and the beast in each of us—in Paul Simon and in each of you who read these words.

When leaders come along who appeal to the better instincts in us, not only are they doing the responsible thing, but they make us feel better and act better.

For example, after World War II the United States assisted Western Europe and a few countries outside of Europe, helping to lift them from their dismal economic plight. People in this country felt good about what we had done. It was a generous act unparalleled by any other national act in history. It rescued Western Europe and in the long run helped the United States economically. But even in the short run it helped us because it made us feel better about ourselves.

Government leaders can tell us, "Look out for yourself and let everyone else take care of themselves." They can add an appeal with ugly racial or regional or national overtones. There is little question about the effectiveness of such an appeal.

But leaders can also be effective urging us to help the unemployed, the handicapped, the hungry in Africa, senior citizens who struggle to make ends meet—appealing to the noble in each of us. Leaders can "win" either way, although those who appeal to fears and hatreds and selfishness sometimes have an easier time of it politically.

But leaders who appeal to the better instincts in us show a wisdom and self-restraint and compassion and common sense that we should applaud. And in some strange way that I shall leave to the philosophers and theologians to fathom, we feel better when our noble instincts are appealed to and when we act upon them.

Not only do we feel better, we build a better society and country and world.

"Democracy Thrives on the Town Meeting Circuit," P.S./Washington, January 5–11, 1986

During my first year in the United States Senate I have visited every county in the state, and almost every ward in Chicago and almost every township in the Cook County suburbs. I held 136 town meetings and attended every other kind of meeting imaginable.

What do you learn in all of these meetings? Perhaps as important as any specific thing you learn, people understand that government is not some distant creature, that they can express their opinions, ask questions, let people in positions of decision-making know what's on their minds. But it is more than that.

For me, it is a chance to sense what people feel. To best serve the people of Illinois, I should not be sitting in Washington simply listening to what the highly paid lobbyists have to say. I need to touch the public pulse, to sense the public mood. And I need to talk to people about their specific problems, some widely known—such as farmers' financial troubles—but some unusual.

In the latter category, for example, were the people from a roller skating rink who say they will be put out of business because of sharply rising insurance liability costs. As I checked into liability costs for roller skating rinks, I learned there are a number of businesses faced with suddenly rising liability insurance costs, rising so rapidly that some small businesses are being forced to close. These include service stations and day care centers and travel agencies and a number of other businesses. I have a staff member working on possible answers.

But our efforts all grew out of a few people from a roller skating rink taking the time to come to a town meeting. I cannot guarantee we will come up with the right answers, but unless we try, harm will come to many small businesses and their employees.

A host of "small things" like that come up in town meetings. On some of these problems I can help and on some I cannot. Even where I am aware of a difficulty—like the farm problem—it reinforces my determination to do something when I talk to a couple who have been hard-working, solid Americans, who believed that if you worked hard you could get ahead. They, and many others like them, have worked hard and now face bankruptcy. It's one thing to read about the farm problem, much different to talk to flesh-and-blood people whose agony is written on their faces and in what they say.

It's one thing to know unemployment statistics, another to talk to a mother who is worried about the mental health of her son because he can't find a job. The people who took time to attend town meetings held in every corner of the state helped me to become a better senator.

Those who came were Republicans and Democrats and independents. Sometimes they praised and sometimes they criticized; sometimes they asked questions and sometimes they made strong statements. Many made excellent suggestions that I have helped enact or that I am still pressing in Congress or with federal agencies. Once we had more than 1,000 people at a town meeting. In three or four cases there were only one dozen present.

But I came away from all of them feeling these meetings were good for me, good for the people who attended and good for the process of democracy.

"Making a Difference," P.S./Washington, October 5–11, 1986

Too many people do not understand that they can have a part in the decisions of government. It may sound obvious to you that in a democracy people can have a strong voice, but I sense that there is a growing part of our population that feels voiceless and helpless.

Our system of financing political campaigns adds to their cynicism.

In a new book, *Citizen Action and the New American Populism*, written by Harry C. Boyte, Heather Booth and Steve Max, the authors write: "If people think that nothing can be done to challenge seriously the shape of decision-making, no one will try. . . . In America today we remember too little about earlier traditions of protest and democratic change. . . . If you don't know that many of the rights and comforts of life that you take for granted today were actually won in [political] conflict, not given as a reward for complacency, how can you believe that you can have power and win now?

"If you don't know of the battles that led to the working day being eight hours instead of 14, or the struggle for public education, or for the right to vote for women, how can you envision changing seemingly overwhelming problems you face today?"

With a gradually shrinking middle class, more and more people find themselves alienated for one reason or another.

The message must be taken to the classroom and voiced on the editorial page and in the pulpit that participation is not only possible, that it is needed. And with participants can come change. Recently one of the major networks broadcast a statement that less than 50 percent of those in our country under 30 years of age will ever own their own homes. If we drift, that may happen. Is it either inevitable or desirable? Absolutely not. But people have to join in the political process or that may be our course.

Is the decline of the family farm inevitable? Is high unemployment our permanent lot? Is it essential that we devote so much more money to nuclear missiles than we do to education or cancer research? Is the deficit an act of God from which we cannot escape? The answer to all of these questions is that we *can* change our course, but we can do it only if—a big if—we get more people interested and participating. But could your voice really make a difference?

The best illustration I have for that is that one of the major reforms of the prison system in Illinois came about because one prisoner—someone who could not vote—sat down and wrote me a letter about the need. I was then in the state legislature and introduced a bill that became law, bringing about significant improvement in the Illinois prison system.

If a prisoner who has lost so many rights can bring about change, so can you. And we need your involvement.

"From an Old Royal Typewriter: 40 Years and Counting," P.S./Washington, June 19–24, 1988

My ever-alert staff tells me that this week marks the 40th anniversary of launching my weekly column. When I was 19 some incredibly courageous people loaned me the money to purchase a small, weekly newspaper in Troy, Illinois, and late in June of 1948 I wrote my first column. It has not been written each week since then. For two years I served in the Army and wrote only occasionally. For short times during other pursuits, I didn't write my column. So it has appeared most of the time, but not all of the time.

I write these columns myself, typing them on an old manual typewriter. I felt somewhat old-fashioned sticking to my old typewriter until I learned that columnist George Will writes his columns with a fountain pen.

Most of the things I have stood for through the years bear up pretty well. I stressed the need for pay-as-you-go government or we would be headed for serious financial problems, never dreaming at that time that we would ever have the kind of deficits we have today.

In 1981, I warned that the tax bill would cause massive deficits, and quoted a former Nixon cabinet member, James Schlesinger, as saying that it would "likely go down in history as the single most irresponsible fiscal action of modern times."

How right and courageous Jim Schlesinger was! That was said at a time when the President [Reagan] assured us that the 1981 tax bill would result in a balanced budget by 1984. The proposal had great popularity.

During these years I've called for more jobs instead of welfare; for Western Europe to share more of the burden for defense of that area; called for long-term care for seniors; and here and there tried to work in a lesson from history, one of my interests.

I'm grateful to people who have suggested ideas for my column, or more often have written me about something and feel that it is worth commenting on. I'm grateful to Pamela Huey and David Carle and others who through the years have had the job of figuring out my illegible handwriting as I corrected and tried to improve the typewriter product.

Whether I have informed anyone else through the process, I have informed myself. It helps me as a legislator. It is easy to get up on the Senate floor and talk on some subject, but putting it in writing requires a little more thought. The discipline of writing, of shifting from a casual observation of truth to making sure something is a fact, of learning just a little more about some subject so I can be sure I am on solid ground—all this has helped me become a better informed public servant. So I shall continue the habit.

"On Being a Senator," P.S./Washington, January 22–28, 1989

Occasionally I read stories about the pressure that a member of the U.S. House or Senate faces: The long hours on the job for those who are conscientious, the need to maintain both a home in Washington, D.C., and in your home state, and other considerations. And there are drawbacks. But the advantages outweigh the drawbacks.

The big advantage is the satisfaction of getting problems solved, of giving opportunity to people, of making our state and our nation and our world a better place. In making a few comments on his retirement, Senator William Proxmire of Wisconsin said, "Just think of a job where your prime responsibility is to do your best to improve your country and the world."

That's the job of a senator. I confess there is also a sense of pride in participating in this process. I was driving in Washington, approaching the Capitol lit up as it is every night, and I said to my daughter, Sheila, riding with me, "I never see that Capitol without getting a thrill out of it." She responded, "The day you don't get a thrill out of it, you ought to quit." She was right.

For someone who is interested in history, as I am, there are many small things that add an important dimension to all of this. Each senator is assigned a desk on the Senate floor, and the Senate curator keeps track of who sits at each desk.

In my four years in the Senate I have sat at three desks. Among those who have preceded me at those desks are Harry Truman, Lyndon Johnson, Robert Kennedy, Robert Taft Sr., Henry Cabot Lodge Jr., Henry Bellmon (now governor of Oklahoma), Harry Byrd Sr., Millard Tydings, Jacob Javits, and Sam Ervin. You may not recognize all of those names, but they are among the most distinguished senators this nation has produced.

I wish I could say I have been at a desk where John Kennedy or Paul Douglas or Hubert Humphrey sat, but being in the same room where they served gives you some sense of history.

The ghosts of the past haunt us a little, as they should.

"A Lesson from 50 Years Ago,"
P.S./Washington, September 3–9, 1989

How close are we to repeating history?

South Africa, with its massive system of racial injustice, came to mind recently while reading some selected writing of the late Sen. Richard Neuberger of Oregon (*They Never Go Back to Pocatello*, edited by Steve Neal, a Chicago journalist).

As a young journalist, Dick Neuberger went to Germany in 1933 and found things strikingly different than the antiseptic tours given by the Nazi guides. Like in the South African situation, many visitors came back from Germany praising the progress Hitler had made. In both cases, many felt the racial oppression was either overplayed in the media or was necessary.

In 1933—six years before the start of World War II—Neuberger wrote:

"Ruthless and relentless as Hitler and his lieutenants are, there is one weapon they fear. The Nazi mayor of a large German town told me his party dreaded economic pressure. At pistol point the storm troopers have forced their victims to deny all stories of atrocities in an attempt to lessen the indignation abroad. They realize a tight international boycott can kill even the monster they have created. A boycott which shuts out German merchandise, reduces passenger lists of German liners, and keeps tourists out of Germany can soon write an end to the most gruesome chapter of modern history by dethroning Hitler and Hitlerism."

Unfortunately, U.S. policymakers, as well as those in Europe, paid no attention to the young journalist's comments. If they had, World War II might have been avoided, with its tragic loss of tens of millions of lives.

The upcoming election in South Africa, in which only whites vote, *could* result in a change of policy, a reversal of direction. The new president, F. W. de Klerk, is apparently more moderate than his predecessor, P. W. Botha, but whether he will have the courage to rid South Africa of its blight of rigid and oppressive racism is not yet clear.

No, the parallels to Hitler's Germany are not all identical. Among other things, in Germany, Catholics and Lutheran leaders were much too silent. In South Africa, all of the major religious leaders have denounced the present system. But one parallel is the same: If courageous leadership does not emerge within South Africa to bring about change, then there is only one way to bring about change—economic muscle. Over the veto of President Reagan, a bipartisan congressional vote overwhelmingly imposed limited U.S. economic sanctions on South Africa.

The Senate a few weeks ago also adopted an amendment of mine, calling on the Bush administration to urge Japan, Great Britain, West Germany and other nations to join in the limited sanctions we already have.

If significant negotiations do not take place soon between the real leaders among the whites and blacks in South Africa, then the United States should strengthen the economic sanctions we have. And we should be a leader on this issue in the United Nations instead of a foot-dragger. As we observe the 50th anniversary of the start of World War II, it is instructive to look back on its lessons. One is that, prior to the war, economic sanctions were not used on Germany and the world experienced massive violence.

If leadership does not come from within South Africa, or from external economic pressure, massive violence inevitably will be the lot of all South Africans, and the bloodshed there is not likely to be confined to the borders of that one nation.

Will we learn from history?

"Choosing Wisely in Matters of War: Some Lessons from History," P.S./Washington, May 12–18, 1991

In the midst of the cheers our armed forces have merited, there are those devastating pictures of some of the 2 million Kurdish refugees the war has caused, and the gnawing uneasiness of knowing that we were presented by the Pentagon with a sanitized war—sanitized by new limits on media coverage and by our inability to see the agony of the 100,000 to 200,000 Iraqis who died in the conflict or of our own casualties.

As I reflected on this, I came across three pertinent quotes, the first two from one *Washington Post* editorial page. Former Secretary of State Henry Kissinger writes: "America does not need to assert either the duty or the capacity to right every injustice by force of arms."

Then I read columnist George Will's reflections on reaching age 50: "To have been born seven months before Pearl Harbor and to turn 50 two months after Desert Storm is to know the centrality of war in America's modern experience." Reflecting is good for us if it does not cause inaction.

On the most recent conflict, I recall the late December meeting five of us in the Senate had with President Bush in which it was clear that he felt it important to launch a military offensive against Saddam Hussein. As we left, he gave each of us a copy of the Amnesty International report on what the Iraqis were doing in Kuwait.

"We can't let them get by with this," he told us.

And now Amnesty International is issuing reports about the abuses taking place in newly free Kuwait. While the most recent reports are somewhat less ominous, I assume they are not being handed out by the White House.

It is much too early to make final judgments on the Gulf War, but my guess is that history will find that we should not have become so cozy with Saddam Hussein during the Iran-Iraq war, that we should have tried sanctions longer before resorting to the use of force, that our military performed superbly once called upon, and that we botched up the postwar situation.

World War II and the Korean War were justified and heroic actions on our part, though the Korean conflict might have been prevented had we been clearer on the matter of aggression.

Historians will not look kindly on what we did in the Vietnam War, though our motivation was good. And the Grenada mini-war is not likely to receive the applause of history. The Panama action will not bring us praise, though historians will not look with any sympathy on the Panamanian dictator, Manuel Noriega. Not in the category of war, but part of history's judgment, will be our eagerness to supply arms to virtually every conflict around the Earth.

Our involvement in wars, whether through our armed forces or our weapons, brings me to the third quotation I read recently from Hermann Goering, Hitler's number two man, at the Nuremberg trials: "Why, of course, people don't want war. Why should some poor slob on a farm want to risk his life in a war when the best he can get out of it is to come back to his farm in one piece?

"Naturally, the common people don't want war: neither in Russia, nor in England, nor for that matter in Germany. That is understood. But after all, it is the leaders of a country who determine the policy, and it is always a simple matter to drag the people along, whether it is a democracy, or a fascist dictatorship, or a parliament, or a communist dictatorship. Voice or no voice, the people can always be brought to the bidding of the leaders. That is easy. All you have to do is to tell them they are being attacked, and denounce the pacifist for lack of patriotism and exposing the country to danger. It works the same in any country."

His words should not paralyze us into inaction, but they should cause pause as we make choices between war and peace, and as we make choices between helping people with arms or economic assistance.

"Standing Up to Evil," P.S./Washington, June 12–18, 1994

I was 15 years old when the invasion of Europe by Allied troops took place, old enough to remember it well, but too young to serve. (A few years later I did serve overseas in the Army.)

Three days before the recent 50th anniversary of D-Day, I visited an American military cemetery in Tunisia in North Africa where 2,800 of the 11,000 Americans who were killed in fighting in Tunisia were buried.

When you see those 2,800 crosses and Stars of David, you reflect on the senselessness of war and the need to prevent those casualties in the future. With each grave marker is the name, rank, military unit and state of residence of the person who died. Thomas M. Dunn and Charles W. Fletcher, both from Illinois, were two of the crosses I saw. Both were young men when they were killed, and I wondered about their families and the agony their families went through.

I am not a pacifist, though I respect those who are. There are times when those who choose a path of violence must be stopped by violence. That was true of Hitler in World War II and it is true of criminals who haunt too many of our communities today.

Each of us has the power to help reduce violence, by example in our families and communities and by supporting public policies that discourage violent "answers" to problems.

One evil man, Adolf Hitler, caused the deaths of millions.

But Hitler did not rise to power on his own. He was aided by a small group of followers and by a much larger group of people in Germany who did not pay much attention to politics.

I'm sure there were people in Germany who said, "Those politicians are all the same. There's no difference among any of them."

BIPARTISANSHIP

"On the Importance of Friendships in the Legislature," Sidelights from Springfield, by State Representative Paul Simon, March 23, 1961

Perhaps you've read newspaper accounts of unusual Republican-Democratic bitterness on the current Springfield scene. Unfortunately, there is much truth to these reports. In House debates there has been more shouting at one another than is usually heard. But that is only part of the picture.

Among members of the legislature a friendship and feeling of comradeship develops that is also a part of state government, and a part of government that the public generally does not see and understand.

Two men may vigorously debate with each other over a measure and then go out and have dinner together. This does not mean that the debate was staged. It does mean that in Springfield (as in Washington) one of the things you learn quickly is that you have to get along with people with whom you disagree. Life would be unbearable hating people who disagree with you, because sooner or later almost everyone disagrees with you on some measure.

Last week—a day after I became the father of a baby daughter—I wanted to leave Springfield for the evening to make a quick trip to Highland, Illinois, to visit my wife at the hospital there. I had promised to speak that evening at a dinner meeting at a hotel in Springfield. Representative Frances Dawson of Evanston graciously agreed to substitute for me, although she and I belong to different political parties and frequently vote in opposition to each other. This working relationship between people of opposing political parties is common.

Last year my car broke down in Pontiac while driving from a Chicago meeting to a Springfield meeting. I was to be the main speaker at a banquet in Springfield and was running on a tight time schedule.

Senator William Harris of Pontiac, not of my political party, lives in Pontiac, and I called on him for help. He loaned me his car, offered to put me up for the night, and in general went out of his way to be agreeable. Part of this is just Bill Harris's friendly nature, but part of this is the feeling of friendship that grows among members of the legislature, a bond that nonmembers rarely understand.

This becomes important to government because it means that men and women who disagree can sit down after a debate, discuss their disagreements with relative calm—and frequently come up with a compromise satisfactory to both. Important legislation rarely passes the way it is introduced. The changes make passage of the measures possible.

These changes—or compromises—are not an immoral compromise of conviction, but a willingness to "take half a loaf rather than a whole loaf." Bitter enemies have a hard time compromising. Friends can.

This working, friendly relationship among people who disagree is an important part of your state government.

"A Grateful Nation Thanks President Ford,"
P.S./Washington, January 16–22, 1977

As President Ford leaves the nation's highest office, all of us—Democrats, Republicans and independents—have much for which we should be grateful to him.

I am among those who supported Jimmy Carter for President, and I believe that President Carter is more likely to provide the economic stimulus this nation needs than Gerald Ford would have, or did provide.

But Gerald Ford inherited the presidency at a time when this nation had lost confidence in itself. For the first time in our 200 years a President had resigned; people had become distrustful of almost everything government did; and all of this disillusionment had been deepened by our experience in Vietnam, where tens of thousands had died for purposes which are not clear.

At that point the nation needed to believe in its leadership, and the people of this nation sensed correctly that the new leader was an honest, sincere man, trying to do his best under extremely trying circumstances.

Not only should history judge that he fit the needs of the nation at that point, but there must be a footnote in history on how graciously he has handled himself since defeat.

Dr. Mark Krug, author and historian, told me the other day that the United States is the only country in the world where by custom the defeated candidate for office congratulates the successful candidate, whether the contest is for the presidency or other political office. That custom helps to bind the nation together.

Ford's final State of the Union address may not have been long on substance, but had class. He left the nation not on a note of bitterness, but of hope. He urged all of us to unite under the new President when his programs are sound, opposing not for the sake of opposition, when there is disagreement.

The applause for his address by Members of Congress—more than 2 to 1 from the Democratic rather than Republican party—was a genuine expression of respect and admiration for a President who had served the nation faithfully.

I believe that by our applause we informally expressed the thanks of a grateful nation.

"Tip o' the Hat to Tip," P.S./Washington, April 30, 1985

Now that I have shifted from the House to the Senate, I trust that these next words will not be considered self-serving. Something has made me feel uneasy for several years; it is the treatment accorded Speaker Thomas P. O'Neill, known generally on Capitol Hill as "Tip."

He is a natural target for cartoonists. His disheveled white hair, his girth, and his cigar make him look like the caricature of an old-time politician. The public image of an old-time politician includes some combination of corruption and serving selfish interest rather than the public interest, and on neither count does the Speaker fit the role.

The combinations of newspaper political cartoons, Republican commercials with an O'Neill look-alike who said outlandish things, and the Speaker's own tendency to say what he thinks—sometimes undiplomatically—have combined to create a public image that is appreciably less favorable than the reality. I have known and worked with him for 11 years. Let me tell you the side of Tip O'Neill you may not know.

He is an old-time politician, not in a corrupt sense at all, but in the best way: He knows how to get things done, and he does them. He is an old-time politician in that he shows up at endless meetings; he "presses the flesh"; he genuinely likes people.

He wants to help people. He got into politics helping the elderly and the handicapped and the unemployed and has been doing it all his life. Give him a choice between helping the unfortunate and pandering to the whims of the powerful, and he comes out on the right side all the time.

He is an old-fashioned patriot. When Ronald Reagan became President the Speaker assured the President that O'Neill would act speedily on the Reagan proposals that the Speaker opposed. Why do that? It was his sense of how the country must operate. He honors the precedents that he knows must be followed; he understands that self-restraint is essential for a democracy to function.

Is he a strong partisan? You bet.

Does he get along personally with those he opposes? Very well.

Is he steeped in the details of legislative proposals? He is not. He's appreciably stronger on this than Ronald Reagan, but not as strong as Jimmy Carter was. But he knows that is not what his position demands. Sam Rayburn and Alben Barkley were not on top of all the details of legislation either. Some great legislators are; Robert Taft and Paul Douglas would be such examples. But most leaders hold office because of a keen sense of what can be done and what cannot be done, not because of intimate knowledge of legislation.

In 1987 the U.S. House of Representatives will have a new Speaker. O'Neill will retire. As time passes there will be more and more appreciation of our good fortune in having "Tip" O'Neill, in the same way public appreciation for Harry Truman gradually grew after he left office. But I am not content to let history make its judgment decades from now.

I have seen enough to know that history's judgment will be kinder than any poll today.

And this is a good time for those of us who know that to say it.

"Extreme Partisanship Fuels Cynicism,"
P.S./Washington, September 3–9, 1995

Why does every poll show so much cynicism toward our government? Some hostility will always be part of a free system, and a certain amount of skepticism—which is less dangerous than cynicism—can be healthy. My own instinct, based on no polls, is that there are two reasons:

One is a failure of government leaders to tell people what may be unpopular but true. Too many "leaders" don't take a stand on any issue until a poll has been taken. They want to please people, no matter what they do or say, and while we all like to please people, you should not vote for a political leader who tells you only what you want to hear.

But a second reason for cynicism is the excessive partisanship that is now part of federal and state governments. I am in my 21st year in the national House and Senate, and there is no question that we are more partisan than when I came—and both political parties share the blame for this.

Illinois State Representative Edward J. Zabrocki Jr. has resigned from that position. He will continue to serve as mayor of Tinley Park, a Chicago suburb. One of his reasons for leaving—the major reason—is excessive partisanship. He is a Republican and proud of it. I am a Democrat and proud of it.

But once elections are behind us, the two political parties should work together for the common good. Some issues will divide the parties on philosophical grounds, but I see us voting now in the U.S. Senate along party lines on trivial and not-so-trivial things that should not divide us. Mayor Zabrocki's statement on leaving the state legislature says: "Politics plays too much of a role in state government."

He also is sharply critical of the excessive negativism of political ads. I agree with him on that too, and sometimes in the heat of a campaign,

I became more negative than I should have been. Candidates should talk candidly about different views they hold, but with respect. When candidates speak negatively of each other in highly sophisticated television, radio and print media, the public tends to believe both sides. "They're all bad," is the conclusion. We have fouled our own nest and hurt our free system of government. The answer has to be self-restraint by candidates and office-holders.

In my years of chairing three subcommittees in the U.S. Senate I don't believe we ever had a party-line vote. That is as much a tribute to my Republican colleagues as it is to those of us who are Democrats. While that required some practical compromises, the public was better served in the long run. I frankly don't know what Ed Zabrocki did as a member of the Illinois House of Representatives.

But perhaps his greatest contribution was to say to political leaders: Let's be a little less partisan.

"ON THE DEATH OF BARRY GOLDWATER," NPR COMMENTARY, JUNE 8, 1998

The death of Senator Barry Goldwater should be noted by those in public office who are eager for success. He succeeded without taking polls and hiring focus groups. Barry Goldwater did and said what he believed to be in the best interest of the nation. I frequently differed with him, but always respected him.

One day on the floor of the Senate Barry came to me and asked, "Do you know where Bowen—B-O-W-E-N—Illinois, is?" I thought I knew every small town in Illinois but I could not place Bowen. He told me his mother was born in Bowen. I looked it up. It is in Hancock County, not far from Quincy, 539 people. I asked the Illinois Highway Department to make a sign: "Welcome to Bowen, the Home of Josephine Williams, the Mother of Senator Barry Goldwater." I presented the sign to the Mayor of Bowen, had a picture taken, then handed the picture to Barry Goldwater on the floor of the Senate. He burst into tears. About two hours later he told me, "I've got to go to Bowen." One Saturday we did, and had a parade though all six blocks or so of Bowen, telling them how much Bowen had meant to his mother. Then about eight years ago Barry's first wife died. He called me and said that he planned to sell his home, but keep his house in Phoenix. But the house that he would sell had many books in it. "I think I'll give them to the library at Bowen," he told me. I responded, "Barry, I don't know if they have a library at Bowen." I checked it out, and they did. Today in that small library at Bowen many of the books are a gift from a United States Senator from Arizona who once ran for President of the United States. But the story should not end there.

I hope some of the young people who see and read those books will be inspired to pursue public service, or at least be responsible citizens who vote and participate. And if they become office holders, I hope they will follow the example of Barry Goldwater and simply ask, "What is in the best interest of my town or country or state or nation?" Not what might get me the most votes or the most campaign contributions.

If they do that, it would please Barry Goldwater, and will help the nation.

"Bush Has a New Opportunity to Build Bipartisanship," *Daily Herald*, January 24, 2001

It is possible that the results of the strange election the nation went through last year will bring a lessening of excessive partisanship, and if so the nation will be well-served by the tight races for the House, Senate and the presidency.

President George W. Bush is sincere in wanting to work together with both political parties. Not only does he say that, but his roots are in that direction. His father and his mother are Republicans, but not wild partisans. A meeting I attended with him Monday at the White House—along with five other Democrats—was a substantial, hour-long discussion. The Senate with its unprecedented 50–50 split could cause endless wrangling, or it could achieve greater bipartisan efforts. In my 22 years on the Washington scene, I saw excessive partisanship grow and grow. No one benefits from that, including the two political parties. The election of Jesse Ventura as governor of Minnesota emerged from that atmosphere.

The public perception is that the two political parties are playing games, rather than asking what is in the nation's best interest. And too often that perception is accurate. There will be—and should be—conflicts where basic political philosophy is at stake. Democrats tend to believe that if you give the average working person enough opportunity so he or she can buy a car, then General Motors will do well, too. Republicans tend to believe that if you give tax incentives to the corporate leaders and to the corporations, the nation will benefit.

As a Democrat, I tend to the former philosophy, but the reality is that we need a balance, and so when the estate tax comes up for debate there will be strong arguments on both sides—and some types of practical compromise, a balance, may be worked out. Where the two political parties need to be stronger is in a willingness to do the unpopular. Political parties should be leading for responsible conduct, not simply popular conduct.

Social Security retirement is a prime example. Both parties, and both presidential candidates, advocated feel-good answers last fall that won't solve the problem. When Social Security first made payments, for several years we had 16 workers for each retiree. We are now down to 3 to 1, and in a few years it will be 2.3 to one. That spells trouble ahead.

It is important that we find solid answers on Social Security, and the two political parties should spend a little less time and effort on bunting and fund-raising dinners, and more time coming to grips with a tough problem like this.

The sooner we tackle it the better. If we wait until it mushrooms into a crisis, then we will hastily pass legislation that probably will not serve the nation well.

The tone of President George W. Bush's first hours in office on the matter of partisanship is sound. His inaugural address had that bipartisan touch. And the meeting I referred to earlier underscored his commitment.

He appointed one Democrat, former Congressman Norman Mineta, as secretary of transportation, and little noticed in most news media, he announced keeping former Sen. George McGovern as our ambassador to the international Food and Agricultural Organization based in Rome. The latter appointment pleased Democrats, as well as Republicans, like former Sen. Bob Dole. But the test for both the president and for congressional leaders will come in the weeks and months to come.

If there is real working together, that will not erupt in headlines. Conflict stills makes the news. It will be hard for the public to sense for a period whether there is more cooperation or whether the old political games are being played. But the people on the scene will know and gradually the public will understand what is happening.

The rule for the president and congressional leaders should be simple:

- Be honest with the public.
- Differ with the opposition when you believe strongly on a matter.
- Do not differ simply because the polls suggest there might be a chance to score a few points with the public.

One other small suggestion: Socialize across party lines more. Whether you are the president or a senator or a House member, invite someone from the opposition to an informal dinner at your home. When you take a trip outside the United States, go out of your way to make it bipartisan.

These are all small things, but they are the lubrication that makes a democracy run more smoothly.

"On Excessive Partisanship," NPR Commentary, May 15, 2001

Excessive partisanship by either major political party tends to turn off the public to the entire political process—and everyone becomes a loser.

Tough talk is not new. Senator James Alexander Reed of Missouri once described President Calvin Coolidge "as dumb and inactive as a New England oyster stranded on the beach in August." I don't know of any Senator who has equaled that invective today.

But what is true is that in Senator Reed's time, the two political parties did work together more, and when difficult issues face the nation, they often joined in producing results that were not popular but good for the nation.

That era precedes our sophisticated polling and was before unscrupulous TV ads that both parties mass-produce today. Any candidate who manages to avoid being attacked in these ads is either far ahead of an opponent or so far behind that the other candidate—usually an incumbent—doesn't bother to get into the political ring with the challenger. But the excesses of these ads, plus their penetrations, result in massive distrust of those who hold office or seek it. These TV ads have added bitterness to the political dialogue, which frequently no longer is much of a dialogue. We should, of course, speak up when we genuinely differ. But we shouldn't differ for the sake of differing.

In the recent township elections (in my small rural township) we had a Democrat and a Republican running against each other for township highway commissioner. I don't know of a Republican or Democratic way to fix holes in our roads and there is no political philosophy at stake. I just want good roads, whether maintained by Republicans or Democrats.

That's the way most people feel about their government, and 90 percent of the issues fundamentally involve no political philosophy. Instead of the two political parties working together on some nuts and bolts issues that require little courage, too often we hold our finger to the wind to try to divine which way the political wind is blowing. And when we can't find issues to differ with one another on, we are sometimes reduced to personal attacks.

Then, everyone loses.

OBSERVATIONS AND LESSONS FROM SOUTHERN ILLINOIS

"Thebes—and National Policy," P.S./Washington, June 6–12, 1976

Most of the citizens of Illinois and of the nation have never heard of Thebes, Illinois, but in that small town (population 450) something happened that ought to be a lesson for the nation.

A river town, it once served as the county seat of Alexander County. On a high bluff in Thebes, overlooking the Mississippi River, stands the old county courthouse, significant because of its classic lines and age, and because that courthouse involved three men famous in our nation's history: Abraham Lincoln, Dred Scott, and John Logan.

Last fall when I paid one of my regular visits to Thebes, I found some people working at restoring the old courthouse. The Pulaski–Alexander County Soil and Water Conservation District had received a grant of $720,000 from the Department of Agriculture for putting rural unemployed people to work, and they used part of it for this project. Administrative costs were approximately 10 percent.

A few days ago I went back to Thebes for the dedication. The courthouse looked great.

By taking people off of welfare and unemployment compensation and giving them an opportunity to do something constructive, that community and this nation have preserved an important historical shrine. Men and women who otherwise would have been drawing money from the federal government for doing nothing had the opportunity to work. Every one of them can look to that bluff and see that fine old courthouse and take great pride in having been part of the reconstruction.

The cost of the Thebes project was $75,000. But if those people had been drawing welfare or unemployment compensation during this period, the cost of that would have been approximately $40,000. They learned good work habits. They were productive.

They spent money at the grocery store and the service station, at the clothing store and fruit stand. The people who operate these small businesses made a little more money—and paid a little more in taxes.

Supervising this project and the expenditure of funds was a group of down-to-earth farmers who served on the Soil and Water Conservation District Board. They received nothing for their efforts except the satisfaction of seeing some of their federal money well spent. With millions unemployed, with $19.4 billion in the federal budget for the next fiscal year for unemployment compensation and about $25 billion for welfare, why don't we do more things like the restoration of the Thebes courthouse all over the nation?

I don't believe in permitting anyone to starve, nor does our country.

And most people on welfare or unemployment compensation would sooner be working.

Let's give them that chance.

We'll be a better nation once we make that move.

"WORLD PROBLEMS AFFECT SOUTHERN ILLINOIS," P.S./WASHINGTON, APRIL 17–23, 1977

"Let's concentrate on our problems in the United States and let the rest of the world take care of itself," a Saline County resident writes. That has great appeal, particularly for an area with above average economic problems like we have in Southern Illinois. But appealing as that sentiment is, it ignores the fact that we are an inter-related world in more ways than most of us realize.

The population problem in Mexico might appear to be one difficulty the United States need not worry about, for example, but look at these figures: There are approximately five million illegal aliens in the United States today, most of them from Mexico. Mexico's population today is 62 million and growing rapidly.

If by the year 2000 their growth rate is reduced to one child for each adult, Mexico's eventual population will be 175 million. Few believe that such a slow-down will be reached by the year 2000. If that slow-down figure is not reached until 2020, Mexico's population will eventually be 270 million—50 million more than the present U.S. population.

If Mexico's population grows to 270 million, with all of the poverty that will inevitably bring, the U.S. illegal alien problems will make today's difficulties look small indeed.

There are eight million unemployed in the United States today. Exactly how many of the five million illegal aliens are part of that total is not clear, but it is a factor. What kind of unemployment problems will we have in 30 years? In 50 years? We could try to make a fortress of that 1,933-mile border, and cut off communications with Mexico and other countries. But one out of every three acres of farm land in the United States and Southern Illinois now goes for export. Those soybeans you will soon see in our fields are a major source of income from other nations to our economy.

One out of every five manufacturing jobs in the United States now comes from exports; one out of every three corporate profit dollars comes from exports. In the last decade our economic dependence on foreign trade has doubled, and it will grow in the future. Even if we could ignore these realities—which we cannot—there is the nuclear reality. The nations of the world now have enough nuclear warheads to theoretically destroy every person on the face of the earth 22 times. If Mexico thought it necessary for survival to produce nuclear bombs, she could do so. But the last thing this world needs is one more member of the nuclear club.

The alternative to sealing ourselves off, to inviting economic and military disaster, is to work with other countries so that all of us together can solve our problems. Then in the U.S. we can achieve economic progress and other nations can also.

That's important for the United States. That's important for Southern Illinois.

"Congressmen Who Served Southern Illinois," P.S./Washington, May 21–27, 1978

The 22 counties which are now the 24th Congressional District in Southern Illinois have had a great variety of representatives in Congress—a variety in quality, background and political affiliation.

The first to represent the area after Illinois achieved statehood was John McLean of Shawneetown, for whom McLean County (the Bloomington area) is named. At that time (1817–19) and through 1835, only one member represented the entire state because Illinois had little population.

Our third congressman, Joseph Duncan of Jacksonville, later became Governor, and as Governor distinguished himself for fighting a foolish scheme to build railroads and canals all over the state. The General Assembly overrode his veto, but Duncan turned out to be right—and legislators like Abraham Lincoln and Stephen A. Douglas were wrong.

The representative in Congress from our area who had the greatest impact on the nation was Lyman Trumbull—a lawyer from Belleville who later went to the Senate. He authored two amendments to the United States Constitution, and served as a friend and counselor to President Lincoln. They had served together in the Illinois State House of Representatives.

The only woman to represent the area, Emily Taft Douglas (1945–47), served as a representative-at-large for the state, including Southern Illinois. The daughter of the famous sculptor Lorado Taft, she authored several books but is more widely known as the wife (and now widow) of Senator Paul H. Douglas, a giant on the Senate side for 18 years.

Several members helped the economic growth of our area, but the two whom many regard as having contributed most in this century would be my predecessor, Kenneth Gray of West Frankfort, and Kent Keller of Ava. One of the most famous, John A. Logan, served as a general in the Civil War and after that was nominated by Ulysses S. Grant for the presidency.

The most scholarly to serve (as an at-large member from the whole state) was T. V. Smith—still quoted often in studies on the political process.

The two with the most unusual names were Napoleon Thistlewood of Cairo and Cecil W. Bishop of Carterville, who preferred to go by the nickname "Runt."

In the list of former Southern Illinois congressmen are those who become state officials and senators, some who came perilously close to landing in prison, and some who made substantial contributions to the nation. As you look over the list, it is probably fairly representative of the nation, with a gradual change in the quality and type of person representing the area in Congress.

For two terms early in the last century, John Reynolds of Belleville represented the area. He became famous for having a bottle of whiskey in one pocket and a Bible in the other, and he pulled out of his pocket whichever he thought would do him the most good with a prospective voter. Some of us feel pretty drab by comparison.

"Marion Will Rise Again," P.S./Washington, June 6–12, 1982

"In every cloud there is a silver lining" is an old saying that we have seen become reality in Southern Illinois. A tornado of incredible force swept through our territory killing 10 people, injuring more than 135, leaving about 1,000 without homes. But in the midst of all the misery and tragedy, two things stand out in my mind:

First, it is miraculous that only 10 people died. Devastation that widespread and complete, hurling cars, houses and signs though the air, setting off hundreds of natural gas leaks, might have caused hundreds of deaths rather than 10. Anyone who saw the damage without knowing the death toll would have had to guess a much higher figure.

Second, the degree and spirit of cooperation which adversity brings out is heartening. In a short time volunteers were there to help people in need, to take care of the many chores that had to be done.

Churches opened up their facilities, the Red Cross and Salvation Army moved in quickly and helped, the National Guard and State Police performed outstanding services—and police in Marion and surrounding communities put in long hours to protect and assist.

Federal officials were on the scene quickly. Mayor Bob Butler and the Marion Chamber of Commerce and labor unions and surviving businesses all pitched in. The utility companies and their employees were superb. The *Marion Daily Republican* was able to publish a special tornado edition that will become a souvenir item.

A host of Southern Illinoisans deserve mention for quiet acts of charity and kindness. For example, much of Marion was without water for drinking or any other purpose. Harry Crisp got his Pepsi-Cola trucks and crew out and they provided free Pepsi-Cola to all who wanted it in the devastated areas.

When I asked the regional manager for Wal-Mart, a major employer in Marion, whether the company intended to re-open he assured me, "We're going to reopen and get back in business just as fast as we can." While all businesses will not be able to reopen, most of the approximately 50 business places which were devastated are doing what Wal-Mart is doing.

Over and over again when I asked people where they were staying, I got answers like: "My sister-in-law took us in." Or: "Some friends took us in." Or: "Some people I hardly know volunteered to have us." The good people of Marion were closing ranks to help each other through the crisis.

I'll always wonder about the ending to one story that day. I asked a man who was moving some furniture if he had been living there. "No," he replied. "This is my father's. My mother and father are divorced and each of them had their place destroyed. The interesting thing is that they are both together again temporarily, living with us."

The tragedies which remain behind the tornado's path are real and the scars that are left will never disappear completely. Approximately 850 people will be out of work for some time. And that brings on added difficulties. But when the *St. Louis Globe-Democrat* interviewed the president of the Marion Chamber of Commerce, J. David Thompson, he responded, "Marion will rise again."

I believe him.

7

Leadership and Courage

EDITOR'S NOTE

Paul Simon articulated a consistent philosophical position on the concept of representation, which was that, as Edmund Burke advocated, the political leader had an obligation to be honest and forthright in his commitment to public service, to cast the hard vote, and then to go home and explain himself to his people. Thus, leadership also entails a central role for public education. The obligation to exhibit that kind of profile in courage was perhaps born in the idealistic young Paul Simon when he watched his Lutheran minister father take a principled and courageous stance against the internment of the Japanese on the West Coast at the height of the World War II scare. It was a lesson he seemed never to forget. It was a high standard, and he spent a career attempting to live up to it. After he left public office, he often lamented the fact that so few modern officeholders seem to have the fortitude to exhibit many "profiles in courage" qualities and that the voters seem to reward those who offer them an easy solution for complicated problems. One of his last books, *Our Culture of Pandering*, was a treatise on this theme, and he deeply believed that the political process demands more than many who seek office are willing to give. He constantly admonished his colleagues to tell the people what they need to hear rather than what they want to hear and to tell them the truth. In that respect, Paul Simon had some very idealistic values, which he tried to play out in a very competitive and often cynical game.

It is not clear whether Simon could have survived electorally in today's world of hyper politics. He lost early in the Democratic presidential nomination contest of 1988; however, he came back and won his second term in the Senate with an overwhelming victory in 1990. Most observers, myself included, believe that he would have won reelection if he had chosen to run for a third term in 1996, although the contest would likely have been a competitive one. Bill Clinton was running for a second term as president that year against Senator Robert Dole. Although Simon was a friend and admirer of Bob Dole's, he would have endorsed Clinton and campaigned with him and would have likely been reelected along with Clinton. Simon's prospects for reelection to a fourth term in 2002 are more problematic. That was the year after the 9/11 terror attacks; George W. Bush was riding a wave of patriotic fervor, and he and the Republicans got a strong "rally around the flag" lift out of the Bush administration's handling of the early stages of the war on terror. It was the year of saber-rattling and a determined buildup toward the invasion of Iraq on March 19, 2003. It was not a good year to be a Democrat running for reelection, and a number of prominent Democrats lost their seat that year. It was not the kind of electoral atmosphere in which Paul Simon thrived, and he may well have chosen to retire that year had he not already exercised that option in the previous round.

More important, Paul Simon was uncomfortable with the requirements of modern campaigns for major public office. A candidate now must raise tens of millions of dollars to be competitive in a big state like Illinois. Simon hated fund-raising, and that was one of the reasons he gave for his retirement in 1996. A candidate has to be always onstage under the watchful eye of the electronic media. Simon was pretty good at that part of the job; he was not intimidated by television and used it to his advantage, even though he was a print media creature at heart. He liked to joke that he had been told that he had a good face for radio. He would have been puzzled by and probably uninterested in Facebook, Twitter, or any of the new social media developments. He was very set in his ways regarding dress, personal style, and image adjustments. No one could imagine him sitting still for any kind of cosmetic makeover. He knew what his image was, and he protected that image and was comfortable with it because it rang true with who he was intrinsically. There was no pretense and no artifice with Paul Simon. I knew him in all kinds of circumstances, and he was always the same guy, no matter what.

He has been missed by his family and friends since he has been gone, and the state and nation lost a unique leader at his death. Paul Simon's career stands as a testament to the best instincts of the American voters and the qualities they are capable of responding positively to in their assessment of the candidates. Simon's brand of leadership is all too rare in today's world, but his career does show that a commitment to public service and to the highest ethical standards can be rewarded by the voters of Illinois. Illinois is famous—or perhaps infamous—for its political corruption and for the criminal convictions of political figures, both high and low. Perhaps understandably, the people of the state have grown tired of some of their leaders and skeptical toward their government. The national mood is no better when significant majorities say they do not trust Congress and disapprove of the job legislators are doing, no matter which party is in charge or when the poll is taken. Paul Simon's example stands as an eloquent counterweight to the pervasive cynicism of today's politics. His writings raised a strong and clear voice on behalf of the principles in which he believed and wanted to impart to others. This book is an attempt to keep that voice alive and to see that his legacy is kept intact and imparted to a new generation and his words renewed for his friends and admirers.

THE NEED FOR COURAGE AND VISION

"FOURTH OF JULY: THE GOOD AND THE BAD,"
P.S./WASHINGTON, JULY 18–24, 1976

Make no mistake about it: This past Fourth of July's celebrations were different, and good. For someone who is involved in leadership in government, there is occasionally this gnawing question: Do people really care? In the Fourth of July celebrations I attended—and I was at six that day—I sensed something good, something solid.

I do not look for the phony patriotism that too often is the mark of the demagogue, who waves the flag while undermining the ideals of this country.

But what I found were decent citizens, in a low-key way showing their genuine affection for this country, in an oft-expressed desire to make it a finer country. Questions were raised: What is happening to our spiritual values? When we have so much that is good in our nation, why can't we do more to make life livable and comfortable for our senior citizens?

And other questions. Questions that George Washington and Thomas Jefferson and the other early leading Americans would have been pleased to hear us asking each other. . . .

The bad part of the Fourth is what did not happen. While there were excellent local programs all over the nation, the spirit of the country is such that we could have used this opportunity to do something really exciting as a nation. But it did not happen.

Fifty years from now or 100 years from now people ought to be able to look back on 1976 and say, "This is what the people of the United States did as a nation to significantly celebrate their 200th anniversary."

History will record some fine local programs. But as a nation we congratulated each other, accepted some symbolic gifts from other countries, had distinguished visitors—and nothing more.

We could have planted a billion trees, or launched a campaign against hunger around the globe, or decided to encourage the arts by having designations such as "poet laureate" in every state, or launched a program of teaching foreign languages, or decided that this is the year that we would implement a guarantee for the chance to go to college for every student with the ability. There were endless possibilities. But we lost that national opportunity. And both political parties are to blame.

Perhaps we were so caught up in Vietnam and Watergate and sex scandals that we did not have the foresight to do it. Whatever the reasons, we erred.

In 1776 we declared our independence, but we really achieved nationhood in 1789 when our Constitution went into effect. While that date is not as clear in our minds as 1776, perhaps that date—200 years later—will give us a chance to redeem ourselves.

"Lifting the National Spirit,"
P.S./Washington, October 21–27, 1979

There is a great deal of talk about the "down" mood of the American public, whatever name you give that mood. "People are disheartened, depressed, and disenchanted," one of my colleagues told me. That is true. But it can be turned around quickly. Let me tell you how I discovered that.

A few weeks ago, traveling in the southern part of my district, I found that the major topic of conversation was not inflation, energy, or the usual concerns. The interstate bridge between Metropolis, Illinois and Paducah, Kentucky had to be closed because of faulty construction and everyone had to go by way of a small bridge at Brookport to get across the Ohio River.

If amid the complaints about what ails this country the closing of a bridge, and the inconvenience that it causes, can suddenly be the chief topic of conversation and complaint, it suggests that our problems are not that deep-seated as far as they affect the spirit of this nation.

Perhaps what we need is a real challenge from the President on inflation and energy, our two most pressing problems. Not a challenge which is simply another speech, more polished oratory. We need something that asks a sacrifice of all of us, for the American public understands that to attack these problems will take sacrifice, but they want to make sure that all of us share in that sacrifice, and not just a few.

Right now I have the uneasy feeling that we have almost surrendered to the OPEC leaders, and many Americans share in that feeling. If the President [Carter] announced cutbacks in oil imports more stringent than those announced so far, and called for a series of oil-saving measures, most Americans would welcome these steps, particularly if there are not some people profiting from our sacrifice. And in the inflation field we yearn for the President to get hold of things, to tell us what needs to be done and what he is doing and make it firm and tough. Be willing to do the unpopular. We want that!

Things can turn around. We can be lifted in spirit just as easily as we get depressed. We do not expect a nation or a world without problems, but we want to have the feeling that there is solid movement and direction in solving them.

It is strange that people talking about a bridge being blocked can be uplifting. But it was.

We want to get the bridge fixed and traffic moving again. We want to get the nation fixed and our spirit moving again.

"What Is Popular May Not Be Right," P.S./Washington, May 10–16, 1987

What's wrong with a lawmaker going along with public opinion and doing what is popular? History is filled with examples of tragedies caused by policymakers who wanted to do what was popular rather than what was right.

Last year every organization I know endorsed the "tax reform" measure. After I indicated on the Senate floor that I would oppose it—I ended up being one of three to vote against it—one of my Senate colleagues came to me and said that while he privately did not think the bill was good, it was so popular that if I voted against it, it would be the end of my political life.

My vote was unpopular, but it is less unpopular today, and by the time most Americans fill out their income tax forms next year it might even be a popular stand. At least it was the right stand.

The wire service recently carried a story that the Tax Foundation says that in 1987 the average American will have to work another 19 days to pay for this year's taxes. How precisely accurate that report may be I do not know. What I do know is that the "tax reform" that everyone swallowed last year means higher taxes from millions of middle-income Americans.

There were some good things about that tax bill, but many more wrong things. It reduced the taxes paid by the wealthiest of Americans from 50 percent to 28 percent, while one-third of middle-income Americans will end up paying more in taxes. That was only one of the many things wrong with that bill.

Other defects:

- It accepts as reality that we are becoming more and more an information and service-oriented society and reduces encouragement for capital intensive manufacturing. The United States cannot maintain its quality of life unless we continue to be a major manufacturing nation.
- It massively overhauled the tax code without reducing the deficit one cent. In fact, it added to the deficit. The deficit is our No. 1 economic problem.
- It reduces the amount a corporation can deduct for research. Anyone who believes that the United States can be competitive against Japan and other nations by cutting back on research has avoided looking at reality.

There are other deficiencies with that measure. And reforming the reform will not be easy, but one of these years it has to happen.

One of the major lessons in all of this for an administration, for Congress, and for the public: Don't get stampeded into supporting something just because every organization you know is for it.

What is popular is not necessarily right.

"Lincoln's Words Still Ring True,"
P.S./Washington, July 19–25, 1987

The current television coverage of the Iran-Contra hearings has prompted some to call Lieutenant Colonel Oliver North a hero. I do not question Colonel North's sincerity nor his patriotism. But he is not an American hero. No one deserves the hero's rank who admits that he lied, shredded evidence and violated the laws of our nation he swore to uphold.

Our heroes should be those who live within the law and serve the public. They are people who are often unsung for their devotion to duty: public servants like teachers, librarians, police officers and firemen.

Colonel North, the President, the attorney general, members of the House and Senate and the public would be wise to listen to the message of a 28-year-old state legislator serving in Springfield, Illinois. In January 1838, he said:

"Let every American, every lover of liberty, every well-wisher to his posterity, swear by the blood of the [American] revolution never to violate in the least particular the laws of this country; and never to tolerate their violation by others . . . Let every man remember that to violate the laws is to trample upon the blood of his father and to tear the charter of his own and his children's liberty. Let reverence for the laws . . . become the political religion of the nation; and let the old and the young, the rich and the poor, the grave and the gay, of all sexes and tongues, and colors and conditions, sacrifice unceasingly upon its altars."

These words, from the pen and tongue of Abraham Lincoln, are as important today as they were then. At that point Lincoln was commenting on mob action that took the law into its hands and killed a newspaper editor who opposed slavery. Neither the mob in the 1830's nor high-ranking public officials in the 1980's should violate the law. Abraham Lincoln was right in 1838 and he is right today.

Phone calls, letters and telegrams have poured into my office from people expressing their opinions about Lieutenant Colonel North. People admire Col. North's devotion to country. Devotion and patriotism are admirable characteristics. But more important than the laudable personal characteristics of one person are larger issues: the accountability of government office holders to the people, and respect for the law.

One woman from Elgin, Illinois sent this telegram: "As a citizen of the United States I am very appreciative of the way in which the Congress is conducting the investigation into the Iran-Contra affair. I particularly appreciate the efforts to help Lt. Col. North understand that he is not above the law."

That is not only true for him. It is true for you and me, for those in the highest positions and those in the lowliest.

"LEE ATWATER AND ABRAHAM LINCOLN: GENEROUS SPIRITS IN TROUBLED TIMES," P.S./WASHINGTON, FEBRUARY 3–9, 1991

I don't ordinarily promote magazines, but the February issue of *Life* has two exceptionally fine articles, one about Abraham Lincoln by Garry Wills and the other by Lee Atwater, former chairman of the Republican National Committee and campaign manager for President Bush in 1988, telling of his battle with a brain tumor.

There was a strange but welcome similarity of spirit to both articles.

Lee Atwater's article was deeply moving. That is an overworked phrase, but it accurately describes what he wrote. It took courage for Lee to have his picture printed in the magazine. I would not have recognized him. But more impressive is the generosity of spirit. Some people shrink in the face of adversity. Lee Atwater has grown.

And, in the process, he helps us grow. Listen, for example, to these words:

"The '80s were about acquiring—acquiring wealth, power, prestige. I know. I acquired more wealth, power and prestige than most. But you can acquire all you want and still feel empty. What power wouldn't I trade for a little more time with my family? What price wouldn't I pay for an evening with friends? It took a deadly illness to put me eye to eye with that truth, but it is a truth that the country, caught up in its ruthless ambitions and moral decay, can learn on my dime. I don't know who will lead us through the '90s, but they must be made to speak to this spiritual vacuum at the heart of American society, this tumor of the soul."

I have a hand-written note from Lee Atwater dated April 10, 1990, written with shaky penmanship. I appreciated receiving that note then, but I appreciate it more after reading this article. In the same magazine is the Garry Wills article about Lincoln, and there is in that article the same generosity of spirit that Lee Atwater shows. (Lee may be a little embarrassed by that Lincoln comparison.) We have had many good presidents, a few great presidents, but only one with the sensitivity that Lincoln showed, both in his actions and in his words.

You would expect the leader of one side in the Civil War, with hatred running deep, in an address to the nation, to say, "We're going to defeat those so-and-so's," but instead he speaks without hatred, "with malice toward none, with charity toward all."

It is that same spirit that somehow must be conveyed to the citizens of Iraq, and indirectly to the Moslem world: That we are in a war, but sensitive to the tragedy that any war causes. If we come across as powerful militarily, but uncaring about the war's tragedies, our political influence in the world will diminish.

We must make clear that we not only can shoot people in the name of justice, but also help people in the name of justice. That's what Abraham Lincoln would do. That is what George Bush should do. And I believe that's what the new and revised edition of Lee Atwater that I respect so much would do.

"The Oklahoma Bombing and the Poison of Hatred," P.S./Washington, April 30–May 6, 1995

Ahead of me the other day was a car with a bumper sticker: "Hatred Is Not a Family Value." Seeing it after the Oklahoma bombing, it seemed an appropriate comment.

A few days after the Oklahoma tragedy, I was at home catching up on my newspaper reading. The *Chicago Tribune* on April 9th, 10 days before the bombing, had a significant headline on a story: "Pennsylvania Slayings Show Hate Groups Know No Bounds."

The people who permitted themselves to become brutes and cause this needless Oklahoma devastation must be vigorously pursued and then prosecuted. That is happening. But they are not alone in their guilt, those who made the bomb and detonated it. Someone poisoned their warped minds with hatred.

People who spread hatred of any kind, toward groups or toward individuals, begin a process that cannot be controlled. "Every action has a reaction," my Dana College psychology professor used to say.

A few years ago I introduced a bill to have the Federal Bureau of Investigation keep track of hate crimes in the nation. That passed and the FBI is now compiling these statistics, with voluntary compliance by local police departments, though it is new enough that many police departments are not yet doing it. But I want to monitor the tracks of the poison of hatred in our system. If the poison in our system is growing, and we know it, then we can deal with it more effectively. The collection of the data is still too new to reach any solid conclusions.

My instinct is that—at best—hatred in our society is not declining, and it may be rising.

People should feel free to disagree with our government, but not hate it; to disagree with the President, but not hate him; to disagree with a family member, but not hate that person.

I confess to some sense of relief when we learned that the persons who played the role of beasts in Oklahoma were not Muslims, because there is an anti-Muslim atmosphere as a result of some extremist actions in the Middle East and the bombing of the World Trade Center.

Remember that those who encourage hatred of Muslims, Jews, Catholics, Latinos, blacks, Armenians, Asians, homosexuals, women or any other group are contributing to events that cannot be controlled. Hatred and bitterness and revenge are passions that harm the persons harboring them, and can harm others. When someone tells a joke making fun of a nationality or a religion or some other group, tactfully let the person telling the story know it is not funny.

And when the balloon of hatred is blown up in front of you, puncture it, before it grows and grows and grows.

"One nation, under God, indivisible" should be more than a phrase. We must reach out to one another with care and respect.

"Major News Stories That You Have Not Seen," P.S./Washington, February 25–March 2, 1996

In his excellent new book, *Breaking the News*, James Fallows says—I believe accurately—that the media are part of the reason for the excessive cynicism that the public harbors about our government and our political process.

Make no mistake about it, the main cause for the cynicism is those in public life who pander, rather than tell people the truth, who provide popular answers rather than the real answers. All of us in public office share some guilt for this.

Fallows is correct when he writes: "The message of today's news coverage is often that the world cannot be understood, shaped or controlled, but merely endured at arm's length." He says much of the writing is like sports coverage: The contest is reported, but not with any real belief that the outcome matters.

A reporter covering a contest between the Chicago Bears and the St. Louis Rams can write whatever he or she wishes and have no impact on the game. But coverage of political matters can have a huge impact on what happens. He makes another point: Journalists tend to cover what is easy to write about. Let me tell you some really important news stories that you have not seen on the front page of any newspaper, heard about on any radio station, or seen on television news:

- The United States is more residentially segregated on the basis of economics than at any time in our nation's history. That means that most Americans are more and more isolated from the poor and their problems, and that is a major reason we have been so unresponsive to the needs of the desperate in our society. Twenty-four percent of our children live in poverty. No other Western industrial nation comes close to that figure, and I believe it is because, unless we are in small towns, we live in economic ghettos.

- The world is headed toward a water crisis. In the next 45 to 60 years the world's population will double, while our water supply will not grow. The World Bank says that in 20 years, 35 nations will face extremely severe problems. Wars over water are coming unless we act, and we are not likely to act unless we know the problem.
- Our future as a nation is being retarded because in the United States elementary and high school students attend school 180 days a year, compared to 243 days in Japan and 240 in Germany, as two examples. If we increased the 180 days to only 210, by the end of high school that would be the equivalent of two additional years of school. We have both a quality problem in education, that many people understand, and a quantity problem, that few understand.
- Less than 1 percent of our college students ever study in another country. All other nations exceed that number, with the exception of North Korea. This short-coming in an increasingly competitive world harms us in trade, science and diplomacy, and probably is responsible for some of the provincial actions of Congress—like being far behind in paying our United Nations dues.
- While the United States spends more on defense than the next eight nations combined, we lag behind all of Western Europe and Japan in foreign economic assistance. Once the United States led the world in foreign aid. Now this takes less than 1 percent of our budget. This is reducing our influence in the world and our ability to stabilize potential problem areas.

Each of the above stories is important to the future of every American, but none of them has received 1/10,000 of the attention of the O. J. Simpson trial. The media should do more than entertain us.

"PUBLIC OPINION SHOULDN'T RULE: LEADERS SHOULD," *DAILY HERALD*, FEBRUARY 14, 2001

In the Lutheran church that I attend, the Sunday Gospel from the book of Luke included these words: "Woe to you when all men speak well of you, for that is how their fathers treated the false prophets." Centuries before the New Testament, the prophet Jeremiah in Jewish Scriptures defined a false prophet as one who simply follows public opinion.

A great temptation in political life is to do what is popular, rather than what is in the best interest of a community, a state, or a nation. Sometimes what is popular and what is right coincide, but they do not always mesh. Don't go to a physician who tells you what you want to hear, and don't support a candidate or public official who tells you only what you want to hear. Too many in public life follow the Groucho Marx philosophy: "These are my principles. If you don't like them, I have others." Groucho spoke in jest. Unfortunately, too many in public life almost say the same thing, but not in jest.

Public officials should listen to people, should understand their problems and concerns. That is why I conducted so many town meetings all over the state when I served as senator. But never once did I take a poll to determine a vote I should cast or a position I should take. Did I always do the right thing and not what was popular? I wish I could reply with a solid "Yes." I am sure that on occasion I rationalized doing the popular. It is a natural temptation. We like the approval of others, not their condemnation.

A small illustration of how public opinion can be wrong: When I supported requiring automobile manufacturers to put seat belts in cars, and then the mandatory use of them, my stand occasionally resulted in a chorus of boos at town meetings. But overwhelming evidence showed that seat belts could save thousands of lives each year, and now we know they have done that and are doing it. Should I have done the popular, rather than the unpopular?

In a similar vein, I supported requiring wearing helmets for motorcycle drivers. It will save lives and reduce the number of paralyzing injuries. But the motorcycle crowd hates my position. At one town meeting, a motorcyclist said, "If we want to commit suicide, we should be able to do it." At that point in our discussion, my patience had worn thin and I unwisely said, "If you can promise me you'll commit suicide in the process, that would generate some votes. But you may end up being paralyzed, costing the taxpayers millions of dollars to sustain you." The next day issue of the motorcycle publication had a headline: "Simon to Motorcyclists: Drop Dead." The reality: My unpopular efforts were aimed at saving their lives.

In her book *Whatever It Takes*, political observer Elizabeth Drew notes: "Politics should be for the purpose of governing."

After World War II, President Harry Truman and Secretary of State George Marshall proposed what became the Marshall Plan, designed to give humanitarian aid and to rescue Western Europe and other areas from communism. The first public opinion poll taken after its proposal showed only 14 percent of the U.S. public supporting the endeavor. Some of that aid went to Germany and Japan, two nations responsible for the deaths of many young Americans during World War II. Today, it is viewed as one of the wisest actions undertaken by our government in the last century. If Harry Truman had governed by responding to polls, our world would look much different—and much worse—today.

The *London Times* four years ago described U.S. government policies as too often motivated by "a shiftless, poll-driven opportunism." In the Republican contest for the presidential nomination, George W. Bush told an Iowa audience: "I don't run polls to tell me what to think. The most important, most influential job in America should be the president, not the president's pollster."

It should be our hope that he follows through on that, and that members of Congress of both political parties do the same. Leaders who follow polls are leaders in name more than reality. The nation needs leadership.

PHILOSOPHY OF LEADERSHIP

"Motives Are Generally Good," P.S./Washington, January 18–24, 1976

They tell a story—not true—about the U.S. ambassador to Austria being awakened by one of his aides about 4 o'clock in the morning and told, "The Soviet ambassador dropped dead about three hours ago." To which the American ambassador responded, "I wonder what his motive was." The story illustrates the tendency to view with suspicion everything done by a political opponent. A certain level of skepticism is understandable, and perhaps healthy. But sometimes it is carried too far.

Essential to the functioning of a free society such as ours is some self-restraint by people and institutions—a self-restraint that grows out of respect for the motives of others.

I see this problem of the bitter critic in a variety of places.

Sometimes it erupts in floor debate in Congress, where there is an excess of rancor. That type of bitterness rarely produces good legislation. A letter I received the other day questioned my patriotism because I did not vote the way the gentleman wanted me to vote on an oil pricing bill. In my opinion he was not properly informed on the measure and my vote is the correct one—but I'm sure he is as loyal to this country as I am. I have seen this questioning of motive in fights over school locations or where a park or industry should be built.

This excessive skepticism erupts in elections, whether for the Presidency or for the school board. Two decades ago the late Sen. Joseph McCarthy got us to suspect each other, to assume the worst instead of something better. Watergate and Vietnam have again renewed that kind of atmosphere.

My immediate reason for writing this column is that three people who advocate a specific cause came into my office recently; they believe that those who oppose them are part of a plot to destroy the country. If you believe something strongly enough, you can fit the facts to your opinion and build up a strong case—at least in your own mind.

If these three people had assumed that their opponents may be just as sincere and dedicated and responsible citizens as they are, it would have taken the bitterness out of their dialogue and would have made me more open to their cause.

This nation—or any community—has no shortage of problems.

There will be, and should be, disagreements as to how to solve those problems.

But we must assume that others may be as sincere as we are, and that sometimes we have made mistakes. If we listen to the opinions of others rather than shouting at them, we might learn and the nation would benefit.

"COMPROMISE: ESSENTIAL TO PROGRESS," P.S./WASHINGTON, JANUARY 25–31, 1976

For many people the word "compromise" has a bad ring to it. And if compromise means abandoning principle, it is bad. But there are practical compromises which are necessary to keep government operating smoothly. If practical compromises are not made, a marriage cannot succeed, a business cannot operate, and democratic government would collapse. Let me give you a practical illustration of how a compromise works.

Recently a measure which authorizes mining for coal on federal lands—under certain restrictions—came before the House. Under the bill, the Secretary of the Interior is authorized to sign leases.

My immediate concern was the Shawnee National Forest. I didn't want some Secretary of the Interior who had never been to Southern Illinois, who perhaps had never even seen a picture of the Shawnee National Forest, to sign some document authorizing strip mining there. It could happen without our knowing about it. Or it could happen that when we finally found out about it, it would be too late to stop.

So I prepared an amendment which said that before the Secretary of the Interior could sign a lease for strip mining on federal lands, the governor of the state involved would have to be notified, and if he objected, the lease would have to be delayed one year, and then the Secretary of the Interior would have to reevaluate the proposal.

That would give a governor a chance to protest and, through the news media and letters to Congress, the public would have a chance to stop something that might do great damage to a national forest.

After drafting the amendment, I told my colleagues in the House about my proposed changes. The chairman of the committee which approved the bill I wanted to amend, Rep. Patsy Mink of Hawaii, told me that she felt it should cover only the national forests, not the other federal lands—which include the grasslands of the West. She thought she could be for my amendment if I made that change. I agreed to it.

Congressman Ken Hechler of West Virginia had a stronger amendment which would have outlawed all strip mining on federal lands in the immediate future. He asked me to let him present his amendment first, and if his failed—which it did—then he would support mine. I agreed.

Congressman Tim Wirth of Colorado felt that the period involved should be six months rather than a year, and Rep. Mink agreed with him; as a subcommittee chairperson and one of the most effective members of the House, Rep. Mink's voice carries considerable weight. I accepted that change. Another clarifying change was suggested during debate. I accepted it. Two members talked to me about other changes which I felt I could not accept.

Debate on my amendment took perhaps 30 minutes on the floor of the House. It carried 39–25. If I had been inflexible and unwilling to compromise, my amendment would have been defeated, and the Shawnee National Forest would have been without this important protection.

I got a little less than I had hoped for, but a small victory was won for the public. And (much as I hate to admit it) perhaps some of those suggestions which I accepted made the amendment a better one for the public.

"Two Unpopular Votes," P.S./Washington, June 26–July 2, 1977

I cast two unpopular votes this past week, and you have a right to know my reasons.

The House voted by a wide margin to prohibit all trade and aid to South Vietnam, Cuba and a few other unpopular countries and to force international organizations to do the same.

I am sure that if these same prohibitions came to a vote in Southern Illinois, they would win overwhelmingly. But I'm also convinced that if the people of Southern Illinois had at their disposal some of the facts that members of the Congress have, they would vote more sensibly than did the majority of my colleagues. There are several issues involved.

First is the fact that Congress should give the President some flexibility in conducting foreign policy. The pendulum between presidential power and congressional power swings back and forth, and thanks to a combination of Watergate and Vietnam, right now Congress is making detailed policy decisions we would be wiser to leave to the President.

For example, what if (to take an extreme example) the House's action carried and became law, and then an earthquake or a terrible hurricane hit Cuba? Thousands are killed and disease and injury are rampant. The nations of the world come to Cuba's aid—with the exception of her wealthy neighbor, the United States. We can't do it because it's against the law.

Prior to our cutting relations with Cuba that island was the number seven purchaser of U.S. agricultural products among the nations of the world. Who gets hurt when we don't trade? Some people in Cuba, yes; but also the farmers in Southern Illinois.

The House action also fails to recognize that there are some differences within the Communist world, and it is in the self-interest of the United States to encourage those differences. The fact that China and the Soviet Union are not getting along right now is one of the major pluses for U.S. security.

There is reason to believe that in the African nation of Angola, Cuba (with troops there) and the Soviets are not in agreement. You even have the strange situation in Angola right now of Cuban troops guarding the Gulf Oil refinery. But by cutting off communication with Cuba, we force that nation closer to the Soviets, and the Soviets—not Cuba—represent the long-run threat to our security. Another nation which fell under the glass eye of the House action is Vietnam.

Unlike Japan in World War II, Vietnam did not attack us. We went over to Vietnam at the invitation of the government then in power and bombed the life out of much of the country.

After World War II there were many voices raised in opposition to helping Japan, but we sensibly helped that nation—and Japan today is one of our most important allies. Whether Vietnam will ever be an ally of the United States I do not know—nor does anyone else. But if there are possibilities of developing friendships, I want to have the President free to do that. The House by its actions has pleased the cheering throngs. My mail will not be pleasant to read after these votes.

But in a world filled with nuclear warheads, we ought to be building bridges of understanding, not blowing them up. The House acted hastily and unwisely. We flunked our test in history.

"IS A CAREER IN PUBLIC SERVICE WORTH IT?," P.S./WASHINGTON, DECEMBER 3–10, 1994

Shortly after announcing that I will retire from the Senate after 1996, a gentleman approached me and asked a simple question: "Should I encourage my 10-year-old to consider entering political life?"

In the quick, passing conversation he added something about the bitterness of politics.

My answer to him and to all parents of 10-year-olds is that if they are talking about non-career participation, then the answer should be a clear yes—and the best way to encourage 10-year-olds is by example: participate yourself.

Political participation is the way we determine the future of our free government, whether those 10-year-olds will be saddled with a huge debt because of our short-sightedness and cowardice; whether those 10-year-olds will have quality educational opportunities; whether those 10-year-olds will grow up in a world of peace and stability.

But I believe the gentleman meant whether he should encourage his son or daughter to make a career of political life, and the answer to that is a little more difficult. My answer is: "Yes, if . . ."

- If that 10-year-old shows a real interest in current events, including politics or in history. Children should not be shoved into a profession. People generally do well at what they enjoy.
- If that 10-year-old shows an ability to get along with people well. I met a young man from Decatur, Ill., 11-year-old Howard Buffett Jr., who someday could make a very successful politician. He is an extrovert. He mixes with people naturally. We are not all suited for every profession, fortunately. Some people can spend a day in a chemical lab and be thoroughly excited by it. For others it would be a chore. The same is true of political life.
- If that young person shows an interest in doing something other than making money. If his or her goal in life is primarily making money, then choose another profession; political life will be a disappointment.
- If there is a genuine sense of wanting to help people. If that gives satisfaction, a political career may be right for him or her. But it is wrong if the person simply wants to *be* a senator or governor

or county commissioner or hold some other office—if the office is
sought solely because of the title and honor, rather than for what
can be done in that office.

- If the person is willing to take criticism and some abuse. More than
most professions, political life is an area where many people believe
strongly they know the right answers and they let you know. That's
the way it should be in a democracy. But frequently those who are
the most certain are the least informed.

In reading over what I have written, I have made it sound too grim.
What I have not added is the great satisfaction a person receives from getting something done that helps people, usually things that do not receive
public attention.

If I were to start over, would I enter public service again?

You bet.

"On Civility," NPR Commentary, July 1, 1997

The term "civility" appears frequently in print these days. Editorial writers
properly decry the trend toward excessive partisanship in Congress. But
that meanness of spirit did not suddenly emerge in the U.S. Congress. It
arose from the ranks of all of us. And the germ carried to Congress is being
nurtured there.

Whether you agree or disagree with the recent decision in the Senate to
change the law on Medicare so that those with higher income will pay a little
more, it was an unusual display of courage—not frequently in abundance
these days—and also an unusual display of bi-partisanship.

We should have open and healthy debate where there are genuine differences, but we should not magnify difference and create unnecessary division
in our society.

The President's appeal at San Diego University to all of us to close the
racial divide is the right appeal. I recently headed an international team
of 104 people from 25 nations that monitored the presidential election in
Croatia. What stuns a visitor to that Balkan area are the sharp divisions and
animosities that still exist between Croats and Serbs and Muslims, divisions
that ultimately and ironically have a religious basis.

More than 10,000 lives lost there are a tragic monument to hatred and a
lack of respect for one another. But those responsible are not simply those
who pulled the triggers. Those who generated the hatred share the blame.

The recent conviction of Timothy McVeigh, found guilty of the Oklahoma City bombing, did not happen in a vacuum. Someone or some few people filled him with so much hatred for our government that he lashed out with his despicable deed. When we nurture hatred rather than understanding, when we tell unfunny jokes that ridicule another race or religion or ethnic group or sexual type, when we needlessly divide people for our own political or personal gain, we do a great disservice to our nation and to humanity.

The very word, "humanity," suggests that to qualify for membership we should be humane.

Essay on Lincoln's Lyceum Speech, *Illinois Heritage*, published by the Illinois State Historical Society, September 3, 1997

Visitors to the Illinois exhibit at the New York World's Fair saw a Disney-created President Abraham Lincoln mannequin stand before them, with mechanically created movements of his arms and lips that made him look almost life-like. When the audience quieted, the Lincoln-like figure spoke to us.

Part of what President Lincoln said at the New York World's Fair were phrases of his familiar to most Americans, but part of what "President" Lincoln said there was not from his years as President, but words from his first Lincolnesque speech, given to the Young Men's Lyceum of Springfield at the age of 28.

What caused Lincoln, a young state legislator, to carefully prepare such a speech?

Seven weeks earlier, a mob in Alton, Illinois, killed Elijah Lovejoy, a Presbyterian minister who edited a newspaper there with strong anti-slavery views. The slaying of Lovejoy stunned Illinois and the nation and around the country—even in the slave-holding states of the south—public officials and newspaper editorials denounced the mob action. But in Illinois, where the abolitionist cause did not generate popularity, most newspapers and almost all public officials were audibly silent, or hinted that Lovejoy brought his death on by his extreme views.

How could that be in Illinois where the Constitution and laws banned slavery?

Illinois technically was a free state. But slavery existed when we became a state and continued for some time afterwards. When Ninian Edwards, father of Lincoln's future brother-in-law, served as territorial governor of Illinois, which did not legally permit slavery, he ran this classified advertisement:

Notice: I have for sale twenty-two slaves, among them are several of both sexes between the years of ten and seventeen . . . I have also for sale a full-blooded horse, a very large English bull and several young ones.

Shadrach Bond, the first Governor of the "free" State of Illinois, had this in his will: "I give to my loving wife, Achsah Bond, all of my personal property . . . my Negro Frank Thomas . . . I give to my daughter Julia Rachel five hundred dollars and my Negro girl Eliza. And to my daughter Achsah Mary five hundred dollars and my Negro girl Harriet and to my wife Achsah I gave all the rest of my Negros."

In 1853—twelve years after Lincoln left the Illinois House of Representatives—Illinois passed a law that a free African American entering the state could be sold into slavery. The mood of Illinois when an angry mob killed Lovejoy was pro-slavery, but not only in Illinois. The state legislatures of Connecticut and New York in the mid-1830s passed resolutions stating that slavery was accepted in the U.S. Constitution and that no state had a right to interfere.

But Lincoln had a different attitude. He spent his first years in Hardin County, Kentucky, where the tax lists of 1811—when Lincoln was two years old—listed 1,007 slaves for purposes of taxation. But earlier, the South Fork Baptist Church split on the basis of slavery, and before Lincoln's birth his parents had joined the Little Mount Anti-Slavery Baptist Church. When they moved to Indiana, they joined a Baptist Church whose pastor had strong anti-slavery views.

Ten months before Lovejoy's slaying, the Illinois House of Representatives adopted a resolution "that the right of property in slaves is sacred . . . (that) we highly disapprove of the formation of abolition societies . . . that the General Government cannot abolish slavery in the District of Columbia." It passed 77–6, Lincoln being one of the six to vote against it. Six weeks later, he and Rep. Dan Stone filed a protest to the passage of the resolution, a rarely used device to register strong disagreement.

Lovejoy's death brought the slavery issue to the fore, particularly in Illinois, because Illinois public officials had been part of an attempt to muzzle Lovejoy.

Threatened with violence regularly, twice the Alton editor's printing equipment had been thrown in the Mississippi River. Community leaders called a general meeting to work out "a compromise" in the volatile atmosphere of Alton. Defending Lovejoy at the large meeting was Edward Beecher, President of Illinois College of Jacksonville, but arrayed against Lovejoy were several public officials including Cyrus Edwards, soon to be the Whig candidate for Governor, and leading the charge, the politically ambitious Attorney General of Illinois, Usher Linder. Linder suggested the compromise: Lovejoy and his family could leave Alton without injury if he would stop publishing his newspaper. Lovejoy declined to accept the compromise in a ringing defense of free speech. He concluded, "If I fall, my grave shall be made in Alton." He lived four more days.

His death shocked the nation. John Quincy Adams called it an earthquake. Protest meetings were held all over the north. At one in a congregational church in Ohio, a young man stood up and said he would devote his life to fighting slavery. His name: John Brown. Another leader of the anti-slavery movement, Wendell Phillips, emerged from a Lovejoy protest meeting. Years later, he wrote: "I can never forget the quick, sharp agony of that hour which brought us the news of Lovejoy's death . . . The gun fired at Lovejoy was like that of Sumter—it shattered a world of dreams. How prudently most men creep into nameless graves while now and then one or two forget themselves into immortality."

However, Illinois had a muted reaction.

And Lincoln, who might have been expected to denounce the mob action immediately, did not, nor did any elected Illinois public official. But seven weeks later, he became the only state office-holder to comment with his speech to the Young Men's Lyceum. Politically cautious, he did not mention Lovejoy but denounced mob action, and everyone present knew why. And here the future Abraham Lincoln can be heard: "Let every man remember that to violate the law is to trample on the blood of his father, and to tear the charter of his own, and his children's liberty. Let reverence for the laws be breathed by every American mother to the lisping babe, that prattles on her lap.

"Let it be taught in schools, in seminaries, and in colleges . . . In short, let it become the *political religion* of the nation; and let the old and the young, the rich and the poor, the grave and the gay, of all sexes and tongues, and colors and conditions, sacrifice unceasingly upon its altars."

"ON SEPTEMBER 11, 2001, ATTACKS,"
NPR COMMENTARY, SEPTEMBER 12, 2001

To say we were stunned by the senseless, tragic events that killed thousands of our people is an understatement. We wonder how twisted minds can find satisfaction is such bloodshed. And then we want to respond. But how? Let me suggest four steps:

First, beef up our intelligence operations. We have been focused too much on the old Soviet Union and not enough on new terrorist groups. As a long-ago veteran of Army intelligence, I can tell you that people in intelligence—like Senators, teachers, journalists, and those in every profession—get in ruts. This operation was not that of an isolated madman in Sacramento, but a complex well-organized effort that we should have penetrated and known about.

Second, respect and protect those in our midst who may have national or cultural ties to those whom we discover are responsible, and within weeks we are likely to know. If, for example, someone living in Afghanistan headed this, that does not mean that those who live in our nation from Afghanistan had anything to do with the tragedy. Their rights should be protected by all of us. In our desire to "do something," sometimes innocent people are harmed. We have had enough innocent people harmed. Let's not compound the tragedy.

Third, as we learn the facts, any nation that harbors or encourages these shameful acts must be dealt with firmly. But we also have to remember that violence breeds violence. The response should be a solid, measured response.

Fourth, all of us will have to pay attention to international affairs. Americans are 4 percent of the world's population. We must learn more and understand more about the other 96 percent. From the most generous nation to those who were poor beyond our borders, we have slipped to dead last among the 21 wealthy nations in what we do to help the world's impoverished. Too often we act without consulting others. We do not intend to convey arrogance, but sometimes because of our insensitivity and disinterest that is the impression we leave with other people.

As a nation we are now united in grief and determination. We must channel that grief and determination so that terrorism shrinks as a world threat, so that our children and grandchildren can live in a safer world.

"REMARKS ON PRESIDENT HARRY TRUMAN," BY SENATOR PAUL SIMON ON RECEIVING THE ANNUAL HARRY TRUMAN AWARD, MAY 2, 2003, AT THE TRUMAN PRESIDENTIAL LIBRARY, INDEPENDENCE, MISSOURI

One of the reasons I am so honored to receive this award is that President Harry Truman had three qualities needed in our government today: integrity and compassion combined with our greatest deficiency, courage.

He took no polls to decide on the Marshall Plan or the integration of the armed forces, both of which were initially immensely unpopular. And when we entered the Korean conflict he did not pander to our greed with a tax cut, but did the sensible and courageous thing—asked for a tax increase, and we went through the Korean conflict with almost no increase in the deficit.

He called on us to provide better education opportunities, improved health care, and to guarantee a job opportunity to all Americans. How far-sighted he appears now.

Too often today's leaders in both political parties are telling us what we want to hear rather than the truth, advocating a course which proclaims that we can drift into greatness without sacrifice on our part, except for those who serve in our armed forces. Drifting without sacrifice is a path to reduce influence for our nation and a diminished future for our children and grandchildren. If I want to improve my house it requires a small sacrifice, and if we want to improve our nation and world it requires a small sacrifice.

John F. Kennedy's famous line rings with a message for us: "Ask not what your country can do for you; ask what you can do for your country."

If I were in the Senate today I would vote against both the Republican and Democratic tax cuts. The projected $400 billion deficit this fiscal year (not counting a huge amount borrowed from the Social Security retirement fund) has a cost of roughly $16 billion a year in interest in perpetuity for which we will receive nothing other than higher interest rates—though we satisfy our desire for something now, we satisfy our immediate greed.

Sixteen billion dollars is approximately 40 percent of what the federal government spends on education.

Harry Truman would point out to us that $16 billion is more than we spend each year on foreign economic non-military assistance. This nation which once led the world with its generosity under the Truman-sponsored Marshall Plan now trails all the other twenty-one wealthy industrial nations in the percentage of our income that goes to help the impoverished beyond our borders. September 11th happened in part because the world now looks at Uncle Sam as "the rich guy on the block who doesn't share his wealth with the world's poor." Other nations do not question our military prowess. We spend more than the next 26 nations combined on defense. Harry Truman served in the Army overseas and so did I. We want an adequate defense. But I also want a warm-hearted nation that recognizes the future of our children is entwined with the future of children in the developing nations.

During Harry Truman's presidency we spent as much as 9 percent of the federal budget on education, compared to 2 percent today. He looked to the future; we look too much to today. His language sometimes lacked polish, but his programs had the words "a better tomorrow" stamped all over them. Too often today's anemic programs that appeal to our greed are covered by a veneer of polished language but they have words "a diminished tomorrow" stamped on them.

Harry Truman represents substance; he showed courage; he grew and helped the nation grow; he looked to the nation's needs not the nation's polls for his programs. How marvelous if future generations could say the same about us.

"LEARNING FROM LESSONS OF THE PAST," NPR COMMENTARY, JULY 22, 2003

The *New York Times* has an article written by Thomas Powers which notes that for the first time in U.S. history our leaders are calling for the assassination of a foreign leader, Saddam Hussein. It is one thing to say he should be captured and brought to the International Criminal Court (which we opposed creating), but calling for the slaying of a leader tips the scales in the direction of international chaos. If we feel justified in calling for the slaying of a leader—or past leader of another nation—many in other countries will feel justified in moving to assassinate our leaders. Both sides will demand revenge. Talk—and actions—like these are popular but unwise.

The *New York Times* article notes: "In April 1986 President Reagan authorized an air raid on the home of Colonel Qaddafi of Libya that spared him but killed his daughter. The Reagan administration never acknowledged that Colonel Qaddafi was the target, nor did it speculate two years later that Libya's bombing of an American jetliner over Lockerbie, Scotland, killing 270 people was Colonel Qaddafi's revenge for the death of his daughter. But the administration got the message: After Lockerbie, Washington relied on legal action to settle the score." Again, that is quoted from the *New York Times*.

What is unquestionably true is that a free system will work within the boundaries of a nation only if the leaders of that nation exercise self-restraint. And I hope it gradually is becoming clearer to international leaders that a world of peace and stability can only come if the leaders of nations exercise self-restraint in dealing with other countries. What has emotional appeal to a domestic audience may be a great disservice to that nation in the long run, if it is based on policies of revenge.

The more the United States calls for the slaying of foreign leaders—even those with a bloody history like Saddam Hussein—the more we invite violent retaliation. We should learn the lesson that history teaches us over and over and over again: Violence breeds violence.

"ON PANDERING," WRITTEN FOR *THE LUTHERAN,* NOVEMBER 2003

Checking into a motel or hotel, frequently you find a small sign on the inside of the door to your room that can be placed outside your room: Do Not Disturb. That sign hangs invisibly but not unnoticed on too many churches.

It is part of what I call *Our Culture of Pandering* in a recently released book in which I look at this cancer of pandering politics, in the media, in education and in religious practices.

Many who read these lines in *The Lutheran* will agree and say to themselves: *They* should stop pandering. That is true. But there is another truth: *We* should create an atmosphere in which such behavior is not rewarded. Let me visit with you briefly about two of the four areas I cover in my book, politics and religion.

Far too many in both political parties tell us over and over what we want to hear, what the latest polls suggest is popular. The words of Jesus in the book of Luke are worth reflecting upon: "Woe to you when all men speak well of you, for that is how their fathers treated the false prophets." Candidates and office-holders who tell you only what is popular, only what you want to hear, are indeed false prophets. Don't go to a physician who tells you only what you want to hear, and don't go to a candidate or office-holder who does the same.

There always has been this tendency to pander, but polling has made it into a science. We now know with great accuracy what the public thinks, and all of us—politicians and non-politicians—prefer plaudits to criticisms, victory to defeat.

In the preface to my book I write: "We have spawned 'leadership' that does not lead, that panders to our whims rather than telling us the truth, that follows the crowd rather than challenging us, that weakens us rather than strengthening us. It is easy to go downhill, and we are now following that easy path. Pandering is not illegal, but it is immoral. It is doing the convenient when the right course demands inconvenience and courage."

Far too many in both political parties are telling us that we can drift into becoming a better nation and creating a better world. Few are suggesting real sacrifice is necessary—unless we serve in the Armed Forces. So, for the first time in the nation's history, we invade another nation creating a conflict—and vote ourselves a tax cut at the same time. That is one example. Unfortunately there are many. The reality is that if I want to improve my house, I have to be willing to make a small sacrifice. And if we want to improve our nation and our world, it will require making small sacrifices. If we are unwilling to make small sacrifices now, eventually we will be forced into making large and bloody sacrifices.

In an address at Southern Illinois University's Carbondale campus, former Conservative leader and Canadian Prime Minister Brian Mulroney said: "We are a generation raised on the bizarre proposition that leadership should be equated with popularity. . . . Presidents and prime ministers are not chosen to seek popularity. They are chosen to provide leadership. There are times when voters must be told not what they want to hear but what they have to know. . . . Time is the ally of leaders who place the defense of principle ahead of the pursuit of popularity."

People who willingly did the unpopular gave us the Marshall Plan and the GI Bill—both of them now viewed as "motherhood and apple pie"— but not when they passed. The first poll taken after Harry Truman and George Marshall called for this big aid program showed only 14 percent of the American public supporting it. Among other nations helped, they were asking us to assist Germany which had just killed many of our sons and brothers and fathers, as well as nurses and other women. And Harry Truman had to deal with a Republican Congress. But the Republican leader on foreign policy, Senator Arthur Vandenberg of Michigan, said that while the President's proposal was unpopular, the Marshall Plan would serve the long-range best interest of the nation and he would support it. We would not have had this crucial program that saved Western Europe from Communism and from hunger without courageous leadership from key people in both political parties, people who were willing to risk their popularity.

The education plan which became known as the GI Bill faced the alternative which public opinion and several veterans organizations favored, a large cash bonus. To the credit of the American Legion, they fought hard for the education program and it emerged from the key House-Senate conference committee by one vote! It turned out to be the most important economic thrust forward for our nation in the last century—and important in the lives of many of you who read these words today because your parents or grandparents benefitted from a college education which many could not have afforded.

But let us not fool ourselves that the world of organized religion is immune from the temptation of pandering.

The cause of much of the conflict in the world today has its roots in religion. Faith can be a powerful force for healing or a powerful force for harm. What is your church doing to reach out to Catholics and Jews and—more important now—Muslims? It does not mean that we accept the beliefs of others, but we should understand them. Political leaders in many nations (including ours) far too often use religion for political purposes rather than quietly practice it. The distortions, the extremism that is found in radicals of all faiths is based on an assumption that *we*—whoever *we* is—have a monopoly on truth and when someone differs, that person is not differing just with the extremists but with God. That, the radicals believe, sometimes demands a violent response.

There are less violent examples of pandering, of abuse of religion, of abuse by failure to apply faith to life.

Here is a test you might try on your church: Take the Judgment Day scene of Matthew 25 where we are asked what we have done for the hungry, the thirsty, the homeless, the poorly clothed, the prisoners. Your church's annual report should, of course, report how many have been baptized, confirmed, married, and buried. But in addition to recording how much money is in the bank, and whether the roof leaks and how much it will cost to repair it, how about also reporting what you have done—or not done—for prisoners, and others listed in Matthew 25?

I read that there are more than 2,500 verses in the New and the Old Testament requiring us to help the hungry and impoverished. I have never counted them, but it clearly is a theme repeated over and over. It is not a theme that I notice many churches pay much attention to. A few congregations are outstanding in what they do. Most churches are outstanding in what they don't do.

Each day, for example, 630 times as many children around the world die each day because of poor quality water than were killed at Columbine High School in Colorado. We were stunned at Columbine High School, as we should have been, but we hardly pay attention to this water-caused tragedy. The United States, which once led the world in aid to the earth's poor, now is dead last among the 22 wealthy industrial nations in the percentage of our income that goes to help impoverished people beyond our borders. Does that reflect on our faith? I believe it does. Is that insensitivity part of the reason that terrorism against us finds it easy to recruit followers? I believe it is. I just received an address by Bernard Rapoport, a Texas business leader, who spoke at Abilene Christian University. He talks about "this ever-increasing greed which seems to be gripping us more tightly day by day." The pattern of greed must be diminished; a pattern of sharing must grow.

In a stimulating book by Robert Putnam, *Bowling Alone*, he notes that people who have a faith affiliation are more likely to be involved in assisting to meet social needs. That is the good news. The bad news is that it is a small fraction of what we could be doing.

It is easy to worship in our mostly middle class churches, to sing hymns and recite prayers, and—let us face it—to feel good about ourselves. We need pastors and lay people who also shake us up.

One day in the local Lutheran church which I attend a man stood up in the middle of the service and started to talk. An usher quickly went down with him and quieted him. I assumed from his conduct that day and visiting with him briefly since then that he has mental problems.

But maybe it was one of the best things that ever happened in our church. Suddenly we were shaken out of our comfort.

Perhaps you can play a role in doing that also.

Appendix

Bibliography

Index

Appendix: Annotated Bibliography of the Books of Paul Simon

1. *Lovejoy: Martyr to Freedom*. St. Louis: Concordia Press, 1964.

Lovejoy was the forerunner of the much more widely known and highly praised *Freedom's Champion: Elijah Lovejoy*, published thirty-one years later. This earlier book was written for a teenage audience and was published by Concordia Press, the publishing arm of the Lutheran church of which Paul Simon was a life-long member. Elijah Lovejoy was a newspaper editor who was also a pastor mostly in and around St. Louis, Missouri. As he matured and observed life in St. Louis, especially the plight of black people and slaves, he became an ardent foe of slavery. He took up the cause on the pages of his newspaper, at first timidly and then with increased vigor and vitriol. As the subtitle indicates, his abolitionist writings ultimately led to his murder by a proslavery mob. This book was intended to be one in a series about early American heroes who could be inspirational figures for young people to learn from and emulate. See item number 15 below for the more completely developed and adult-oriented edition of this work.

2. *Lincoln's Preparation for Greatness: The Illinois Legislature Years*. Norman: University of Oklahoma Press, 1965. Reissued, Champaign: University of Illinois Press, 1971.

Many people believe that this is Paul Simon's best book, and it is certainly the most scholarly one. It is filled with references to primary documents and with detailed footnotes. Simon went to the library and sought out books on Lincoln's early years in Springfield and on his legislative career. To his surprise, he found that out of the long list of works on Lincoln, there was no book covering the era of the young Abe Lincoln's career in New Salem and Springfield. So, Simon decided to write one himself. How did Lincoln get into politics, and what kind of politician was he in the rough and tumble of Illinois politics that swirled around the state capital in Springfield? This is the story of a surprisingly practical politician who learned to ply his trade in state politics at a time when there was plenty of intrigue and even outright corruption in Illinois. While Lincoln was pragmatic and worked hard to represent his people and get the job done for them, he also had solid Whig principles that he adhered to as he sought to be a successful legislator. Simon paints Lincoln as an effective legislator who was not above bargaining, deal making, and logrolling but who was incorruptible and principled in his maneuvering through the legislative labyrinth. As the title implies, there is much in the story of the young Abraham Lincoln in Springfield that prepared him to become perhaps the greatest president in U.S. history. Simon contends that if you want to understand Lincoln in Washington, you must first understand Lincoln in Springfield.

3. *A Hungry World*. St. Louis: Concordia Press, 1966.

This third book of Simon's shows that world hunger was an early interest of his, and it was a cause he followed and wrote about throughout his public career. Like the first Lovejoy book, this one was published by Concordia Press for the Lutheran church. The young Paul Simon couched his writings in an explicitly Christian context, and he makes hunger, whether in India or the United States, a moral issue that he felt should compel a response from religious people. If feeding the poor is not a Christian obligation, endorsed by the Gospels, what is, asks Simon rhetorically. He notes the irony of too much food and too much obesity in the United States juxtaposed against a backdrop of pervasive hunger throughout the world and even in some places in America. The influence of his early background, especially growing up in the home of a Lutheran pastor and missionary to China, is everywhere evident in this work. It is clearly the precursor to the much more ambitious and more famous volume *The Politics of World Hunger* that Paul published with his brother, Arthur, in 1973.

4. *Protestant-Catholic Marriages Can Succeed* (with Jeanne Hurley Simon). New York: Association Press, Published by the National Board of the YMCA, 1967.

Paul Simon was a Lutheran and Jeanne Hurley was a Catholic when they first met as young and aspiring legislators in the Illinois House of Representatives. Jeanne, one of a small number of women elected to the

House in that era, was from a suburban Chicago district, while Paul was the brash corruption fighter from the Metro-East area downstate. As Jeanne tells it, she was looking for a Catholic Paul Simon, and he was looking for a Lutheran Jeanne Hurley. It finally dawned on them that they could have a "mixed marriage" and put aside their differences while still holding onto their original denominational identities. The Simons became the epitome of a committed Christian couple, and this story covers the early years, telling how they started on a journey that lasted for almost forty years. They offer much advice for other couples who might be considering a similar mixed marriage and recommend studying the other partner's religion with respect and with a spirit of mutual exploration of the important faith-based issues. This is one practical form of the pluralism and ecumenicalism that has always marked American life. Both qualities were deep commitments of Paul and Jeanne's. This book is about the importance of communication and mutual respect within the intimacy of marriage and also about trying to take the Christian message seriously and applying it to daily life.

5. *You Want to Change the World? So Change It!* New York: Thomas Nelson, 1971.
    This book was published in the Youth Forum Series, which was a series designed to give good advice to young people from a Christian perspective. Other notable authors who contributed to this monograph series included Martin Marty, the scholar and church historian, and Andrew Greeley, the Catholic priest who became a leading public intellectual. The purpose of the series was to address real world problems from a religious and moral point of view, and the theme throughout Simon's book is that the key to living out one's faith is service to others: "The Christian faith is a doing faith" (35). The book is filled with practical advice on how to achieve change in a peaceful manner.
    You Want to Change the World? was published one year after the tragic deaths of young people at Kent State and Jackson State in May 1970 as they were protesting the war in Vietnam. At the time of writing, Paul was fresh from having refereed some of the conflicts on college campuses engendered by the war; for example, he met with the faculty, staff, and students of Southern Illinois University Carbondale in the wake of the antiwar demonstrations and riots on campus in May 1970, and he tried to negotiate some positive solutions to the problems he found there. Simon gives advice on how to take youthful enthusiasm and idealism and channel those impulses in positive directions. He was lieutenant governor of Illinois at the time and drew on many of his experiences in public office, particularly in acting as the state's "ombudsman" in executing his duties. He provides many case

studies of change and reform that he had participated in as he and his office tried to solve practical problems for the people of Illinois.

In that era, it was mostly those on the political Left who were the most engaged and outraged at the policies of the national government. Interestingly, today it is mostly those on the political Right who express those feelings most adamantly and aggressively. Simon's advice is timely and cogent for both sides. Simon frequently stated that the American people have little knowledge about our national history, and he advocated learning from history. The characters and some of the issues have changed since the early 1970s, but fundamentally, otherwise, not much has changed with respect to mass ignorance of history and our inability to learn from it in the United States today. Simon was one of the few political leaders of his day who studied history carefully and seriously sought to learn and teach from the lessons he gleaned from his readings.

6. *The Politics of World Hunger: Grass-Roots Politics and World Poverty* (with Arthur Simon). New York: Harper's Magazine Press, 1973.

Coauthored with Arthur Simon, Paul's brother and the former president of Bread for the World, this book lays out a systematic and compelling case advocating that the United States must try to address the scourge of world hunger. Paul and Arthur also provide many practical suggestions as to how ordinary Americans can help. Simply put, it is the right thing to do from a moral and religious perspective. If that does not move you, then consider self-interest, because a hungry world is a dangerous world. In a nation where many people are too well fed, or at least consume too many calories daily, the Simon brothers provide a compelling explanation for how we can do better and why we should try to address the worldwide phenomenon of hunger and malnutrition. In addition, malnutrition is directly related to the expanding gap between the rich and the poor and the gap between the rich nations and the underdeveloped world. This book ranges from considering the implications for individual responsibility and decision making to macroeconomics and trade policy. It is particularly clear in making recommendations for changes in U.S. food, foreign aid, and agricultural policy and is one of the most widely recognized and quoted books that Simon wrote.

7. *The Tongue-Tied American: Confronting the Foreign Language Crisis*. New York: Continuum Books, 1980.

This is one of Paul Simon's most influential works. It was particularly well received and widely quoted in academic institutions where the teaching of foreign languages is a calling and a cause dear to the hearts of those who teach in elementary and secondary schools and in the colleges and universities. Simon became perhaps the foremost advocate among all major elected officials at the federal level for the cause of language education. He maintained that increasing our facility with languages other than English was literally a matter of national security survival as well as a dire necessity in an emerging global economy. Americans tend to be a parochial people, secure in the knowledge that many others speak English and have to deal with the United States as the largest economy in the world. Simon provides both a trenchant indictment of our failure as a nation to recognize the need for teaching and learning foreign languages and a compelling case for increasing the role that language instruction should play in the education of American students, from K–12 all the way through graduate school. While the teaching of foreign languages has increased marginally today, the United States remains the most monolingual of any of the developed nations in the world. Our military and state departments still have acute problems recruiting and retaining those with critical language skills, and our businesses and industries still depend on finding people in other countries who can speak English in order to make deals with those operating in the global economy. Simon's critique of American education still rings true today.

8. *The Once and Future Democrats: Strategies for Change.* New York: Continuum Books, 1982.

This book was written just after the Democrats had suffered a devastating electoral loss of the presidency as Ronald Reagan defeated Jimmy Carter decisively in the 1980 election. The Democrats were reeling from that loss and from the deep internal divisions that had been revealed and exacerbated by that campaign. The internal factionalism of the Democratic Party was particularly evident in the run-up to the 1980 national convention in New York and in the convention itself as the Carter forces tried to fight off the challenge from Senator Edward Kennedy, who tried to unseat Carter as the party's presidential nominee. As a result, there was lingering bad blood within the party and a variety of very different views on how to face the future and develop an agenda that both factions could adhere to in the electoral battles to come. Parties routinely face such internal divisions and public soul-searching after a serious national defeat, and 1980–82 was no exception for the Democrats. In this book, Simon weighs in with his advice and his "Strategies for Change." He challenges the concept of there being a "conservative mandate" in the Reagan victory. Instead, he contends that

1980 was a personal victory for Reagan as a candidate and a personal loss for Carter, a position that has been validated by much subsequent empirical research. The book was published in 1982, and by that time, many of the major Reagan policies were clear, most notably a very large tax cut for those with the highest incomes, a large defense buildup, and budget cuts in many domestic programs such as school lunches and public sector jobs such as those provided by the CETA program. Simon was opposed to much of the Reagan agenda, and he articulates a compelling critique of those policies. He also offers clear alternatives that he urges his fellow Democrats to adopt. This is the classic role for the "out party" or the loyal opposition—to provide a critique of the ruling party and to offer alternatives. Simon presses other Democrats to also fulfill that role and to offer other ideas. This book is vintage Paul Simon the Progressive, who believed that government must actively regulate the marketplace and provide a balance wheel against the abuses of corporate power as well as be a positive force in the lives of ordinary people and especially in the lives of the powerless and the dispossessed. In short, it was the pure "anti-Reagan" book for its time.

9. *The Glass House: Politics and Morality in the Nation's Capital*. New York: Continuum Books, 1984.

At the time of publication, near the end of Ronald Reagan's first term, Simon had been in the U.S. House for nine years, after serving fourteen years in the Illinois General Assembly and then as lieutenant governor of Illinois. *The Glass House* provides his reflections on the application of ethics and morality in politics and policy-making, topics that had become timely and compelling with the rise of the "religious Right" during that era. Simon was a leader widely respected for his high ethical standards and keen sense of morality. Yet he came under intense fire from some on the Right who claimed the mantle of morality in pursuit of policies that Simon did not support. Here he asserts that it is not always clear or easy to know what the application of morality requires in the policy realm. The problems and the solutions may be ambiguous and may require a certain amount of compromise, according to Simon. One must remember that this was the era when the "Moral Majority" was riding high and leaders like Jerry Falwell and Pat Robertson were advocating an aggressive agenda reflecting their religious views as applied to the public policy–making process. Their worldview was all black and white. Simon dissented vigorously from that view. He believed that most members of Congress were highly ethical people individually, despite the bad reputation of Congress at that time. (It is interesting to note that Congress was held in as much popular disdain then as it is now, in 2012.) Simon also believed that Congress as an institution did not always work very well, and he had a number of institutional and procedural reforms he thought would make it a better and more effective instrument for realizing the public interest. *The Glass House* offers a good sample of Paul Simon as the Public Intellectual, the term that would be applicable to him today.

10. *Beginnings: Senator Paul Simon Speaks to Young Americans.* New York: Continuum Books, 1986.

Beginnings provides a series of short homilies for the young. It is the kind of book a young Abe Lincoln or a young John Adams might have read and profited from in much earlier generations. It is also the kind of book that Paul Simon would have read and internalized as he grew up in the earnest Lutheran household of Martin and Ruth Simon. *Beginnings* helps define the kinds of character traits that Simon believed should be ingrained in the hearts and minds of young people the world over. It is a manual for good citizenship, which was always one of Simon's keen interests throughout his career.

11. *Let's Put America Back to Work.* Chicago: Bonus Books, 1987.

Paul Simon was always a firm advocate for increasing the employment opportunities for ordinary Americans. He was for a variety of policy stimulants designed to increase private sector jobs; however, if the private sector was not providing the jobs in sufficient numbers, Simon was a strong proponent for public sector jobs. He maintained that there was plenty of work that needed to be done and that public sector jobs could address many of the public needs for infrastructure and services. State parks, hiking trails, lodges, bridges, city parks, bike paths, urban recreational centers, and a wide variety of infrastructure projects needed to be built and maintained, and service was needed in hospitals, nursing homes, recreational programs, urban and rural schools, prisons, and mental institutions as well as in the military. Simon believed it was much better to have the government pay for people to do such projects and perform such services than to pay them welfare for not working. He was a great admirer of the WPA and the CCC, which Franklin Roosevelt used during the New Deal to help his fellow citizens regain employment and to combat the ravages of the Great Depression. We are having a debate today over the role of government in rebuilding the infrastructure and the role such a massive effort could play in providing a stimulus for the economy. This book is highly relevant to that debate. *Let's Put America Back to Work* is also eloquent is explaining and documenting the many positive psychological benefits that accrue to those who have jobs and the very negative and debilitating effects of unemployment. In all these respects, the book is still relevant and cogent for addressing today's unemployment dilemma.

12. *Winners and Losers: The 1988 Race for the Presidency—One Candidate's Perspective.* New York: Continuum Books, 1989.

As many readers know, Paul Simon sought the Democratic nomination to run for president in 1988; this is his insider story. Its companion book is *Codename Scarlett*, written simultaneously by Jeanne Simon, which tells the story of the candidate's wife and frequent surrogate as she and the family hit the campaign trail to try to ensure that Paul Simon would win his party's nomination. The two books nicely complement each other and provide contrasting perspectives on the spouses' experiences during the campaign.

It was truly a family affair as both children, Sheila and Martin, and the new son-in-law, Perry Knop, worked hard for Paul's nomination. In fact, Sheila and Perry spent their honeymoon campaigning for Paul in Iowa. Paul Simon and his family traveled the nation, raised millions of dollars, made countless speeches, shook tens of thousands of hands, and participated in multiple candidate debates in the fall of 1987 and the winter of 1988. They ultimately fell short of their goal because of a late start, limited resources, staff shortages, and a message that was not compelling enough with enough voters to prevail in the Democratic primaries and caucuses. Simon counted heavily on an early victory in the Iowa caucuses, and the campaign focused most of its attention and resources on that first-in-the-nation contest. However, Simon lost narrowly to Richard Gephardt from neighboring Missouri. Both Simon and Gephardt then lost the New Hampshire primary to Michael Dukakis, who was governor of Massachusetts at that time. Dukakis went on to become the Democratic Party's nominee in 1988, but he lost to George H. W. Bush in the general election in November. Out of the early contests, Simon ultimately won only the primary in his home state of Illinois. That victory proved to be too little, too late.

One might think that he could have become bitter and disheartened by this disappointment. If so, one would be wrong. Paul Simon recounts this contest as one of the most enlightening and encouraging experiences of his long political life. He is remarkably upbeat and positive about having his shot at the greatest prize in American politics, even though he fell rather far short of attaining that goal. Simon is critical of some of the players and some of the processes by which we select our presidential nominees. For example, he was particularly critical of the media and their fixation on the personalities and the trivial stories of the campaign, and he was troubled by the amounts of money that must be raised in order to be competitive. However, he was energized about the education and enlightenment he received from his travels and meetings with countless ordinary Americans across the country. In Paul Simon's lexicon, the only "losers" are those who choose to stand aside and not become engaged.

13. *Advice and Consent: Clarence Thomas, Robert Bork, and the Intriguing History of the Supreme Court's Nomination Battles.* Washington, D.C.: National Press Books, 1992.

Senate fights over the nomination of new justices to the U.S. Supreme Court are not new. Nominations have always been a potential threat, as Lyndon Johnson found out in 1968 when Republicans refused to allow his nomination of Abe Fortas to be chief justice to even come to a vote; however, one could certainly argue that such fights really started in earnest and became much more the norm with the nomination fights over Robert Bork in 1987 and Clarence Thomas in 1991. Since then, most nominations from presidents of both parties have become the occasion for recurring conflict over the composition and direction of the Supreme Court as the nation has become more ideologically polarized and each president has tried to ensure that the Supreme Court would help shape his legacy, or at least not overthrow the major policies he supported.

Simon was in the middle of the Bork and Thomas nomination battles as a member, and the only non-lawyer member, of the Senate Judiciary Committee. Simon believed that there had to be a better way. He advocated that the president should seek advice from the Senate and others before he sent the name up to the Hill for confirmation, and he maintained that presidents had come to expect consent without first seeking advice on which justice they should name. He believed that the confirmation process had become too partisan and too polarized. He voted, for example, against William Rehnquist to be chief justice but in favor of Antonin Scalia, despite having serious doubts about the Scalia nomination because of Scalia's deep public commitment to his ideological views. This book is almost as timely today as it was when it was first published.

14. *We Can Do Better: How to Save America's Future—An Open Letter to President Clinton.* Bethesda, Md.: National Press Books, 1994.

It is notable that the foreword to this book was written by former senator Paul Tsongas. Both Tsongas and Simon were social liberals who were also deficit hawks. Both believed in the Balanced Budget Amendment and that the United States was borrowing too much money. In so doing, we were mortgaging the future of our children and grandchildren, according to Simon and Tsongas.

This book is directly addressed to President Bill Clinton, who was two years into his first term, and it is all about families, especially couched in terms of what would be good for the Simon and Clinton children. Some of Clinton's priorities and his strengths and weaknesses were becoming well known by then, and Simon addresses a number of those, often fairly candidly and pointedly. Characteristically, Simon urges Clinton to be bold in his leadership and to be willing to make the hard choices, even if they are not the popular choices. Simon believed that too many grave national problems had not been addressed during the Reagan and Bush years, and he feared that these problems were also not likely to be addressed by Clinton if the president only lurched from crisis to crisis, which is what most presidents do. Health care, crowded prisons, public schools that did not educate a modern workforce, adult illiteracy, and a decaying national infrastructure were all big problems that Simon urged Clinton to tackle. Of course, both Clintons—the president and the first lady—did spend the first half of his first term trying to attack the problems of the health care system, but they could not even get Congress to vote on their proposals.

This book is Simon playing the classic Edmund Burke role as the "trustee" or the leader who follows his conscience and convictions and tries to educate his people to see the wisdom of a sometimes-unpopular stance. While the particulars of many of the policies have changed, a number of the basic and generic problems remain today. For example, health care was a huge issue then, and it has dominated the first three years of the Obama administration seventeen years later. The need for a national energy policy was compelling then, and it has been an insurmountable challenge for President Obama. It is very difficult to tackle the large issues in a system that is stacked on the side of the status quo and that mostly lends itself to slow and incremental change. Simon was often critical of this system and restive under its limitations. In this book, Simon is particularly complimentary of Clinton for his leadership in achieving tax increases and spending cuts in the 1993 Budget Act and for his leadership in passing NAFTA, which Simon supported. On the other hand, he is very critical of Clinton for his tendency to seek incremental and middle-of-the-road measures, especially after the Democrats lost their majorities in Congress in 1994. Of course, without a majority in both houses of Congress, it is almost impossible for any Democratic president to attain his policy objectives, and it takes a supermajority of sixty votes in the Senate. Many of the criticisms of Clinton in the early 1990s are being heard from Progressive Democrats in the 2008–12 Obama administration era, indicating that there is a timeless quality to the dilemmas of leadership and the limitations of the political system discussed in this book.

15. *Freedom's Champion: Elijah Lovejoy*. Carbondale: Southern Illinois University Press, 1995.

This is one of Paul Simon's most influential books. It is also a revised edition of the earlier and much shorter book on the same subject written for teenagers and published in 1964. The senator was a newspaperman before he went into politics, and *Freedom's Champion* tells a great story about a notable newspaperman and his defense of the First Amendment. Lovejoy, from Alton, Illinois, was one of the first martyrs to the cause of the free press. He fought a brave battle on the side of the abolitionists and railed against slavery in an area where that message was widely and often violently rebuffed. This was an era routinely marked by lawlessness and mob rule, even in downtown St. Louis. Missouri was a slave state, and this book paints a grim picture of what life was like in a state and city where human beings were routinely bought and sold at public auction and families split and sold like so many cattle. Slaves were frequently abused and even hung on a tree or burned at the stake for the most trivial offenses against white people. Some of the newspaper accounts of this atavistic violence are sickening.

Most of the book is set in St. Louis, although Lovejoy ultimately moved to Alton to get away from his reputation as an abolitionist and as one who simply felt compelled to speak out against the sins of the "peculiar institution" of slavery. Lovejoy did not start out as an abolitionist, or even as one who was very interested in the subject of slavery or in the plight of black people. However, the longer he observed the abuses of those who surrounded him and the more he thought about slavery from a Christian perspective, the more he spoke out against it. The more he spoke out and the more pointed his criticism became, the more the supporters of slavery hated him and vowed to take revenge. The more they abused him, the more Lovejoy became convinced that he was doing the right thing and that he could not and should not be silenced. Lovejoy was ultimately killed by a mob in Alton and his newspaper sacked. It was the third time that his printing presses and his other equipment had been destroyed, and on this occasion the mob action resulted in Lovejoy's death from at least five gunshot wounds from perhaps as many different sources. Simon clearly admired Lovejoy, although he admitted that Lovejoy was a difficult and complicated man. The title, *Freedom's Champion*, indicates the great respect and admiration that Simon had for his subject. In his autobiography, Paul Simon wrote that this book was his favorite among all those he published.

16. *The Dollar Crisis: A Blueprint to Help Rebuild the American Dream* (with Ross Perot). Arlington, Tex.: Summit Publishing Group, 1996.

At first glance, Paul Simon and Ross Perot would seem an unlikely couple to team up on a book, no matter what the subject. Certainly there was much, particularly in the realm of social policy, on which they disagreed. They were also quite different in temperament. However, they had one area of profound agreement and deep conviction: the pernicious effect of the accumulating national debt. More than anything else, this was Perot's signature issue when he ran for president in 1992. Perot received 19 percent of the popular vote that year, the highest percentage for a third party candidate since Theodore Roosevelt in 1912. Paul Simon had always called himself a "pay as you go Democrat," and this was one of the major planks in his platform when he sought the presidency in 1988. Both men were convinced that we were borrowing too much money, both individually and most notably as a nation. Indeed, pressure from Perot helped push Bill Clinton's policies in the 1993 Tax and Budget Bill that he worked through a reluctant Congress that year over the determined opposition of a united Republican Party and a nervous bunch of congressional Democrats. That bill, in turn, contributed materially to the Clinton era budget surplus in 1998–2000, the only federal budget surplus years in recent history.

Perot and Simon explore a lot of good things that they believed would flow from a balanced budget: rapid jobs creation, lower interest rates, low and sustainable rates of inflation, lower taxes, and better educational opportunities for the nation's young people. Most of those good things were ultimately realized during the 1990s, thus making this book seem prescient. This debate over the need for a balanced budget and how to obtain it is still very relevant in an era when the budget deficit has once again soared under the twin pressures of tax reductions and increased spending for defense and domestic programs and reduced revenues from a deep recession and tax cuts. Whether to start on reducing the national deficit before the baneful effects of the 2008 recession recede or to keep priming the pump with federal dollars until the economy heals is the much-debated current dilemma, one foreshadowed by this book.

17. *Tapped Out: The Coming World Crisis in Water and What We Can Do About It*. New York: Welcome Rain Publishers, 1998.

The subject of *Tapped Out* is one that Paul Simon was most passionate about and that consumed much of his energy and attention after he left the U.S. Senate. In the book, he issues a clarion call to the nation to wake up to the importance of clean water and to understand its critical importance in world affairs as well as in the life of our nation. Simon became a self-taught expert on the many aspects of water policy and one of the most widely recognized voices favoring the adoption of policies that would both expand the supply of potable water as well as ensure its distribution in more equitable ways. He was also a keen advocate for water conservation measures. He warns that water is so essential to so many facets of human life that its scarcity threatens regional stability in many parts of the globe. He was convinced that the wars of the future could well be fought out over water rights even more than over access to carbon-based fuels, which tends to be the major flash point in world politics today. He also recounts the great hardship that befalls those, particularly children, who are denied access to pure water. Literally millions die or are sickened each year because of drinking and using contaminated water. Simon covers many successful experiments in the United States and abroad that were designed to increase the supply and availability of potable water. He is particularly optimistic about the potential for desalination, although he recognizes the very real obstacles it faces in the attempts to lower the energy inputs necessary to produce fresh water. This book became a cover story for *Parade Magazine* on August 23, 1998. Through that story, Simon gained a national and international audience for his water policy views. Simon was one of the leading advocates for more rational water policies at the time of his death. This is certainly one of Paul Simon's most important and influential books.

18. *P.S.: The Autobiography of Paul Simon*. Chicago: Bonus Books, 1999.

This is the story of Paul Simon's life from the early years all the way through his last position as the founding director of the Paul Simon Public Policy Institute at Southern Illinois University Carbondale. This book offers important insights into Simon's early life and experiences as they shaped the mature man and public servant. The story of the early years is particularly focused on the profound influence that Simon's parents, and especially his father, Martin, had on shaping his character and values. Martin and Ruth Simon were Lutheran missionaries to China in the 1930s. After they returned to the United States and settled in Paul's birthplace of Eugene, Oregon, they lived for a time the prosaic lives of a pastor's family, and his father became a leader in Lutheran church circles. Paul's recollection of the stance that his father took against the Japanese relocation movement on the West Coast during World War II and of the personal embarrassment his father caused the young Paul Simon seems to be a particularly poignant and cogent insight into the ways Simon grew to look at the world of politics and public policy through the moral lens of his father's eyes. It is ironic and satisfying to note that one of Simon's guest speakers at the Paul Simon Public Policy Institute at SIUC was Fred Korematsu, the Japanese American who challenged President Roosevelt's relocation policy and who won recognition much later for the injustices that had been done, in the name of national security, to the tens of thousands of his compatriots who were taken from their homes and located in internment camps at the start of World War II. This story is just one of many that Simon's autobiography tells about the events and people who influenced his life and shaped his views and values. A commitment to public life and the necessity for government to counterbalance the other large forces, particularly corporations and the interest groups endemic to American politics, is a constantly recurring theme. This book offers the best insight into the thinking and commitments of Paul Simon the ultimate Progressive, who wanted the power of government used for the greater good of the most people, and explores the foundation of some very conservative personal values that have long shaped American life and that certainly shaped Paul Simon's life.

19. *How to Get into Politics—and Why: A Reader* (with Michael Dukakis). Wilmington, Mass.: Great Source Education Group, a Division of Houghton Mifflin Company, 2000.

Paul Simon and Michael Dukakis ran against each other for the Democratic Party's nomination for president in 1988; Dukakis won. Later, they teamed up to write this book for young people. It reflects the deep commitment both men exhibited to politics and public service throughout their lives. Certainly the advice to get involved and try to make a difference is found in virtually all of Paul Simon's writings and speeches, and it is a commitment shared no less enthusiastically by Michael Dukakis, who was governor of Massachusetts when he ran for president. The titles of the chapters that each contributed are revealing: Dukakis titled his "A Fulfilling Life"; Simon, "If You Believe in Something." They also recruited an all-star bipartisan cast of political luminaries and leaders—including Dick Armey, Willie Brown, Federico Peña, Al Simpson, Dianne Feinstein, Kay Bailey Hutchison, Elizabeth Dole, Mark Hatfield, Mario Cuomo, Sandra Day O'Connor, Phil Gramm, Carol Moseley-Braun, Olympia Snowe, and other notables—to contribute chapters on how and why they first got involved in politics and on what advice they would offer to young people. Their contributions are interesting and inspirational, short and pithy, and are the kinds of readings that could be assigned usefully to either high school or college students of any generation.

20. *Healing America: Values and Vision for the 21st Century*. Maryknoll, N.Y.: Orbis Press, 2003.

This book was written in the wake of the September 11, 2001, terrorist attacks on the United States. In it, Simon poses the question of what should be the response of the United States to the bombings in New York and Pennsylvania and at the Pentagon. Simon recommends a measured path that stresses increased understanding between ethnic, religious, nationality, and racial groups and that seeks reconciliation rather than revenge. This is signature Paul Simon writing. He advocates a level of political discourse and personal empathy for others that would tax ordinary mortals. The book was published by the Maryknoll Fathers and Brothers, who say they seek "to explore the global dimensions of the Christian faith and mission, to invite dialogue with diverse cultures and religious traditions, and to serve the cause of reconciliation and peace" (ii). Paul Simon's words in this book are those of a committed and compassionate Christian who was taught these basic values by devout Lutheran parents. Not surprisingly, the strictures given in this book to the American people and to our leaders about what should be our response in the face of evil were not followed by the federal government. Instead, we went off to two wars, which were instrumental in the killing of hundreds of thousands of people and whose baneful consequences are still being felt in the United States and the world today.

21. *Our Culture of Pandering*. Carbondale: Southern Illinois University Press, 2003.

Simon was always interested in the concept of leadership and in the qualities that leaders should exhibit. Above all, he advocated that leaders should have vision and courage. In this book, he indicts many leaders for their excessive timidity and constant concern with maintaining their office and power base rather than with making a genuine commitment to getting things done. According to Simon, many leaders are guilty of pandering to the fears, ignorance, and more petty instincts of their followers. There are always leaders who will pander and people who want to be pandered to and who will reward such behavior in their leaders. It is a corrosive bargain. This pandering is what undercuts most political and governmental institutions in modern America and prevents them from making the hard, but wise, decisions and choices for the long term and the greater good. Instead, the focus for too many in politics is on the immediate goal of getting reelected, and the focus for those in business is the next quarterly earnings statement. Simon charged that this pandering is endemic not only in politics but also in the media, religion, and education. Simon's constant advice is for leaders to have courage and to be audacious in making great long-range plans for their country and for their constituents. He believed that if leaders wanted to get things done and to lead, rather than simply focus on reelection and the timid politics that often results from such a myopic view, the whole political system would be the better for this commitment and courage.

22. *Fifty-Two Simple Ways to Make a Difference*. Minneapolis: Augsburg Books, 2004.

This last book of Paul Simon's was published after his death in December 2003. It is the quintessential Paul Simon, who above all always worked at making a difference and toward a better day. His creed was personal service and a deep commitment to his fellow mortals. He tried to make a difference in the lives of those he represented and those he met, whether it was in the hundreds of town hall meetings in his district and state, in his constituency offices, in a cab in Chicago, at the St. Louis airport, or in the checkout at Arnold's Market on Carbondale's south side. Paul Simon was always meeting people and learning their stories. He also was an inveterate policy wonk and was convinced that wise and rational public policies could make all the difference in his community, the state, the nation, and the world. He pursued the public policies that he thought would make the world a safer, more peaceful, and more prosperous place.

Paul Simon was a doer and an activist. He urged his fellow citizens to roll up their sleeves and to get their hands dirty in service to larger and nobler causes. This book contains fifty-two practical ideas—one for each week of the year, if one chooses to apply them that way. In an era marked by cynicism and disengagement, one that Harvard political scientist Robert Putnam characterized in his *Bowling Alone* book, Paul Simon urged people to join a league, find a place of service, get involved, and make a difference. Look around your community and see what the needs are, then search for a way to address those needs. Find friends, neighbors, and like-minded people who will join you in the common civic effort. It is somehow fitting that Paul closed with these timeless themes, the credo by which he lived his public life for well over five decades. The book summarizes the defining commitments of a life well lived and well invested in public service.

Bibliography

Balz, Dan, et al. *Landmark: The Inside Story of America's New Health-Care Law and What It Means for us All.* New York: Public Affairs Press, 2010.

Hartley, Robert E. *Paul Simon: The Political Journey of an Illinois Original.* Carbondale: Southern Illinois University Press, 2009.

Kenney, David, and Robert E. Hartley. 2003. *An Uncertain Tradition: U.S. Senators from Illinois.* Carbondale: Southern Illinois University Press, 2003.

Morgenthau, Hans J. *Politics among Nations: The Struggle for Power and Peace.* 4th ed. New York: Alfred A. Knopf, 1966.

Nye, Joseph S., Jr. *Soft Power: The Means to Success in World Politics.* New York: Public Affairs Books, 2004.

Pensoneau, Taylor. *Governor Richard Ogilvie: In the Interest of the State.* Carbondale: Southern Illinois University Press, 1997.

Pensoneau, Taylor, and Bob Ellis. *Dan Walker: The Glory and the Tragedy.* Evansville, Ind.: Smith-Collins Company, 1993.

Putnam, Robert. *Bowling Alone: The Collapse and Revival of American Community.* New York: Simon and Schuster, 2000.

Simon, Paul. "Are We Running Dry?" *Parade Magazine*, August 23, 1998.

——. *Our Culture of Pandering.* Carbondale: Southern Illinois University Press, 2003.

——. *P.S.: The Autobiography of Paul Simon.* Chicago: Bonus Books, 1999.

Trani, Eugene P. "The Man and the Land: The Politics of Paul Simon and Southern Illinois, 1950–1973." *The Simon Review.* Paper #21, July. Carbondale, Ill.: The Paul Simon Public Policy Institute, 2010.

Index

John S. Jackson is a professor of political science emeritus at Southern Illinois University Carbondale (SIUC), and he is currently a visiting professor at the Paul Simon Public Policy Institute (PSPPI). A native of Waldo, Arkansas, Jackson holds a PhD in political science from Vanderbilt University in Nashville, Tennessee; an MA from Baylor University, Waco, Texas; and a BA from Ouachita Baptist University in Arkadelphia, Arkansas. He came to Carbondale in 1969 as a lecturer in the Department of Government. Jackson held numerous leadership positions during his career of over forty years at SIUC. These included associate dean and acting dean of the graduate school, associate dean and dean of the College of Liberal Arts, vice chancellor for academic affairs, provost, and interim chancellor. Jackson has published extensively in the academic journals in his field as well as in a variety of other outlets. He has published three books on presidential elections, presidential primaries, and national conventions. In addition, he originated and is the editor of *The Simon Review* papers, which are published by the PSPPI. Jackson is a frequent commentator on politics for both print and electronic media. He was a longtime friend and supporter of Paul Simon's and did some of the senator's early polling for him.